Peripheries
and Center

In the quest to meet the summit of our potential, it is my firm conviction that our American Constitution will serve future generations with all their complexities, as it has the current generation and the generations of our forebears.

RICHARD B. RUSSELL

THE RICHARD B. RUSSELL LECTURE SERIES

The Richard B. Russell Foundation and the University of Georgia have joined in establishing this lecture series to honor the late Senator Russell. The Richard B. Russell Lectures will extend through the 1980s, addressing the Bicentennial of the Federal Constitution and encompassing the Charter of the University of Georgia in 1785. The Russell Lectures are scheduled for each year during this decade, at which time a distinguished guest of the University of Georgia will present three addresses on some notable aspect of the Constitution.

Jack P. Greene

Peripheries and Center

Constitutional Development in the Extended Polities of the British Empire and the United States, 1607–1788

THE RICHARD B. RUSSELL LECTURES
NUMBER TWO

The University of Georgia Press
Athens and London

© 1986 by the University of Georgia Press
Athens, Georgia 30602

Set in Palatino
The paper in this book meets the guidelines for
permanence and durability of the Committee on
Production Guidelines for Book Longevity of the
Council on Library Resources.

Printed in the United States of America

90 89 88 87 86   5 4 3 2 1

Library of Congress Cataloging in Publication Data

Greene, Jack P.
  Peripheries and center.

  (The Richard B. Russell lectures; no. 2)
  Bibliography: p.
  Includes index.
    1. Great Britain—Colonies—Administration—
History—17th century.   2. Great Britain—Colonies—
Administration—History—18th century.   3. United
States—Politics and government—Colonial period, ca.
1600–1775.   4. United States—Politics and government—
Revolution, 1775–1783.   5. United States—Politics and
government—1783–1789.   I. Title.   II. Series.
JV1062.G74   1987   321.03   86-7802
ISBN 0-8203-0878-1 (alk. paper)

FOR JOHN RICHARD ALDEN
who generously indulged a young student whose research interests were far removed from his own and who continues to set an example of scholarly productivity, lucidity, and judgment to which his students can only aspire.

Contents

PREFACE ix

PROLOGUE 1

Book One: A Problem Experienced, 1607–1763

CHAPTER ONE
In Quest of Periphery Dependence: Crown and
Colonies 7

CHAPTER TWO
In Quest of Periphery Rights: Local Roots of
Constitutional Change 19

CHAPTER THREE
An Ambiguous Accommodation: Liberty, Prerogative,
and the Imperial Constitution, 1713–1763 43

CHAPTER FOUR
Parliament and the Colonies 55

Book Two: A Problem Defined, 1764–1776

CHAPTER FIVE
Definitions of Empire, 1764–1766 79

CHAPTER SIX
Parliament, Crown, and Colonial Rights, 1767–1773 105

CHAPTER SEVEN
Disintegration of Empire, 1773–1776 129

Book Three: A Problem Resolved, 1776–1788

CHAPTER EIGHT
A Confederation of States, 1776–1783 153

Contents

CHAPTER NINE
In Quest of a Republican Empire: Creating a New Center,
1783–1788 181

EPILOGUE 212

NOTES 219

INDEX 267

Preface

This book seeks to trace and analyze the developing structures and theories of constitutional organization in the extended polities of both the early modern British Empire and the revolutionary United States between the founding of Virginia in 1607 and the adoption of the federal Constitution in 1788. The term *extended polity* is used as an analytic category to apply to the far-flung associations of separate political entities represented by the early modern overseas European empires. Unlike either the unitary or the contiguous confederations of states that then existed in Europe, this new category of *modern* political organization posed unfamiliar new questions about constitutional relationships among the several distinct units of which such organizations were composed. How these basic organizational questions were experienced and confronted in the British American context is the particular subject considered in the pages that follow.

Ever since the mid-1960s, when I first came across Edward Shils's important essay on the subject,[1] I have found the conceptual distinction between *center* and *periphery* especially useful as a framework for understanding a variety of aspects of the relationship between metropolis and colonies in the early modern British Empire as well as between dominant (and usually older) areas and subordinate (and usually newer) areas of settlement within individual colonies and regions. As my title suggests, this distinction is central to the analysis that follows. It both provides the framework for that analysis and is intended to highlight the locational bases of differences in situation and points of view in relation to constitutional developments within the empire and the United States.

Constitutional history has not excited much interest among early American historians in recent decades. Although early modern English historians have continued to turn out important work on the constitutional development of England during the seventeenth and early eighteenth centuries, colonial historians have neither produced a comparable body of work about British America nor shown much interest in absorbing the findings of recent English constitutional historians. Indeed, except for Peter S. Onuf's excellent new study of the role of interstate relations in American constitutional development between 1775 and 1787 and the extremely important recent work of several legal historians, including Barbara A. Black, Thomas C. Grey, William E. Nelson, and John Phillip Reid,[2] almost all work of significance on the subject has been incidental to the influential studies of revolutionary political ideology done in the 1960s by Bernard Bailyn and Gordon S. Wood. For the years before 1760, however, neither Bailyn nor Wood gave any systematic attention either to constitutional developments in the colonies or to the changing character of constitutional thought about the nature of the empire. Even for the period after 1763, they focused primarily upon the employment, domestication, and elaboration of the civic humanist tradition in American republican thought and devoted relatively little space to problems of constitutional organization.[3]

The contention of this volume is that such problems were fundamental to both colonial and revolutionary constitutional concerns. This view represents something of a return to the emphases of an older generation of historians, including especially two people whose work I have long admired, Andrew C. McLaughlin and Charles H. McIlwain. With McLaughlin, this volume stresses the continuity of constitutional issues from the colonial period through the Revolution. With McIlwain, it emphasizes the fluidity and unsettled character of the constitutional situation within the empire, the parallels between the colonial and Irish constitutional situations in regard to Britain, the continuing importance of custom in colonial constitutional developments, the novelty of parliamentary claims to jurisdiction over the internal affairs of the colonies in the 1760s, and the powerful customary foundations for the colonial constitutional case as it gradually took shape between 1764 and 1775.[4]

In many of its more important features, this book may be considered an elaboration of the broad framework sketched out or implied by those two scholars. In its more detailed and systematic analysis of the development of colonial constitutions both in practice and theory in the North American and West Indian colonies, the evolution of American thought about the constitutional situation of the colonies between 1764 and 1775, and the interplay between experience and perception in the emergence of American ideas about federal-state relations between 1776 and 1788 it builds on these older works at the same time that it has been informed by more recent scholarship.[5]

In several important respects, however, the volume departs from this older tradition. First, it distinguishes sharply among the three sets of operative constitutions in the British Empire: the British constitution, the specific constitutions of individual colonies, and the emerging imperial constitution. Second, it places considerably more stress on the experiential foundations of changing constitutional perceptions. Third, it puts much heavier emphasis upon both the local roots of constitutional authority within the empire and the consensual basis of constitutional arrangements, including especially the role of peripheral areas in defining those arrangements.

Indeed, contrary to the work of many recent historians, the analysis that follows assumes that, so far from being authoritative, pronouncements from the centers of early modern extended polities like the British Empire acquired constitutional legitimacy for the whole only through implicit or explicit ratification by the peripheries. Had Britain had the requisite coercive resources, which it did not, it presumably could have enforced the views of the center in all the peripheral areas of the empire. To have secured obedience through force, however, would have constituted an admission of the absence or breakdown of authority, which, as most contemporary political thinkers in the British-American world were acutely aware, was always a function of opinion.

In practice, then, political and constitutional arrangements within the extended polities of both the early modern British Empire and the new United States were founded upon the consent of their many constituent components. That is, local sanction from the peripheries was essential to endow any position of the center with constitutional authority—and vice versa. Constitutional customs and doctrines could emanate from either the center or the peripheries, but they could not attain full constitutional authority outside the area of emanation—or for the empire as a whole—until they had been accepted by all parties to which they might apply.

Both in its origins and in its results, the American Revolution provides a classic illustration of the truth of these observations. Between 1765 and 1776, the metropolis simply could not secure colonial consent to its emerging view of the constitutional structure of the empire without resorting to force, and when, after nearly eight years of war, its will and resources proved inadequate to that task, it had no alternative but to permit the former colonies to go their own independent ways. With this experience behind them, political leaders of the

United States in the 1770s and 1780s automatically understood that no new center for the American union could be constituted without the formal and explicit consent of all the several entities that composed that union.

The book developed out of an invitation from the Richard B. Russell Lecture Committee to offer the second in an annual series of lectures on aspects of American constitutional history at the University of Georgia. Although my first research was on the constitutional development of the early modern British Empire, constitutional history has not been central to my interests since the early 1960s. But I have never lost my affection for the subject and was delighted to have an opportunity to draw together, develop at greater length, and place in a more general context several ideas that I have had about the subject in the intervening years. Representing a considerable expansion of the three lectures I presented in Athens in the winter of 1983 under the title "Power, Authority, and the Problem of Center-Periphery Relations in Anglo-American Constitutional Development, 1607–1789," the book that follows builds upon and borrows freely from several of my previously published articles and essays.[6]

Several people have assisted in its preparation. Joyce Chaplin and Mary Gwaltney helped gather materials. Elizabeth Paynter typed the first half of the manuscript. Trevor Burnard checked for typographical errors and footnote inconsistencies. Avihu Zakai read the first four chapters, and Peter Onuf the entire manuscript. Both offered useful suggestions for improvement and saved me from some errors. Elizabeth Paynter and Trevor Burnard read proof. Jacqueline Megan Greene did the index. The book was completed while I was a member of the Institute for Advanced Study in Princeton during the academic year 1985–86.

Jack P. Greene
Princeton, New Jersey
October 31, 1985

Peripheries
and Center

Prologue

When on June 19, 1787, in a committee of the whole, the delegates to the Federal Convention in Philadelphia took up the question of whether a new national government should be established, the Pennsylvania lawyer and legal theorist James Wilson was the first to speak. "In all extensive empires," he declared in expressing his opposition to any proposal that would "annihilate the state governments," "a subdivision of power is necessary." Without appropriate "subordinate jurisdictions" to take responsibility for all those many "purposes [to] which [the authority and competence of the central government] . . . could not reach," no "general government," he observed, could possibly govern such "a great extent of territory" as the United States. No other delegate disputed Wilson on this point. But it was far easier for them all to agree that the United States was "too extensive for a single Gov[ernmen]t" than to achieve a consensus on how authority should be divided between the central government and the states.[1] As James Madison subsequently reported in reviewing the work of the convention for Thomas Jefferson, "the due partition of power, between the General and local Governments, was perhaps of all [questions confronting the convention], the most nice and difficult."[2]

Madison's report could scarcely have surprised Jefferson. The problems of how and where, in Madison's words, to "draw the line of demarkation which would give to the General Government every power requisite for general purposes, and leave to the States every power which might be most beneficially administered to them" was not a new one for Americans in 1787.[3] These essentially constitutional problems had become increasingly familiar to the emerging nation-states of western Europe during the late medieval and early modern periods as they sought to extend their hegemony from core areas—centers—outward, first over contiguous areas and then over more distant territories—peripheries.[4]

Most often, this objective was accomplished by direct incorporation of new areas into the political system of the center. Through incorporation, the center consolidated its authority over the peripheries while the peripheries became immediate, if by no means usually equal or well-assimilated, participants in the central polity. As the historical sociologist Michael Hechter has shown in the case of England, this process of "internal colonialism" produced markedly unequal results because wealth, capacity, and power tended to concentrate in the center to the socioeconomic and cultural disadvantage of the Celtic fringe, which included Cornwall, Wales, and Scotland after 1707.[5] But these peripheries at least had a direct political voice in the decisions that produced and sanctioned their disadvantaged condition.

The situation was different with Ireland. Partly because of its physical separation across the Irish Sea and partly because the stubborn resistance of the native Irish had, prior to the early seventeenth century, prevented the English from establishing their influence beyond the Pale, a relatively small area adjacent to Dublin, Ireland, unlike Cornwall, Wales, and, later, Scotland, was not incorporated into the realm for several centuries. Until it was subjected to a parliamentary union with Great Britain in 1800, it remained theoretically a separate kingdom, a dominion of the English crown with its own semi-autonomous constitutional system. As we shall see later in more detail, the English government's relationship with Ireland provided some direct experience in dealing with the problem of how to exert and maintain its authority within an extended polity, not every part of which was fully and formally incorporated into the central government. But this problem appeared in a new and considerably different form as a result of the decision to authorize the settlement of subordinate colonies in America. Initially taken in a tentative way during the closing decades of the sixteenth century, this decision had by 1750 resulted in the creation of twenty-three separate British colonies on the western rim of the Atlantic. Nine additional British colonies were set up in America over the following quarter century. Like Ireland, each of these colonies was, for all practical purposes, a separate satellite state that existed in an ambiguous relationship to the central state to which it was attached.[6]

Throughout the long period from the establishment of England's first successful colony in Virginia in 1607 to the Declaration of Independence in 1776, British people on opposite sides of the Atlantic repeatedly found themselves at odds over the question of how, in Edmund Burke's words, "the strong presiding power, that is so useful towards the conservation of a vast, disconnected, infinitely diversified empire" could be reconciled with the "liberty and safety of the [several separate] provinces" in America.[7] That they never succeeded in resolving this problem in a way that was acceptable to people both at the center and in the peripheries was vividly indicated by its centrality in the long and intense series of disputes between Britain and the colonies from 1764 to 1776.

Certainly the most important and intractable issue in those disputes, this problem was by no means resolved for the Americans by separation from Britain. Rather, it continued to perplex the new United States during the Revolution and the Confederation period. If in the British Empire the metropolis had claimed too much power to render the rights of the colonies secure, the Articles of Confederation, the country's first national constitution, gave the national government far too little authority to supply it with the "strong presiding power" thought by leaders at the center to be necessary for the perpetuation of a national union. Among the many concerns that animated the movement for constitutional change during the 1780s, few were so powerful as the growing realization that, no less than the constitution of the British Empire, the Articles of Confederation had failed to resolve this classic difficulty of the extended polity.

In the pages that follow I will trace the search for a solution to this problem from the beginnings of settlement through the adoption of the Federal Constitution in 1787–88. I will argue that this search was a significant and persistent concern for British-Americans in their relations with the metropolis before 1776 and with each other thereafter and that it provides an underlying unity to early American constitutional history from the colonial through the early national periods.

Book One

A Problem Experienced, 1607–1763

Chapter One

In Quest of Periphery Dependence: Crown and Colonies

Establishment of colonies in America presented the English government with a wide range of practical political problems, every one of which also had important theoretical implications. Notwithstanding that they were both persistent and of crucial importance to the lives of the people involved, throughout the first century and a half of settlement many of these problems proved to be exceedingly difficult not only of resolution but even of definition. Indeed, they can perhaps be most accurately characterized as problems that were repeatedly experienced and at least partially grasped but by no means fully defined and certainly not resolved to the mutual satisfaction of all concerned parties. What these problems were, how they were experienced and understood, and how they affected the constitutional development of the British Empire between 1607 and 1763 are the subjects of this and the succeeding three chapters.

Perhaps the most basic question raised by the creation of American colonies was precisely what these colonies were. By the early seventeenth century, the English had had extensive experience in dealing with areas that, though parts of the monarch's dominions, were not physically attached to the realm of England. These included Anjou, Acquitaine, Gascony, the Channel Islands of Guernsey and Jersey, Wales, Ireland, and the Isle of Man, the first three of which had by 1600 long since passed out of the monarch's control. Most of the dominions of this "medieval empire" had come to the monarchy through inheritance, but two—Wales and Ireland—had been acquired by conquest. Each was adjacent to or reasonably close to England, well-peopled with non-English inhabitants, and possessed of its own peculiar socioeconomic, legal, and political traditions that differed from and were to varying extents independent of those of England. Of them all, only Wales had been fully incorporated into the realm of England and then not until 1536. The rest were a series of small satellite states bound together by their mutual connection with the monarchy and its advisers either in the conciliar parliaments of the Middle Ages or in the Privy Council under the Tudors. With the accession of James I in 1603, Scotland came into this loose association of political entities, although before the Act of Union in 1707 it was explicitly and formally independent of the realm—as opposed to the monarchy—of England.[1]

The American colonies differed from these old dominions in many crucial respects. First, and by no means least important, they were three thousand miles away. Second, although all but one or two island colonies had significant native populations at the time of initial settlement, population density was low relative to the most fully occupied areas of Europe, much of the land was uncultivated and therefore according to contemporary European theory "waste" and available for colonization, and the natives were both pagan and, the English thought, culturally less advanced than most Europeans. Showing very little interest in absorbing the natives, the English preferred to displace them through physical expulsion, purchase of their land, or both. Thus, unlike the monarch's dominions on the eastern side of the Atlantic, those in America to an important degree were composed of emigrants from the British Isles and their descendants, new settler populations in places from which the old populations had been or soon would be almost entirely removed. The very newness of these new societies—the absence of long-settled local traditions, institutions, and patterns of social relations—constituted still a third important distinction between them and the various components of the English monarchy's medieval empire.

The new plantations of English and Scots established in Ireland under Elizabeth and the first two Stuarts were in several respects similar to the American colonies. But they differed in two important ways. First, they were established on territories conquered from a people that was numerous, Christian, and, by European standards, civilized. Second, the English and Scottish immigrants and their increase became a majority only in a few localities and thus had to live in the midst of a numerically superior and often hostile native population.[2] To be sure, a few of the American colonies had, like Ireland, also been conquered. Previously settled by colonists from rival European societies, Jamaica had been wrested from the Spanish in 1655, New York from the Dutch in 1664, and Nova Scotia and half of St. Christopher from the French in 1713. Except in Jamaica, from which all of the Spanish settlers fled following the English conquest, many of the old inhabitants of these colonies chose to remain under English governance. In contrast to the situation in Ireland, however, incoming immigrants from the British Isles quickly became a majority and eventually established their political and cultural predominance over the earlier inhabitants.

If the American colonies differed in these ways from the monarch's more ancient dominions in the British Isles and Europe, they were also somewhat different from most other colonies with which contemporaries were familiar. Colonization had, of course, been a familiar phenomenon in antiquity. As early modern Europeans understood these early colonies, those of Greece had been autonomous settlements in previously unoccupied lands by surplus population from Greece itself, and the Roman, as one eighteenth-century commentator remarked, had been "planted among vanquished nations to over-awe, and hold them in subjection."[3] The plantations in Ireland bore some strong resemblances to the Roman prototype as, many English people believed, did the contemporary Spanish colonies in Mexico and Peru. Similarly, some of the Anglo-American colonies were initially conceived and at least to some extent actually functioned for a time much like the garrison settlements on the English frontiers and in Ireland.[4]

But observers early recognized that the colonies in America were unlike either of these ancient models. Unlike the Greeks, they did not have de jure autonomy; unlike the Romans, they were not primarily concerned with "keep[ing] conquered Countries in Subjection." Rather, like most of the early modern European colonies in America, they were groups of people who, with the authorization of the monarch, settled in vacant or lightly occupied places for the specific purposes of cultivating the land and promoting trade "for the good of themselves and that [of the] state they belong[ed] to." Thus "intended to increase the Wealth and Power of the[ir] native Kingdom," these "Colonies of Commerce," people gradually came to perceive, were an entirely "new species of colonizing, of modern date, and differing essentially from every other species of colonizing that is known."[5]

There is some evidence that in the early days of colonization, metropolitan officials hoped that the colonies eventually might be "firmly incorporate[d] into this Commonwealth" of England in the manner of Wales.[6] But they soon recognized that distance made such a goal unfeasible with the result that the American colonies, like the monarchy's older non-English territories, soon came to be thought of not as "Part of the Realm of England" but as "Separate and Distinct Dominions." In this conception, each colony was thus a separate corporate entity, a body politic authorized by the crown, with jurisdiction over a well-defined body of territory and its own distinctive institutions, laws, customs, and, eventually, history and identity—all of which reflected its peculiar "Circumstances . . . in respect of its Soil, Situation, Inhabitants, and Commerce."[7]

Separateness did not, of course, mean independence. Although the colonies were "distinct . . . dominions" and not actually part of the English realm, they were nevertheless, virtually all metropolitan officials agreed, also "dependent . . . dominions." *Dependence*, to quote Dr. Samuel Johnson's *Dictionary*, was a "state of hanging down from a supporter," a condition that implied both weakness and subordination in relationship to some person, body, or institution that was stronger or more competent and superior. Precisely because wives, children, servants, and other dependents who could neither sustain nor defend themselves had to rely on husbands, fathers, masters, or patrons to support and protect them, they were not independent but, in the terminology of the age, were "at the disposal or under the sovereignty of" those upon whom they relied. Dependency was, however, a relative state. Although metropolitan officials could agree that the colonies were dependent entities, they found the further questions of in what ways and to what extent they were dependent and how much actual autonomy or independence such dependent institutions might enjoy far more difficult to answer.[8]

The basic objectives of the English in establishing colonies dictated that these questions would not be easily resolved. As they said in the case of Virginia, English officials authorized colonies in expectation of "the great advantages both of honor and profitt which this Crowne and state might receive from . . . set[t]led and well ordered plantation[s]." The American colonies were thus, as many later observers affirmed, "first planted on *Commercial Views*" with trade and profit as "their first principle." To obtain these goals at minimal costs to itself and the nation, the monarchy encouraged private adventurers—either organized into chartered companies or acting as lord proprietors—to sponsor colonies by granting them exclusive title to vast areas of land and "sundrie verie large immunities and priviledges," including extensive self-governing powers and, in many cases, special economic concessions. Such arrangements were similar to those earlier used in the expansion of England into the Celtic fringe, where the monarchy had granted local magnates in places such as Chester and Durham a large measure of autonomy in return for their continuing fealty. Lacking the fiscal resources to enable them to undertake such territorial expansion on their own, English monarchs had no other means by which to establish the legitimacy of their claims to both new territories and, certainly no less important, the allegiance of the inhabitants of those territories.[9]

But the colonies differed from English border areas in three important respects. First, they were far more distant. Second, they did not have settled native populations that could be easily mobilized to achieve the objectives of the colonizers. Third, the new predominantly English settlers brought with them English traditions of law and governance, which put a high premium upon individual and local corporate liberties and autonomy. Tudor England, as Kenneth R. Andrews has remarked, was "a largely self-governing society—under the crown," and the "increase in governance" through the establishment of many "new local institutions that tied the counties [more closely] to the center" during the century following the accession of Elizabeth does not seem to have seriously dampened "the fierce, full-hearted localism" that both supported and encouraged those local self-governing tendencies. One important consequence of this deeply etched "characteristic of early modern English society" was what Andrews refers to as a powerful "tendency towards self-government in the emergent empire." At the same time that the sponsors of the several colonial enterprises invariably proved to be both "particularly jealous of" their "autonomy and resistant to royal interference," they found that they could not recruit settlers for such distant and unfamiliar areas in numbers sufficient to meet their objectives without generous guarantees of self-governing rights and concessions in the form of access to land and, occasionally, temporary exemption from taxation and other public obligations.[10]

Thus, on both levels—between the monarchy and the sponsors on one hand and between the sponsors and individual colonists on the other—English colonization depended initially upon a series of reciprocal agreements, or, in the formal theoretical language of the day, contracts that permitted the sponsors and the individual colonists a generous amount of political freedom and wide latitude to pursue their own personal objectives in return for extending the dominions of the sponsors and the monarchy over vast new areas in America. The "charter" privileges thus enjoyed by the colonists, which in virtually every case included "a liberty of enacting among themselves such laws as they think convenient," provided the basis in each colony for a "Particular Constitucion." As William Penn remarked, each of these constitutions was both specially "adapted to" a specific "People and Place" and constituted a form of possession that, most colonists seemed to have come to believe, was at least "as much Property as Soil." Precisely because people in possession of property in the English-speaking world were, by definition, both independent and autonomous, this conception of the colonial constitutions (and the liberties they embodied and protected) as property carried with it powerful connotations of corporate independence for the entities involved.[11]

Notwithstanding these connotations and the extensive self-governing powers actually exercised by the colonies under their charters, English monarchs and their advisers never wavered in their insistence that "such inferiour dominion[s]" had to remain subordinate to the "Dominion Superiour." Nevertheless, although the monarchy assumed direct control over Virginia in 1625 after the courts had vacated the charter of the Virginia Company and asserted its intention to provide "one uniforme Course of Government" for all of the English plantations in America, it did not, before the 1660s, make any concerted or comprehensive effort to restrict the self-governing privileges granted to the colonies in their charters. In fact, it made several similar grants to new colonies between 1660 and 1680. The result was that the early colonists, as a later writer remarked, "grew up . . . in a spirit of independence and self-reliance." By the middle of the seventeenth century after only a few decades of settlement, they already had become thoroughly accustomed—as well as attached—to what they referred to as "their *ould liberties and privileges.*" Thus during the Interregnum, on February 18, 1651, the pro-royalist government of Barbados denounced Parliament's effort to assert its jurisdiction over the island and to curtail its close trading connections with the Dutch as an attempt to reduce the colony to slavery and as an unwarranted attack upon its *"freedom, safety, and well-being."*[12]

That the metropolitan government intended to reduce the colonies to what it called an "absolute obedience to the King's authority" became ever more evident beginning with the Restoration of Charles II in 1660. Between 1651 and 1696, Parliament enacted a series of navigation acts designed to define the economic relationship between England and the colonies; to eliminate colonial trade with rival foreign powers, especially the Dutch; and, insofar as possible, to subordinate the economies of the colonies to that of the metropolis.[13] The difficulty of securing colonial compliance with these measures as well as a growing recognition of the colonies' commercial and strategic importance to the parent state had by the mid-1670s persuaded metropolitan authorities that these distant and semiautonomous colonies on the outermost peripheries of the English Empire needed to be fixed much more firmly within the orbit—and the control—of the center. The consequence was a movement to reconstruct the political relationship between the monarchy and the colonies in a way that would both significantly enhance the power of the crown at the center and weaken the effective authority of local institutions in the peripheries.

This centripetal movement began in earnest in 1675 with the creation of the Lords of Trade, a permanent committee of the Privy Council responsible for overseeing the colonies. For a decade, until it lost its authority to the Privy Council under James II, this body, assisted by a permanent staff and a host of new crown officers in the colonies, provided, for the first time since the beginnings of English colonization nearly three-quarters of a century earlier, vigorous and systematic metropolitan supervision over the colonies. In a concerted effort to secure colonial obedience to royal authority and the navigation acts, the Lords of Trade developed a comprehensive program with three general objectives.[14]

The first was simply to strengthen the monarchy's hand in the four existing royal colonies: Virginia; Jamaica, which had been captured from the Spanish in 1655; and Barbados and the Leeward Islands, which had passed from proprietary to royal control in 1663. In pursuit of this objective, the Lords of Trade tried to bring the king's governors in the colonies under much stricter regulation. Not only did it insist upon more frequent and fuller reports on a wide range of activities within the colonies, but it also put the governors under much more detailed and rigid regulations than ever before by greatly expanding in scope and specificity the royal instructions given to governors to direct them in their conduct of government.

Equally important in regard to the royal colonies, the Lords of Trade set out to curtail the extensive powers of the elected legislative assemblies, which it perceived as the primary vehicles for colonial resistance to metropolitan policy. Derived in large part from the dependence of the governors upon the assemblies for money, both for their own personal support and for all normal expenses of government, the power of the assemblies extended over virtually all aspects of colonial government; and the assumption of such full and complete legislative authority had already led colonial legislators to the heady conclusion that each assembly was the "epitome of the [English] House of Commons."[15]

To render royal governors less dependent upon the assemblies, the Lords of Trade sought to persuade the assemblies of Virginia and Jamaica to follow the examples of those of Barbados and the Leeward Islands, which, in 1663 and 1664, respectively, had voted a permanent revenue from which the salaries of the governor and other royal officials as well as many ordinary expenses of government could be drawn. This effort, which was successful in Virginia and unsuccessful in Jamaica, was accompanied by a direct assault upon the legislative powers of the assemblies in which the Lords of Trade attempted unsuccessfully to apply Poynings's Law—which required the crown's prior approval of all laws passed by the Irish Parliament—to Jamaica and Virginia.

The second broad objective of the Lords of Trade was to prevent the creation of any more private colonies and to convert those already in existence into royal colonies. Upon its recommendation, the New Hampshire towns were separated from Massachusetts Bay in 1679 and made a royal colony. Although the Lords of Trade was unable to block Charles II's grant of Pennsylvania to William Penn in 1681, it did secure the insertion in the Pennsylvania charter of a series of limitations that subjected Penn to much stricter controls than any of his predecessors. In 1684, the Lords of Trade also initiated a general assault upon the charters of the private colonies in the metropolitan courts that resulted in the forfeiture of the charters of Bermuda and Massachusetts Bay.

A logical extension of the previous two, the third objective of the Lords of Trade was to consolidate the colonies into three general governments. Presided over by viceregal representatives of the monarch, these governments were to be altogether unhampered by representative assemblies. This objective, evidently inspired at least in part by Colbert's contemporary reforms in the French colonial system, was in the air as early as 1678. In 1686, after the accession of James II, who shared with the Lords of Trade an antipathy to private colonies and colonial representative institutions, it resulted in the establishment of the Dominion of New England, intended to include all of the colonies from Maine south to Pennsylvania.

Attempts to implement this centralizing program forcibly raised a series of issues about the relationship of metropolis and colonies that were never satisfactorily resolved before the American Revolution. The precise nature of these issues and the ways they affected metropolitan-colonial relations will be explored more fully in subsequent chapters. At this point, it is sufficient to indicate that the crown's new Restoration colonial policy provoked a profound mistrust of central authority among the colonists and stimulated a variety of efforts in the peripheries to find explicit legal defenses to protect the colonies from such wholesale intrusions of metropolitan power.

None of the colonies denied that they were dependent upon the English monarchy; but they did insist that their dependence did not deprive them of their rights as Englishmen, which they had claimed on the basis of inheritance and royal charters at least from the early 1620s. Thus did the first Maryland Assembly assert in 1638 "that all the Inhabitants of this Province . . . shall have and enjoy all such rights liberties immunities priviledges and free customs within this Province as any naturall born subject of England hath . . . in the Realm of England."[16]

As it became more and more clear that the new metropolitan policies undermined their claims to those rights, colonial leaders both opposed those policies and demanded that the inhabitants of the colonies be guaranteed the rights of Englishmen. Between 1675 and

1695, this demand was explicit in a variety of efforts by colonial legislatures to secure measures that would serve as formal legal guarantees of their constituents' rights to English liberties and privileges. These included Virginia's attempt to obtain a new charter from the Crown in 1675–76; documents such as the Bill of Privileges drawn up by the Jamaica Assembly in 1677 and the Charter of Liberties enacted by the first New York Assembly in 1683; manifestos adopted in Massachusetts, New York, and Maryland in 1688–89 when, inspired by the Glorious Revolution at home, groups of colonists seized power from existing officials in behalf of William III; and the rash of attempts by the legislatures of Virginia, New York, Massachusetts, South Carolina, and Maryland between 1691 and 1696 to pass measures in imitation of Parliament's 1689 Declaration of Rights. In fact, the Glorious Revolution was widely interpreted in the colonies as a common struggle to secure the rights of Englishmen both in the center and the peripheries of the English-speaking world.[17]

For a few years after the Revolution, it appeared that metropolitan authorities might adopt a more permissive posture toward the colonies. Neither William III nor his advisers showed any disposition to revive the Dominion of New England, which had been overthrown by the New Englanders in the wake of the revolution, or to govern the colonies without representative assemblies. In 1691 they granted a new charter to Massachusetts Bay, albeit one severely limiting the colony's self-governing powers, and in 1694 they restored Pennsylvania, which they had taken over in 1692, to William Penn.

But it soon became clear that the underlying goals of metropolitan colonial policy had not changed. In 1696, Parliament passed a new and stricter navigation act, the first of several commercial regulations it would enact for the colonies over the next six decades, and the crown created the Board of Trade to assume the duties earlier handled by the defunct Lords of Trade. Confronted with persistent reports of colonial violations of the navigation acts as well as problems in trying to mobilize the colonies to contribute to their mutual defense during the first two intercolonial wars, the Board of Trade sought to enhance metropolitan authority in the colonies through many of the same policies pursued by its predecessor in the 1670s and 1680s. Thus it endeavored to limit the autonomy of the royal colonies by securing permanent revenues and restricting the authority of the colonial assemblies; it sought to eliminate the private colonies by recalling their charters and converting them to royal colonies; and it advocated consolidating the colonies into one or more general governments so that they might be more easily controlled from London and better able to defend themselves.

Although the crown assumed the administration of several private colonies when the proprietors of New Jersey (1702), the Bahamas (1717), and the two Carolinas (1729) voluntarily relinquished their self-governing privileges, a combination of colonial resistance and lack of domestic political support in Britain combined to frustrate most of the board's efforts to achieve these objectives during its first quarter century of existence, and, although it continued to pursue these same objectives, albeit with somewhat less vigor, it enjoyed even less success during the so-called period of salutary neglect when Sir Robert Walpole was at the head of the British government. Nor would it obtain a more favorable hearing for its proposals until mid-century, after the second series of colonial wars had once again seemed to underline the desirability of tighter metropolitan controls over the colonies.

A century of efforts to reconstruct the relationship between the metropolis and the colonies in ways that would render the peripheries more securely dependent upon the center had thus by no means been fully successful. In the economic realm, the colonies had gradually come to accommodate to the navigation acts during the first half of the eighteenth century. Especially after 1715, there was very little of the overt resistance to those measures that had been so often manifested over the previous seventy years of their existence. Yet this compliance was selective: the colonists continued to ignore or to evade those regulations that seemed, as one royal official in the colonies complained, to hinder "the growth and prosperity of their little commonwealths."[18] Thus merchants in the middle colonies and New England did not hesitate to violate the Molasses Act of 1733, which, they correctly felt, discriminated against them in favor of West Indian sugar interests. By contrast, in the political realm there was considerable open controversy, much of which revealed the colonists' continued resistance to metropolitan efforts to bring them under stricter control and underlined the fact that in most colonies the political authority of the center remained infinitely weaker and much less secure than British officials and their colonial representatives would have preferred.

Between 1660 and 1760 metropolitan authorities had not managed to render the colonies as dependent as they would have liked; but in pursuit of this general policy objective they had articulated a cluster of overlapping working assumptions about the nature of the relationship between Britain and the colonies—between the center and the peripheries of the British Empire. The first and most fundamental of these assumptions was simply that the colonies were dependent entities, an idea that was at the heart of the familiar parent-child metaphor that was increasingly employed to describe the metropolitan-colonial connection. This metaphor implied both a need for protection and obligations of obedience on the part of the colonists. A second assumption was that the primary reason for the existence of the colonies was to contribute to the well-being of the parent state. The third was that the political systems of the colonies had to be and were subordinate to the government of Britain. Within metropolitan circles, these assumptions had come to be so widely accepted as to make them virtually unchallengeable.

The colonists did not in principle deny the validity of any of these assumptions, but they showed by their behavior a profound concern over how such concepts as *dependence* and *subordination* were to be applied to their situation. More specifically, they worried over how their relationship with Britain affected their rights as Englishmen and whether those rights and the corporate and individual interests those rights had been devised to protect could be secured to English people living in dependent and distant polities. To an important extent, the constitutional development of the early modern British Empire and of the several colonies associated with it evolved out of the debates and controversies over these questions.

Chapter Two

In Quest of Periphery
Rights: Local Roots of
Constitutional Change

The many efforts to impose metropolitan controls upon the colonies after 1650 gave rise to a seemingly endless series of controversies over the balance of authority between the center and the peripheries within the expanding Anglophone empire. Persisting for the next century and a quarter, these controversies initially focused to an important degree upon the commercial restrictions imposed by Parliament in the navigation acts. Few colonies went so far in their opposition to these measures as Barbados. Having previously been consistently unfriendly to Parliament in its struggle with Charles I during the English Civil War, many of the leading inhabitants joined together in 1651 to condemn the first navigation act as an unwarranted intrusion upon the colony's economic autonomy. Denouncing the measure as subversive of *"the freedom, safety, and well-being of this island,"* the Barbadians directly challenged the legitimacy of any parliamentary limitations upon their trade and vowed never to submit to any law that would "deny or forbid" the "Netherlanders . . . or any other nation, the freedom of our harbours, and the protection of our Laws, by which they may continue, if they please, all freedom of commerce and traffick with us."[1]

That no other colony issued so dramatic a challenge to Parliament's authority to regulate colonial economic life did not mean that hostility to Parliament and resentment against its economic controls did not run deep everywhere in the American colonies. In 1689, Edward Littleton, a Barbadian planter, expressed what seems to have been a widely shared view. "In former daies," he declared in *The Groans of the Plantations*, published in London, "we were under the pleasing sound of Priviledges and Immunities, of which a free Trade was one, though we counted That, a Right and not a Priviledge. . . . Now those things are vanisht and forgotten. . . . All the Care now is, to pare us close, and keep us low. We dread to be mention'd in an Act of Parliament; because it is alwaies to do us Mischief."[2]

Over time, however, colonial concern tended to fix not upon Parliament's efforts to turn the economies of the colonies into channels thought to be most profitable to the metropolis, efforts the colonies eventually came to accept, but upon the crown's claims to extensive authority over and within the colonies. As the colonists gradually came to understand the situation, these claims "for making the Crown absolute in America" had been first articulated under the Stuarts, monarchs, as one colonist later remarked, "who carried the notions of kingly RIGHT and kingly POWER to . . . a blasphemous height, and set . . . little value on the liberties of the people." In England, Parliament had imposed explicit restrictions upon the crown's prerogative following the Glorious Revolution. But these restrictions did not extend to the colonies. Thus, long after the crown had given up its rights to veto laws, to prorogue and dissolve legislative bodies and determine the frequency of their meetings, to dismiss judges at pleasure, and to create courts in Britain itself, it continued to claim and actually to exert such authority for its governors in the colonies. Moreover, it also continued to claim and to exercise authority to disallow colonial laws without the consent of the "Plantation Assemblys by whom they were made," which, as one colonial pointed out, could "not be done in [any of] the rest of [the crown's] . . . Dominions." The result was that the crown claimed far greater power over the colonists than "over any other of [its] . . . Subjects."[3]

That metropolitan authorities thought "it necessary [that] the King should be more Absolute in the Plantations than he is in *England*" was a source of enormous unease in the colonies. As an anonymous Jamaican declared in 1714, it seemed wholly inexplicable "that in all the Revolutions of State and Changes of the Ministry" in England since the Restoration "the several Colonies which compose the *British* Empire in *America*" and were inhabited by supposedly freeborn Englishmen "should . . . lye still so much neglected, under such a precarious Government and greivous [sic] Administration, as they have, for the most part, labour'd under, both before and since the late signal Revolution." Indeed, from the perspective of that revolution in which the rights and privileges of subjects in England had been so fully

"confirmed; and the knavish Chicanes, and crafty Inventions, that
were introduced [by the later Stuarts] to deprive the Subject of his
Rights . . . abolished," it seemed especially grievous "that a Governour of any Colony . . . so far distant from the Seat of Redress
. . . should be vested with a Power to govern, in a more absolute and
unlimited manner there, than even the Queen herself can, according
to Law, or ever did attempt to exercise in *Great Britain.*"[4]

Nor were the dangers of this situation merely imaginary. The histories of the colonies were replete with instances in which "Temporary
and Mercenary Governours," lacking in many cases even a remote
sense of identity of interests with the colonists, had used their "extraordinary powers" to "squeeze Provinces, and make the most they
can of them, during their Time of Administration." "Intent upon
nothing but their own private Gain" and made "haughty and inso-
lent" by their exaggerated powers, plantation governors, the colonists claimed, had repeatedly "usurped more Authority than [even
theoretically] belonged to them" and committed all sorts of "oppression and rapine" under "Colour of his Majestie[']s Authority." Thus,
"to the great Terror and grievous Oppression of the Inhabitants" in
Antigua, had Daniel Parke "frequently . . . use[d] . . . Her Majesty's
Troops in executing Warrants and other Civil Process[es]" and,
through such acts of "Tyranny and Oppression," thereby sought to
"bear down and discourage People from any Opposition to him in his
lustful Attempts." Thus, in New Jersey, had Edward Hyde, Viscount
Cornbury, treated the people "not as Free-Men who were to be Governed by Laws, but as Slaves, of whose Persons and Estates he had
the sole power of disposing." Thus, in one place after another, had
governors by "various kinds of injustices and oppression, . . . sordid
mercenary measures . . . [and] . . . , mean things" managed to turn
"a flourishing Colony [into] a very poor one."[5]

Of course, colonial leaders were the first to admit that not all governors were weak or corrupt. Most of them perhaps were "Men of pure
Hearts, clear Heads, and clean Hands, experienc'd in Business, and
Men of [independent] Interest." Nor do many colonists seem to have
doubted that the king, as James Otis, the Massachusetts lawyer and
political writer, asserted in 1762, intended for "all his Plantation Governors [to] follow his royal example, in a wise and strict adherence to the
principles of the British Constitution." Whatever the king's intentions,
however, the "vast Influence" of colonial governors "over the Liber-

ties, Properties, and Estates of . . . every Man under [their] . . . Government[s]" meant that it was all too easy for them to "make Tyranny their Glory" and to "introduce [their] . . . own Will, as . . . Law." "Though possibly practised in *Morrocco,* where the moral Right all Men have to be happy and free, is destroyed by all being subservient to the Will of One," such potential for the exertion of "Arbitrary Power," an anonymous New Englander protested in 1749, had been "unknown in our Mother Country, since the glorious Revolution of 1688." "No sensible man," a Pennsylvanian observed in restating one of the most hallowed maxims of British political culture, could "think it safe that a power, which" was so liable to "be *abused,* should be left [thus] *indefinite.*" The Glorious Revolution had guaranteed that in Britain kings would thenceforth be "made for the good of the people, and not the people for them." If British kings were thus restrained, so also, Otis remarked acidly, "plantation Governor's [sic] should be."[6]

To defend themselves against wanton exertions of power by the crown's officers, the colonists relied primarily upon their inherited rights as Englishmen. As we have seen, in most colonies they had laid claim to those rights within a few years after their arrival in America, and during the last half of the seventeenth century they worked out an elaborate argument to strengthen those early claims. According to this argument, the original settlers and their descendants were all equally "honest free-born Subjects of England," who, with authorization from the English monarchy, had voluntarily left their "native country" for "a waste and howling wilderness." "*With great danger to our persons, and with great charge and trouble,*" they said, they had turned that wilderness into thriving and well-inhabited settlements and had thereby, at little cost to the English government, significantly "enlarged the *English* Trade and Empire" and brought "*England* . . . its greatest Riches and Prosperity."

While they were thus creating this new and valuable "*English* Empire in *America,*" they retained their English identity and remained, as a Barbadian declared in 1698, "no other but *English* Men: . . . your Countrey-Men, your Kindred and Relations," who, said another, "pretended to have as good *English* Bloud in our Veins, as some of those that we left behind us." It followed that their continuing identity as Englishmen entitled them to all the "hereditary Rights" of English subjects, rights they could not lose merely "by Transporting themselves" to America and rights that had been confirmed to them by their charters and were secured by their respective civil governments. To be in any way diminished in those rights simply because of their "great Distance . . . from the Fountain of Justice," they believed, would deprive them of "their Birthright and the Benefits of the Laws and Priviledges of *English* Men" and reduce them to a species of "slavery far exceeding all that [any of] the English nation hath yet suffered."[7]

But it was far easier for inhabitants of distant and dependent colonies to lay claim to the rights of Englishmen than it was for them actually to secure them. They knew—it was "a received Opinion"— that "Right without Power to maintain it" was "the Derision and Sport of Tyrants," and the quest to secure those rights against the power of the center was everywhere an enduring feature of colonial political life. In general, leaders of individual colonies pursued this quest along two parallel lines. First, they sought explicit guarantees of the rights of colonists to the laws of England. Second, they sought to enhance the authority of the elected assemblies. In the colonies, as well as in the metropolis, they hoped, law and parliaments would be the bulwarks of the people's liberties and properties.[8]

The colonists' quest for explicit guarantees of their right to English laws was a recurrent subject of debate for more than half a century beginning around 1670. This debate turned around two questions: first, whether the colonists were entitled to English laws, and, second, if so, to what laws.

At the root of the debate over the former question was the problem of whether the colonies were conquered countries. In 1607, in *Calvin's Case*, Sir Edward Coke had laid down the opinion that conquered countries, such as Ireland, could be governed according to the will of the king, who, though presumably bound to govern "according to natural equity," might or might not introduce the laws of England. Although the early Stuarts proceeded in some respects to treat Virginia, the Irish plantations, and the other colonies as "conquered" countries, there were obvious doubts about whether colonies of Englishmen settled in the "vacant" spaces of America fitted this definition. Thus in 1670 Chief Justice John Vaughan (in a report of *Craw* v. *Ramsey*) distinguished between dominions acquired by conquest and those acquired by colonization. But the implications of Vaughan's distinction were not fully spelled out until 1694, when, in the case of

Dutton v. *Howell* relating to a dispute in Barbados, Sir Bartholomew Shower, one of the lawyers, argued that as "a new settlement of *Englishmen* by the King's consent in an uninhabited country" Barbados was not a conquered territory. Whereas, according to the doctrine of *Calvin's Case*, the inhabitants of a conquered country were entitled to the privileges of English law only if they had been extended to them by the monarch, those in a newly settled colony of Englishmen, Shower contended, enjoyed those privileges as their birthright. The House of Lords, the tribunal in the case, ultimately ruled against Shower's view, and metropolitan judicial and legal officers continued in many instances to consider the colonies as conquered territories. But the Privy Council ultimately reaffirmed Shower's argument in 1722, when it determined in a widely reported case that "an uninhabited country newly found out, and inhabited by the *English*," as presumably were most of the American colonies, could not be treated as a conquered territory but had "to be governed by the laws of England."[9]

But the simple fact was that that none of these ad hoc decisions and arguments settled the question. As late as the 1760s there was still enormous confusion in the metropolis over whether the colonies had been acquired through settlement or, as such a widely respected authority as Sir William Blackstone affirmed, had been "principally . . . obtained . . . by right of conquest." This continuing confusion was vividly revealed at the close of the Seven Years' War, when British officials were establishing regulations for governing the ceded islands of Dominica, Grenada, St. Vincent, and Tobago obtained from France in the Treaty of Paris of 1763. "While those Islands were deemed Conquered Countries and subject to the King's Prerogative Royal by the Ministers on the first Floor," complained William Knox, later undersecretary of state for the colonies, "the Ministers on the second were considering them as British Colonies and investing the Inhabitants with all the privileges of Englishmen," and the "Privy Council which was intended by the Constitution to control the other Departments sanctified the absurdity by lending it's [sic] Authority to both Propositions." Few colonists shared this confusion. They did not dispute that many of the colonies had initially been conquered from the Indians or from rival foreign powers. But they insisted that the subsequent occupation of those colonies "by natural-born subjects of England" clearly entitled their inhabitants "to the benefit of all the laws of England . . . and the rights of Englishmen."[10]

When the colonists claimed the benefit of English laws, they were referring primarily, as the Jamaica legislature declared in 1677, to all those "laws and statutes heretofore made and used in our native country, the Kingdom of England, for the public weal of the same, and all the liberties immunities and privileges contained therein." These liberties included especially those basic protections, confirmed by Magna Charta and the Petition of Right, against imprisonment, loss of life, or dispossession of property without due process of law and exemption from taxation without consent. As noted earlier, between 1670 and 1700 the legislatures of several colonies had sought explicit confirmations of those rights in new charters, public declarations, and statutes, and these efforts continued during the early years of the eighteenth century, particularly in Jamaica, where, perhaps because the colony had been acquired by conquest, the inhabitants were expecially anxious to have some positive codification of their rights, and in Maryland, where antiproprietary leaders viewed English laws as a bulwark against possible arbitrary rule by the proprietor. This determination, in the words of the Duke of Portland, who acted as governor of Jamaica in the mid-1720s, "to be as near as can be, upon the foott of H[is] M[ajesty's] English subjects" in England finally succeeded in Jamaica in 1729. After a long battle, the legislature managed, in return for granting the crown a permanent revenue of £8,000 per year, to obtain metropolitan approval for a clause declaring "all such laws, and statutes of England as have been at any time esteemed, introduced, used, accepted, or received, as laws of this Island . . . to be and continue laws of this His Majesty's Island of Jamaica for ever."[11]

But Jamaica's success was exceptional. Most metropolitan officials, judges, and lawyers opposed such efforts, partly because of fears that they would diminish the royal prerogative in the colonies and partly because "so much of the English law" was either directed to purely local concerns or so full of those "artificial refinements and distinctions incident to the property of a great and commercial people" as to be "[in]applicable to . . . the condition of an infant Colony."[12]

Even had every judge and lawyer in Britain agreed that the colonists were entitled to English laws, however, there remained the extremely difficult question of precisely what English laws might apply in the colonies. English law was a complex combination of common law practices as applied by the courts and statute law enacted by Parliament. When either metropolitan judges and lawyers or colonial theorists declared that colonies of Englishmen had to be governed by English laws, did they mean the common law, the statute law, or both? Did they mean only those laws in force in England before the settlement of the colonies or also those in use thereafter?

The New York and New Jersey judge and lawyer Lewis Morris spelled out the dimensions of this complex problem in a tract published in 1734. "The Extent of the Laws of *England* into the Plantations," he wrote, "has been a Question often Debated, but never satisfactorily resolv'd. Some thought the common Law only, some that the common and statute both, did extend; those of the first Opinion were puz[z]led to tell what period of the common Law extended; and how it could extend, without the help of those Statutes esteemed declaratory or explanatory of the common Law. . . . Those who held that both common and Statute Law extended were as much puz[z]led to tell, what periods of Time were to be taken in? Whether the Time of the Imbarkation of the first People of any Colony? Or at the [several] different Imbarkations? Or that Statutes . . . made [after the colonies had been settled] . . . were binding in the Plantations as well as in England" unless the colonies were actually named in them?[13]

No doubt in an effort to clarify this confused situation, Richard West, the Board of Trade's legal counsel, had ruled fourteen years earlier in 1720 that the "Common Law of England is the Common Law of the Plantations, and all Statutes in affirmance of the Common Law pass'd in England antecedent to the settlement of any Colony are in force in that Colony unlesse there is some private Act to the contrary, tho' no Statutes made since those settlements are there in force unlesse the Colonies are particularly mention'd." In 1722, the Privy Council reiterated West's ruling in a memorandum. But such pronouncements did not have the weight of positive law and did not, in Morris's words, produce "a clear and satisfactory Resolution" of the enduring questions of "how far, and in what Sence, the Laws of *England* do extend and are in Force in the Plantations." Nor was any such resolution forthcoming in subsequent decades.[14]

As Knox observed, the continuing failure of officials at the center to make a systematic and effective effort to clarify this ambiguous situation left local institutions in the peripheries with wide latitude and primary responsibility for determining which English "Laws the People in any Colony were to be governed by." Some colonial writers and political leaders—notably in Jamaica, Maryland, and New York— sought to obtain the maximum benefits of English law by contending that all English statutes that did not specifically exclude the colonies applied to them. But the most prevalent opinion in the colonies seems to have been that only English statutes that specifically mentioned the colonies and English common law, insofar as it was applicable to local conditions, were in force. The corollary of this position was that English statutes that did not explictly mention the colonies were not in force unless, as Sir William Keith, a former governor of Pennsylvania, reported in 1726, they had been formally "brought over by some Act of Assembly in that Colony, where they are pleaded." Thus, during the century before the American Revolution, the colonial assemblies had gradually, in Knox's words, "assumed the authority of deciding which" general English statutes "should be of force, and which not, and by an Act of their own declared Acts of Parliament binding or useless as they judged proper."[15]

But these formal enactments by the legislatures do not appear to have limited colonial courts in their use of English law. Rather, during the last half century of the colonial period, lawyers and judges seem to have applied all kinds of English law—the common law, presettlement statutes, and postsettlement statutes that both did and, at least in some instances, did not specifically mention the colonies—as it suited local and temporal needs and conditions. In so doing, local legal and judicial officials followed the strategy pursued during the late seventeenth and early eighteenth centuries by the Jamaicans when they were unable to secure metropolitan approval for a statute to secure the benefits of English laws to the colony: they "pronounce[d] and admit[ted] in their Courts of Justice these English Laws [to be] in Force in the Island" with the deliberate intention of making them "after a Series of Years . . . freely Operate as Customs" that through "Prescription and long Usage" would acquire "the Effect and Value of Written Laws." Through this process, they fashioned a legal system for each colony that, as Sir William Gooch, lieutenant governor of Virginia from 1727 to 1749, observed, was both "exactly suited to the Circumstances of the Respective Governments, and as near as possible [as] it can be, conformable to the Laws and Customs of England." The colonies thus gradually gained in practice what they had, except in a few cases, been unable to obtain by statute: traditional English legal guarantees of life, liberty, and property. This development no doubt helps to account for the virtual disappearance of colonial attempts to secure such laws after the mid-1730s.[16]

That after more than a century they still had not managed to obtain positive legal confirmation of their entitlement to such rights, however, that it was yet impossible, as one perceptive observer had lamented way back in 1701, to "tell what is Law, and what is not in the Plantations" with the result that the colonists were "left in the dark, in one of the most considerable Points of our Rights; and [were] too often obliged to depend upon the Crooked Cord of a Judge's Discretion, in Matters of the greatest Moment and Value," continued as a latent concern among the colonists. This concern might no longer be deemed "a great Unhappiness," "one of the most material Grievances which the Subjects in America have just Cause to complain of." That it continued to be productive of a lingering unease, however, was powerfully evidenced during the 1760s and 1770s by the frequency and vehemence of colonial denials that the colonies were "under the circumstances of a conquered country" or were without the benefits of "the common law, and such general statutes of England as are securative of the rights and liberties of the subject."[17]

Much more enduring was a second issue, the issue, in the words of an anonymous Virginian in 1701, of "how far the Legislative Authority is in the Assemblies of the several Colonies." "Of late Years," he explained, "great Doubts have been raised" about "whether they have Power to make certain Acts or Ordinances in the nature of by-Laws only; or, whether they can make Acts of Attainder, Naturalization, for set[t]ling or disposing of Titles to Lands within their own Jurisdiction, and other things of the like Nature; and where Necessity requires, make such Acts as best suit the Circumstances and Constitution of the Country, even tho' in some Particulars, they plainly differ from the Laws of England." Disputes over such questions, the writer remarked, had run "very high in the late Reigns." He probably would have found it especially appalling that they would continue to "run very high" right down to the American Revolution.[18]

That the colonists had right to legislative assemblies and that those assemblies did indeed have legislative power were not in dispute. Those rights and powers had been conveyed to most colonies by their early charters from the crown or, for those few colonies like Jamaica and New Hampshire that never had charters, by the royal commissions to the first governors. These early grants were repeatedly reaffirmed in all the royal colonies—whether or not they had charters—

by clauses in the governors' commissions empowering them "to summon and call General Assemblies of the . . . Freeholders and Planters within your Government, according to the Laws and Usages of Our said Province" and with such assemblies to exercise "full Power and Authority to make, constitute and ordain Laws, Statutes and Ordinances for the Public Peace, Welfare and good Government of Our said Province, and of the People and Inhabitants thereof." That acts of these assemblies were "of the same effect" in the colonies as was an act of Parliament in Britain had been affirmed by the crown's law officers as early as 1703.[19]

Except for the brief experiment with absolute government for the Dominion of New England under James II from 1684 to 1689, metropolitan officials never attempted to govern in the colonies without representative institutions and invariably expressed their intentions that the colonists' "religion, liberties and properties should be inviolably preserved to them" through their assemblies. "By their several Constitutions," the Board of Trade informed the House of Lords in 1733, "All these Colonies . . . have the power of making Laws for their better government and support." By definition, the board thus implied, British colonies enjoyed representative institutions, and Dr. William Douglass, the Boston essayist and historian, could in 1749 credibly refer to those few English "Settlements with a Governor only . . . such [as] . . . *Newfoundland, Nova-Scotia, Hudson's Bay,* and *Georgia*" as "not [yet fully] colonized." Because they had no assembly, these plantations, according to Douglass, lacked the "Essence of a *British* Constitution." This same point was echoed just a few years later by discontented Nova Scotians, who complained that the absence of a "legislative power" deprived them "of those priviledges and civil rights which the people of the other colonies enjoy." The crown's law officers agreed and ruled in 1755 that no laws could be enacted in Nova Scotia without a legislative assembly, a ruling that led three years later to the establishment of such a body in that colony.[20]

The question was thus not whether the assemblies had lawmaking power but how extensive that power was. Although the Navigation Act of 1696 declared "illegal, null and void" any colonial law that was contrary to any of the navigation acts, the only express reservation in the colonial charters and governors' commissions was the provision that laws could "not be repugnant, but [had to be] as near as may be, agreeable to the Laws and Statutes of this Our Kingdom of Great Britain." This "nonrepugnancy" clause formed the legal basis for the review of colonial legislation by the king and Privy Council. Governors of all of the colonies except Maryland, Connecticut, and Rhode Island, which were exempt from the requirement by their charters, were obliged to transmit all laws to London, where the Privy Council could either disallow or confirm them according to whether they were or were not deemed to be repugnant to British law. Even laws from the three exempt colonies could, upon appeal from colonial courts, come before the Privy Council for review in its judicial capacity and were subject to invalidation if they were judged not to be "agreeable to the Laws of England."[21]

Although some colonial advocates tried to argue that the nonrepugnancy requirement applied only to those colonial laws that were contrary to British laws that had been made explicitly for the colonies, the Privy Council employed a much wider construction. But it did not insist that colonial laws be identical to those of England. On the contrary, it recognized the validity of the argument, made by the New England agent Jeremiah Dummer among others, that "Every Country has Circumstances peculiar to it self in respect of its Soil, Situation, Inhabitants, and Commerce" and that, as the governor and company of Rhode Island urged, "the various circumstances of the time and place and people doe often make it necessary to enact and establish Laws different [from], though not repugnant, to the Laws of England."[22]

With so few express restrictions upon their legislative authority, it is scarcely surprising that the colonial assemblies interpreted that authority very broadly. They were encouraged in this impulse by two conditions. First was their distance from the metropolis and the need for a broad range of laws and regulations to organize and reorganize the new environments they were elected to serve. Second was their inherited ideas about the function of representative bodies in the English world. That these ideas were applicable to their local situations had been powerfully reinforced by the largely successful effort by metropolitan authorities following the Restoration to substitute something resembling an English model of government for the welter of existing political forms that had grown up in the colonies during the first six decades of the seventeenth century and, more especially, by the explicit analogy drawn by those authorities between king, Lords, and Commons in England on the one hand and the governors, councils, and assemblies in the colonies on the other.

By the early eighteenth century, the inhabitants of the colonies took great pride that their "Form of Government" was "as nigh as conveniently can be to that of *England*." Just as the governors were invested with all the prerogatives of the king, and the councils performed the functions of the House of Lords as a middle or "*Aristocratical*" branch of the legislature, so did the lower houses conceive of themselves as being "upon the very same foot" with the House of Commons in Great Britain. "'Tis well known," wrote a Pennsylvanian in 1728 in repeating what had already become a commonplace, "that the Assemblies in the *English*-Plantations are formed on the Plan of an *English* Parliament: And as the Methods of Proceedings in *Westminster-Hall* are made a Rule to us, in our *Courts of Justice*, so our *Assemblies* in like manner take their Rules from the *House of Commons* there." Thus did the several colonial assemblies "proceed to do Business, choosing Committees, and in all other Respects imitating the House of Commons in *England* as nigh as possible."[23]

But it was not only the procedures and the forms of the House of Commons that the assemblies sought to copy in their efforts "to Assimilate themselves as near as possible to that August Body." Because the assemblies held "the same rank, in the system of" their "own constitution[s], as a British House of Commons does, in that of our mother Country," because they were "called by the same authority," derived their "power from the same source, [were] instituted for the same ends, and [were] governed by the same forms," colonial leaders insisted that it was "not only Reasonable but Necessary that the Assemblies in our Colonies, should be vested with the same Powers and Privileges there, as the Parliament have in England." In their efforts thus to make themselves "an epitome of the house of Commons," the assemblies "insisted on [retaining] the Sole Power of raising and disposing of all Publick Monies." Except in four colonies—Barbados, the Leeward Islands, Virginia, and Jamaica—they refused to vote permanent revenues to support the colonial civil establishments lest such votes deprive them of "the greatest Security of their Rights and Privileges: *Viz.* Their Power of Deprivation, which is the greatest Check against . . . absolute Government." Less successfully, they tried to secure the right to frequent sessions and the powers of adjournment and control over their internal affairs—all on the grounds that the English House of Commons enjoyed such authority.[24]

Precisely because the king's governors claimed to "be more Absolute in the Plantations than" the king himself was "in England," because some governors actually sought to use their exorbitant powers to increase the prerogative at the expense of liberty, the lower houses not only insisted on "conform[ing] themselves, as near as they possibly can, in all Matters, wherein the Rights and Liberties of the People are any Ways concern'd, to the Pattern and Example of the *Honourable House of Commons in* Great Britain." They also found themselves—and were frequently and correctly accused of—trying to secure checks on the prerogative and power over executive affairs that were "very contrary to the Usage of Parliaments in *England*" and went well beyond any exercised by the House of Commons. Thus in most colonies they assumed the power of appointing many executive officers, including especially those who were responsible for collecting and dispersing public revenues. As one South Carolinian noted in 1710, " 'tis a received Opinion among them, that the Power of appointing, examining, censuring, and displacing those who have the public Money in their Hands, is much better lodg'd in the" assembly "than in the Hands of any Governour, for Reasons generally [well-]Known in *America*." "To commit the absolute Disposition of our public Funds, to Men, on whose Actions they have no Check, or Controul," said a Pennsylvanian in the late 1750s, "would . . . be the height of political madness in our Assemblies." Wisely considering "the Frailty and Passions of Men, how difficult it is for those in Power to keep themselves within Bounds, and how inclin'd they are to Resentment," the assemblies, "tho' they never endeavoured to abridge their Governour's Power of doing Good, yet, by" these "and other Methods, they have aimed at leaving them as few Opportunities of doing Hurt as is possible."[25]

The assemblies' quest for power created serious problems for governors and their supporters in the colonies and for colonial officials in London. Already by the 1670s, metropolitan representatives were condemning the assemblies for trying "to grasp all power." By the early eighteenth century, governors were complaining, frequently and stridently, that the assemblies had "extorted so many powers from" their "predecessors, that there" was "now hardly enough left to keep the peace, much less to maintain the decent respect and regard that is due to the Queen's servant." The assemblies "not only claim[ed] . . . all such priviledges as" were "enjoyed by the House of Commons of Great Britain, but . . . even attempt[ed] to grasp at more power than any House of Commons ever yet exercised." While they were sitting, they acted as if "all power and authority was only in their hands," and, it was charged, they seemed determined "to divest the administration . . . of all . . . power and authority and to lodge it in the Assembly."[26]

By the middle of the eighteenth century, the situation had reportedly deteriorated still further. Metropolitan supporters in the colonies widely lamented that the assemblies had been so "long nibbling at the Prerogative[s] of the Crown" and had made such "a great progress" in their designs that they had "got[ten] the whole administration into their Hands" and thereby wholly destroyed "the political balance in which consists the strength and beauty of the British Constitution[al]" tradition and thrown "all the Weights that should trim and poise" the constitution "into the Scale of the People." "Instead of drawing nearer to the *mixt Forms*" of the British constitution, as they might have been expected to have done as the colonies increased in population and wealth, the colonial governments were becoming more and more like "*pure Republic[s]*," in which the assemblies exercised "such unrestrained Powers and Privileges" that they "seem[ed] even to claim a kind of Independency of their Mother-Country" and to act as if they were "not accountable for" their "Proceedings, to any Superior Powers," "no, not even to the King."[27]

If, as Knox remarked, the assemblies had little difficulty in baffling "the feeble attempts of the Royal Power" within the colonies, metropolitan officials both in the colonies and at home never accepted the legitimacy of these developments. The assemblies might indeed have lawmaking power within the colonies. According to metropolitan theory, however, their very existence depended not upon their constituents' inherent rights as Englishmen but upon the favor of the crown as extended to them by royal charter or some other official document such as the king's commission or instructions to his governors. The Lords of Trade articulated the official position in 1679 during the controversy over the metropolitan attempt to apply Poyning's Law to Jamaica and Virginia. Declaring that the colonists could not "pretend to greater privileges than those [specifically] granted them by Charter or

Act under the Great Seal," that body condemned the colonial assemblies for "regard[ing] as a right what was granted [only] as a favour" and denied that such "temporary and experimental constitutions" as the crown had thus far extended to the colonies could ever be regarded "as a resignation and devolution to them of the royal authority."[28]

Repeatedly affirmed over the next eighty years by the crown's law officers in London, this doctrine served as the favorite defense for colonial executives trying to combat the assemblies' pretensions to full legislative powers in the colonies. If, as metropolitan partisans affirmed, the colonies enjoyed their legislative privileges "from the Grace and Favour of the Crowne alone" and if the royal charters and commissions were the sole basis of "the *Constitution of Government*" in the colonies and "the only Thing[s]" that gave the assemblies "the Power of making Laws of any kind," then several conclusions followed: first, that "*without* the grace of the crown" the colonies would "have no legislative power at all"; second, that whatever legislative powers they did enjoy were neither "inherent" nor "*original*" but merely "derivative" in nature; third, that the assemblies had no "right to exercise the power[s] given them, in express *Contradiction* to the directions of the crown"; and, fourth, that the continued existence of the assemblies depended wholly upon the sufferance of the crown.[29]

The clear implication of this line of argument was that the crown might "change the Constitution[s]" of the colonies whenever and however it saw fit. Before it could alter the constitutions of the charter colonies, it had to have the sanction of the metropolitan courts or a parliamentary statute. But royal colonies did not even have that much protection. Because their constitutions depended on the crown's commissions to its governors and because those commissions were "revocable at pleasure, all the powers contained in it," metropolitan supporters asserted, "might be also revoked by The King's sole Authority." As the only "Giver of the Authority" by which they acted, the crown, according to the logic of this argument, had every right to "put Bounds or Limitations upon [the] . . . Rights and Privileges" of the assemblies in the royal colonies and to "alter them at Pleasure." By "*prerogative* . . . alone," a New York partisan of this position taunted assembly defenders, "you are ruled, . . . the Royal Pleasure . . . is your Magna Charta." "Our Constitution is the Queen's Creature," declared another writer of the same persuasion. "Without any Regard to Magna Charta," he contended, the colonists might "be Ruled and Governed, by such wayes and methods, as the Person who wears [the] . . . Crowne . . . shall think most proper and convenient." So far from being "*sui Juris*," then, the colonial assemblies, metropolitan adherents thus claimed, might be eliminated altogether and the power to make laws for the colonies vested in the crown's governors and councils.[30]

For any institutions that were on such a precarious legal footing "to claim an absolute legislative Power within themselves" seemed absurd to metropolitan authorities. Incapable of "enact[ing] at their own will and pleasure what they think fit," the assemblies, they believed, could by no means "pretend to have an equal power with the parliament of England" and would "never be allowed to assume those privileges which the House of Commons are entitled to justly here, upon principles that neither can, nor must be applied to the assemblies of the colonies." The "wisdom and regularity of a British parliament" might indeed provide "very fit patterns, so far as they" were "imitable by" assemblies in "dependent dominions" and so long as those assemblies did not grasp after more than their legitimate share of authority. But such "inferior Bodies, who" were "the express Creation of another," obviously had "no Right to deduce their Privileges from the Lex Parliamenti of the House of Commons of England." Rather, they could pretend to no greater authority than that "of making temporary By-Laws" for "the good Government of their [respective] Corporation[s]," regulations that by definition could not transgress "the legal Prerogative of the Crown." Thus, those assemblies that "declared themselves a House of Commons . . . assumed all the Privileges of it, and acted [even] with a more unlimited Authority" deserved only scorn as the unwitting tools of "a few designing and malicious Men," who, "quite intoxicated" with their own dreams of personal power and suffering from "a wanton Uneasiness under Authority," stirred up their mostly rude and ignorant fellow members to engage in "unnecessary Questions & Disputes about *Powers* & *Dignities*," their claims for which were wholly without legal foundation.[31]

In the colonies, however, few other than metropolitan representatives and their supporters accepted this argument. Denying that they were to be considered as nothing more than "new Clay in the Potter's Hand," most colonial political leaders emphatically rejected the "slavish . . . position . . . that we have no Constitution in the Colonies, but what the king is pleased to give us" and challenged the notion that their constitutions, including their rights to representative government, were founded only on royal charters and commissions. Partisans of those few colonies that still retained charters through the middle decades of the eighteenth century praised their "Precious CHARTER[S]" as those "great Hedge[s] which Providence has planted round our natural Rights." As Edward Rawson pointed out in 1691 in justifying the overthrow of the Dominion of New England in Massachusetts Bay, the charters might indeed be considered as "an Original Contract between the King and the first Planters" by which the king had promised them that "if they at their own cost and charge would subdue a Wilderness, and enlarge his Dominions, they and their Posterity after them should enjoy such Priviledges as are in their Charters expressed." But colonial partisans insisted, in paraphrasing Sir Edward Coke, "that Oracle of the Law," that the charters, like Magna Charta itself, were only "declaratory of *Old Rights,* and not . . . Grant[s] of *new ones.*" A charter, the New York assembly told Governor William Burnett in August 1728, merely confirmed "Rights and Privileges inherent in Us, in common with [all] . . . his Majesty's Free-born Natural Subjects." No less than in Britain itself, the colonists thus argued, the inhabitants of *"America* have a just Claim to the *hereditary Rights* of *British* Subjects." Accompanying "every *British* Subject . . . wheresoever he wanders or rests; so long as he is within the Pale of the *British* Dominions, and is true to his Allegiance," these "inherent" rights, as one colonial writer defined them, included the right "to have a Property of his own, in his Estate, Person and Reputation; subject only to Laws enacted by his own Concurrence, either in Person or by his Representatives."[32]

Quite apart from whether it still had or ever had had a charter, therefore, every colony, as "the Progeney of" Britain, therefore had "an undoubted Right to the Liberties of its' [sic] Mother Country." Because the colonists were thus entitled to "the same *fundamental Rights, Privileges,* and *Liberties*" as the "People of *England,*" "no difference [could be] made, between the Rights and conditions of subjects in the colonies, and those in England." Because their rights ultimately rested upon "the same *grand Charter* with the People of *England,*" moreover, the colonists believed, their claims to those rights were every bit as secure as the king's title to the crown, which was founded on precisely the same document. In the colonies, as in

Britain, "the *Prerogatives of the Crown,* and the *People['] s Liberty*" were thus "regulated by and under the Protection of the *same* [fundamental] *Laws.*" Even more recently than the issuance of the charters, various colonists pointed out, their entitlement to these rights had been confirmed both by the crown's law officers and, in 1740, by Parliament itself in an act offering naturalization to foreigners after seven years' residence in the colonies. This act, James Otis later contended, constituted a "plain declaration of the British parliament, that the subjects in the colonies" were "intitled to all the privileges of the people of Great Britain."[33]

Of all the rights thus inherited by and confirmed to these distant colonies, none was considered more valuable than the rights, in the words of New York Justice William Smith in 1734, "*to choose the Laws by which we will be governed*" and "*to be governed only by such Laws.*" Colonial writers were fond of quoting Sir William Jones, attorney general under Charles II, that the king "could no more grant a commission to levy money on his subjects in the plantations, without their consent by an assembly, than they could discharge themselves from their allegiance." If the colonial legislatures thus existed by virtue not of royal charters or commissions but of the colonists' "right to participate in the legislative power," it followed that because their distance prevented them from being represented in the British Parliament and having "Laws made for them . . . from Home" they "must therefore have new Laws from a legislature of their own." Both law and necessity thus dictated that the colonies should have "a perfect *internal* Liberty, as to the Choice of their own Laws, and in all other Matters that" were "*purely* provincial." Precisely because "the Colonies themselves," as a West Indian remarked during the last decade of the seventeenth century, were the "proper Judges of what they suffer, want, and would have" and because the colonists' "minds must best appear in [their] generall Assemblies," it seemed to the assemblies that there could be no "Reasonable Objection" to those bodies in "any . . . British Colonies . . . Exercising" a "Legislative power in its full Extent . . . within their own Jurisdiction[s]" so long as they did "not act contrary to the laws of Great Britain." "What . . . may be done by the Legislature there," declared a Jamaican in the mid-1740s, "may be done by the Legislature Here."[34]

Assembly partisans in this debate relied not only on the colonists' inherent rights as Englishmen but also upon custom, usage, and prescription. Custom had enormous authority in the British constitutional tradition. The British constitution was itself based as much upon custom as upon statute law, and the *"Common Law of England"* was *"*nothing else but the *Common Custome* of the *Realm."* Sir John Davies, attorney general of Ireland, provided the classic statement on the authority and character of custom in 1612 in the preface to his law reports. Custom, he explained, "taketh beginning and groweth to perfection in this manner: When a reasonable act once done is found to be good and beneficiall to the people, and agreeable to their nature and disposition, then they do use it, and practise it again and again, and so by often iteration and multiplication of the act, it becometh a *Custome,* and being continued, without interruption, time out of mind, it obtaineth the force of a *Law."* This *"Customary Law,"* Davies continued, was "the most perfect and most excellent, and without comparison the best, to make and preserve a Commonwealth" because "a *Custome* doth never become a Law to bind the people, untill it hath been tried and approved time out of Mind, during all which time, there did arise no inconvenience, for if it had been found inconvenient at any time, it had been used no longer, but had been interrupted, and consequently it had lost the virtue and force of a Law." Like the law of nature, Davies explained, custom was thus *"Jus non Scriptum,* being written only in the Heart of Man," and it was necessarily "better than all the written Laws in the World, to make Men honest and happy in this Life." Not just the common law but Parliament itself derived its authority from the force of custom, and, within Parliament, both the House of Lords and the House of Commons operated on the basis of their "own [customary] laws, the *lex parliam[enti],"* which defined their privileges and their place in the constitution in relation to each other and to the king.[35]

With the rise of the doctrine of parliamentary supremacy during the seven or eight decades after the Glorious Revolution, parliamentary statutes gradually came to be seen as taking precedence over custom. As a result, in Britain, J.G.A. Pocock has noted, "the concept of custom, and of English institutions as founded on custom," received less and less emphasis until it was revived by Edmund Burke during the last quarter of the eighteenth century. Yet, even in Britain, custom continued to be accorded considerable weight in the courts, in local legal and social relations, and in the works of some political and legal writers. Thus did the Cambridge legal theorist Thomas Rutherforth stress the customary roots of both the common law and the constitution in his mid-eighteenth-century *Institutes of Natural Law.* Echoing Davies, Rutherforth emphasized the legal force of custom. "Whatever usage has obtained in any civil society may be presumed to be agreeable to the sense of such society, and to have obtained with its consent," he wrote, and "whatever is consented to by a civil society, becomes a law of such society; and, consequently, any usage which has obtained for time immemorial, is established into a law by prescription." The same was true with regard to constitutions of government, the surest, sometimes the only, guide to which, according to Rutherforth, was to be found in "usage or continued practice" as revealed "in the history, records, or standing customs of the nation." Precisely because civil constitutions were so deeply rooted in custom, they could, Rutherforth stressed, obviously also be changed by usage and prescription. "Laws may be repealed, customs may be established into laws, civil constitutions of government may be altered, subjects may enlarge their privileges, governors may extend their prerogative . . . by such tacit agreement as this of prescription." For "whatever constitution . . . might appear, from former usage to have been established in any civil society," Rutherforth declared, "a different or contrary usage, after it obtains, will afford the same evidence, that the governors and the people have mutually agreed to change the constitution."[36]

Whether the colonies had "been long enough set[t]led" to be able to claim "their Liberties and Privileges by [such] immemorial Custom" was a matter of some doubt, even among assembly partisans. Yet in asserting that their right to representative institutions was inherent in them as Englishmen, the colonists were claiming, as Justice Joseph Murray of New York declared in 1734, that the assemblies derived "their Power or Authority . . . from the *common Custom and Laws of England,* claimed as an *English-man['*]s *Birth Right,* and as having been such, by *Immemorial Custom in England;* and tho' the People" in the colonies could not "claim this by *Immemorial Custom* here, yet as being part of the Dominions of *England,* they are intitled to the like *Powers* and *Authorities* here, that their fellow Subjects have, or are intitled to, in their *Mother Country,* by *Immemorial Custom.*"[37]

From very early on, however, colonists defended their rights to assemblies on the basis not just of English but of their own custom. Less than twenty years after the establishment of an assembly in Jamaica,

Chief Justice Samuel Long of that colony argued against the metropolitan attempt to apply Poynings's Law to Jamaica on the grounds that "it was against law and justice to alter the constitution Jamaica had so long lived under" and that, having been already "governed . . . for 16 or 17 years by . . . laws . . . of their own making," they could not then be governed in any other way. Leaders in Massachusetts Bay similarly objected to the Dominion of New England, arguing that the elimination of representative institutions not only "destroy[ed] the Fundamentals of . . . English . . . Government" in Massachusetts but was also against the "constant usage" of the colony as it had been practiced for almost fifty years. By the early 1720s, it was common for colonists to defend their right to "make laws to govern themselves" on the basis of "Ancient Custom" or "uninterrupted practice," which in some colonies by that time ran "well nigh to an hundred years," and to assert that they could not be governed "otherwise than According to the useage and Custom of the Country since the first Set[t]lement thereof." "One would think," wrote Connecticut governor Jonathan Law in 1728, that rights "of so antient standing"—constituting a "universal custom" stretching back "beyond the memory of man" to the very beginnings of the colonies—"would . . . have the like foundation with the general and particular customs in England."[38]

On the basis of custom—both English and local—colonial political leaders justified not only the existence of the assemblies but also their claims to full legislative powers and to rights peculiar to their specific polities. The assemblies had authority to exercise "a Legislative power in its full[est] extent," James Knight, a former attorney general of Jamaica, announced in the mid-1740s, in part because over a long period of time they had "in Fact Exercised a Legislative Power in almost every Instance, wherein it is possible to be Exercised." Similarly, although colonists themselves insisted that "the constitution[s] of the British colonies" had to be "modelled . . . in as near a conformity as possible to [that of] the mother country," they had no qualms in defending the assemblies' claims to peculiar rights and privileges that deviated from metropolitan norms on the basis of "Perpetual Usage," "established custom," or "Length of practice." Like the British Parliament, each assembly, this position implied, had its own peculiar "Lex & Consuetudo Parliamenti," a set of privileges and powers that rested primarily upon the authority of immemorial custom as it had developed over time in the colonies. When they were "general, and . . . long continued," explained Jonathan Blenman, attorney general of Barbados, in 1742, such "particular Customs and Usages" became "in a manner *Lex Loci*" and were "not at once to be overthrown, merely because they happened to be various from those of *England*." Because "every Country" had its own "peculiar . . . Situation, Inhabitants, and Commerce," it was "altogether as absurd, to prescribe [exactly] the same form of government to people [so] differently circumstanced, as to pretend to fortify all sorts of places on the same model," which, one Pennsylvanian explained in 1755, was precisely why the crown had "thought fit to allow different Constitutions to different Colonies." On many occasions, especially in the charter colonies, colonists actually justified some of their more peculiar customary rights and constitutional arrangements as improvements upon the British model.[39]

The crown's law officers and even the Board of Trade occasionally admitted "that some *advantageous customs* have prevailed and were long enjoyed, as privileges, by the people in America" and sometimes took the position that "what has been usually done by" the "Assemblies, may have by that usage, acquired a sanction in matters not directly repugnant to the authority, and prerogative of the Crown." Some officials also expressed doubts about the political wisdom of "impeach[ing] rights [thus] heretofore granted and enjoyed." But the usual metropolitan attitude was that, no matter how long they had prevailed, such customary deviations from British practice and prescription were "unconstitutional" "Blemish[es]" upon the colonial polities, that they had no real legal standing, and that they might be altered by the unilateral action of the metropolitan government, especially when they represented obvious encroachments upon the prerogatives of the crown. Quoting Coke, however, colonial protagonists argued that the crown could "lose a right by never having inforced" it and questioned the crown's authority to infringe rights that had "been long settled and established."[40]

Whether the crown could—or could not—alter colonial rights and privileges established through usage and founded on either custom or the colonists' presumed inherent rights as Englishmen was certainly the single most divisive issue separating metropolis and colonies during the seven decades following the Glorious Revolution. That issue was at the heart of the recurring controversies over the applicability of English law in the colonies and the status of the colonial assemblies, controversies that exemplified the continuing struggle between the center and the peripheries over their competing demands for control and autonomy. By its very persistence, this ongoing struggle vividly demonstrated that the intractable question of the distribution of power in the ever-extending polity known as the British Empire had never been resolved to the satisfaction of both metropolis and colonies.

Chapter Three

An Ambiguous Accommodation: Liberty, Prerogative, and the Imperial Constitution, 1713–1763

"The chiefest Thing wanting to make the Inhabitants of these Plantations happy," an anonymous Virginian told his English readers in 1701, "is a good Constitution of Government." By a good constitution, he explained, he meant one that would not only settle the nagging questions of "what is Law, and what is not in the Plantations" and "how far the Legislative Authority is in the Assemblies of the several Colonies" but settle them in such a way as to leave the colonies with "a Just and Equal Government." Such a constitution, he insisted, was necessary to guarantee the colonists the equal and impartial administration of justice and the full enjoyment of "their Liberties and Estates" that were the proud distinguishing marks of Englishmen whether they remained at home or lived in distant colonies. But the crown's continuing claims for "*a more absolute Power in the Plantations than in* England" meant that the colonists would never be able to extract such formal and explicit guarantees from metropolitan authorities. That "a Regular Settlement" of this question had "never yet been made," that, as another writer phrased it, the precise "bounds between the chief power and the people" in the colonies, between metropolitan authority and colonial rights, had never been explicitly settled, left the British-American world with two competing definitions of the constitutional situation within the expanding British

Empire and remained a source of deep anxiety for both colonial leaders and metropolitan authorities.[1]

If the colonists never succeeded in persuading crown officials in London to establish a "regular Constitution of Government" for the British Empire that explicitly and formally put the colonists on an equal footing with Englishmen with respect to their liberties and property, in actual practice, the crown's claims for greater authority in the colonies than it exercised in Britain were mitigated by a variety of factors. These included distance, inherited traditions of governance, metropolitan reluctance to commit substantial resources to colonial administration, and the extraordinary success of the empire.

In the early 1720s in a passage in *Cato's Letters* that many later writers on the colonies would find worthy of quotation, John Trenchard and Thomas Gordon remarked that distant colonies could be kept dependent upon their parent states either "by Force" or by "using them well." Unlike later empires, however, the early modern British Empire was not held together by force. Before 1760, metropolitan authorities sometimes considered using force to control the colonies and even wished that they had larger forces in the colonies for that purpose. With the significant exception of the small army that was sent to Virginia to suppress Bacon's Rebellion in the late 1670s, however, the few military units stationed by the metropolitan government in the colonies were intended not to police but to defend the colonies against attacks either from the colonies of rival powers or from their own slaves. The defensive character of the British army in America is obvious. There were much larger numbers of troops in the more exposed Caribbean colonies than on the continent, and those few troops on the continent were strategically placed in zones where the potential for attack from French Canada or Louisiana or Spanish Florida was greatest.[2]

Without a much larger force than they either had or could afford to have in the colonies, the British government had no other choice in its efforts to retain the dependence of the colonies than to use them well. That "public opinion sets bounds to every government," that no government could function, as Burke put it, "without regard to the general opinion of those who were to be governed," was a truism among political theorists during the early modern era; and although those people who were most closely involved in colonial administration in

London often demanded tighter controls over the colonies, during the seven decades following the Glorious Revolution the metropolitan government never made a sustained effort to govern the colonies in ways that were at serious variance with colonial opinion. Despite much bluster from the Board of Trade and governors and other royal and proprietary officials in the colonies, the metropolitan government consistently governed the colonies in such a way as to reveal that it had no intention of trying "to streighten or oppress them."[3]

Indeed, especially over the decades following the close of the first series of intercolonial wars between 1689 and 1713, the growth of the British colonies in population, wealth, and strategic importance was so rapid in comparison with that of the American colonies of rival European nations that by the middle of the eighteenth century it had become a widely accepted "Maxim" among British colonial experts "that *Liberty and Encouragement*" were "the *Basis of [successful] colonies.*" The remarkable development of the British colonies exceeded that of other European colonies, it was often asserted, precisely because they had been so "very singularly indulged in many respects above [the colonies of] all other nations; particularly in the power of making laws" for themselves. Along with "Plenty of good land," Adam Smith wrote in his section on the "Causes of Prosperity of New Colonies" in *The Wealth of Nations*, "liberty to manage their own affairs [in] their own way" was one of "the two great causes of the prosperity" of the British colonies in America. If, as another writer declared, "those free systems of provincial government" that encouraged such a demonstrable "regard to the rights of men" were what primarily "distinguished the English colonies above all others," it followed that "nothing but our arbitrary treatment of them and our misgovernment" could "make them otherwise than beneficial to the nation in general."[4]

The lax administration thus thought to have been in some major part responsible for the rapid growth of the colonies was especially evident during the long ministry of Sir Robert Walpole from 1721 until 1742, and it derived largely from the application to colonial affairs of many of the underlying principles and techniques he had employed with such brilliant success in managing domestic affairs. To avoid any issues involving fundamentals and all debates over basic principles, to restrict the active role of government as much as possible and act only when it was expedient or necessary to do so, to attempt to bind potentially disruptive groups to the administration by catering to their interests, to seek to adjust all disputes by compromise and manipulation, and, if a choice had to be made between competing interests, always to align the government with the strongest—each of these characteristically Walpolean modes of procedure inevitably spilled over into and affected the handling of the colonies.

Based on a clear recognition that the continued prosperity of the colonies—which had been such an important "Cause of enriching this Nation"—depended to some considerable degree upon their having, as one writer put it, "a Government . . . as Easy & Mild as possible to invite people to Settle under it" and to keep them happy once they were there, the new metropolitan posture toward the colonies was succinctly characterized by Charles Delafaye, one of Walpole's subordinates. "One would not Strain any Point," Delafaye warned Governor Francis Nicholson of South Carolina early in Walpole's administration, "where it can be of no Service to our King and Country, and will Create Enemys to one[']s Self." To promote the economic well-being of the empire in general and, not incidentally, to avoid political difficulties for the administration at home thus became the central objectives of British colonial policy in the decades after 1720. Although the Board of Trade continued to press for measures that would bring the colonies under closer metropolitan supervision, it regularly failed to get full ministerial support for its recommendations during these years.[5]

Walpole's tendency to let the colonies proceed on their own without much interference from the central administration in London except in matters that were of serious and pressing concern to powerful interest groups in Britain actually gave colonial governors more room for political maneuver than they had had at any time since the Restoration. For those governors operating from an actual or potential position of political strength, this relaxation of pressure meant that they could pursue the "real Advantage" of the parent state without having to be constantly on guard against reprimands from home for failing to enforce the "long established Maxims" of the Board of Trade. Those with significant patronage at their command were able to distribute the growing number of royal offices in the colonies to influential members of local elites and thereby parry opposition to British policy and secure support from a critical segment of colonial society. This was precisely the course of action through which Walpole had solidified his political control in Britain. Ever since the 1670s, however, metropolitan officials had been slowly taking into their own hands the patronage to most key offices in the colonies with the result that most governors controlled the appointment to few offices and thus had few of the utilitarian resources through which they might have enhanced metropolitan authority in the colonies. By thus depriving them of their "only means of rewarding Merit and creating and [exerting] Influence," governors complained, metropolitan officials had assigned them the task of preserving British authority "without giving [them] the power of performance."[6]

Under these conditions, many governors chose simply not to "consider any Thing further than how to sit easy" and to be careful "to do nothing, which upon a fair hearing . . . can be blamed." Because the surest way to "sit easy" was to reach a political accommodation with local interests, they frequently aligned themselves with dominant political factions in the colonies. Such governors sought to avoid disputes with the assemblies by taking special care not to challenge their customary privileges and, if necessary, even quietly giving way before their demands. As a consequence, royal and proprietary governors in many colonies were fully integrated into the local political community and came to identify and to be identified as much with the interests of the colonies as with those of the metropolis. This co-option, this domestication, of metropolitan governors significantly eased tensions between the center and the peripheries: the personal prestige and sometimes even the political influence of governors actually increased, and the assemblies contented themselves with the rather large amount of de facto power they could wield whenever it became necessary to do so.[7]

In this situation, the character of the long struggle over the distribution of authority within the British Empire changed substantially. Although the colonial assemblies did not usually shrink from any challenges from representatives of the center to the rights of people and institutions within their respective jurisdictions, they virtually ceased to demand the explicit recognition of those rights they had so often sought between 1660 and 1720. Thereafter, the unstated strategy of the assemblies seems to have been to secure local rights against the power of the center in much the same way that those rights had been achieved within the metropolis itself: through practice and usage that with the implicit acquiescence of the center would gradually acquire the sanction of custom. The effort of the Jamaica Assembly in the 1720s to obtain the crown's specific acknowledgment that Jamaicans were entitled to all the rights of Englishmen in return for voting a perpetual revenue to the crown was notable because it was the last such attempt by any assembly before the disturbances that immediately preceded the American Revolution.

Ever since the establishment of the colonies, their inhabitants mostly through their assemblies had been slowly building their own local inheritances and "Establishing the Constitution[s] of their Countrey[s]" on what they hoped was a firm foundation that would secure their inherited rights as Englishmen. Initially, it was entirely plausible for metropolitan officials to think of the colonies as "so many petty Corporations at a distance" with degrees of local authority equivalent only to those of "municipal corporations" in England. "As the colonies [had] prospered and increased to a numerous and mighty people, spreading over a great tract of the globe," however, they had gradually, in their "Corporate Capacity[s]," become full and distinct "Communities, deriving their Authority from the Crown." Under these conditions, as Edmund Burke remarked, "it was natural that they should attribute to [their] assemblies, so respectable in their formal constitution, some part of the dignity of the great nations which they represented."[8]

Metropolitan officials might speak derisively of these assemblies' pretensions "to have an equal power with the parliament of England." They might insist that these assemblies would never be "suffer[ed] . . . to erect themselves into the power, and authority, of the British House of Commons." But the case was that during the century and a half after the first establishment of the colonies, the assemblies had changed the constitutions of those colonies much in the same manner as Parliament was at the very same time changing the constitution of Britain. Thus the assemblies were no longer limited to making by-laws but "made acts of all sorts and in all cases whatsoever. They levied money, not for parochial purposes, but upon regular grants to the crown, following all the rules and principles of a parliament to which they approached every day more and more nearly." In comparison with the British House of Commons, these "Plantation Assemblies" might indeed be "circumscribed by very narrow Bounds." They did not, after all, preside over "a great and independent empire." But if these "little Senate[s]" did not have "all" the authority of Parliament, they nonetheless were, as James Otis said in the case of the Massachusetts House of Representatives, "the great council of this province, as the British parliament is of the kingdom" of Great Britain. "However contemptuously some . . . affect[ed] to speak of" them, they were thus, Otis implied, the most important and certainly the most cherished components of the colonists' "Ancient Constitution[s]."[9]

Notwithstanding the very great extent to which officials at the center had acquiesced in the many changes that had helped to shape these "long established Constitutions in [the] Colonies," they never came to regard those constitutions as fixed and inviolable. On the contrary, as a later observer acidly remarked, while they suffered "the real and substantial Authority of the British Government . . . to be sapped, and at length overturned" within the colonies, metropolitan authorities constantly "kept up in words" their "high Claims of Prerogative." Indeed, those claims became more strident over time.[10]

Almost from the beginnings of English colonization, people at the center had worried that as the distant colonies became stronger and more powerful they would seek to shake off their dependence upon the metropolis. Increasingly during the first half of the eighteenth century, such fears as well as a growing awareness of the economic and strategic importance of the colonies to Britain had led to demands for the crown "to revise the Constitutions of the Settlements abroad, and to regulate them" by restricting the scope of their local legislative powers and compelling them "to follow the commands sent them by your Majesty." Invariably, these demands to bring the colonies under a more "absolute and immediate dependancy" became more vociferous during wartime, when colonial resistance to or incomplete compliance with defense requisitions and directions from London underlined for people at the center the tenuousness of metropolitan controls in the colonies and made them acutely aware of the extent to which the enforcement of metropolitan measures in the colonies depended upon the approval of colonial governments.[11]

During the late 1740s, London authorities responded to this situation by undertaking a new and reasonably systematic campaign to bring the colonies under closer supervision by reducing their autonomy and, if necessary, remodeling their constitutions. To achieve these ends, crown officials initially relied almost entirely upon traditional instruments of metropolitan control, including legislative review and royal instructions. Their efforts evoked considerable colonial resentment over the expanded use of the royal veto of colonial laws. Even more seriously, perhaps, they revived and intensified a long-standing controversy over the legal force of crown and proprietary instructions in the colonies. As a consequence, during the 1750s and early 1760s, attention on both sides of the Atlantic focused ever more directly upon the continuing tensions within the British Empire between central control and periphery rights.[12]

At various times following the Glorious Revolution, metropolitan officials had sought through formal instructions to colonial governors to achieve a variety of objectives, many of which were intended to curtail the powers of the assemblies while maintaining the authority of the prerogative in the colonies. Thus they instructed governors not to consent to the passage of temporary laws that would expire before they could be reviewed in London, to insist upon the inclusion of suspending clauses in any legislation that seemed to interfere with the royal prerogative or the navigation acts, not to permit the assemblies to determine their internal constitutions or to enjoy traditional parliamentary privileges, to make sure that the royal-appointed upper houses exercised equal rights with the assemblies in framing money bills, to secure from the assemblies permanent revenues so that governors and other members of the colonial civil establishments would not be dependent on the assemblies for their support, to deny the assemblies the power to nominate or to appoint persons to executive offices, and to pass no bills for the emission of paper currencies.[13]

The assumption behind both these instructions and the insistence that they were binding upon the colonies was, as one official phrased it early in the eighteenth century, that legislative authority in the colonies operated "within the limits of the Governor's commission and Her Majesty's instructions." As William Knox would subsequently explain, because, according to metropolitan theory, the constitutions of the royal colonies derived from the crown's commissions to his governors and because each of those commissions specifically directed the governor to "guide himself by the Instructions he . . . therewith receive[d] and also by such other Instructions as he receive[d] [t]hereafter," crown officials invariably took the position that the king's instructions were "part of the Commission itself, and of equal authority." In Maryland and Pennsylvania, provincial officials used the same argument to urge the constitutional character of proprietary instructions.[14]

Just as few colonial leaders were disposed to admit that the royal commission was the sole basis of their local constitutions, so also did they deny that the instructions had any constitutional status. Commissions at least had been passed under the great seal in Britain and were routinely entered into the public records of the colonies. But instructions passed only under the lesser authority of the privy seal and, upon the explicit directions of metropolitan authorities, were usually "kept secret by the Governor[s]." Thus, colonial advocates pointed out, for the colonists to accord constitutional standing to instructions would constitute an open admission that, as one writer phrased it, the colonies were "without any Constitution at all, and could have no permanent form of Government, but might have one secretly modelled by the King's Ministers and privately introduced, without their ever being able to know what it was." In proprietary colonies, the same objections were made to instructions from the proprietors.[15]

Because almost no colonial leaders were willing to admit that the colonies were "without any Constitution at all, and could have no permanent form of Government," it is not surprising that governors of both royal and proprietary colonies never had much success in securing compliance with any instructions opposed by the assemblies. Time after time, officials in the colonies complained that those bodies showed "no regard . . . to H[is] M[ajesty's] Instructions." In defense of this behavior, assemblies argued that they had no obligation to comply with what one writer referred to as "*unconstitutional Instructions*," by which they meant instructions that were either contrary to existing colonial statutes or were incompatible with either the colonists' inherent rights as Englishmen or the customary powers and privileges of their assemblies. As the New Jersey Assembly pointed out in 1707, the "last clause of the *Petition of Right*" had stipulated that the crown's servants were obliged to act "according to Law, and not otherwise."[16]

Similar arguments served as the basis for the colonies' adamant opposition to the crown's expanded use of instructions after 1748. As a South Carolinian explained in 1756, the crown's instructions might be obligatory upon governors and councils "because, if either should disregard them, they might be immediately displaced." But, colonial advocates argued, no instruction could bind the inhabitants of any colony "unless the people whom it concerns, adopt[ed] it, and their representatives, in their legislative capacity, confirm[ed] it by a law." For, they contended, if instructions not thus ratified by the people's representatives "should be laws and rules to the people, . . . then there would be no need of assemblies, and all our laws and taxes might be made by an instruction." For the king to "make his instructions the rule and measure of the people's obedience" would be "to govern by Instructions and not by Laws" and thereby to make "his will their only law." If, as the colonists believed, each assembly had "the same freedom and independence of legislature, as the parliament of Great Britain has," then it followed that it could not "be governed, directed, restrained or restricted, by any posterior instructions or commands" that diminished that legislative "freedom and independence."[17]

But these arguments carried little weight in the metropolis. "You Americans have wrong Ideas of the Nature of your Constitution," Lord Granville, president of the Privy Council throughout the 1750s, told Benjamin Franklin in 1757, "you contend that the King's Instructions to his Governors are not Laws, and think yourselves at Liberty to disregard them at your own Discretion. But, those Instructions," Granville insisted, could not be thus treated "as *not binding,* and *no Law* . . . they are first drawn up by grave and wise Men learned in the Laws and Constitutions of the Nation; they are then brought to the [Privy] Council Board, where they are solemnly weigh'd and maturely consider'd, and after receiving such Amendments as are found proper and necessary, they are agreed upon and establish'd. The Council is *over all* the Colonies," Granville continued: "The King and Council is THE LEGISLATOR of the Colonies; and when his Majesty's Instructions come there, they are the LAW OF THE LAND; *they are,* said his L——p, repeating it, the Law of the Land, and as such *ought to be* OBEYED." Given the depth and extent of colonial opposition to this view, however, there was no way for officials at the center to ensure that the crown's instructions would be thus "OBEYED" in the peripheries.[18]

This stalemate over the question of whether royal and proprietary instructions were binding upon the colonies was emblematic of the ongoing struggle within the British Empire over how power should be allocated between the center and the peripheries. For the first time in many decades, metropolitan officials, beginning in 1748, had made a concerted effort to bring the peripheries more thoroughly under the authority of the center. Although the colonial assemblies had been able to thwart most of their specific initiatives, the assemblies' success in this regard in no way diminished metropolitan determination to augment the authority of the center in the colonies. Rather, as Benjamin Franklin reported from London in 1759, a decade of failure and frustration had left "the Ministers and great Men here" more persuaded than ever that the colonies had "too many and too great Privileges" and that it was "not only the Interest of the Crown but of the Nation to reduce them" by "Clipping the Wings of Assemblies in their Claims of all the Privileges of a House of Commons" and reducing the colonies to an "absolute Subjection to Orders sent from hence in the Shape of Instructions."[19]

This continuing "zeal" among metropolitan authorities "for making the Crown absolute in America" more and more caused "informed" and "sensible Men" on the opposite side of the Atlantic to "look . . . with Jealousy and Distrust upon the Royal Authority." By reminding colonial leaders that the crown had not abandoned its claims for a more unlimited power in the colonies than it enjoyed at home and reviving inherited memories of "the arbitrary reigns of a Charles and a James . . . when prerogative was unlimited, and liberty undefined," it enhanced the colonists' awareness that "nothing but a free and independent Assembly" could give them adequate "protection against arbitrary power" and intensified their determination to hold "fast [to] those Privileges," including especially their inherent rights to strong representative assemblies, "that tend[ed] to balance . . . or keep . . . down" the power of the crown.[20]

Thus stirred by new fears that "the natural, and legal, and constitutional rights of the people" in the colonies might "be annihilated," colonial leaders responded to this campaign with intense resentment that the crown's servants in the colonies should yet "be so infatuated, as to seek every occasion for alarming the fears, and exciting the jealousy, of his majesty's subjects; by endeavouring, to extend the prerogative, and advance the power, of the Crown, to the diminution, if not the total extinction, of the *natural* and *indisputable rights* of the people" in the colonies. Whether their constitutions would ever be settled or would be constantly exposed "to a *perpetual mutability*," whether metropolitan authorities would ever "*explicitly* . . . acknowledge, and put out of farther danger of unconstitutional attempts" the "*essential* rights of the people," in the colonies were persistent and worrisome questions for the colonists during the late 1750s and early 1760s.[21]

In 1724, the crown's law officers had complained that "so many things, of no little consequence" to the constitutions of the colonies, were still "left in [such] great uncertainty, at this day." Forty years later, such an observation was still appropriate. Whereas the colonists lamented that the constitutions of the colonies were yet "so imperfect, in numberless instances, that the rights of the people lie, even now, at the mere mercy of their Governours" and profoundly wished that "our Liberties & Privileges as free born British Subjects were once properly defin'd," metropolitan authorities were more than ever persuaded that they should, could at any time, and had every "right to [re]moddle the Constitution[s]" of the colonies in such a way as finally to set "some bounds" to the inflated privileges and extensive autonomy of the distant and increasingly valuable colonies. This wide divergence of opinion powerfully illustrates the fact that even as late as the early 1760s the problem of the distribution of power within the British Empire had, though constantly experienced, not yet been resolved.[22]

Chapter Four

Parliament and the Colonies

In relations between the colonies and the home government before the mid-1760s, Parliament's authority over the colonies was an infinitely less important issue than that of the crown. When, in 1649, during the Interregnum, the House of Commons asserted its authority not just over the realm of England but over "all the Dominions and Territories thereunto belonging," significant proportions of the populations of Barbados and Virginia, both predominantly royalist strongholds, resisted. In defense of their actions, the Barbadians explicitly raised the issue that would bring the British Empire into open conflict 120 years later: no legislation without representation. Any effort to bind them "to the Government and Lordship of a Parliament in which we have no Representatives, or persons chosen by us, for there to propound and consent to what might be needful to us, as also to oppose and dispute all what should tend to our disadvantage and harm," they protested, "would be a slavery far exceeding all that [any other part of] the English nation hath yet suffered." Similarly, over the next fifty years, several colonies resisted the navigation acts at least partly on the grounds that the removal of their inhabitants out of England had simultaneously left them without any of "those privileges in the Parliament of England which their fathers had" and deprived Parliament of any further legislative authority over them.[1]

But there were no such bold assertions from any of the colonies during the seventy-five years following the Glorious Revolution; and the virtual absence of any systematic attention either in the center or in the peripheries to the nature of Parliament's specific relationship to the colonies stands in pointed contrast to the seemingly perpetual debates over the extent to which royal authority was or was not limited in the colonies by charters, customs, and the colonists' rights as Britons. The meaning of this silence is the subject of this chapter.

During the late Middle Ages, both the House of Lords and the House of Commons, as Robert L. Schuyler has explained, functioned less as modern legislative bodies with independent initiating powers than as advisers of or counselors to the king. This essentially conciliar role was not very different from that of the king's own appointed Privy Council under the Tudors. As the crown's advisers, both Parliament and the Privy Council made regulations for the crown's dominions outside the realm of England. In practice, however, most such regulations were the work not of the king-in-Parliament but of the king-in-council, which also heard appeals from all of the king's external dominions. Nevertheless, the king-in-Parliament did occasionally legislate for the dominions, and this custom of occasional legislation gradually, as in the case of Ireland, "evolved into a legally recognized right"—recognized at least within England.[2]

With the establishment of the American colonies, Parliament simply assumed that it could legislate for the colonies, and although the Stuarts, who still had veto power, were cautious not to let Parliament assert too wide a jurisdiction in the colonial sphere, and although the colonies, like the king's external dominions in the medieval empire, generally came to be considered possessions of the crown and not parts of the realm, throughout the seventeenth century Parliament did upon occasion bind both Ireland and the American colonies through acts that specifically applied to them, most notably in the case of the colonies, as already indicated, in the series of navigation acts adopted between 1651 and 1696. Nevertheless, throughout the seventeenth century the king-in-council, not the king-in-Parliament, assumed most of the burden for overseeing the administration of both Ireland and the colonies.[3]

But the founding and development of the American colonies took place in a period of "great constitutional change," a period that, in A. F. M. Madden's words, saw "a shift of balance between king and parliament" from a situation of "royal dictatorship" under Henry VIII to "one of parliamentary omnicompetence" by the time of George III. Britain's was "a polity ruled by convention," and its constitution, as H. T. Dickinson has emphasized, "was the product of time and the result of specific responses to practical problems." "Not fixed and immutable," it "developed almost imperceptibly through the ages" through custom, usage, and precedent. During the seventeenth century, Parliament had sought, with modest success, to diminish the relative authority of the crown by appeals to fundamental law and "customary restraints on arbitrary power," the Whig case against unlimited prerogative being based on an "ideology of customary law, regulated monarchy and immemorial Parliamentary right." From the early 1640s on, as Corinne C. Weston has shown, radical advocates of the expansion of parliamentary power had invoked the coordination principle in lawmaking in an effort to redefine the "relationships between the king and the two houses of Parliament by elevating the two houses at the expense of the king." A "theory of shared legal sovereignty by which the two houses became the predominant partners in lawmaking," this doctrine held that sovereignty rested not in the king alone but in the king-in-Parliament.[4]

But the diminution of the king's power within England during the seventeenth century was relatively minor compared to that which took place in the wake of the Glorious Revolution. As a result of that revolution, the principle of coordination was enshrined as the new orthodoxy. As Jennifer Carter has observed, England now "had a monarch depending on a parliamentary title, and a constitution based on [parliamentary] law." The "two salient features of the post-Revolution constitution were, first, that however much it was disguised a parliamentary monarchy had replaced a divine right monarchy; and, secondly, that since 1689 the monarch had learned somehow to live with Parliament." As Carter has emphasized, however, these developments were by no means a "foregone conclusion" at the time of the Glorious Revolution. Only gradually over the next half century did Parliament grow from what Burke called "a mere representative of the people, and a guardian of popular privileges for its own immediate constituents . . . into a mighty sovereign," from a body that was not simply "a control on the crown on its own behalf" to one that, as Burke put it, "communicated a sort of strength to the royal authority." As several historians recently have pointed out, the "concept of a sovereign parliament" had not been "reasonably foreseeable in 1689," was largely "a development of the mid-eighteenth century," and was only just "hardening into an orthodoxy" during the 1760s. The effect of this great constitutional change, Dickinson has noted, was to transform the ancient "doctrine of non-resistance from a buttress of divine right monarchy into the strongest defence of an existing constitution, whatever form it might take." Increasingly during the eighteenth century, the constitution came to be seen—in Britain—as virtually identical with Parliament itself: the constitution became precisely what Parliament said it was. That this "Modern Constitution" was both a recent development and "infinitely better than the Ancient Constitution" were widely recognized by contemporaries within the British political nation.[5]

Precisely what this domestic constitutional change at the center meant for the peripheries was never explicitly worked out. Much evidence suggests that the colonists recognized and accepted the growing omnipotence of Parliament within Britain.[6] How they regarded Parliament's authority over the rest of the empire is much more problematic. No American produced a treatise comparable to William Molyneux's *The Case of Ireland's Being Bound by Acts of Parliament in England Stated,* a 1698 publication which, as the title implies, argued that Ireland was a separate kingdom with its own parliament and that the English Parliament had no jurisdiction over it.[7]

Some contemporary reports, however, suggested that at least some prominent colonials questioned Parliament's legislative capacity in the colonies. In May 1744, for example, William Fairfield, speaker-elect of the Massachusetts House of Representatives, was said to have "openly in his Discourse bid Defiance to the Act of Parliament then lately pass'd for the Suppression of the *Land Bank* Scheme" in Massachusetts Bay. Similarly, Governor Stephen Hopkins of Rhode Island allegedly declared in July 1757 "that the King & Parliament had no more Right to make Laws for us than the Mohawks" and that whatever might be said "concerning the Arbitrary Despotic Government of the Kingdom of France, yet nothing could be more tyrannical, than our being Obliged by Acts of Parliament To which we were not parties to the making; and in which we were not Represented." That such notions were not limited to Fairfield and Hopkins was charged by the Earl of Loudoun, the king's first commander in chief of forces in America. In December 1756, he complained to his London superiors that it was "very common for the people in the Lower and more inhabited Country [in America] to say" that "they would be glad to see any Man durst Offer to put an English Act of Parliament in Force in this country."[8]

But such attitudes seem to have been unusual. From very early in the eighteenth century, most colonial political leaders appear to have admitted the legitimacy of acts of Parliament in which the colonies were "particularly named," even when they "abhor[red] the very thought of them." Upon a few occasions and when it was for their own advantage, some people even argued that certain acts of Parliament that did not specifically mention the colonies, such as the Act of Toleration, were actually in force there.[9] Similarly, people on the losing side of an argument in the colonies several times threatened to appeal to Parliament for redress of grievances on the grounds that its members, having "been in the Practice of these Things for Ages past," were obviously "better Judges . . . than we who are but of Yesterday." Thus in the 1730s and 1740s people who opposed the Massachusetts Assembly's measures for emitting paper money urged "the supreme Legislature[,] the *Parliament of Great Britain*," to take some "*summary Method[s]*" to "abridge the Plantations of this Privilege which they have assumed, of making their *publick Bills of Credit, a Tender.*" If people sometimes looked to Parliament for redress against colonial assemblies, the assemblies themselves occasionally appealed to Parliament against what they regarded as the arbitrary behavior of the crown. For example, in 1701 the Jamaica Assembly tried to address the English House of Commons against what it took to be the arbitrary behavior of Governor Sir William Beeston, and in the early 1730s, some Massachusetts leaders advocated an appeal to Parliament to protect the colony from measures, "projected by the Crown," which they regarded as "inconsistent with the Liberties of their Country."[10]

If the range of colonial attitudes reveals enormous uncertainty in the colonies over the relationship of Parliament to the British dominions on the American periphery, few in Britain following the Glorious Revolution had any doubt that Parliament had the right to legislate for the colonies whenever it chose to do so. Throughout the eighteenth century, Parliament continued to pass legislation affecting the external commerce and sometimes even the internal economies of the colonies. Metropolitan authorities proposed parliamentary intervention in several other areas. When the Board of Trade concluded early in the eighteenth century that the private colonies would have to be brought under the direct supervision of the crown if they were ever to be properly subordinated to the metropolis, it automatically assumed that the recall of the charters would be handled by parliamentary statute.

Parliament's competence in this area would have been denied by Charles II or James II. After 1688, however, metropolitan administrators counted on the assistance of Parliament to handle difficult colonial situations. Between 1701 and 1715 they brought four separate bills into Parliament calling for the resumption of the private colonies by the crown. Because of the opposition of the proprietors, a genuine reluctance by many members of Parliament to tamper with private property, the vagaries of party politics, and, after the beginning of Queen Anne's war in 1702, an uncertain international situation that made any measure likely to produce discontent in the colonies seem highly imprudent, none of these bills got a full hearing and all failed to pass. Nevertheless, no one in Britain questioned the authority of Parliament to act in this area.[11]

Also during the early decades of the eighteenth century, the refusal of some colonial legislatures to comply with royal requests twice brought demands from metropolitan authorities for parliamentary intervention into the internal administration of specific colonies. First, when the New York Assembly failed to vote as large a salary to Governor Robert Hunter as stipulated by his instructions or to provide salaries for other executive officials, the Privy Council, upon the recommendation of the Board of Trade, took the unprecedented step in March 1711 of threatening to bring before Parliament a bill "for Enacting a Standing Revenue . . . within the Province of New York for the Support of the Governor there, and the necessary Expenses of the Government" if the assembly would not itself provide the "Necessary Support." Although the board repeated this threat several times and the Privy Council twice ordered bills to be brought before the House of Commons, the assembly stood firm for over two years. Finally, Hunter, despairing of ever getting any effective backing from London, agreed to a compromise in the summer of 1713 that led to the resolution of the conflict and the abandonment by metropolitan authorities of any plans to turn to Parliament.[12]

Similarly, during the late 1720s and early 1730s, when the Massachusetts House of Representatives repeatedly refused to comply with the crown's directions to vote a permanent salary for the royal governor, the Board of Trade, in desperation, threatened in early 1729 to turn to Parliament. When the Massachusetts House would not yield, however, the board again was unable to carry through on its threats and in 1736 finally abandoned the cause and permitted the governor to accept annual grants from the House.[13]

The Board of Trade's failure to bring its recommendations for a permanent revenue for either New York or Massachusetts before Parliament was followed during the 1730s and 1740s by Parliament's refusal on three separate occasions to use its legislative authority to strengthen royal authority in the colonies. In 1734, a House of Lords committee proposed a bill to prevent any colonial laws from taking effect until they had been approved by the crown, but the Lords never formulated this proposal into a bill. Similarly, two bills to regulate colonial paper currencies considered by the House of Commons in 1744 and 1749 contained clauses that would have given royal instructions the force of law in the colonies. When these clauses provoked a "general opposition" from the colonial agents in London, however, the Commons dropped both bills, and the currency law it finally did enact in 1751 included no such provision.[14]

Parliament's reluctance to act on these and earlier matters affecting the charters and internal administration of the colonies contrasted pointedly with its willingness to legislate upon a wide range of other problems. During the first six decades of the eighteenth century, it passed legislation to encourage the production of naval stores (1706) and indigo (1748) in the colonies, to regulate the value of foreign coin (1708), to restrict colonial manufacture of hats (1732) and iron (1750), to make it easier for metropolitan creditors to secure payment of colonial debts (1732), to discourage trade with foreign sugar islands (1733), to prohibit private banks of issue in the colonies (1741), and to forbid the emission of legal tender paper money in the four New England Colonies (1751). Although it also enacted a few measures of concern to the colonies as a whole, including statutes to establish a colonial post office (1710) and to provide for the naturalization of foreigners who migrated to the colonies (1740), Parliament, as Martin Bladen, a member of Parliament and of the Board of Trade, observed in 1739, in practice had thus very largely limited its activities with regard to the colonies to "laying Duties on their Produce, and with Enacting Laws, to secure the Advantage of their Commerce to Us."[15]

By not legislating on the noneconomic and internal affairs of the colonies, Parliament was acting toward them very much as it acted toward Ireland. In response to repeated claims by Irish leaders for exemption from its authority, Parliament passed a Declaratory Act in 1720 asserting its jurisdiction over Ireland in "all cases whatsoever." As J. C. Beckett has emphasized, however, Parliament continued thereafter, as it had done since the Tudor period, to exert its right to legislate for Ireland "with great caution." After 1720, as before, British legislation for Ireland "was, in fact, very largely economic or administrative," and the crown, as had long been its custom, usually sought the concurrence of the Irish Parliament to any British statutes that applied specifically to Ireland. According to Beckett, "there was never any question of taxing Ireland by British legislation; and even in less vital matters ministers were very unwilling to stir up trouble by using the authority of a British statute to over-ride the will of the Irish Parliament."[16]

Nor did the British Parliament customarily legislate on Irish internal affairs. With a "nervous regard for Irish opinion" and a grave "apprehensive[ness] of the consequences that might follow rash punitive measures," the British government in Ireland occasionally threatened to take unpopular measures but repeatedly backed down in the face of Irish resistance. The result was that the constitutional relationship between Ireland and Great Britain underwent "a practical change, due to the pressure of political circumstances." Even the application of Poyning's Law "became little more than formal," and the British Parliament rarely legislated in areas likely to produce a "popular clamour" in Ireland. And in Ireland, as in America, British trade laws were routinely evaded by smuggling whenever they were regarded as unfairly detrimental to Irish interests.[17]

In recent years, there has been a growing trend for scholars to suggest that in resisting parliamentary authority during the 1760s and 1770s, the American colonies were "reject[ing] the results of" the Glorious Revolution. But there are major difficulties with this argument. The ascendancy of Parliament within Britain and the eventual triumph of the doctrine of parliamentary omnipotence during the mid-eighteenth century may have been the most important results of that revolution, but they were by no means the only ones. Within Britain, as Jennifer Carter has pointed out, another consequence of the revolution, was "a distinct, though not complete, withdrawal of central authority from local affairs." Earlier in the seventeenth century, Charles I had undertaken an extensive effort to exert the authority of the central government over county and local affairs in both the civil and the religious realms, and, although this effort was interrupted during the Civil War, the later Stuarts resumed it after the Restoration. "Perhaps nothing done in the 1680s by Charles II and

James II," Carter has noted, "caused so much reaction against them as their interference with local privilege and the accustomed pattern of existing hierarchies—in counties, in corporations, or in university colleges." At least in the short run, the revolution effectively put an end to this effort and thereby created the conditions necessary for "the typical eighteenth-century situation of gentry and aristocratic independence in the localities." Within Britain, the localities, along with the people who dominated them, enjoyed much less interference from the central government than they had at any time under the Stuart monarchy. During the eighty years following the Glorious Revolution, Britain seems to have experienced a significant redistribution of power to the localities as English, Welsh, and (after 1707) Scottish counties became what Edward Shils has referred to as "pockets of approximate independence." The same development was evident in Britain's more distant peripheries in Ireland and America, and this localization of power ensured that, in contrast to contemporary continental monarchies, Britain's expanding nation-state and overseas empire would not be founded on "methods of centralisation and absolutism."[18]

In both Ireland and the American colonies, the growth of parliamentary institutions during the eighteenth century epitomized this development. Before the Glorious Revolution, the Irish Parliament had convened only rarely. Though it met somewhat more frequently under Charles I, there were only three Irish parliaments under Elizabeth and only one under both James I and Charles II. Between 1666 and 1692, it did not meet at all. Hence, as Beckett has noted, "the Irish parliament as we know it in the eighteenth century begins in 1692," when the ascendancy of the Protestant population as a result of the revolution enabled it "to take a more independent line than formerly," while the insufficiency of the crown's hereditary revenues to meet the usual costs of government provided it with an opportunity "to assert its rights, even against England," in exchange for granting funds to make up the difference. As a result of these developments, the Irish Parliament beginning in 1692 both met regularly and developed a vigorous "spirit of independence." Chapters 2 and 3 have described comparable developments in the American colonies.[19]

For the development of the British Empire as a whole, then, perhaps the most important results of the Glorious Revolution were the localization of power and the growth of parliamentary institutions, not just within Britain but also in Ireland and the American colonies. At the same time that the British Parliament was growing "into a mighty sovereign," Ireland and the American colonies, "advancing by equal steps, and governed by the same necessity," had, as Burke would subsequently remark in relation to the American colonies, "formed within themselves, either by royal instruction or royal charter, assemblies so exceedingly resembling a parliament, in all their forms, functions, and powers, that it was impossible they should not imbibe some opinion of a similar authority." To be sure, there were very important distinctions among these British legislatures. Those in Britain and Ireland had a House of Lords and the representative portions of the legislature were both much larger and considerably less representative than the colonial lower houses. At the same time, both the Irish Parliament, through the operation of Poyning's Law, and the colonial assemblies, through the process of metropolitan review of colonial legislation, had far more serious restrictions upon their legislative power than had the British Parliament.[20]

Notwithstanding these differences, the growth in the power of all these bodies during the eighteenth century depended upon the same circumstance: the crown's inability to cover either the normal costs of government or extraordinary wartime expenses without formal grants from local legislative bodies. Moreover, they all performed the same legislative functions within their respective political societies. It was therefore entirely reasonable for the political nations in both Ireland and the colonies to assume that their "mimic parliament[s]" rested upon the same "Foundations" and had the same rights and powers within their several political jurisdictions as did the British Parliament within Britain. "The parliament of Great-Britain, and the general assembly (or parliament) of . . . any American Province," the South Carolina merchant Christopher Gadsden declared in the early 1760s, "though they differ widely with regard to the extent of their different spheres of action, and the latter's may be called a sphere within the former's, yet they differ not an iota" in their functions. There was therefore no reason, added an anonymous contemporary from Maryland, why "the same Rights cannot be common to both, where they may be exercised without clashing or interfering with one another."[21]

Just as the growth of parliamentary power after 1689 had changed the constitution of Britain in fundamental ways, so also had similar developments in Ireland and the colonies altered the constitutions there. Throughout the British Empire, both at the center and in the peripheries, constitutions were customary. That is, in the best English constitutional tradition, they were all the products of evolving usage. In Burke's words, they had been slowly "formed by imperceptible habits, and old custom, the great support of all governments in the world." "No Government ever was built at once or by the rules of architecture, but like an old house at 20 times up & down & irregular," observed Sir George Saville, an English member of Parliament in the 1760s, in commenting on the nature of constitutional change within the British Empire: "I believe," he continued, that "principles have less to do than we suppose. The Critics['] rules were made after the poems. The Rules of architecture after ye houses, Grammar after language and governments go *per hookum & crookum* & then we demonstrate it *per bookum*. There is not that argument or practice so bad that you may have precedents for it."[22]

If by the early 1760s the British, Irish, and American colonial constitutions were thus all well "established by long custom and . . . sanctioned by accepted usage," the unformulated and unasked question was whether in the process of changing the constitutions of their respective political jurisdictions, these legislatures were also changing the constitution of the whole to which they all belonged. Without as yet having formulated a coherent and fully articulated sense of empire, the British political nation had not, before the 1760s, developed any explicit concept of an imperial constitution. Indeed, the tendency within Britain was to conflate the British constitution with the imperial constitution. Yet the absence of the concept did not mean that an imperial constitution did not exist or was not being slowly formed through the same evolutionary process that was shaping and reshaping the constitutions of the several entities that composed the British Empire. As Burke would subsequently remark, during the eighteenth century an imperial constitution had gradually evolved out of "mere neglect; possibly from the natural operation of things, which, left to themselves, generally fall into their proper order." In this constitution, as Andrew C. McLaughlin, the doyen of American constitutional historians, pointed out a half century ago, the metropolitan government exercised general powers that "from the necessity of the case . . . could not well be exercised by [Ireland or] the colonies—the post-office, naturalization, war and peace, foreign affairs, intercolonial and foreign commerce, establishment of new colonies, etc." and the Irish and American colonial governments exerted de facto and virtually exclusive jurisdiction over all matters of purely local concern, including matters of taxation.[23]

This arrangement meant that people in the peripheries, Irishmen and American colonists, were subject to what Burke called a "double legislature." Because the legislature at the center and those in the peripheries usually operated in rather well-defined and distinct spheres, however, they did not, in Burke's words, "very grossly or systematically clash." Because Parliament thus usually limited its actions with regard to the colonies to the general or external sphere and was so obviously not "clearly *informed [about]* . . . the Constitutions and Governments [with]in the Colonies," and the crown, through its governors and its powers of legislative and judicial review, exerted the predominant role in metropolitan interactions with the colonies, the colonists, as Barbara Black has argued persuasively, could reasonably develop a sense that the colonies were primarily "the king's dominions" and that Parliament's involvement with them was "essentially conciliar"—that is, advisory to, reinforcive of, and operating through the crown—much as had been its relationship with the medieval empire. Inasmuch as Parliament's colonial authority thus derived from the crown, it followed that as the colonial assemblies had succeeded in reducing the crown's authority in the colonies, they had also diminished the authority of Parliament and that the developing constitution of the empire was, as the seventeenth-century English constitution had been in theory, a constitution of "principled limitation," in which by long custom Parliament's authority did not usually extend to the internal affairs of the colonies and virtually all segments of the empire enjoyed "the benefits of government by consent" in matters pertaining to their own particular interior concerns.[24]

This is not to suggest that colonists thought of the colonies as "Independent State[s]" or yet even of their assemblies as bodies "politick coeordinate with (claimeing equal powers) and consequently independent of the Great Councell of the Realme." But colonial leaders certainly understood that their precise relationship to Parliament remained unsettled. Benjamin Franklin spoke for many colonists during the Stamp Act crisis when he questioned the extent of Parliament's jurisdiction over the colonies. "Planted in times when the powers of parliament were not supposed so extensive as they are become since the Revolution" and "in lands and countries where the parliament had not then the least jurisdiction," all of the colonies except Georgia and Nova Scotia, Franklin pointed out, had been settled without "*any money* granted by parliament" by people who, with "permission from the crown, purchased or conquered the territory, at the expence of their own private treasure and blood." "These territories," Franklin contended, "thus became *new* dominions *of the crown,* settled under royal charters, that formed their several governments and constitutions, on which the parliament was *never consulted;* or had the *least participation."* Like the Irish settlers, the American colonists "from the beginning," Franklin noted, had had "their separate parliaments, called modestly assemblies: by these chiefly our Kings have governed them. How far, and in what particulars, they are *subordinate* and *subject* to the British parliament; or whether they may not, if the King pleases, be governed as *domains of the crown,* without that parliament, are points newly agitated, [and] never yet . . . thoroughly considered and settled."[25]

In the absence of such a thorough consideration, the colonists' experience taught them that, "since the Settlement made at the *Revolution,"* the constitutions of the colonies, no less than that of Britain itself, had entered "*a new Aera"* in which "the main strong lines" of "the people's rights (including Americans)" had "been more particularly pointed out and established." Far from rejecting the results of the Glorious Revolution, colonists simply assumed that they were entitled to all its benefits. As a result of the revolution, they felt, their "Liberties & Constitution[s]" had been "secur'd & establish'd upon [just as] . . . firm and lasting [a] foundation" as had been those of Britons in the home islands. Based "on the same rational, constitutional foundation" laid down during the revolutionary settlement, Parliament and the assemblies, colonial leaders could reasonably surmise, differed from each other "ONLY as a greater circle from a less[er]."[26]

According to the practice of the extended polity of the British Empire as it had developed during the three-quarters of a century following the Glorious Revolution, there were thus three separate constitutions. First, there was a British constitution for the central state and its immediate dependencies, including Cornwall, Wales, and, after 1707, Scotland. Second, there were separate provincial constitutions for

Ireland and for each of the colonies in America. Third, there was an as yet undefined, even unacknowledged, imperial constitution—the constitution of the British Empire—according to the practice of which authority was distributed in an as yet uncodified and not very clearly understood way between the center and the peripheries with Parliament exercising power over general concerns and the local legislatures handling local affairs within their respective jurisdictions.

Practice to the contrary notwithstanding, no one in power in Britain accepted *in theory* any limitations upon the authority of Parliament to act in the colonial sphere. Parliament might hesitate to undertake any measure that would raise "a general opposition from our colonies and plantations," as it did during the 1740s, when the crown proposed legislation to make royal instructions law in the colonies and as it repeatedly did in Irish affairs. Through such restraint, Parliament acknowledged the truth of the old political adage that government was founded on the consent of the governed. But metropolitan authorities, in both the colonies and Britain, never doubted that Parliament had authority to take any action it thought necessary with regard to the colonies, even to the point of "alter[ing] . . . or intirely abolish[ing]" any "Concessions or Constitutions" formerly "granted by any of the Kings of England, or the first proprietors" if they thought those "Concessions or Constitutions inconvenient or Injurious" to the metropolis. Even those who believed that the crown could not of its own authority change the constitutions of the colonies in any fundamental way also thought that there was absolutely no "mischief" that could not "be remedied . . . by act of parliament of Great Britain." As occasion required, Parliament could levy taxes to defray the cost of the internal administration of specific colonies, revoke charters, new "moddle the Constitution[s] of those governments," or, otherwise abridge the colonies of the "many valuable Privileges which they enjoy[ed]" in exactly the same way as it had ostensibly already done in the case of Ireland with the Declaratory Act of 1720. "In all *British* Cases and over all Persons according to the *British* Constitution," they were convinced, the "Legislature of *Great-Britain*" was "absolutely supreme and the *Dernieir Resort*" not just for Britain but for the entire British Empire.[27]

By the time the outbreak of the Seven Years' War in the mid-1750s forced them to suspend the campaign begun in the late

1740s to tighten metropolitan controls over the colonies, crown officers in Britain had decided that they would never be able to accomplish their objectives with the prerogative powers at their command. Their largely ineffective efforts to enhance crown authority in the colonies during the six years from 1748 to 1754 had taught them that "no other Authority than that of the British Parliament" would either "be regarded by the Colonys, or be able to awe them into acquiescence." Increasingly, during these prewar years, frustration had driven them to threaten the intervention of Parliament to force colonial compliance with metropolitan commands. Except in the case of the Currency Act of 1751, however, metropolitan ministries had proven reluctant to involve Parliament in their reform efforts. During the war the failure of several colonies to support the military effort and the renewed encroachments of the colonial assemblies upon the crown's authority brought forth a veritable chorus of demands for Parliament to intervene in colonial governance. There were proposals for Parliament to form "a Parliamentary Union" among the colonies for their defense, to tax the colonies to pay the costs of the war, to curtail colonial trading with the enemy, and to act to "restore ye Authority of ye Crown & settle ye Rights of ye People according to the true Spirit of ye British Constitution."[28]

That Parliament might indeed act to shore up metropolitan authority in the colonies was suggested in 1757. The House of Commons intervened in the purely domestic affairs of a colony for the first time since 1733 in May of that year, when, with the full approval of the crown, it censured the Jamaica Assembly for making extravagant constitutional claims while resisting instructions from London. The possibility that metropolitan authorities might take similar actions with regard to other colonies was strongly suggested by the pains they took to inform all of the colonies of the Commons' action in this important precedent.[29]

Whether a more extensive exertion of parliamentary authority over the colonies would be readily accepted by the colonists seems not to have been doubted in Britain, and many colonials, especially those who held crown offices or otherwise supported the executive in its contest with the local legislatures, agreed that there would be "no contending" with Parliament. That august body, they believed, had the power and the right to do whatever it thought necessary with regard to the colonies. It could pass measures "for their better Regulation," even to the point of abridging the colonists of their "Privileges & put[ting them] . . . under a more Despotick Govern[men]t." "A *British* Parliament," Governor Lewis Morris told the New Jersey Assembly in April 1745, could "abolish any Constitution in the Plantations that they deem inconvenient or disadvantageous to the . . . Nation" as a whole.[30]

How the colonists might respond if Parliament did indeed try to legislate for the colonies in unaccustomed ways might have been predicted from their reactions to earlier proposals for such measures. When Parliament was considering legislation to resume the charters of the private colonies during the first decades of the eighteenth century, Jeremiah Dummer, agent for the New England charter colonies, produced the most systematic colonial commentary on Parliament's authority over the colonies before the 1760s. In *A Defence of the New-England Charters*, first published in London in 1721, Dummer admitted that Parliament's "Legislative Power" was "absolute and unaccountable, and [that] King, Lords and Commons" might "do what they please[d]." But, he added, in elaborating a point that would be frequently made by partisans of the colonies between 1764 and 1776, "the Question here is not about *Power*, but *Right: And shall not the Supream Judicature of all the Nation do right?*" Denying that it was "right" for colonies, which had "no Representatives in Parliament," to be "censur'd and depriv'd" of their rights by that body, Dummer suggested "that what the Parliament can't do justly, they can't do at all." "The higher the Power is," he concluded, "the greater [the] Caution is to be us'd in the Execution of it."[31]

The colonists' view of an unjust action was revealed during the 1740s, when Parliament was considering legislation to make royal instructions law in the colonies. Such legislation, the colonists contended, was "*contrary to the Constitution[s] of Great Britain & of the Plantations*" and "*inconsistent with the Liberties & Privileges inherent in an Englishman whilst he is in a Brittish Dominion.*" By subjecting them to "a Despotick Power vested in the Crown," such a measure, they protested, would deprive them of their "inestimable privilege of" being "governed by the laws of their own making" and "annihilate all the Legislative Power" formerly exercised by the colonies. Such a measure, asserted William Bollan, agent for Massachusetts in London, "was plainly . . . an unconstitutional attempt" that would "wholly subvert" the "Constitution[s] of the Colonies."[32]

The colonists were implying in these protests that, as the New Jersey Assembly resolved in 1745, Parliament had no right through legislation thus to encroach "upon *the fundamental Constitution[s]*" of the colonies or to alter "*the Concessions made to the first Settlers . . . by his Majesty's Royal Ancestors.*" Although no colonists at this time seem to have explicitly denied that Parliament, as well as the assemblies, could legislate for the internal affairs of the colonies, the obvious logic of their argument was that legislation without representation was a violation of the entire British constitutional tradition as it had evolved in both Britain and the colonies and that Parliament therefore had no authority over the internal concerns of the colonies. Certainly, this was the obvious inference behind the assertion, made by the historian Daniel Neal in his 1720 *History of New-England,* that because the inhabitants of Massachusetts had been guaranteed "all *English* liberties" by the 1691 charter, they could "be touched by no Law, by no Tax, but of their own making."[33]

Adherents to this emerging colonial interpretation of the eighteenth-century British and imperial constitutions had obviously not accepted the postrevolutionary metropolitan concept of a constitution based on parliamentary supremacy. Rather, they were espousing the older seventeenth-century theory of a constitution of customary restraints on arbitrary power, a theory that seemed to them to be more compatible with—and more explanatory of—their own constitutional experience both within the colonies and with regard to metropolitan-colonial relationships within the empire at large. Questioning whether Parliament had "a Right to enact any Thing contrary to a fundamental Part of the British Constitution," they argued that Magna Charta and the Petition of Right were expressive of "*reserv'd Rights*" that were antecedent to and therefore binding upon Parliament. "To imagine that a Parliament is Omnipotent, or may do any Thing," a Freeholder argued in the *Maryland Gazette* in February 1748, was "a vulgar Mistake . . . for . . . they can't alter the Constitution. There are certain Powers, Rights, and Privileges invested in every Branch of the Legislature, by the Constitution," he explained, "no Part of which can be given up by any of them without breaking thro' that Constitution, which is the Basis of the whole." "Even the Authority of Parliament," concluded another writer in accordance with the best seventeenth-century thought on the subject, "is circumscribed by Law, and has its Bounds."[34]

The practical question, of course, was what agency could prevent

Parliament from trampling upon these fundamental rights whenever it decided to do so: in the words of another Maryland writer, "Who, or what, can disable the Legislature?" Though some colonial thinkers suggested in early hints of the later concept of judicial review that the courts might do so, colonial thinkers could come up with no better answer than the people themselves. Strictly speaking, observed still a third Maryland author who quoted extensively from John Locke, it was untrue that the legislative power was *"accountable to no Power of Earth."* Although he admitted that there was *"no Power on Earth* (that is, no Body politic, entrusted by the Society) *superior to the legislative Power,"* he insisted that that power was always limited by the willingness of the governed to obey it. Legislative power was therefore always "accountable to the *Community,"* members of which could judge whether the legislature "acted agreeably to . . . *Reason* [and to] . . . the *Fundamental Rule[s] of society"* and withhold support from any measures that "Breach[ed] the *Constitution."* But the emerging imperial constitution contained no formal and theoretically neutral mechanism to which people in the peripheries could appeal against an erring Parliament.[35]

In this situation, colonists could do little else but hope that "so great" a body as the British Parliament would take no action that by "preparing Slavery to us would give a presedent" that could subsequently be used "against themselves." Although some people fretted lest after the war Parliament should try "to make general Colony Laws" that would "deeply . . . enter into our *Constitution[s]* and affect our most *valuable Priviledges,"* most seemed to have remained far more fearful of attacks upon their rights and constitutions from the "long hand of the Prerogative" than from Parliament. Indeed, rather than thinking of Parliament as a source of danger or as a competitor to their own legislative jurisdictions, they seem to have regarded it, in the phrase of Christopher Gadsden, as "their best and most interested friends" in Britain, the ultimate protector of colonial, as well as British, rights and privileges, and a body to which they could appeal for help if the crown persisted in its efforts to violate their established constitutions.[36]

Acting in their executive capacity, the crown's ministers might very well, as they had so often done in the past, through either ignorance or malice, take up oppressive measures against the colonies. But colonial writers cited the House of Commons' condemnation of the Earl of

Clarendon under Charles II for having tried to introduce "an arbitrary government *in[to] his Majesty's . . . plantations*" as evidence that *"that August Assembly,* the Protectors of English Liberties," would never lend its weight "to enforce illegal or arbitrary orders" or, indeed, to *"do any thing that shall be to our disadvantage."* Parliament's refusal in 1744 and 1749 to give the royal instructions the force in law in the colonies seemed to confirm this opinion. When "the clause [for that purpose] was thrown out by the Commons," Franklin later recalled, "we adored them as our friends and [as] friends of liberty." The wide-spread feeling seems to have been that Parliament simply had too much wisdom and too much regard for the preservation of British liberty—in the colonies as well as in Britain—ever to interfere with the jurisdictions of its sister parliaments, the colonial legislatures. The ministry did not again try to enlist Parliament in its schemes to make instructions laws in the colonies, Franklin believed, because it feared that if it permitted Parliament to "meddle at all with the Government of the Colonies," it "would establish more Liberty in the Colonies" at the expense of the powers and prerogatives of the crown.[37]

Of course, this roseate view ignored some powerful evidence pointing in the opposite direction. Especially foreboding were the implications behind the precise wording of the House of Commons' condemnation of the Jamaica Assembly in 1757. Whereas a committee report had denounced the assembly's claims as "illegal unconstitutional and dirogatory of the Rights of the Crown and People of Great Britain," William Knox later recounted, the House of Commons itself "ordered the Word *Unconstitutional* to be struck out, and [in its place] inserted [the phrase] *repugnant to His Majesty's Commission to His Governor of the said Island."* The grounds for this change, "as it was said in the Debate and reported in America, where I then was, and well remember the alarm it excited," Knox wrote, was that "the Island had no Constitution but the King's Commission." By this change in wording, the House of Commons in effect subscribed to the crown's long-standing contention that, as Knox put it, "the Colonys have no Constitution, but that the mode of Government in each of them depends upon the good pleasure of the King, as expressed in his Commission, and Instructions to his Governor."[38]

The colonists' failure to give major weight to such evidence provides impressive testimony to their basic trust in Parliament, which, it is clear in retrospect, was founded on Parliament's not having acted toward the colonies before the 1760s in ways that could be perceived as unusual, arbitrary, or threatening. Indeed, because it had almost entirely refrained from interfering in internal colonial matters, Parliament had done precisely the opposite. So long as Parliament continued to take only a limited role in colonial affairs and otherwise to behave in ways to which colonists had become accustomed, they had little cause to be jealous of, much less to challenge, its authority. But the colonists' failure to challenge Parliament's authority did not mean that they had accepted it "in all cases whatsoever," as the Irish Declaratory Act asserted. Nor did their high regard for Parliament by any means suggest that they had endorsed the doctrine of parliamentary omnipotence that was then gaining ascendance in Britain as a result of what C. H. McIlwain has called the "unforeseen constitutional consequences" of the Glorious Revolution. Because Parliament had never tried to intrude into their internal affairs in any sustained or serious way, they had never been required to consider the legitimacy of its authority to do so. Neither by explicit declaration nor by long-standing practice had they ever accepted—or rejected—the doctrine of parliamentary omnipotence insofar as it extended to the colonies. However thoroughly it had come to be accepted in Britain as an essential attribute of the British constitution, that doctrine could not, without colonial acceptance, become an established principle of the emerging imperial constitution, that cluster of conventions that defined and structured relationships between the center and the peripheries in the mid-eighteenth-century British Empire.[39]

Even though Parliament's precise relationship to the colonies had, in Franklin's words, "never yet [been] . . . thoroughly considered and settled," well before the 1760s it could be viewed from two well-articulated and opposing perspectives. One, the perspective of the center, derived from the metropolitan understanding of the nature of the British constitution as it had evolved since the Glorious Revolution. The other, from the peripheries, was shaped by the colonists' experience with their own local constitutions and the developing imperial constitution. The weight of recent historical argument has been that the perspective of the center was the "correct" one. But this interpretation falls into the trap too infrequently avoided by historians of equating correctness with centrality and strength. As subsequent events would prove, the position of the center on this question could never enjoy unchallenged supremacy—or be regarded as correct—until it had been ratified through either explicit consent or implicit acquiescence in the peripheries.[40]

That the colonists would not readily ratify the doctrine of parliamentary omnipotence could easily be surmised from the thrust of their own constitutional thought between 1660 and 1760. Their view of the constitution was developmental in the sense that they saw their own constitutions and, by implication, the constitution of the empire as moving in the same direction as had the British constitution in the wake of the Glorious Revolution: that is, toward increasing limitations upon prerogative power and greater security for individual and corporate rights under the protection of a strong legislature. According to this view, further gains in the direction of still greater limitations and security could still be achieved but those already made could not—constitutionally, at least—be lost. From this perspective, any effort to impose the principle of unlimited parliamentary authority upon the colonies was bound to appear to the colonists as retrogressive and unacceptable.

In this unsettled and uncodified situation, practice was the best, indeed, the only, guide to what was "constitutional" in relations between center and peripheries within the empire, and, as McLaughlin pointed out in the 1930s, the British Empire "as a practical working system" was characterized "by diversification and not by centralization." According to metropolitan theory, the central government in London "had complete and unalloyed power." In "actual *practice*," however, "the empire of the mid-eighteenth century was a diversified empire" with power "actually distributed [among] and exercised by various governments." Ireland and the American dominions "had long existed" as "bodies, corporate, constituent members of the Empire," each with its own constitution and a government "with many powers and with actual authority." Each inhabitant of both Ireland and the American colonies thus lived under two governments, one imperial in scope and exercising full general powers over foreign affairs, war and peace, and external trade and the other a colonial government that "was peculiarly his own." Although the several colonial governments were by no means "in possession of complete authority," they had long exercised actual and virtually exclusive jurisdiction over almost all matters of purely local concern.[41]

To a remarkable extent, the colonial legislatures, like Parliament in

Britain, exercised full legislative powers over their respective jurisdictions. They claimed those powers on the basis of their constituents' inherited rights as Britons not to be subjected to any laws passed without their consent, on their having actually exercised those powers, according to their customary constitutions, for many decades and in some cases for over a century, and on metropolitan confirmation of their rights to those powers through either explicit charters or long-standing custom. Because the metropolitan government never explicitly admitted in theory what had developed in practice, however, the authority of the assemblies in the peripheries vis-à-vis that of the crown and the Parliament at the center remained in an uncertain state as late as the 1760s. Meanwhile, notwithstanding this lack of theoretical resolution or agreement as to the actual and customary distribution of power within the empire, the empire continued to function in practice with a clear demarcation of authority, with virtually all internal matters being handled by the colonial governments and most external affairs and matters of general concern by the metropolitan government.

Book Two

A Problem
Defined,
1764–1776

Chapter Five
Definitions of Empire, 1764–1766

When the Seven Years' War ended in 1763, the only certainty about constitutional arrangements within the large, extended polity that constituted the early modern British Empire was their uncertainty. The balance of authority between the center and the peripheries remained undefined. Recurrent disputes over the extent of the crown's colonial authority had left that issue unresolved, and the nature of Parliament's relation to the colonies had never been explicitly examined. As Massachusetts Governor Francis Bernard remarked in August 1764, the relationship of the "Subordinate Governments . . . to the Sovereign power" had "never been formally settled" and was certainly not "generally understood."[1]

Parliament's efforts to impose taxes on the colonies in the mid-1760s precipitated the first intensive and systematic exploration of this problem on either side of the Atlantic. Ostensibly, the issue raised by these efforts, especially by the Stamp Act of 1765, was no more than whether, in the succinct words of Bernard, "America shall or shall not be Subject to the Legislature of Great Britain." But the controversy rapidly moved on to a more general level. In the process, it provoked a broad-ranging consideration of fundamental issues involving the nature of the constitutional relationship between Britain and the colonies and the distribution of power within the empire. Far from producing either a theoretical or a practical resolution of these issues, however, the Stamp Act crisis of 1764–66 revealed a deep rift in understanding between the center and the peripheries that would never be bridged within the structure of the empire.[2]

Historians have tended to agree that the administration of George Grenville had no doubts about the legitimacy of its actions when it initiated these efforts in the late winter of 1764. But Grenville's speech introducing his American measures suggests otherwise. No M.P. rose to challenge the legitimacy of his proposals. Indeed, one observer reported that they "gained the applause of the *whole* House." Yet, by acknowledging that "the path" might be "thorny," Grenville betrayed both an awareness of the novelty of those proposals and a pronounced uneasiness about the negative reception they might receive in the colonies. As Bernard would later remark, Grenville and his aides could scarcely have failed to realize "that such an Innovation as a Parliamentary Taxation would cause a great Alarm & meet with much Opposition in most parts of America."[3]

Some metropolitan supporters later admitted that the Stamp Act was the "first Instance of parliament's imposing an internal tax upon the colonies for the single purpose of a revenue." For at least three decades, however, metropolitan officials had casually assumed that Parliament's colonial authority was unlimited. For over a century, Parliament had routinely laid duties upon colonial exports and imports for the purposes of regulating trade. But it was also true that parliamentary legislation for the colonies had been confined almost entirely to commercial and other economic regulations of general scope. The only precedent for a tax for any other purpose was the Post Office Act of 1710, and that measure, as William Beckford, the wealthy Jamaican sugar planter and M.P., noted on the floor of the House of Commons, had "certainly [been] for the convenience of the colonies themselves." If there were no clear precedents for Parliament's taxing the colonies for revenue before the Stamp Act, neither had anyone ever explicitly articulated a theoretical justification for the exertion of parliamentary authority in that area.[4]

Because of the traditional link between taxation and representation in British constitutional thought and practice, this problem was potentially troublesome—for metropolitans as much as for colonials. Indeed, metropolitan disquiet over this problem was clearly revealed during the Stamp Act crisis by proposals from several writers for colonial representation in Parliament. More important, the Grenville administration itself implicitly acknowledged the importance of this problem by the pains it took to deal with it. During the winter of 1764–65 in the months preceding the final passage of the Stamp Act, Grenville's lieutenant, Thomas Whately, ingeniously developed the doctrine of virtual representation, according to which the colonists, like those individuals and groups who resided in Britain but had no voice in elections, were nonetheless *virtually* represented in Parliament.[5]

When Grenville first brought the proposal for colonial stamp duties before Parliament the previous March, however, neither he nor Whately had apparently yet applied this doctrine to the colonies, and he tried to finesse the problem created by the lack of colonial representation in Parliament with a simple—and categorical—assertion of Parliament's right. Indeed, by insisting on that occasion that Britain had "an inherent right to lay inland duties there," Grenville himself first raised the question of parliamentary right. In addition, by going out of his way to assert that the "very sovereignty of this kingdom depends [up]on it," he also managed to establish the framework within which most metropolitans would subsequently consider the issue by ensuring that they would thenceforth interpret colonial opposition to the exertion of that right as a challenge not simply to the authority of Parliament per se but to the sovereignty of the metropolis in general.[6]

As soon as it was raised, the specter of parliamentary taxation stimulated "great inquiry and some apparent puzzle" in the colonies. That it was both "new and unprecedented" most colonial leaders seemed to agree. In the "long period of more than one hundred and fifty years" since the founding of the colonies, the Pennsylvania lawyer John Dickinson subsequently remarked, "no statute was ever [previously] passed [by the British Parliament] for the sole purpose of raising a revenue on the colonies." If, however, the entire subject "had never been canvassed before" and was "yet new to the whole British Nation," few colonists seem to have doubted that, at least from their perspective in the peripheries, it was obviously unconstitutional.[7]

Beginning with their earliest protests against the proposed Stamp Act, they insisted that no community of Englishmen and their descendants could be taxed without their consent, an exemption they claimed "as their Right" and not "as a *Privilege.*" "To be subject to no . . . taxation . . . but [that] which is authorized by the representative body of each society in concert with the representative of the crown presiding over it," declared the Barbados Assembly, was "a privilege which we imagined the subjects of Great Britain had been particularly entitled to in every settlement, however distant, of the British Empire as a birthright and blessing indeed capable of making every settlement, even the most distant of that Empire[,] grateful to a

British spirit." Throughout the entire British world, the colonists asserted, in the peripheries as well as at the center, representation was the only basis for the authority to tax. Because Parliament represented only the inhabitants of Britain, it necessarily followed that its taxing power did "not extend . . . to such parts of the British dominions as are not represented in that grand legislature of the nation."[8]

They dismissed the idea of virtual representation out of hand. Founded on no more secure foundation than "a Defect in the Constitution of England," namely, the "Want of a full Representation in Parliament of all the People of England," the "Phantasie of virtual Representation," they declared, was obviously a "far-fetched" notion "of late date" that had been fabricated for the sole purpose of arguing the colonists "out of their civil Rights." If they were virtually represented in 1765, the colonists contended, they must always have been so, and if they had always been represented, why for a century and more, as one anonymous writer asked, had "the Mother Country . . . continually applied to the assemblies of the various provinces, whenever she wanted their assistance?" Indeed, he queried, why in the first place had she granted "a provincial legislature to her Colonies, and from the time of their first existence, invest[ed them] . . . with the sole power of internal taxation?"[9]

Besides, they complained, the very concept was incompatible with that ancient and basic British constitutional principle that no tax could be "justly laid on any People . . . when the People taxed have not contributed to the Law, and agreed by their Representatives to receive it." Quoting Joseph Addison to show that in the British tradition true liberty always required a community of interest between legislators and constituents, an anonymous Barbadian pointed out that this notion of a "common interest" was so fundamental to the British constitution that it even extended "beyond the legislative Line, into the civil Administration of Justice. Juries to determine on a Point of Life and Property," he observed, "must come in a Manner qualified for the Office, by having lived in the Neighbourhood of the Party" under prosecution. Thus, in "Cases of [both] Taxations and Verdicts," he noted, a "Man's Neighbours alone" were, according to British constitutional practice, the only people who had "an exclusive Right to determine all his Questions." Hence, it seemed evident to this writer that virtual representation was "a Notion no less absurd than virtual Neighbourhood would be, if set up in a Court of Law." "*To have any*

Authority," he concluded in quoting David Hume, *"a Law . . . must be derived from a Legislature* WHICH HAS A RIGHT*"*; for a legislature to have a right, it had to have a common interest and a direct connection with the people for whom it presumed to legislate.[10]

For people in the peripheries of an extended polity like that of the early modern British Empire, this emphasis upon the local foundations of both legislative and judicial authority made sense, and, whatever Parliament might declare, few colonists had any doubt that their rights as Englishmen demanded both that they be exempt from taxes levied in a distant metropolis without their consent and that their own local assemblies have an exclusive power to tax them. Indeed, as most colonial leaders seem to have recognized, the "exclusive Right" of the assemblies to tax the colonies constituted "what the Lawyers call the very Git of the Colony Argument."[11]

In analyzing the colonial response to the Stamp Act crisis, most scholars have tended to treat the colonists' claims as demands for their individual rights as Englishmen, as indeed they were. But this emphasis has tended to obscure the very important extent to which, especially during the Stamp Act crisis, the colonists seem to have believed that, as Robert W. Tucker and David C. Hendrickson have recently reminded us, "there could be no effective guarantee of individual rights without the effective guarantee of collective rights (or powers)," which they thought of as virtually synonymous with "the rights of the provincial assemblies." As was stressed in earlier chapters, the status and authority of the assemblies had "always been the central issue in the imperal-colonial relationship." Whereas earlier the conflict had been between the assemblies and the crown, it was now between the assemblies and Parliament. In view of the close relationship in colonial thinking between individual rights and corporate rights, it is by no means an exaggeration to argue, as do Tucker and Hendrickson, " that the central issue raised by the measures of the Grenville ministry concerned the role and power of the provincial assembly."[12]

Throughout the Stamp Act crisis, colonial spokesmen put enormous stress upon the traditional conception of their assemblies as the primary guardians of both the individual liberties of their constituents and the corporate rights of the colonies. Noting that it was precisely because their great distance from the metropolis had prevented them from being either fully incorporated into the British nation or represented in the metropolitan Parliament that "their own assemblies" had been "established in its stead," they insisted that each of their own local legislatures enjoyed full legislative authority and exclusive power to tax within its respective jurisdiction. "As the legislative, deliberative body" in each colony, the assembly, in the words of former Massachusetts Governor Thomas Pownall, represented the collective "will of that province or colony."[13]

This identification of individual rights with the corporate rights of the assemblies ran right through the entire colonial argument. Thus the Connecticut Assembly argued against Parliamentary taxation on the grounds that it would both deprive its constituents of "that fundamental privilege of Englishmen whereby, in special, they are denominated a free people" and, no less important, leave them with "no more than a show of legislation." "May it not be truly said in this case," it asked, "that the Assemblies in the colonies will have left no other power or authority, and the people no other freedom, estates, or privileges than what may truly be called a tenancy at will; that they [will] have exchanged, or rather lost, those privileges and rights which, according to the national constitution, were their birthright and inheritance, for such a disagreeable tenancy?"[14]

But the colonists based their claims for exemption from parliamentary taxation not merely on "their right to the general principles of the British constitution" and certainly not just on "the [many] royal declaration[s] and grant[s] in their favor" in their charters from the crown. They also grounded those claims on "Prescription, or long Usage, which," they insisted, was "generally understood to give Right." "Ever since the first establishment of . . . civil government" in the colonies "to the present time," they argued, "for more than 100 years," they had "uniformly exercised and enjoyed the privileges of imposing and raising their own taxes, in their provincial assemblies"; and those privileges, they asserted, had been "constantly . . . acknowledged, and allowed to be just in the claim and use thereof by the crown, the ministry, and the Parliament." Originally confirmed "by *solemn acts* of government," their rights, one writer declared in language redolent of the colonists' ancient disputes with crown authorities, had thus subsequently been "sanctified by successive usage, grounded upon a generous reliance on English Faith and Compact, and that usage—ratified by repeated authoritative acquiesence." Such "constant and uninterrupted usage and custom," it seemed to them, was, in the best traditions of English constitutional development, "sufficient of itself to make a constitution." In these appeals to their rights as Englishmen, their charters, and long-standing custom, colonial spokesmen were merely turning against Parliament the defenses they and their ancestors had developed over the previous century to protect colonial rights against abuses of prerogative.[15]

Whatever the sources of the legislative authority of the assemblies, the most significant questions posed by the new intrusion of Parliament into the domestic affairs of the colonies—the most vital issues raised by the Stamp Act crisis vis-à-vis the constitutional organization of the early modern British Empire—were how extensive that authority was and how it related to the authority of the British Parliament. Few colonists could accept the metropolitan position that there were no limits to Parliament's colonial authority. They did not deny that Parliament's power was extraordinary. They knew that, at least within Britain, its privileges were then "as undetermined as were formerly the Prerogatives of the Crown." Just as the prerogative had eventually been "fixed and settled," however, "So in like Manner," they believed, "ought all other Claims of Privilege to be," including those of Parliament. "Power of every Sort has its Boundary," an anonymous Barbadian declared in arguing that it "would tend to the Happiness of all English Subjects" if Parliament's "Privileges were as well known and ascertained as the Prerogatives of the Crown." "To presume to adjust the boundaries of the power of Parliament" might be beyond its competence, the Massachusetts House of Representatives admitted in October 1765, but it had no doubt that "boundaries there undoubtedly are."[16]

In trying to fix for themselves the boundaries of parliamentary authority, colonial spokesmen carefully distinguished between power and authority. For a legislature to have "Authority," they argued, it "must have a Right over the Persons whomsoever it may affect," and such a right, they believed, could only be "derived by Compact, and must have a legal and open Commencement" that "carried with it not only Marks of Notoriety, but of the Consent of all Parties." Nor, they contended, could that compact be changed without the mutual consent of *all* parties. Consent was thus not merely "a bare Circumstance to the Rise and vesting of Authority." It was "the very Essence of . . . Jurisdiction." Without it, a legislature had no authority, and its actions could be "supported on no other Base than Power." However great had been the increase in Parliament's authority as a result of the constitutional changes that had occurred in England since the founding of the colonies, those changes were perforce confined to the "People of England only" and had "nothing to do with" the colonies—unless the colonists had themselves consented to them. Great as was the "Power of Parliament," its colonial authority was therefore necessarily confined to those areas in which the colonies had given their consent.[17]

But what were these areas and how could they be described? A few colonists concluded that there were no areas in which Parliament had "lawful authority over" the colonies. The delegation of legislative power to the colonies, they believed, had to be "considered not only as uncurrent with, but as exclusive of all parliamentary participation in the *proper subjects* of their legislation, that is to say, in cases not repugnant to the laws of Great-Britain." According to this line of argument, Parliament had "no power but what is delegated to them by their constituents," and because those constituents had "no power over our liberty and property," it followed both that the authority of Parliament was "(over these things at least) . . . purely local, and confined to the places they are chosen to represent," and, as at least one writer asserted, that any exertion of that authority over the colonies was "most inconsistent with civil liberty."[18]

But most colonists took a far more cautious approach to this subject. They neither claimed "an independent legislature" nor denied that the colonies were "all subordinate to and dependent upon the mother country." Rather, most seem to have agreed with the Maryland lawyer Daniel Dulany that because the colonies were "dependent upon Great Britain," the "supreme authority vested in the King, Lords, and Commons" could "justly be exercised to secure, or preserve their dependence whenever necessary for that purpose." Such authority, wrote Dulany, "results from and is implied in the idea of the relation subsisting between England and her colonies." As Dulany quickly added, however, there could "very well exist a *dependence* . . . without absolute *vassalage* and *slavery*," and he was persuaded that the extent of that dependence could be located in "what the superior may *rightfully* control or compel, and in what the inferior ought to be at liberty to act without control or compulsion."[19]

The colonies might thus, as the Virginia lawyer Richard Bland acknowledged, be "subordinate to the Authority of Parliament," but they were subordinate only "in Degree" and "not absolutely so." "When powers compatible with the relation between the superior and inferior have by express compact been granted to and accepted by the latter, and have been, after that compact, repeatedly recognized by the former—when they may be exercised effectually upon every occasion without injury to that relation—," Dulany explained, "the authority of the superior can't properly interpose, for by the powers vested in the inferior is the superior limited." As free-born Britons, the colonists assumed, they could not be subjected to any but what Bland referred to as "a constitutional Subordination" to the parent state.[20]

But what was the nature of that "constitutional Subordination"? Where should the line be drawn between the authority of Parliament at the center and that of the colonial legislatures in the peripheries? The traditional view has been that during the Stamp Act crisis the colonists drew that line between taxation and legislation, that they denied Parliament's authority to tax the colonies for revenue but not its authority to legislate for the colonies. That neither the Stamp Act Congress nor many of the assemblies explicitly commented on Parliament's authority outside the realm of taxation seems to support this argument. Probably because "the issue of the day was taxation" and "Parliament at this time was not attempting to interfere in" other aspects of the internal affairs of the colonies, these bodies, as Edmund S. Morgan has observed, saw no need to consider Parliament's legislative authority in other areas, and "what the colonies insisted on most vigorously was that Parliament's supreme legislative authority did not include the right to tax." But the failure of most of these bodies to challenge Parliament's legislative authority outside the area of taxation by no means constituted an admission of that authority, especially in view of the explicit denial of that authority by several official bodies.[21]

Indeed, there is considerable evidence to suggest that the colonists' strong initial impulse was to exclude Parliament from all jurisdiction over the domestic affairs of the colonies. They claimed a right not merely to no taxation without representation but to no legislation without representation. Thus did the Connecticut Assembly in the summer of 1764 in its protest against the proposed stamp duties invoke that "fundamental principle of the British constitution that 'NO LAW CAN BE MADE OR ABROGATED WITHOUT THE CONSENT OF THE PEOPLE BY THEIR

REPRESENTATIVES.'" Thus did the Virginia Assembly in its petition to the king the following December claim for its constituents the "ancient and inestimable Right of being governed by such Laws respecting their internal Polity and Taxation as are derived from their own Consent"—a claim that was reiterated by the Virginia House of Burgesses when it adopted Patrick Henry's defiant resolutions in May 1765 and was repeated in one form or another in public resolutions by the legislatures of Rhode Island, Maryland, and Connecticut in September and October. Although the Massachusetts Assembly did not go so far in its resolutions against the Stamp Act, it unequivocally asserted, in a late October message to Governor Bernard its right to make laws for the province's "internal government and taxation." And that authority, it added, had "been never. . . questioned; but has been constantly recognized by the King and Parliament."[22]

Precisely what the several assemblies were claiming in 1764–66 when they denied Parliament's authority to pass laws respecting the internal polity of the colonies can be surmised from contemporary comment by several prominent political writers. These included the Virginians Richard Bland and Landon Carter, Rhode Island's elected governor, Stephen Hopkins, and the Massachusetts political leader Samuel Adams. An analysis of the works of these and other writers suggests that, as Bernard Bailyn has emphasized, the supposed colonial distinction between taxation and legislation was less important to the colonial attempt to demarcate the jurisdictional boundaries between Parliament and the colonial assemblies than the distinction between "'internal' and 'external' spheres of government."[23]

Bland provided the most extensive and systematic exploration of this distinction. In *The Colonel Dismounted*, published in late October 1764, just a few weeks before the Virginia Assembly prepared to petition against the proposed stamp duties, he argued that because Virginians were entitled to all of the "liberties and privileges of English subjects, they must necessarily have a legal constitution," which he defined as "a legislature composed in part of the representatives of the people who may enact laws for the INTERNAL government of the colony and suitable to its various circumstances and occasions." "Without such a representative," Bland made "bold enough to say, no law can be made." Thus, by definition, Parliament, in which the colonists were not represented, had no authority to pass laws for the "INTERNAL government" of the colonies without blatantly violating "the most valuable part" of the colonists' "Birthright" as Englishmen, the right "of being governed by laws made with our own consent." The constitution, said Bland, demanded that Parliament be excluded from "all power" over any colony "but such as respects its EXTERNAL government," and, he observed in a pointed reference to the proposed stamp duties, any law "respecting our INTERNAL polity which may hereafter be imposed on us by act of Parliament is arbitrary, as depriving us of our rights, and may be opposed."[24]

Fifteen months later, early in 1766, after Parliament had passed the Stamp Act and it had met with widespread colonial resistance, Bland enlarged upon this position in a second pamphlet, *An Inquiry Into the Rights of the British Colonies*. Once again claiming for the colonists the authority "of directing their *internal* Government by Laws made with their Consent," he argued that each colony was "a distinct State, independent, as to their *internal* Government, of the original Kingdom, but united with her, as to their *external* Polity, in the closest and most intimate LEAGUE AND AMITY, under the same Allegiance, and enjoying the Benefits of a reciprocal Intercourse." Though Bland did not make clear in either pamphlet exactly what matters were subsumed under the terms *internal* and *external*, his clear implication was that Parliament's authority—to legislate as well as to tax—stopped short of the Atlantic coast of the colonies and did not extend over any affairs relating exclusively to the internal life of the colonies. Such matters, according to Bland's formulation, were the exclusive preserve of the colonial assemblies. Implicitly, at least, Landon Carter, Bland's associate in the Virginia House of Burgesses, subscribed to the same general argument when, in four separate essays against the Stamp Act, he vigorously pressed the colonists' claim "of being solely governed and taxed by Laws made with the Consent of the Majority of their own Representatives, according to an Englishman's inherent Birthright."[25]

Nor were these Virginians peculiar in explicitly arguing that the limitations on Parliament's colonial authority extended to all of the internal affairs of the colonies, and not just to taxation. "The general superintending Power of the Parliament over the whole British Empire," four members of the Massachusetts Assembly, including Samuel Adams and James Otis, wrote a London correspondent in December 1765, "is clearly admitted here, so far as in our Circumstances is consistent with the Enjoyment of our essential Rights, as Freemen, and British Subjects." As Adams emphasized, however, that "general superintending Power" did not extend to the internal affairs of the colonies. Claiming "an exclusive Right to make Laws for our own internal Government & Taxation," Adams argued that if the colonists were "indeed . . . British Subjects, (& they never can brook to be thought any thing less) it seems necessary that they should exercise this Power within themselves; for they are not represented in the British Parliam[en]t & their great Distance renders it impracticable." Only if each legislature within the empire had an exclusive legislative authority within its own jurisdiction, the Massachusetts Assembly declared in elaborating this point, would it be possible to ensure "that equality [of rights and status] which ought ever to subsist among all his Majesty's subjects in his wide extended empire."[26]

Stephen Hopkins carried this point still farther. "In an imperial state, which consists of many separate governments each of which hath peculiar privileges and of which kind it is evident that the empire of Great Britain is," Hopkins observed, "no single part, though greater than another part, is by that superiority entitled to make laws for or to tax such lesser part." That was the reason, Hopkins believed, why each of the colonies had to have "a legislature within itself to take care of its interests and provide for its peace and internal government." Yet, like Bland and the Massachusetts representatives, he recognized that there were "many things of a more general nature, quite out of the reach of these particular legislatures, which it is necessary should be regulated, ordered, and governed." Among these "matters of a general nature," Hopkins included regulations concerning the commerce and good order of "the whole British empire, taken collectively," including "those grand instruments of commerce," money and paper credit. With regard to all such general matters, he thought it "absolutely necessary" to have "a general power to direct them, some supreme and overruling authority with power to make laws and form regulations for the good of all, and to compel their execution and observation." Within the British Empire, this general power, according to Hopkins, could be lodged only in the British Parliament.[27]

All of these writers thus agreed that, although Parliament had to have jurisdiction over what the New York pamphleteer William Hicks referred to as "all such general Regulations as could not be effected by the single Powers of any one Colony," the internal and purely provincial affairs of the colonies should remain under the exclusive authority of the assemblies. So long as Parliament confined its regulations to "restrictions on navigation, commerce, or other external regulations," they reasoned, the "legislatures of the colonies" would be "left entire" and "the internal government, powers of taxing for its support, an exemption from being taxed without consent, and [all] other immunities which legally belong[ed] to the subjects of each colony agreeable to their own particular constitutions" would thereby, according to the "general principles of the British constitution," remain "secure and untouched." To govern the colonies *according to the principles of the national constitution*," they thus insisted, required that they be *"vested with authority of legislation"* over all provincial matters *"and have right to be represented in their Assemblies, in whom [alone] that authority"* was *"lodged."*[28]

The underlying implications of the conception of the empire suggested by these writers were, perhaps, most clearly spelled out by one of the colonists' supporters in Britain. "Our Constitution is so tender of the Rights and Liberties of the Subject," wrote the anonymous author of *A Vindication of the Rights of the Americans* in 1765, "that the People of *England* have their Repr[esentative]s, the *Scotch* theirs, the *Welsh* theirs, the *Irish* theirs, [and] the *Americans* theirs, for they have Assemblies and Parliaments, each of which represent the Bulk of the People, of that Generality, or Division, for which such Assembly or Parliament is appointed to be held." The reason why it was "necessary to have so many Houses of Representatives in the several Departments of Government" was "obvious." "In extensive Territories not confined to one Island, or one Continent, but dispersed through a great Part of the Globe," he explained, "the Laws cannot be put into execution, nor the Rights of the People preserved, without their being arranged into several Classes" of coordinate legislatures, each, presumably, having exclusive jurisdiction over the internal affairs of the territory for which it was responsible.[29]

As Tucker and Hendrickson have remarked, the "distinction between imperial and provincial purposes, between general and local areas of concern, between external and internal objects—the appeal, in other words, to principles recognizably federal, came naturally to men on both sides of the Atlantic when forced, during the crisis brought on by the Stamp Act, to articulate the character of the imperial constitution." Such distinctions effectively described the pragmatic and customary distribution of authority and functions within the empire as it had developed over the past century and a half. The colonists could not deny that Parliament had, during that time, occasionally passed statutes that "by express words" extended to the colonies. Some writers attempted to explain those acts as measures submitted to at an early point in the history of the colonies when the settlers were "too much employ'd by their necessary Avocations, to examine much into the Minutiae of Government," and few had any doubt that such measures, though perhaps justified by "political reasons," were "in some measure an exception from the general rule by which British subjects (according to the constitution) are governed." Yet they had to admit that parliamentary restraints on colonial trade, commerce, and manufacturing were "what has been customary, and therefore chearfully submitted to." Historians have generally failed to realize that, according to British constitutional tradition, custom itself was a form of consent. But it was precisely because colonial submission to these general, external measures had been so long *customary* that they obviously could not, strictly speaking, be taken as violations of the fundamental principle of no legislation without consent.[30]

When Britain's American "Provinces [thus] claim[ed] an exclusive Power of making Laws for their internal Polity and Government," they were, then, simply asserting their right to what they had long enjoyed: as one writer phrased it as early as 1741, "a perfect *internal* Liberty, as to the Choice of their own Laws, and in all other Matters that are *purely* provincial; under a *Salvo* of their inviolable Allegiance [to the crown], and Complyance with the Acts of Navigation." Notwithstanding metropolitan efforts over the previous century and a half to limit the extent of local self-government in the peripheries of the empire, "local provincial authority," as Bailyn has noted, "continued to characterize" colonial governance. In the exercise of metropolitan authority, crown and Parliament had, in fact, usually "touched only the outer fringes of colonial life" and dealt only "with matters obviously beyond the competence of any lesser authority" and with "the final review of actions initiated and sustained by colonial authorities." As Bailyn has remarked, all other powers—the vast area of "residual authority" that both constituted "the 'internal police' of the community" and "included most of the substance of everyday life"—"were enjoyed, in fact if not in constitutional theory, by local, colonial organs of government."[31]

In view of this situation, it was only natural for the colonists to conclude that, insofar as their respective internal affairs were concerned, there could be "no proper subordination of one part [of the empire] to another." "It has been a grand Error of the present Times to consider separate Governments as one," complained a Barbadian pamphleteer at the conclusion of the Stamp Act crisis. But there was "no natural Impediment," he added, "to my Imagination's suggesting to me a Form of Government in the People Abroad, as little connected with that of the English, as the Count[r]ies or Soils themselves which both People inhabit." Even though "Our Governments . . . are founded on similar Principles," he concluded, "this is no Reason that in all Points, whether similar or not, the Stronger must give Law." On the contrary. "In a confederacy of states, independent of each other, yet united under one head, such as I conceive the British empire at present to be," declared an anonymous writer in the *Pennsylvania Journal* in March 1766, "all the powers of legislation may subsist full and compleat in each part, and their respective legislatures be absolutely independent of each other."[32]

Although this analysis treated the crisis of the imperial constitution largely as a problem of identifying the proper allocation of authority, colonial spokesmen did not entirely ignore the knotty issue of sovereignty. The reader will recall that Grenville and his supporters had from the beginning seen that issue as fundamental, and from the point of view of the metropolis it would always remain "the intractable core of the controversy." At first, the colonists had some difficulty in dealing with the metropolitan charge that by challenging the authority of Parliament they were denying the authority of Britain. Indeed, many writers who denied Parliament's right to tax the colonies seemed to go out of their way to acknowledge its sovereign authority over the colonies. Eventually sensing the inherent contradictions in that position, however, a few writers explicitly denounced it. Thus, charged Philalethes in a New York newspaper in May 1766, those who had admitted "a sovereign jurisdiction in the Parliament over the Colonies, in all other respects but that of imposing internal taxes, for the purposes of raising a revenue" had thereby "betrayed the liberties of America."[33]

Looking at the whole subject more closely, a few proponents of the colonies focused more directly upon the question of precisely in what sense "*the people of America*" were "dependant on the *people of Britain*." They quickly concluded that, as Stephen Hopkins emphatically wrote, it would be "absurd to suppose that the common people of Great Britain have a sovereign and absolute authority over their fellow subjects in America, or [indeed] any sort of power whatsoever over them." And if it could not be shown that the inhabitants of the center were sovereign over those in the peripheries, it was "still more absurd to suppose," wrote Hopkins, that they could "give a power to their representatives which they have not themselves." If Parliament had "not receive[d] this authority from their constituents," Hopkins concluded, "it will be difficult to tell by what means" it "obtained it, except it be vested in them by mere superiority and power."[34]

But if Parliament was not sovereign over the colonies, what was the connection between the colonies and Britain? Building on John Locke's notion of the natural right of people "to quit the Society of which they are Members, and to retire to another Country," Richard Bland worked out an elaborate answer to this question. "When Men exercise this Right, and withdraw themselves from their Country," Bland argued, "they recover their natural Freedom and Independence: The Jurisdiction and Sovereignty of the State they have quitted ceases; and if they unite, and by common Consent take Possession of a new Country, and form themselves into a political Society, they become a sovereign State, independent of the State from which they separated." "No Part of the Kingdom of *England*" and, at the time of settlement, still "possessed by a savage People, scattered through the Country, who were not subject to the *English* Dominion, nor owed Obedience to its Laws," America, Bland asserted, was thus an "independent Country . . . settled by *Englishmen* at their own Expense" on the basis of a "Compact with the Sovereign of the Nation, to remove into a new Country, and to form a civil Establishment upon the Terms of the Compact." When he used the term "Sovereign of the Nation," Bland was pointedly referring to the king alone—and not to the king-in-Parliament.[35]

Bland was only one of many writers who thus suggested that the colonies had "no civil connection [with Britain], but by means of the King as the bond of union and the sovereign of *both*." As the person who had initially granted the colonists "License . . . to remove into a *new* Country, and to settle therein," the king, and not Parliament, these writers concluded, was "*sovereign* and *supreme* over the Colonies." Again, this conclusion conformed with colonial experience. The colonies, as James Otis observed, had always been and still were "entirely subject to the Crown." No laws could be made without the crown's consent "as sovereign," and, because he thus exercised "an actual supremacy . . . in every Legislation," there seemed to be no need for "a supreme Legislature, to which all other Powers must be subordinate." From these conclusions, it followed that the "Kingdom of Great-Britain" could claim no "*sovereignty* or *supremacy*" over the colonies."[36]

A few writers pointed to the relationship between Hanover and Britain as a model for that between the colonies and the metropolis. Although the colonists "still remain[ed] under the most sacred tie, the subject[s] of the *King* of Great Britain," Britannus Americanus remarked in the *Boston Gazette* in the late winter of 1765, the "people of England could have no more political connection with them or power and jurisdiction over them, than they now have with or over the people of Hanover, who are also subjects of the same King." Just as the Hanoverians "continued to be governed by their own Laws, under the general Superintendance and Controul of the supreme Magistrate in England, and his lawful Deputies and Officers abroad," declared another writer, so "with Respect to the Parliament, and the Power of imposing Taxes" should "all the Dominions of the Prince . . . be on one and the same Footing." The colonists were thus "utterly unaccountable to, and uncontroulable by the *people* of Great-Britain, or any body of them whatever." Because the king was the "sovereign of America, distinct from the power and authority of the parliament of Great-Britain," an anonymous New York pamphleteer asserted, also in 1765, "no body, or set of men, but your assemblies or parliament here . . . can lay any tax, tallage or impositions whatsoever within this your dominion of America."[37]

If, at the beginning of the Stamp Act crisis, the questions, in Franklin's words, of "how far, and in what particulars" the colonies were "*subordinate* and *subject* to the British parliament" were "points newly agitated [and] never yet . . . throughly considered," that was no longer the case by the time of the repeal of the Stamp Act in the late winter of 1766. Over the preceding two years, the colonists had slowly begun to construct what John Adams called "a formal, logical, and technical definition" of the imperial constitution under which they lived. As a result of this "great inquiry," they had learned that, as Richard Bland put it, it was "in vain to search into the civil Constitution of *England* for Directions in fixing the proper Connexion between the Colonies and the Mother Kingdom." The main underlying principles of that constitution were certainly relevant to their inquiry, but the British Constitution was not, in and of itself, suitable as the constitution for an "extended and diversified" empire.[38]

Instead, in their efforts to understand the nature of the relationship between Britain and the colonies, the colonists turned for guidance to the traditional rights of Englishmen and to their own experience with the actual pattern of customary relations within the empire as they had developed over the previous century and a half. They agreed with the Cambridge natural law theorist Thomas Rutherforth that the best "way of determining what form [of constitution] has been established in any particular nation" was to examine "the history and customs of that nation. A knowledge of its present customs will inform us what constitution of government obtains now," Rutherforth wrote, "and a knowledge of its history will inform us by what means this constitution was introduced or established." Indeed, one of the central conclusions of their inquiry—and one of the arguments they pressed most vigorously in their claims against the intrusion of parliamentary authority in the colonies—was that, like Britain itself, both the individual colonies and the empire as a whole had long-standing constitutional traditions that, at least from the point of view of the peripheries, seemed to supply legitimacy to their determined efforts to resist what Bland referred to as this "new System of Placing *Great Britain* as the Centre of Attraction to the Colonies."[39]

In 1764–66, only the most advanced thinkers among the colonists were willing to argue that Parliament had *no* role in either the imperial or the several colonial constitutions, to suggest that there was "no *dependence* or relation" between Britain and the colonies except "only that we are all the common subjects of the same King." All colonial protests did, however, have in common a clear concern to fix the boundaries between the authority of the center and that of the peripheries, between the power of Parliament and that of the colonial assemblies. If Parliament had a constitutional role in the empire, they were persuaded, that role had to be limited. They were virtually unanimous in agreeing that that role did not include authority to tax the colonies for revenue, and a substantial body of sentiment also held that it did not include authority to legislate for the internal affairs of the colonies.[40]

Whether they drew the jurisdictional boundaries between taxation and legislation or between internal and external spheres of authority, the attempt to draw them implied a conception of the empire in which authority was not concentrated in the center but was distributed among several distinct polities within the empire, much in the manner of the old English medieval empire and of the American federal system contrived in 1787. An expression of an impulse, manifest in the peripheries since the earliest days of English colonization, "to suffer as little interference by the metropolis as possible [in their internal affairs] while still remaining within the protective framework of the empire," this conception also strongly implied both the existence of a pragmatic distribution of authority among those polities and the need for some definition of exactly how those powers were distributed and precisely what underlying principles determined the system of distribution.[41]

The colonial case against the Stamp Act got a mixed reception in Britain. Better than most later historians, several metropolitan commentators realized that some colonists had not just challenged Parliament's authority to tax but had carried their objections "so far, as to dispute in great measure, [its] . . . Power of making *any* Law[s] whatever, that can be considered as affecting the Colonies *internally*." They also recognized that each assembly pretended "to an equality with the British parliament, and" allowed "no laws binding but those, which" were "imposed by itself." Few disputed "that the Colonists of any particular Province, have, in what Relates to their *internal Police*, a Right to make Laws, by their Representatives, on the same Principles, as the *British-Parliament*, provided" that they were "not repugnant to the Laws of their Mother-Country." Some writers were even willing to acknowledge that the assembly in each colony was both a "better judge of its own province than" Parliament ever could be and enjoyed "an exclusive legislative right" for "the conclusive regulating of their internal affairs." Moreover, in insisting that Parliament alone was competent to oversee and therefore had to maintain its authority to regulate "all general Affairs concerning the Colonies, as a *collective* Body, with Respect to *Trade* and *Commerce*, and all other Matters of a *general* Nature and Tendency," such people, in effect, also endorsed the colonial distinction between internal and external spheres of authority, with the former belonging to the colonial assemblies and the latter to Parliament.[42]

To people who thought in these terms, the relationship between the British and the Irish parliaments seemed to be an appropriate model for the connection between Parliament and the assemblies, an analogy that appeared to gain power because the constitutions of Ireland and the colonies were "not greatly dissimilar." To be sure, Parliament had "plainly asserted" its sovereignty over Ireland. But it had also been "very cautious in the exercise of it, particularly with respect to internal taxation." In fact, Parliament had "constantly left to" the Irish "legislature the power of imposing taxes and regulations for the defence and interior police of the country." What the Irish example seemed to suggest was thus that, though the "legislative authority of every country must, in the nature of things, be all-powerful," "justice and wisdom ought, and will restrain the exercise of that power," and metropolitan "controll should be exercised with due regard to all privileges, laws, and judicatures." In short, as one writer observed, it was "a presumptuous, as well as unpopular thing, to depart from the antient forms of a state, and to go out of the usual road of government; and, without absolute necessity, should never be done." Wherever possible, the example of Ireland seemed to indicate, government should "every where" be carried on "in the usual constitutional channel, without infringing or violating the rights and franchises of any part of the British subjects." In Ireland, as in America, the "usual constitutional channel" seemed to be to give the local legislature effective control over all internal affairs.[43]

But most people in Britain seem not to have understood that the colonists' challenge to parliamentary authority went beyond the realm of taxation, and even with regard to this more restricted conception of the colonial position, only a few men in Parliament agreed with the colonists that there were limits upon Parliament's colonial authority. Chief among them were William Pitt in the Commons and Lord Camden, former attorney general and then chief justice of common pleas, in the Lords. Although Camden admitted that "the sovereign authority, the omnipotence of the legislature," was "a favourable [favorite?] doctrine," he argued that there were "some things it cannot do." Specifically, he declared, it could not act "contrary to the fundamental laws of nature, contrary to the fundamental laws of this constitution." In this formulation, Camden implicitly distinguished between ordinary law and fundamental law. Deriving either "from the Law of Reason and of Nature" or "from [the] Custom and Usage our own Constitution," fundamental law consisted of those "public laws" that "prescribe[d] the form, and establish[ed] the constitutional power of the legislative body of the society." As Rutherforth had earlier remarked, such laws had been "usually understood to bind the legislative body itself, and not to be alterable by its authority."[44]

Among these fundamental laws, Camden, Pitt, and others of like mind argued, was the ancient British principle of no taxation without representation. Out of respect for this fundamental law, they contended, Parliament had "never levied Internal Taxes on any subject without their own consent." "The Commons of *America*, represented in their several assemblies, have ever been in possession of the exercise of this, their constitutional right, of giving and granting their own money," Pitt asserted. "At the same time," he noted, "this kingdom, as the supreme governing and legislative power, has always bound the colonies by her laws, by her regulations, and restrictions in trade, in navigation, in manufactures—in every thing, except that of taking their money out of their pockets without their consent." If few colonists had explicitly distinguished between Parliament's authority to tax and its authority to legislate for the colonies, for Pitt and Camden that distinction was thus crucial. In Pitt's words, it was "essentially necessary to liberty."[45]

Although there was substantial support in the pamphlet literature for these and similar arguments against the exertion of parliamentary power in the colonies,[46] few people in power found such arguments persuasive. They both rejected the colonists' contention that they were not represented in Parliament and dismissed the argument that charters and custom exempted the colonies from parliamentary taxation. They acknowledged that the crown could grant charters that would protect the colonists "from violence or impositions, which might be attempted by authority of the prerogative of the crown" and thereby secure the "colonies . . . from the despotism of the crown." But they emphatically denied that "the constitution of Great Britain" empowered the crown to "grant an exemption to any subject of Great Britain, from the jurisdiction of Parliament." Because the constitution acknowledged "no authority superior to the legislature, consisting of king, lords, and commons," they argued, the crown constituted "but a part of the British sovereignty." "Considered as the executive power," the crown, by itself, obviously could neither "controul the legislature, nor dispense with its acts," much less put the colonies "out of the subjection to the *summum Imperium* of Great Britain." For that reason, it was evident both that "no Charter from the Crown" could "possibly supersede the Right of the whole Legislature" and that the king could not possibly "govern the Colonies, independent of his British parliament."[47]

Nor did custom seem to offer any more solid support for the colonial cause. At least some metropolitan commentators admitted that the "long uninterrupted *Custom* and *Usage* in the Colonies, of taxing themselves by Representatives of their own choosing; and also the *Non-usage* of the *British* Parliament in that particular" might appear to have become "a kind of possessory Right" that, in turn, "might naturally induce Persons, perhaps not thoroughly acquainted with the Nature and Constitution of our Parliament, to imagine the sole right of laying Taxes, belonged to themselves." From the perspective of the metropolis, however, the logic of the emerging constitution of parliamentary supremacy seemed to render absurd all suggestions of customary restraints upon the authority of Parliament. Any custom or usage to the contrary notwithstanding, "upon the principles of the Revolution," Parliament was "the only natural, constitutional Seat of *compleat* Jurisdiction in the Kingdom" and that jurisdiction necessarily extended not just throughout the home islands but "over the property and person of every inhabitant of a British colony" as well.[48]

In making these arguments, metropolitan supporters revealed considerable confusion over the ancient question of the precise legal status of the colonies. Most seem to have fallen back on the position traditionally taken by crown officials in their recurring polemics with colonial assemblies over the previous century: that the colonies were equivalent merely to domestic corporations within Britain and as such could "have no . . . Pretence" to any "legal or constitutional Existence which" might "entitle them to greater Privileges than . . . the Corporations in this Kingdom enjoy[ed] by their respective Charters of Incorporation." According to this argument, "the mighty Powers of" the colonies' "little Assemblies" consisted of nothing more than a "Licence or Authority, flowing from the royal Prerogative of the Crown, to frame such Laws and Regulations, for the Management of their own domestick Concerns, as may best answer the Ends of their Institution." Such limited powers could not possibly justify the colonies even in claiming "an Exemption from . . . parliamentary Authority," much less operate "to erect them into that State of Independency" that would justify their "placing their *Indulgencies* in Competition with *Privileges,* Or, in other Words, setting up their *Bye-Laws* in Opposition to *Acts of Parliament.*"[49]

Not everyone adhered to such a limited conception of the colonies. Thus, Sir William Blackstone, in his celebrated and widely read *Commentaries on the Law of England,* the first volume of which was published while the Stamp Act was under consideration, characterized the colonies, like Ireland, as "distinct, though dependent dominions." Even those who thought of the colonies in this more expansive sense, however, tended to emphasize their dependence rather more than their distinctiveness. As Grenville declared in his speech introducing the Stamp Act, "all colonies" were "subject to the dominion of the mother country, whether they" were "a colony of the freest or the most absolute government." The very word *colony,* echoed Charles Townshend in the brief debate that followed, implied "subordination."[50].

The predominant argument in Britain was sounded by Lords Mansfield, Northington, and Lyttleton in early February 1766 in the House of Lords debate on the repeal of the Stamp Act. In specific answer to Camden, Mansfield flatly declared that, "as to the power of making laws," Parliament represented "the whole British empire" and had "authority to bind every part and every subject without the least distinction" in matters of taxation as well as legislation. That the colonists, as a result of their situation, did not "have a right to vote" for members of Parliament, according to Mansfield, meant not that they were exempt from Parliament's authority but only that they were "more emphatically subjects of Great Britain than those without the realm." "A free and extended empire," wrote an anonymous pamphleteer in making the same point, "are incompatible: to think they are not is a perfect solecism in politicks."[51]

From this point of view, colonial claims for exemption from parliamentary taxation seemed, as Grenville had defined them when he first proposed to levy stamp duties on the colonies, to be nothing less than a challenge to British sovereignty. As it had gradually developed over the previous century and a half, the conventional conception of sovereignty was that in all polities, including "an Empire, extended and diversified, like that of *Great-Britain,*" there had to be, as Blackstone wrote, "a supreme, irresistible, absolute uncontrolled authority, in which the *jura summi imperii,* or the rights of sovereignty reside[d]" and, as another writer asserted, "to which all other *Powers* should be *subordinate[d]*." Because, most contemporaries seem to have believed, the king-in-Parliament was sovereign in the British polity, it could accept no restrictions upon its authority without relinquishing the sovereignty of the nation over the colonies. By definition, there could be no limitation upon a supreme authority. It was either complete or nonexistent. For that reason, it seemed obvious that the king-in-Parliament had full authority over all matters relating to all Britons everywhere. And for the same reason, it also seemed evident that no clear line could be drawn between Parliament's power to legislate for the colonies and its power to tax them. As Grenville noted early in the controversy, the claim of the colonists "not to be taxed but by their representatives" applied with equal force "to all laws in general," and if Parliament could not legislate for the colonies, the British nation no longer had any control over them. As the Connecticut agent Jared Ingersoll reported to his constituents in February 1765, the metropolitan establishment regarded the power to tax as "a necessary part of every Supreme Legislative Authority" and believed that "if they have not that Power over America, they have none, & then America is at once a Kingdom of itself."[52]

In the metropolitan view, there was thus no distribution but a concentration of authority within the empire: "as the sovereign of the whole," the king-in-Parliament had "control over the whole British empire." To most metropolitans, in fact, the colonial position appeared incomprehensible because it seemed to imply the existence of more than one sovereign authority within a single state, and sovereignty, according to conventional theory, could not be divided. An "Imperium in imperio"—a sovereign authority within a sovereign authority—was a contradiction in terms. As Lyttleton put it, the colonies were either "part of the dominions of the Crown of Great Britain" and therefore "proper objects of our legislature" or they were "small independent communities," each operating under its own sovereign authority. There was, according to metropolitan theory, no middle ground between these two extremes. Even those who, like Lord Egmont, held that the supreme power in any polity could delegate "to other subordinate powers a part of itself" and that, in such cases, "time" would "give to these subordinate powers a right of prescription" that could not be recalled "excepting only in the utmost emergency," also believed that "when the exigencies of government required it," Parliament, by virtue of its "supreme, absolute and un-limited" power, could levy taxes "upon the People not by right of their having *representatives* but [by virtue of their] . . . being *subjects* to the Government."[53]

The strength of colonial opposition to the Stamp Act forced Parliament to retract it, but repeal was accompanied by passage of the Declaratory Act, modeled on the Irish Declaratory Act of 1720 and asserting Parliament's authority "to bind the colonies and people of America . . . in all cases whatsoever." But this fiat from the center by no means resolved the question of the distribution of authority within the empire. Even though the Declaratory Act stated that Parliament "retain[ed] the idea of right," people in the metropolis realized that "the circumstances of the repeal" stood as "convincing proof that . . . parliament" could not "execute it" and made it possible for the colonists to interpret repeal as "a full renunciation of the right" that left the colonies "at *full liberty.*" At the same time, the Declaratory Act powerfully impressed upon the colonists that Parliament had kept the door open to some future attempt to force them to acknowledge "Par-liament's Right to tax us . . . or that in every other Respect but Taxa-tion, they have an absolute Right to make Laws to bind us without our own Consent."[54]

As Colonel Isaac Barre announced in the House of Commons early in 1766, the Stamp Act crisis had thus provoked "the people of Amer-ica to reason . . . closely upon the relative rights of this country and that," and the undefined and "loose texture" of Britain's "extended and diversified" empire had fostered the development of two widely divergent interpretations of how authority was distributed between the center and the peripheries. Whereas most people in the metropo-lis thought the empire a unitary state "organized on the principle of devolution" with "sovereignty . . . vested in Parliament" and the au-thority of the colonies consisting "merely of privileges" that were al-ways "subject to the discretion of Parliament and could, *in extremis,* be curtailed," most people in the colonies thought of the empire as being "predominantly federal in practice" with the authority of the center limited by the authority it had delegated to the peripheries.[55]

In this situation, many people on both sides of the Atlantic called for a permanent resolution of the constitutional issues raised by the Stamp Act, a solution that would "discover such Means of perfect and stable Connection with the Colonies, as may secure a just Authority over them, and at the same Time, preserve inviolable, the Privileges and Immunities" of the colonies. Some observers called for the creation of an intercolonial Parliament with full authority to tax and to attend to the general concerns of the colonies; others, with the example of the Stamp Act Congress before them, feared the establishment of such "a dangerous federal union" among the colonies. In the meantime, having learned from the crisis that the metropolitan government was too weak to force the peripheries to comply with measures the people there did not support, the colonists, as Francis Bernard reported from Boston in November 1765, "seem[ed] to be resolved that their Idea of their relation to Great Britain however extravagant various & inconsistent" should "be the standard of it." At least in regard to the "new" questions posed by the Stamp Act, the crisis of the imperial constitution in 1764-66 had taught them, as a New York writer phrased it, that "the People of England" understood "them not a whit better that we do in America."[56]

Chapter Six

Parliament, Crown, and Colonial Rights, 1767–1773

If the Stamp Act crisis "first led the colonists into [systematic] Enquiries concerning the nature of their political situation," its resolution in early 1766 by no means put an end to those inquiries. Indeed, Parliament's renewed efforts early in 1767 to tax the colonies through the Townshend Acts quickly reopened the question. For the next six years, people on both sides of the Atlantic further explored the difficult problem, in the words of Jonathan Shipley, bishop of St. Asaph in 1773, of "by what bond of union shall be hold together members of this great empire, dispersed and scattered as they lie over the face of the earth"? Agreement was widespread that this question was "as arduous and important . . . as ever the English government was engaged in." But as they dug ever deeper into the subordinate questions of how far the authority of Parliament extended over the colonies and "how far, if at all," the colonies were "subject to the controul of the parent state," people of all persuasions revealed a fundamental ambivalence about the implications of their findings. On the one hand, they desperately hoped that, once it was "better understood," the "political relation between the colonists and the mother country" would be settled to the mutual satisfaction of all parties. On the other, they were deeply afraid that the continued exploration of that relationship would produce results that would be detrimental to the very "continuance of the structure of the empire."[1]

During the crisis over the Townshend Acts, these fears helped to account for a considerable amount of pragmatic flexibility that was manifest, on both sides, by a pronounced concern to contain the dispute within a narrow compass. At the same time, however, the length and intensity of the dispute pushed some analysts on the colonial side to think through the nature of the connection between Britain and the colonies more thoroughly than anyone had ever done before. Although these thinkers regarded their conclusions as no more than an articulation and rationalization of long-standing practice, they represented a radical challenge to the metropolitan belief in Parliament's supremacy over the entire empire, a belief that, for most members of the metropolitan political nation, continued to be nonnegotiable.

Notwithstanding a palpable crystallization of informed colonial opinion around this emerging and, from the perspective of the center, radical view of the constitutional organization of the empire, the spirit of conciliation ran so deep that constituted authorities in no colony officially endorsed it during the Townshend Act crisis. Indeed, Parliament's repeal of most of the Townshend duties in 1770 and the rapid subsidence of overt colonial opposition to Parliament over the next three years provided dramatic testimony to the depth of that spirit. Yet those same years were also marked by a revival of the much older controversy over the scope of the crown's prerogative powers in the colonies. This revival underlined the fundamental problem of the distribution of authority between the center and the peripheries as a continuing major source of tension between metropolis and colonies.

Throughout the first phase of this controversy, the vast majority of people in the metropolitan establishment, in both Britain and the colonies, adhered strictly to the position articulated by Grenville and his supporters during the Stamp Act crisis. To be sure, a few people thought it unwise for Parliament to "endeavour to enforce novel measures and regulate old established regulations" in ways that would seem to be "innovating upon what" the colonists "thought their usages, and customs." Still others, mostly members of the minority Rockingham party that had engineered the settlement of 1766, insisted that it was possible "to maintain the due authority of the mother country, and yet satisfy the demands of the Americans" merely by adhering to the spirit of that settlement. Thus, as Edmund Burke argued in May 1770, Parliament had no need to tax the colonies because the Declaratory Act already "sufficiently establish[ed] the sovereignty of this country over its plantations and colonies." If, however, a few people, like the Rockinghams, consistently argued for lenient measures on "ground[s] of expediency," virtually no one in the British establishment was willing, as the Connecticut agent William Samuel Johnson reported to his constituents in the fall of 1768, to discuss "the principle of right, it being almost universally" believed to have been "completely settled by the late Declaratory Act."[2]

Interpreting all suggestions for any limitations upon Parliament's colonial authority as a challenge to the British constitution of parliamentary supremacy and to the sovereignty of the metropolis over the colonies, they continued to insist, as they had throughout the Stamp Act crisis, that sovereignty was indivisible. "*Sovereignty*," declared Allan Ramsay, a polemicist with connections to George III, in 1768, "admits of no degrees, it is always *supreme*, and to level it, is, in effect, to destroy it." In every community, wrote Richard Phelps, an undersecretary of state, there had to be both "an unlimited authority lodged somewhere . . . and an unreserved obedience to that authority required of every individual." Without such a sovereign authority, Phelps believed, a polity would lack that essential "attracting power" by which "both those who rule[d] and those who obey[ed]" were drawn "to the same common centre." William Knox spelled out the full implications of this line of reasoning in his influential *The Controversy Between Great Britain and her Colonies Reviewed*, published in 1769. "If the authority of the legislature be not in one instance equally supreme over the Colonies as it is over the people of England," Knox wrote, "then are not the Colonies of the same community with the people of England. All distinctions," he continued, "destroy this union; and if it can be shown in any particular to be dissolved, it must be so in all instances whatever."[3]

From this emerging metropolitan perspective, both the distinction between taxation and legislation made by Chatham and Camden during the Stamp Act crisis and the colonial argument that compacts made with the crown exempted them from parliamentary taxation seemed thoroughly untenable. "Legislation and taxation," Lord Hillsborough, secretary of state for the colonies, declared in 1768 in a typical remark, "were essentially connected and would stand and fall together." The king, "being a limited monarch," asserted Richard Hussey in the House of Commons in 1769, could not "for a moment release" the colonies "from the sovereign power of this country." One of "the great fundamental principles of the Government of Great Britain," the crown's incapacity to grant any "dispensation from the laws of the land, and the authority of parliament," without the concurrence of the other two branches of the legislature could not be violated, an anonymous pamphleteer insisted, without dissolving the constitution and annihilating the most important foundation of British liberty. In Hillsborough's words, the colonial contention that the crown had granted the colonies a "power of absolute legislation . . . tended to the absurdity of introducing [an] *imperium in imperio*, and to create" within the empire a series of "independent state[s]," an arrangement he roundly condemned as nothing less than a "polytheism in politics."[4]

Maintaining "the supremacy and legislative authority of Parliament" in its fullest extent over the colonies thus continued to be viewed by most members of the metropolitan establishment as "essential to the existence of the empire." If this "great constitutional point" were ever given up, if Britain ever permitted the colonists, who were "already proprietors of the soil," to "govern themselves in the same manner that she is governed," if their assemblies were ever allowed to enjoy all "rights of national legislation," they would "be, then, necessarily, possessed of every qualification of sovereignty; and in every respect . . . free and independent of Great Britain." For the colonists to deny Parliament's authority to tax them was thus also "to deny her sovereignty," and to deny her sovereignty was "to change their political existence: and in place of sons and provinces of their mother country, to become aliens: and to form themselves into a mother country, and an independent nation." In Knox's words, there was "no alternative: either the colonies are a part of the community of Great Britain, or they are in a state of nature with respect to her, and in no case can be subject to the jurisdiction of that legislative power which represents her community, which is the British parliament." The colonies, added Phelps, "must either acknowledge the legislative power of Great Britain in its full extent, or set themselves up as independent states."[5]

Indeed, from the vantage point of London, colonial opposition to the Townshend measures seemed to betray nothing less than a "high and imperious ambition of being themselves, a nation of independent states." Their resolves against parliamentary taxation looked little short of a series of colonial "Declaratory Act[s] . . . against the Declaratory Act of Great Britain," and their economic sanctions against the metropolis suggested that the colonists already thought of Britain and the colonies as "independent nations at war with each other." Such behavior, one writer charged, could only be the product of a deep-seated "desire of managing their own affairs more to their own advantage, than what they think can be accomplished, under the government . . . of Great Britain."[6]

Such alarming impulses unleashed a demand within the metropolitan establishment to determine, in the words of Hans Stanley in a House of Commons debate in November 1768, precisely "what we were, what the Americans were," and there was a surprisingly narrow range of opinion on this subject. As Allan Ramsay pointed out, the colonists strongly preferred to use "the word *Colony*" to refer to their polities because, he charged, it carried connotations of "a degree of independency." But most people seem to have agreed with Ramsay that, strictly speaking, those polities were "not properly *colonies* either in word or deed. Their most ancient English and legal name," Ramsay contended, was "*plantations*, and they have always been, in fact, *provinces*, governed by a lieutenant or governor, sent by the King of Great Britain, and recalled by him at pleasure." Although people recognized that metropolitan failure to establish "any system of government, natural and proper to their situation and condition, as provinces" was the reason why the colonists had by "uninterrupted habit . . . come to think their corporation assemblies to be no less than parliaments" and "emboldened [them] . . . to grasp at national and independent legislation and government," few had any doubt that, as Ramsay declared, the "plain truth" was "that those countries, let them be called *plantations, settlements, colonies,* or by what other name they will," were "from their nature and situation, only subordinate parts of the empire of Britain."[7]

From this perspective, the British Empire seemed to be a unicentric polity in which, as Thomas Pownall put it, "the realm . . . [and] government of Great Britain [w]as the Sovereign, and the Colonies . . . the subject, without full participation in the Constitution" and "bound implicitly to obey the orders of the [metropolitan] government." In view of the "inherent pre-eminence" of the parent state in this arrangement and the colonies' status as nothing more than "so many appendages or factories to this kingdom, devoted solely to the emprovement of its particular interest, wealth, and power, and without any rights or privileges which" were "not perfectly consistent with the attainment of those desired objects," any suggestion that "each petty colony" might actually have a "right to be [Britain's] . . . equal" seemed ludicrous.[8]

In short, both because the "interest of a part" always had "to give way to the interest of the whole" and because, within the extended British Empire, Great Britain was itself "that whole; and her colonies . . . but that part," it followed that "North America must be governed as a province, if Great Britain be inclined to govern her at all." One segment of metropolitan opinion even advocated using military force to secure colonial obedience, and there was powerful sentiment that it was absolutely necessary to "fix the nature, power, and extent of the colony assemblies, so, that, they may never be mistaken, hereafter, for parliaments: but known and universally acknowledged as corporate bodies, only, having power to propose laws for the internal police of that colony," with those laws being liable to approval by the crown "as usual; and always subject to the revisal and alteration of parliament."[9]

Notwithstanding this tendency to define the controversy in such extreme terms, metropolitan authorities resisted the impulse to take sweeping coercive measures against the colonies during the crisis over the Townshend Acts. Sensing the expediency of Pownall's declaration that *"You may exert power over, but you can never govern an unwilling people,"* they instead took in 1770 what they regarded as a conciliatory approach. At the same time that they indicated that they would seek no new parliamentary taxes and guided through Parliament a repeal of most of the Townshend duties, they retained the tax on tea to stand as a symbol of Parliament's colonial authority.[10]

If anything, the urge toward conciliation during the crisis over the Townshend Acts was even more powerful in the colonies. On both sides of the Atlantic, John Dickinson's *Letters from a Farmer in Pennsylvania*, published in 1767, was certainly the most widely circulated expression of colonial opinion. "By no means fond of inflammatory measures," Dickinson had chaired the committee of the Pennsylvania Assembly that had drafted the Pennsylvania resolves against the Stamp Act in September 1765, the first set of resolutions by any colonial assembly that did not explicitly couple taxation and internal polity as areas over which the colonial legislatures had exclusive jurisdiction. The following month, Dickinson also took a prominent role in drafting the Declaration of the Stamp Act Congress, which made similarly limited claims. With his *Letters,* as well as with these earlier documents, Dickinson obviously intended to confine the controversy within the narrowest possible bounds.[11]

To that end, he addressed his pamphlet exclusively to the issue of the moment—Parliament's right to tax the colonies for revenue—and did not consider the wider problems of the relationship between metropolis and colonies, the extent and nature of metropolitan sovereignty over the colonies, or the distribution of authority within the empire. Thus, although he denounced all parliamentary attempts to tax the colonies for revenue as unwarranted efforts "to erect a new Sovereignty over the Colonies with Power inconsistent with Liberty or Freedom" and warned that colonial submission to those efforts would eventually reduce "these colonies . . . into [the] 'COMMON CORPORATIONS'" that "their enemies, in the debates concerning the repeal of the *Stamp Act,* [had] *strenuously insisted they were,*" Dickinson was careful to separate himself from those colonists who during the Stamp Act crisis had seemed to suggest that the colonies were separate states. "He who considers these provinces as states distinct from the *British Empire,*" he declared, "has very slender notions of *justice,* or of their *interests.* We are but parts of a *whole;* and therefore there must exist a power somewhere, to preside, and preserve the connection in due order. This power," he acknowledged, "is lodged in the parliament."[12]

Of course, in granting Parliament this general presiding power, Dickinson also took pains to point out that the colonists could only be "as much dependent on *Great Britain,* as a perfectly free people can be on another." Neither the maintenance of Parliament's "legal power to make laws for preserving" the dependence of the colonies nor "the relation between a mother country and her colonies," Dickinson insisted, required that "she should raise money on them without their consent." Contrary to what many historians have assumed, however, he did not explicitly admit Parliament's authority over all matters except taxation for revenue. Rather, he specifically restricted Parliament's presiding authority to those areas in which it had customarily exerted colonial jurisdiction: to measures intended "to regulate trade, and preserve or promote a mutually beneficial intercourse between the several constituent parts of the empire." At the same time, he maintained a discreet silence on the question of whether Parliament might legislate for the internal affairs of the colonies.[13]

Nevertheless, by focusing debate so closely upon the narrow question of taxation, Dickinson helped to deescalate the controversy. The widespread acceptance of his definition of the situation seems both to have inhibited free and wide-ranging discussion of the nature of the metropolitan-colonial relationship such as had occurred during the Stamp Act crisis and to have been in no small part responsible for confining all but a few official colonial challenges to parliamentary authority during the late 1760s and very early 1770s to the single issue of taxation for revenue. Indeed, the Virginia legislature was one of the few colonial assemblies that explicitly continued to assert its exclusive authority over matters of internal polity as well as taxation.[14]

If during the crisis over the Townshend Acts, most colonial assemblies, as the Massachusetts legislator Thomas Cushing later observed, "Acquiesced in the distinction between Taxation and Legislation and were disposed to Confine the dispute to that of Taxation only and entirely to wave the other as a subject of too delicate a Nature," a number of thinkers in both the colonies and Britain took a much deeper look at the controversy and concluded, as Benjamin Franklin wrote his son in March 1768, that, although "Something might be made of either of the extremes; that Parliament has a power to make *all laws* for us, or that it has a power to make *no laws* for us," "no middle doctrine" of the kind proposed by Dickinson could successfully be maintained. Worried about the long-term effects of the "spirit of compliance and moderation" represented by the mainstream colonial response to the Townshend Acts, such people developed an interpretation of the relationship between Britain and the colonies that was much closer to the arguments set forth by Richard Bland, Stephen Hopkins, and other advanced thinkers in the mid-1760s than to the conciliatory views of Dickinson.[15]

This interpretation proceeded from three underlying assumptions. The first was that Parliament's claims to colonial jurisdiction had to be proved and could "not [simply be] take[n] . . . for granted" or permitted to rest on "the monstrous idea of a *Virtual Representation*." The second was that the "civil constitution" of Britain "by no means" determined "the connection which ought to be established between the parent country and her colonies, nor the duties reciprocally incumbent on each other." The third was that the history of the colonies and of their relationship to the metropolis was the most authoritative guide to the exact nature of that connection.[16]

In examining the history of the colonies, these writers were specifically concerned to refute the metropolitan contention that the crown in its executive capacity had no authority to grant any of its subjects an exemption from parliamentary authority. Elaborating on points that had been widely canvassed during the Stamp Act crisis, they pointed out that, with the exception of Jamaica and New York, both of which had subsequently been accorded English privileges, and those areas in Canada, Florida, and the Caribbean that had been acquired as a result of the Seven Years' War, the colonies were not conquered territories but settlements of "free People" who, with the consent of the crown, had merely exercised their natural and "just Right to" emigrate and "separate themselves" from their old society.[17]

These writers had no doubt that the crown had acted legally in giving its consent to these undertakings. "From the earliest times, down to the present," declared Gervase Parker Bushe, a metropolitan sympathetic with the colonists, "the disposition of foreign territory belonging to Great Britain" had "always been vested in the Executive." If, as it had repeatedly done, the crown could legally cede territory to foreign powers, why, Bushe asked rhetorically, could it not also fix "the terms, on which its present and future inhabitants should continue the subjects of Great Britain? Where it could have relinquished *all* the authority possessed by Great Britain," he contended, "certainly it could relinquish a *part* of that authority. Where it could make a *total alienation,* to enemies, even, surely it could make a *modified grant,* to subjects."[18]

If the crown thus had "a Constitutional Right" both to grant the colonists "an accession of foreign Territory, which he had a legal Right to alienate from the Crown and Realm," and to "permit them to enter into a second Community," then it also followed that it had authority to enter into formal constitutional compacts with them. By these instruments, as Franklin put it, the colonists "voluntarily engaged to remain the King's Subjects, though in a foreign Country," in return for the crown's recognition of their traditional rights as Englishmen, including especially the right to have "a Share in the Power of making those Laws which they are to be governed by." With these compacts, each group of colonists became in effect a separate "body politic" with "power to make all laws and ordinances for the well governing of the people." Because their "distant situation" made "it impossible for" them either "to be represented in the [metropolitan] parliament . . . or to be governed from thence," these new polities had to have "a distinct intire Civil Government, of like Powers, Pre-eminence, and Jurisdictions, (conforming to the like Rights, Privileges, Immunities, Franchises, and Civil Liberties,) as" were "established in the *British* Government, respecting the *British* Subject within the Realm." To this end, the "formation of legislatures" with "full and absolute powers" of "legislation and taxation" became "the first object of attention in the colonies."[19]

At no point in this process had Parliament taken any role. As Franklin noted, the first two Stuarts "Governed their Colonies, as they Governed their Dominions in France, without the Participation of Parliament." Having "had no hand in their Settlement," Parliament, Franklin insisted, "was never so much as consulted about their Constitution . . . took no kind of Notice of them till many Years after they were established," and "never attempted to meddle with the Government of them, till that Period when it destroy'd the Constitution of all Parts of the Empire, and usurp'd a Power over Scotland, Ireland, Lords and King." Throughout this early period, before "that revolution in provincial policy, which produced the act of navigation," added an anonymous Briton who claimed to have resided in the colonies for more than two decades, the colonies "not only considered themselves, but were considered by the king, parliament, and people of England, as free distinct states, not depending on the parliament of this kingdom, though owing allegiance to its sovereign, and intitled to a free unrestrained trade to all nations, with a positive exemption from every species of taxation, by any authority but that of their own assemblies."[20]

The early history of the colonies thus seemed to confirm the view that the act of emigration and the establishment of a new polity had effectively "annihilate[d] the sovereignty and jurisdiction of the abandoned society," that Parliament's "Jurisdiction did not extend out of the Realm," and that the colonists were, therefore, exempted from its authority "as soon as they landed out of its Jurisdiction." So long as the colonists had resided within the realm of England "as a collective Part of its Inhabitants, and received Protection from its Laws and Government, no Power whatever could possibly exempt them from Obedience to its Legislative Authority." But, they argued, "this Obligation to Obedience . . . naturally ceased on their Separation from" the realm. They willingly admitted that the king's prerogative extended "indiscriminately, to all States owing him Allegiance." Yet they contended that the legislative power, being derived entirely from the inhabitants of the state over which it presided, was "necessarily confined within the State itself." A "Subjection to Acts of Parliament" was thus, as Franklin declared, "no part" of the colonies' "original Constitution[s]."[21]

Nor had subsequent events changed this situation to any important extent. "By the act of navigation, and several subsequent . . . regulations" during and after the Restoration, Parliament had indeed circumscribed the "commerce of the colonies with foreign nations." "From the aera of their settlement to the last war," however, it had never made "any attempt . . . to regulate their internal policy or legislation, or impose taxes upon them." As a result, even those colonies founded after the Restoration had been "undertaken in full confidence and expectation of being perfectly independant of the parliament of this kingdom, except in commercial regulations only." Indeed, in Franklin's view, Parliament's failure in the wake of the Glorious Revolution to act in a more extensive sphere with regard to the colonies itself constituted sufficient refutation of the metropolitan contention that the early histories of the colonies were irrelevant because the revolution had established Parliament's authority over "all parts of the British dominions." Just as the revolution had "made no alteration in the nature of the union then subsisting between England and Scotland," Franklin wrote to the *London Chronicle,* so it had not changed the relationship "between England and her colonies; for after that period, there was not any attempt made to alter their internal governments: but that their legislative power and administration of justice remained unaltered." What, according to Franklin, "very strongly" continued to mark "the independence of the Americans on the British Parliament" was "that it has never been thought of, to make the House of Lords the ultimate resort in their appeals in law, as is the case from Ireland, the King in council remaining to this day sole arbiter."[22]

Even if the crown did not initially have authority to grant the colonies independence from parliamentary authority, however, the fact

that Parliament, "for more than a century," had both "constantly recognized and assented to the King's Prerogative Right of permitting
his subjects to withdraw themselves from the Realm, and the Jurisdiction of its Laws," and permitted the colonists "a long uninterrupted
enjoyment" of "the privileges originally granted by charter" seemed,
as one writer asserted in reminding metropolitan readers of the traditional importance of custom in English constitutional law, "alone sufficient to render all their claims valid, agreeable to the laws of this
kingdom." "Is there not a term," asked Bushe in invoking the same
tradition, "after which uninterrupted possession confers a right?
Have not the Colonists possessed their charters, much longer than
that term? Have they not dedicated their lives and fortunes to the
improvement of that country, from a dependance upon the validity of
their title? Have not the British Parliament seen and acquiesced in
their doing so?" According to this line of reasoning, Parliament,
through its inaction, had at once "confirmed *sub silentia*" the rights
originally granted by charter and strengthened those rights by according them both "a Parliamentary sanction, as well as a title by prescription."[23]

History and usage thus seemed to make clear that the colonies had
never been "incorporated with Great Britain in a legislative capacity."
This being the case, it seemed equally obvious that the colonies could
not suddenly be treated as a mere collection of individual emigrants
from Britain. Rather, reasoned William Hicks, they ought to "be considered as so many different countries of the same kingdom, the
nature of whose situation prevents them joining in the general council, and reduces them to a necessity of applying to their Prince for the
establishment of such a partial polity as may be the best adapted to
their particular circumstances." In effect, said Samuel Adams, each
colony was "a separate body politick" whose inhabitants had "a right
equal to that of the people of Great Britain to make laws for themselves, and are no more than they, subject to the controul of any legislature but their own." As "Separate states (all self-governing communities)," it appeared evident both that the colonies "must be considered as independent of the legal parliamentary power of Great Britain" and that the metropolitan Parliament had no authority to "make
laws for their internal government."[24]

According to this line of argument, Great Britain and the British
Empire were distinct political entities. As the Georgia minister Johan

Joachim Zubly explained, the British Empire was a far "more extensive word, and should not be confounded with the kingdom of Great Britain." Rather, it was a "confederal" polity that consisted of both the home islands and a number of "extrinsic Dominions," including "several islands and other distant countries, asunder in different parts of the globe." As the "head of this great body," England was "called the mother country" and "all the settled inhabitants of this vast empire" were "called Englishmen." But those phrases by no means implied that the empire was "a single state." Rather, each of its many separate entities had a "legislative power . . . within itself," and "the several legislative bodies of Great-Britain, Ireland and the British Colonies" were "perfectly distinct, and entirely independent upon each other."[25]

If, however, the British Empire was not a unitary state and if legislative power within it was both distributed among "*a number of self-governing states*" and, within each of those states, confined within its territorial limits, its several constituent parts were nevertheless, in Franklin's words, "all *united in allegiance to one Prince, and to the common law.*" If they were "absolutely free from any obedience to the *power of the British Legislature,*" they were bound "to the Power of the Crown." If they did "not [have] the same legislatures," they did "have the same king." Moreover, if, as this developing position suggested, the several polities of the empire were "only connected, as England and Scotland were before the Union, by having one common Sovereign," then it followed that the colonies and other parts of the king's "extended dominions" were "*not* part of the Dominions *of England.*" As nothing more than "a Dominion itself," England could not, in fact, have dominions. Nor could "Subjects of one Part of the King's Dominions" possibly have any legitimate claim to be "Sovereigns over the King's Subjects in another Part of his Dominions."[26]

Such an analysis disturbed those who preferred to think of the entire British world as a single "compacted empire." "Disuniting the subjects of the Crown, and splitting the widely-extended territories" of the "empire into so many distinct and separate states, independent of, and co-ordinate with, each other, and connected together by no other tie but that of owing allegiance to the same Sovereign," decried one writer, was to put the colonies and Ireland in precisely the same "relation in which Hanover has stood to Great-Britain ever since the accession of the present royal family." But its exponents strongly denied that there was anything new in their view of the organization of the empire. "Our Kings," Franklin declared in 1769, "have ever had Dominions not subject to the English Parliament," and he cited a long list of precedents from the French provinces under the Norman monarchs to contemporary Hanover.[27]

In the view of its proponents, however, the real virtue of this emerging conception lay not in its foundations in past practice but in its appropriateness for the governance of an extended polity. The "Excellency of the Invention of Colony Government, by separate independent Legislatures," Franklin wrote in 1769, was that it permitted "the remotest Parts of a great Empire" to be "as well governed as the Center." By guaranteeing maximum autonomy to peripheral states and thereby helping to prevent wholesale "Misrule, Oppressions of Proconsuls, and Discontents and Rebellions" in those areas, the authority of the British monarch seemed to be infinitely expandable, capable, in Franklin's words, of being "extended without Inconvenience over Territories of any Dimensions how great soever." From the vantage point of the peripheries, an important additional benefit of this constitutional organization was that, whenever the several parts of the polity had "different and opposite Ideas of Justice or Propriety," they could each follow the course dictated by "their own Opinions" and interests so long as they did "not interfere with the common Good." Nor did there seem to be much danger that the centrifugal impulses inherent in such a system would get out of hand. With "the restraining power [securely] lodged in" its hands, the crown would, Hicks declared, always be in a position to ensure that no part would act against "the general welfare of the whole."[28]

This conception of the British Empire as consisting, in Benjamin Prescott's words, "of a great and glorious King, with a Number of distinct Governments, alike subjected to his royal Scepter, and each governed by its own Laws" also seemed to its proponents to offer a solution to the problem of the indivisibility of sovereignty. Posed by metropolitan protagonists during the earliest days of the Stamp Act controversy, the logical dilemma of "an *imperium in imperio*" had remained at the heart of metropolitan resistance to colonial claims for exemption from parliamentary authority. According to the emerging conception of empire among the most advanced defenders of the colonies, however, sovereignty within the extended polity of the British Empire resided not in Britain and not in the king-in-Parliament but in the institution of the monarchy alone. In the imperial realm, according to these writers, the theory of coordination, of the legal sovereignty of the king-in-Parliament, did not apply.[29]

Franklin was an early and insistent exponent of this view. "All of the Colonies," he explained to the Scottish philosopher Lord Kames in February 1767, "acknowledge the King as their Sovereign: His Governors there represent his Person. Laws are made by their Assemblies or little Parliaments, with the Governor's Assent, subject to the King's Pleasure to confirm or annul them." "The Sovereignty of the King," Franklin observed, was "therefore easily understood." Because the colonies "totally disclaim[ed] all subordination to, and dependence upon, the two inferior estates of their mother country," however, notions like the "*Sovereignty of Parliament,* and the *Sovereignty of this Nation* over the Colonies" appeared to people like Franklin to be both without any clear legal foundations and unnecessary. "The freemen settled in *America,*" Hicks declared, "may preserve themselves absolutely independant of their fellow subjects who more immediately surround the throne, and yet discharge, with the strictest fidelity, all their duties to their sovereign" monarch.[30]

To its proponents, this view of the empire as "many states under one Sovereign" seemed thoroughly defensible on the basis both of the terms of the colonial charters and the customary constitutional arrangements that had grown up since the establishment of the colonies. No country, declared Edward Bancroft, had "a better Title to its Constitution, than . . . the Colonies." Thus, when Grenville and his supporters "artfully endeavoured to confound the original distinctions which the colonies derived from their charters; and [to] contract them within the limits of this kingdom, and consequently within the extent of parliamentary jurisdiction," they were claiming for Parliament an authority to "make Laws relating to Persons and Societies of Men" who simply were "not within their Jurisdiction." By thus attempting to "arrogate to themselves" a "jurisdiction so infinitely extensive, and so little capable of limitation," these would-be "sovereigns of the new-discovered world" had at once invaded the rights of both the people in the peripheries and the king and thereby tried fundamentally to alter the constitution of the empire.[31]

To prove that such acts were indeed unconstitutional, colonial advocates, as they had done during the Stamp Act crisis, invoked the hallowed British doctrine of consent. Because the mutual "consent *of* [all] . . . the contracting parties*" was required to change the terms of any constitutional contract and because each of the colonies was founded on the basis of a "compact between the King and the people of the colony who were *out of the realm* of Great Britain," wrote Franklin, "there existed nowhere on earth a power to alter it" without the colonists' "formal and express Consent, which," as Edward Bancroft insisted, had "never been given." "In a Dispute between two Partys about Rights," declared Franklin, the mere "Declaration of one Party can never be suppos'd to bind the other."[32]

The explicit assumption behind this position was that, far from having authority to change the constitution of any part of the British world, Parliament was "limited and circumscribed by the constitution that formed it, and from whence it derives its authority." Ridiculing the modern metropolitan idea "that an act of parliament when once passed . . . becomes a part of the constitution," colonial proponents quoted the Swiss natural law theorist Emmerich de Vattel to prove that " 'the supreme legislative [power] cannot change the constitution.' " Great Britain, declared the Georgia minister Johan Joachim Zubly in 1769, had "not only a Parliament, which is the supreme legislature, but also a constitution," and "the now Parliament," Zubly insisted, derived "its authority and power from the constitution, and not the constitution from Parliament." Whatever authority Parliament might possess over either the center or the peripheries of the British Empire therefore necessarily had to be "agreeable to the constitution."[33]

Although the colonists could thus make a strong case that for over a century and a half they had without interruption "been trusted in a good measure with the entire management of their affairs," the doctrine of usage on which their developing conception of the empire rested so heavily cut two ways. If Parliament had no role whatever in their early history and if subsequently it had not customarily interfered in their internal affairs, they could not deny that from the mid-seventeenth century on, Parliament had "exercised its Authority in the Colonies, for regulating their Trade, and afterwards for directing their exterior Policy." Furthermore, they had to admit that even though Parliament's authority had "in some Instances been executed with great Partiality to Britain and Prejudice to the Colonies," they had "nevertheless always submitted to it" and thereby "consented to consider themselves as united to Great Britain in a commercial capacity, and to have their trade governed by its parliament."[34]

Such an arrangement not only had the sanction of custom but seemed to be dictated by "the circumstances of the times, and complications of the British Empire." As the Irish peer Sir Hercules Langrishe put it, the extended character of the empire rendered it "*in some measure* . . . necessary, that a general superintending power should be somewhere deposited, for the arbitration of commerce, and for directing, restraining, and regulating the *external* relations between the different members of the empire," and few disputed the contention that that power could not "reside any where with such propriety, as in the British legislature." But they insisted that although this general regulating power was "indeed a great power" that enabled Parliament to "restrain the external operations of the whole" extended British polity, they denied that it could be used to "abridge the *internal* liberty of a single man," much less that of an entire colony. Whatever the general superintending authority of Parliament, the Massachusetts House of Representatives wrote George III in 1768, it could not violate "the fundamental Rights of Nature & the Constitution to which your Majesty[']s happy Subjects in all parts of your Empire conceive they have a just & equitable Claim."[35]

Derived from a century and a half of experience, custom thus seemed to prescribe a clear allocation of authority within the broad, extended polity of the early modern British Empire, an allocation precisely along the lines identified by Bland and other colonial writers during the Stamp Act crisis. The many provincial governments, Ireland in the near-periphery and the several colonies in the distant American periphery, had full jurisdiction over their own particular local and internal affairs, while the metropolitan government at the center had authority over all general matters, including the external relations of the several provincial governments. As Pownall noted, this division of authority seemed to have been "established by invariable prescription from the [colonies'] first establishment."[36]

From the point of view of the peripheries, the logic of this pragmatic and long-established division of authority seemed to leave no doubt that, though "the authority of parliament in its proper extent" was indeed "justly supreme," the "same ought to be said of the general assemblies of the colonies." That is, as Governor William Pitkin of Connecticut declared in 1768, no "superintending supreme power in the British Parliament to regulate and direct the general affairs of the empire" could deprive the colonists of the "essential privileges" of their constitutions as defined by charters, inheritance, and custom. In both Britain and the colonies, declared an anonymous metropolitan writer who was sympathetic to the colonial argument, "the king has his prerogative and the subjects their rights, and in both the people as their supreme privilege, have the exclusive right of granting their own property" and otherwise governing themselves in all matters relating to their own internal concerns. In "an empire of freemen, no power," declared Zubly, was "absolute but that of the laws, and," he noted in an important addendum, the only laws that carried such absolute authority were those "to which they that are bound by them have consented."[37]

Notwithstanding the antiquity of the colonists' acquiescence in the exertion of parliamentary authority over their external affairs, however, the logic of the doctrine of no legislation without representation led a few people to question that authority as well. Such people did not deny that Parliament could "propose regulations for the trade, and restrictions for the manufactures of those by whom they were appointed" in Britain. But they questioned how, in the words of the New York writer William Hicks, "they can, with any face of equity[,] resolve to extend those regulations to those from whom they have received no *delegated power*"? Other writers agreed. So long as they were unrepresented in Parliament, an anonymous metropolitan pamphleteer argued in 1769, the colonists could, "with equal justice and propriety, dispute" Parliament's "right of legislation in general." "Perfect political liberty," observed Gervase Parker Bushe, consisted "in not being subject to any laws, but such as we have consented to, by ourselves, or by our representatives." "The very spirit of the constitution," said both the Rhode Islander Silas Downer and the New Yorker William Hicks, required that the colonists should not be subject "to *any* laws, but those which they themselves have made, by *regular agreement* with the deputy of the Crown, properly authorized for that purpose." In short, as Franklin asserted as early as 1766 in paraphrasing and parodying the Declaratory Act, Parliament had "not never had, and of Right never can have without our Consent, given either before or after[,] Power to make Laws of sufficient Force to bind the Subjects of America in any Case, whatever."[38]

If, as the logic of the developing colonial argument thus seemed to indicate, the colonies were wholly independent of Parliament, there existed no properly constituted authority either to legislate on matters relating to the general affairs of the empire or to settle disputes among its component entities. To resolve this problem, a number of people called for some formal legislative union among Britain, Ireland, and the colonies. Though Franklin later changed his mind about the desirability of such a union, during the crisis over the Townshend Acts he joined Thomas Pownall and Francis Maseres in calling for a full "consolidating Union, by a fair and equal Representation of all the Parts of this Empire in Parliament." Others, including William Hicks, more cautiously advocated only a limited legislative union, with the peripheries having "representation in parliament for the purposes of commerce [or other matters of general concern] only." According to these proposals, most fully articulated by an anonymous writer in New York in 1768, local legislatures in every part of the empire would continue to have authority over all "their own provincial legislation," while *One Central Parliament* representing the Whole" would be responsible for all "Matters of *national* Concern (Such as Protection, Defence, Regulation of Trade and naval Concerns, [and] all such Matters as may properly be deemed *national,* or such as concern the Benefit and Welfare of the Whole)."[39]

But such schemes had little support on either side of the controversy. Insisting that Parliament already had full legislative authority over the colonies, most members of the metropolitan establishment thought them unnecessary. Worried that limited representation in such a distant institution would only lend legitimacy to metropolitan efforts to curtail autonomy in the peripheries, most colonials thought them unwise. The latter continued to believe that it was absolutely "necessary to settle a Constitution for the Colonies" and to advocate an explicit settlement that would, by determining the nature of the colonies' connection to the metropolis and "ascertaining the relative Rights and Duties of each," fix the constitution of the empire upon "an equitable and permanent Basis," and the former continued to resist any suggestion for constitutional change that would in any way limit the omnipotence of Parliament.[40]

In the absence of any impartial tribunal to settle constitutional disputes between the center and the peripheries, there was, as Pownall lamented in 1768, "no means of deciding the controversy" by law. "Every act you have taken," Burke pointed out to his colleagues in Parliament in May 1770, "has got a contrary act," and the resulting constitutional impasse left metropolitan leaders with no fully satisfactory course of action. Unwilling to give in, they were, as yet, also unwilling to resort to force. They still understood the power of the old political adage that, in the words of Burke, there was "no such thing as governing the whole body of the people contrary to their inclinations," that, as Lord John Cavendish told Parliament, "dominion without the affection of the governed" was "not worth having." Such considerations were behind Parliament's decision in the spring of 1770 to repeal all the Townshend duties except the tax on tea. This essentially political resolution of the crisis in effect went back to the settlement adopted by the Rockingham party in 1766. That is, it left the issue of the extent of Parliament's colonial authority to rest on the Declaratory Act and token taxes on sugar products and tea, with an implicit understanding that, as in the case of Ireland, Parliament would not thenceforth levy any further taxes on the colonies.[41]

Like the Stamp Act crisis, the controversy over the Townshend Acts had helped to illuminate still further the ancient question of how, within the extended polity of the British Empire, authority was distributed between center and peripheries. To be sure, it produced little change in the metropolitan position as it had been articulated in 1764–66, and the conciliatory thrust of both Dickinson's *Letters from a Pennsylvania Farmer* and most of the official colonial protests helped to obscure the radical drift of sentiment among spokesmen in both America and Britain who supported the colonial side. Pursuing the logic of the customary constitutional arrangements that had obtained in the empire over the previous century, a great many writers between 1767 and 1770 had worked out detailed arguments to prove what a few colonial thinkers had already implied in 1764–66: that the British Empire was a loose association of distinct political entities under a common king, each of which had its own legislature with exclusive jurisdiction over its own internal affairs. A few writers during these years even challenged Parliament's competence to legislate on matters relating to the general affairs of the empire. As in 1764–66, a major constitutional crisis had thus functioned to intensify, rather than to resolve, differences in interpretations of the constitutional organization of the empire.

Nevertheless, repeal of the Townshend Acts brought a temporary respite from the turmoil that had beset metropolitan-colonial relations over the previous six years. For the next three and a half years, debate over the respective jurisdictions of Parliament and the peripheral legislatures in Ireland and the American colonies fell into temporary abeyance. Yet throughout the early 1770s, constitutional relations within the empire remained troubled. Beginning with the Stamp Act crisis, the long-standing conflicts over the relative balance between prerogative power and colonial rights, conflicts that had been an endemic feature of metropolitan-colonial relations ever since the middle of the seventeenth century, had been subordinated to the new and more pressing debate over the extent of Parliament's colonial authority. To be sure, the older conflict had never fully disappeared. Indeed, not since the late 1740s had there been so many serious controversies between metropolitan authorities and local legislatures as there were in the years just before and during the Stamp Act crisis.

During the early 1760s, there were several major confrontations over the extent of the king's prerogative in the colonies. Though they were often intensely fought, most of these, like the altercation that occurred in Massachusetts in the fall of 1762 over Governor Francis Bernard's attempts to expend public funds without legislative authorization, were soon over. In a few instances, however, these disputes lasted for years and seriously disrupted provincial political life. Such was the case in New York, where, throughout the early 1760s, a debilitating battle occurred between Lieutenant Governor Cadwallader Colden and local leaders over two related issues. First was the question of whether the crown should appoint judges during good behavior, as it had done in Britain since the Revolution Settlement, or, as metropolitan authorities insisted, only during the crown's pleasure. Second was the issue of whether the governor and council could, on appeal, overrule jury decisions.[42]

Similarly prolonged and even more intense disputes left both South Carolina and Jamaica without operative legislatures for long periods and were resolved only by the resignation or removal of the royal governors. In the former, government was virtually halted for more than nineteen months beginning in the spring of 1762 when Governor Thomas Boone attempted to interfere with what the Commons regarded as its exclusive right to judge the legitimacy of the elections of its own members. In the latter, Governor William Henry Lyttelton's efforts to restrict the customary parliamentary privilege that exempted assembly members from suits at law during legislative sessions produced a profound deadlock that lasted from December 1764 through the summer of 1766. That deadlock was probably the primary reason why the Jamaica Assembly failed to enter a formal protest against the Stamp Act.[43]

Underlining the persistence of the long-standing tensions between metropolitan authorities in the center and the local legislatures in the peripheries, these battles all revolved around the familiar issues of the previous century: whether the royal prerogative in the colonies should be placed under the same restraints it had been subjected to in Britain in the wake of the Glorious Revolution, whether royal instructions had constitutional standing, whether the rights of British people in the colonies were equal to those who continued to reside in the home islands, whether colonial legislatures were entitled to the same privileges and powers enjoyed by the metropolitan House of Commons, and whether usage had the same constitutional authority in the colonies as it had traditionally had in Britain. Underlying these battles, moreover, were the same old fears. Metropolitan authorities worried that the continual grasping after power by these distant colonial legislatures would eventually erode all control from the center; colonial leaders were anxious lest the crown's continuing efforts to extend the "prerogative beyond all bounds" would sooner or later cheat the colonists "out of their liberties" and thereby degrade them "from the rank of Englishmen" to "a condition of slavery."[44]

Throughout the last half of the 1760s, this ancient contest between prerogative and liberty was superseded or at least pushed into the background by the debate over Parliament's relationship to the colonies. Coincident with the repeal of most of the Townshend duties, however, a new series of quarrels arose over the scope of the crown's colonial authority, quarrels that punctuated the so-called period of quiet during the early 1770s and revealed that the debate over the extent of the crown's prerogative in the colonies was still hotly contested. Major controversies developed in Georgia, Maryland, and North Carolina, respectively, over the governor's right to reject the Georgia Commons' choice as speaker, the governor's authority to set the fees of public officers without legislative approval, and the North Carolina Assembly's authority to establish the right of its constituents to attach the property of nonresidents in suits for debts. Much more serious were quarrels in Massachusetts over the governor's right to transfer the meetings of the legislature from the traditional site at Boston to Cambridge and in South Carolina over the Commons' authority to issue money from the treasury without executive approval. With the former lasting for over two years and the latter for five, both of these contests resulted in long interruptions in the legislative process and, like the more limited controversies in Georgia and North Carolina, revolved around metropolitan efforts to use royal instructions to curb the power of local assemblies.[45]

In one sense, these controversies were simply the latest rounds in the long contest between central prerogative power and local colonial rights as championed by provincial assemblies. From the 1670s on and more systematically since the late 1740s, the "Governing of Colonies by Instructions," as Franklin observed in January 1772, had "long been a favourite Point with Ministers" in the metropolis. Ministers had indeed made so many "daring and injurious attempt[s] to raise and establish a despotic power over them" that, as the Maryland lawyer Charles Carroll of Carrollton remarked during the fee controversy in Maryland in May 1773, it had long since become "a common observation confirmed by general experience" that any "claim in the colony-governments of an extraordinary power as . . . part of the prerogative" was "sure to meet with the encouragement and support of the ministry in Great-Britain."[46]

From the perspective of the crises over the Stamp and Townshend Acts and the debate over Parliament's new pretensions to authority over the internal affairs of the colonies, however, these old questions about the crown's relationship acquired a new and heightened urgency in the colonies. If, as an impressive number of colonial spokesmen had begun to argue during the late 1760s, sovereignty within the empire rested not in the crown-in-Parliament but in the crown alone, it became especially important for the colonists to establish the boundaries not just of parliamentary but also of royal authority in the colonies. For that reason, colonial defenders in all of the battles of the early 1770s revealed a pronounced tendency to build upon their own particular local constitutional heritages to argue, as their predecessors in earlier generations had often done, that, no less than in Britain itself, the crown's authority—the freedom of its "will"—in the colonies had been effectively limited over the previous century by specific idiosyncratic constitutional developments in each of the colonies. Again just as in Britain, these developments had led, colonial leaders believed, irreversibly in the direction of increasing authority in the hands of the local legislatures and greater restrictions on the prerogatives of the crown. By this process, they argued, the rights of the inhabitants in the peripheries had gradually been secured against the power of the center.

As refined and elaborated during the contests of the early 1770s, this view of colonial constitutional history powerfully helped to reinforce traditional views of the colonial legislatures as both the primary guardians of the local rights of the corporate entites over which they presided and, like Parliament in Britain, as the dynamic forces in shaping the colonial constitutions. Insofar as the constitution of the empire was concerned, this emphasis upon the peculiarity and integrity of the several colonial constitutions certainly constituted, as Peter S. Onuf has noted, a vigorous "defense of constitutional multiplicity" that had profound implications for the ongoing debate over the nature of sovereignty within the empire. For, together with the emerging conviction that Parliament had no authority over the colonies, the renewed contention that the crown's authority in the peripheries was also limited by local constitutions as they had emerged out of not just the colonists' inherited rights as Englishmen and their charters but also local usage and custom pushed the colonists still further in the direction of a wholly new conception of sovereignty in an extended polity like the early modern British Empire. That conception implied that ultimate constitutional authority—sovereignty—lay not in any institution or collection of institutions at the center of the empire but in the separate constitutions of each of the many separate political entities that composed the empire.[47]

Chapter Seven

Disintegration of Empire, 1773–1776

When Parliament's passage of the Tea Act in May 1773 revived the dispute over its colonial authority, colonial resistance to that measure provoked the crisis that would, in a mere two and a half years, lead to the dismemberment of the early modern British Empire. At no time during this crisis did either side show much disposition to compromise. As each quickly took a determined stand upon the position marked out by its most extreme proponents during the previous crises, the spirit of conciliation that had marked the crisis over the Townshend Acts rapidly gave way to complete intransigence. While the metropolitan political nation refused to back down from its insistence that the king-in-Parliament was the supreme sovereign of the empire, the colonial assemblies and the First and Second Continental Congresses, composed of delegates from the thirteen colonies from New Hampshire south to Georgia, gave official sanction to views that had previously been held only by private individuals, views that had been developed by Franklin and others during the late 1760s and early 1770s and called for complete colonial autonomy over internal affairs. By 1776, what had begun as yet another crisis over Parliament's right to tax the colonies had become a crisis over whether the colonies would become independent, and the empire foundered over the inability of the center and the peripheries to agree on a formula for governance that would give the peripheries of that extended polity the same rights and control over their domestic affairs that was enjoyed by the center.

In both Britain and the colonies, supporters of Parliament's right to legislate for the colonies insisted, as they had ever since the beginning of the controversy during the Stamp Act crisis, that the British Empire, consisting of Great Britain *and* all its territories, was a single state composed of "ONE people, ruled by ONE constitution, and governed by ONE King." Arguing that the early Stuarts, no less than postrevolutionary kings, had always been "under the control of the other parts of the legislative power" and therefore had no authority to exempt the colonists from Parliament's jurisdiction, they held that the colonists were "subjects of the Kings of England, not as the inhabitants of Guyenne formerly were, or as those of Hanover now are, but subjects of an English parliamentary King." As such, like all other Englishmen, they necessarily owed obedience to parliamentary statutes.[1]

Reiterating the same central contentions that had underlain their argument from the beginning, they continued to interpret the controversy as a dispute over sovereignty. Dismissing the doctrine of no legislation without representation as "an obsolete maxim" that had no applicability to the distant parts of an extended polity like the British Empire, they persisted in asserting that "No maxim of policy" was "more universally admitted, than that a supreme and uncontroulable power must exist somewhere in every state." In the British Empire, they insisted, that power was vested "in King, Lords, and Commons, under the collective appellation of the Legislature," which as James Macpherson phrased it, was merely "another name for the Constitution of State," was, "in fact, the State itself."[2]

Thus, if the colonists refused obedience to Parliament, they were "no longer Subjects, but rebels" who, by arrogating "to themselves all the functions of Sovereignty," were obviously endeavoring to put themselves "on the footing of a Sovereign State." "The question between them and Great Britain," then, as Macpherson gravely noted in summarizing the dominant position within the metropolitan political nation, was nothing less than "dependence or independence, connection or no connection." With "no common Principle to rest upon, no common Medium to appeal to," wrote Josiah Tucker, the dispute seemed to have no middle ground. To admit any qualification in "the controuling right of the British legislature over the colonies," its proponents devoutly believed, would mean nothing less than the abandonment of "the whole of our authority over the Americans."[3]

Not everyone in Britain viewed the situation in terms of such polar options. Jonathan Shipley and Edmund Burke, for example, thought that no drastic remedies were required. Arguing that it was "unnecessary to lay down the limits of sovereignty and obedience," they believed that imperial harmony could yet be restored simply by a return to "lenient and conciliating measures." But others saw the crisis as an opportunity for constitutional reform, which, by explicitly incorporating the traditional British principle of consent into the constitutional structure of the empire, would serve as a via media between "absolute obedience in the colonies to be taxed by parliament, and their total independence on the parent state from which they are descended."[4]

There were two quite different approaches to this task. The first, which had been widely canvassed during previous crises, was that no major innovations were necessary. Its advocates believed that a medium could be found either in the example of the customary relationship between Britain and Ireland or in the explicit codification of existing divisions of authority. Either way, this approach involved the establishment of what Thomas Pownall called "A LINE OF PACIFICATION" based upon the by now familiar distinction between internal and external spheres of authority. According to this formulation, the colonies, with respect to their "interior rights, within the bounds of their corporation[s]," would have the same "absolute and sovereign" authority "as the government of the mother country hath within its realm," and the metropolitan government would retain "*supreme sovereign power*" over all matters involving the external affairs of the empire. As Pownall explained in elaborating upon the views he had set forth at the time of the controversy over the Townshend Acts, this arrangement was far from new. Rather, it merely gave explicit sanction to the very "*line of the administration of the government of England, towards the Colonies, and of their obedience towards its supreme empire, for near a century and a half.*" Furthermore, another writer declared, such long and successful usage made it clear that according internal autonomy to the colonies would "no more" lead "to their independency, than the possession of those [same] privileges" had led "to the independency of Ireland."[5]

What was new in this formulation was Pownall's perception that the new European colonies of the early modern era represented a new species of political entity that, through usage, had developed a distinctive form of government, which Pownall referred to as "a mixed or COLONIAL GOVERNMENT." Neither, as many colonists now contended, "*states sui juris*" with "external as well as internal sovereign jurisdiction" nor, as most people in the metropolitan political nation seemed to agree, merely *"communities within the state* of Great Britain," colonial governments, in Pownall's view, were something in between. Less free than national and more free than provincial governments, this new species of polity had gradually emerged to meet the specific conditions of governance in a wide, extended polity.[6]

A second approach to constitutional reform involved more sweeping measures. Believing that the metropolitan establishment had so far "evade[d] a fair discussion of *the question of right,"* its advocates held that the long and increasingly acrimonious conflict made it clear that "the constitution of the Colonies must be [wholly] new-modelled." As one anonymous writer of this persuasion declared, the "question should be, not what the constitution was, or is, but what present circumstances considered, it ought to be." According to this view, which had support among conservative Americans as well as liberal metropolitans, the most effective way to make sure that the doctrine of consent obtained in the peripheries as well as at the center of the empire was to create a central American Parliament that, while leaving the specifically local affairs of the colonies in the hands of their *"little Parliaments,"* would have jurisdiction over such matters of general concern as expenditures for defense.[7]

Following Parliament's passage of the Coercive Acts in the spring of 1774, most opinion leaders in America certainly agreed with those metropolitan writers who thought that the time had come for constitutional reform. "For nine successive years," one metropolitan writer complained in 1774, the colonists had "been impoliticly kept in a state of continual training." In quick succession, the Stamp and Townshend acts had forced them to examine their constitutional "situation more closely and critically than they had ever done" before. In the process, they conducted a "thorough examination" of questions that had not previously been so intensively and "accurately canvassed," fundamental questions concerning those important points relating to "the bounds of power and of obedience" within the empire that, as Baron Rokeby remarked, were "in all governments" better left "unsettled and undetermined."[8]

As a result of "their eager researches after that information which was so essentially necessary to the preservation of their liberties," they had gradually acquired during the years of crisis beginning in 1764 a far "better understanding" of the "nature of their political situation." By 1770, in fact, they had, as individual thinkers and writers, already worked out an elaborate and fully formed body of theory designed to secure colonial rights against metropolitan power. In 1774, during the early stages of what would become the crisis of independence, that body of theory needed only the sanction of constituted authority to make it the official position of the several colonies. That sanction was supplied by the actions of the First and Second Continental Congresses in 1774–75 and the endorsement of those actions by the local legislative bodies of the thirteen protesting colonies.[9]

The colonial position, as it was enunciated in mid-1774 and elaborated over the next two years, was founded on a complete rejection of the prevailing metropolitan theory of an omnipotent Parliament, a theory that was "evidently of [such] a modern structure" that it was not "even now an established idea on either side of the *Atlantic*." By ignoring the vital and traditional British constitutional principle of consent, of no legislation without representation, this "dreadful novelty," supporters of the colonial position declared, was at total variance with both "the ancient rights of the people" and "the settled, notorious, invariable practice of" imperial governance within the empire over the previous century and a half.[10]

No less important, when applied to distant and unrepresented colonies, this "modern doctrine," it seemed to the colonists, obviously also represented "a total contradiction to every principle laid down at the time of the [Glorious] Revolution, as the rules by which the rights and privileges of every branch of our legislature were to be governed for ever." Indeed, by its insistence upon exerting a "*supreme jurisdiction*" over the colonies, Parliament seemed not merely to be violating the most essential principles of the Glorious Revolution but actually to have assumed and to be acting upon precisely the same "high prerogative doctrine[s]" against which that revolution had been undertaken. Thus, the colonists believed, if, by resisting Parliament, they had become rebels, they were "rebels in the same way, and for the same reasons that the people of Britain were rebels, for supporting the Revolution." That is, they were merely acting to defend rights that they had "possessed for about two hundred years."[11]

If, as the colonists and many people in the metropolis believed, the most important legacy of the Glorious Revolution was freedom from arbitrary government, then the experience of the past ten years had taught them that their right to share in that legacy could never be secure unless they enjoyed full autonomy over their own internal affairs. As their metropolitan proponent John Cartwright remarked, they were simply "too far removed to be governed on . . . [revolutionary] principles of freedom by the mother country." Indeed, they could now see clearly that it was precisely "because no man thought at that time that the *English* Parliament" could possibly be "a constitutional or adequate Legislature in ordinary, for Dominions beyond Sea" that the crown had initially granted "*Ireland* . . . a Parliament of her own" and then established assemblies in each of the colonies. Having from the beginning been "considered as being out of the jurisdiction of parliament," the king's many external dominions in America and Ireland had thus had to have their own legislatures, each of which necessarily enjoyed "supreme power of legislation" over its respective locality. There was no other way either "to supply the want of . . . [a legislative] jurisdiction" or to guarantee that Englishmen in distant countries would continue to enjoy English liberties.[12]

By 1774, few people in America thus any longer had any doubt that, over the previous decade, it had "been clearly and fully proved that the Assemblies or Parliaments of the *British* Colonies in *America*" had "an exclusive right, not only of taxation, but of legislation also; and that the *British* Parliament, so far from having a right to make laws binding upon those Colonies in all cases whatsoever," had "really no just right to make any laws at all binding upon the Colonies." Far from being subject to the "supreme" authority of Parliament, most American leaders now believed, the colonies had "always enjoyed a supreme Legislature of their own, and . . . always claimed an exemption from the jurisdiction of a *British* Parliament." Not the king-in-Parliament, wrote the Virginian Thomson Mason, but the "King, at the head of his respective *American* Assemblies," constituted "the Supreme Legislature of the Colonies." Parliament's claim in the Declaratory Act "to regulate our internal police, give, take away, change, and infringe, our Constitutions and Charters," one speaker told a general meeting at Lewes, Delaware, in July 1774, was nothing more than a "lawless usurpation."[13]

Whether Parliament had any authority even over the external affairs of the colonies was now a point of contention among colonial resistance leaders. Already during the Townshend Acts crisis, some colonial supporters, as Sir John Dalrymple correctly charged, had begun to advance "the extravagant doctrines that" the colonies were "not bound by the Navigation Laws, and that" they were "even independent of Parliament altogether." By 1774, many of the most influential tracts, including those written by James Wilson of Pennsylvania and Thomas Jefferson of Virginia, unequivocably took this position. The legislative authority of each of the many independent legislatures within the empire, including Parliament, wrote Wilson, was necessarily "confined within . . . local bounds" and could not be imposed upon any of the other areas of the empire without their consent. During the early stages of the crisis of independence, however, most American leaders seemed still to have believed that Parliament did have authority over external affairs and, as both Alexander Hamilton and John Adams pointed out, that that authority derived from the "long usage and uninterrupted acquiescence" by which the colonists, since the middle of the seventeenth century, had given their "implied consent" to the navigation acts and other trade regulations.[14]

But if few of their protagonists yet claimed for the colonists "external as well as internal sovereign jurisdiction" as "independent nations," virtually everyone now agreed with those people who had begun to argue during the late 1760s that "all the different members of the British Empire" were "distinct states, independent of each other, but connected together under the same sovereign." Upon close examination, they had discovered that, as an entity "composed of extensive and dispersed Dominions," the empire was "in some degree a new case" in political history that had to "be governed . . . more by its own circumstances, and by the genius of our peculiar Constitution, than by abstract notions of government." Separated by vast distances, "inhabited by different people, [living] under distinct constitutions of government, with different customs, laws and interests," its several constituent elements could not possibly be considered as a single civil state. Rather, each part had to be "considered as a [distinct] people, not a set of individuals." Presided over by its own legislature, each of these corporate entities was a separate realm that was entirely independent of all the others. According to this line of thought, no part of the empire was subordinate to any other part. As Franklin had remarked in 1770, there was thus no dependence among the several parts of the empire, "only a *Connection,* of which the King is the common Link."[15]

Indeed, to the colonists' few defenders in Britain, this dispersion of authority seemed not to be a defect but a necessary and viable solution to the problem of governance in an extended polity. Recognizing that it had "always been a most arduous task to govern distant provinces, with even a tolerable appearance of justice," they agreed with John Dickinson, who quoted the Italian political thinker Cesare Beccaria to the effect that "an over grown republic" like the British Empire could "only be saved from despotism by sub-dividing it into a number of confederate republics." "If an empire be too large, and its parts too widely separated by immense oceans, or other impediments, to admit of being governed on the principles essentially belonging to all free governments," argued John Cartwright, it was "an overgrown empire, and ought to be divided before it fall into pieces." As in all "large bodies," the "immutable condition, the eternal law, of extensive and detached empire," Burke declared in expanding upon this theme, was that "the circulation of power must be less vigorous at the extremes." Even a despot like the sultan of Turkey, Burke explained, understood that "the force and vigor of his authority in his centre . . . derived from a prudent relaxation in all his borders" and therefore governed his distant provinces "with a loose rein," in order that he might "govern [them] at all."[16]

George Johnstone, former governor of West Florida, took this theme even farther in several speeches in Parliament. Arguing that the British colonies had "flourished more than others" precisely because Britain had "found out the secret of carrying freedom to the distant parts of the empire," Johnstone asked his fellow M.P.s to "consider that the very first principles of good government in this wide-extended dominion, consist in subdividing the empire into many parts, and giving to each individual an immediate interest, that the community to which he belongs should be well-regulated. This is the principle," Johnstone declared, "upon which our ancestors established those different colonies or communities; this is the principle upon which they have flourished so long and so prosperously; this is the principle on which alone they can be well governed at such a distance from the seat of the empire." Before they tried to run "the different privileges belonging to the various parts of the empire into one common mass of power," therefore, Johnstone urged his listeners to recall that "the great maxim to be learned from the history of our colonization" was to "let men manage their own affairs; they will do it better on the spot," he contended, "than those at a distance . . . can possibly do it for them."[17]

In view of the success of the empire, in view of the "riches and power, men and money," and "credit and honour in the world," which "the detached parts of its dominions" contributed to "the centre of government," both Americans and their supporters in Britain regarded it as absurd for the metropolis to risk so many palpable advantages in pursuit of what increasingly appeared to them to be nothing more than an academic and irrelevant political abstraction. To the vast majority of the metropolitan political nation, the "grand" question in dispute might very well appear to be "Whether or not the British parliament . . . hath the right of sovereignty over North America." Throughout the prerevolutionary debates, however, most colonial leaders had resisted such reductionism and had endeavored, unsuccessfully, to focus debate upon the seemingly more tractable and certainly less abstract problem of how power was or should be allocated in a polity composed of several related but nonetheless distinct corporate entities. For the colonists, resolution of their dispute with the metropolis had never seemed to require much more than the rationalization of existing political arrangements within the empire.[18]

For them, the "great solecism of an *imperium in imperio*" seemed, as James Iredell declared, to be little more than "a narrow and pedantic . . . point of speculation," a "scholastic and trifling refinement," that had no relevance to the situation at hand. The claim "that two independent legislatures cannot exist in the community," George Johnstone observed, demonstrated "a perfect ignorance of the history of civil society" and a complete misunderstanding of the workings of the empire. "Mankind are constantly quoting some trite maxim, and appealing to their limited theory in politics, while they reject established facts," he complained. For colonial supporters, however, "custom and continual usage" were invariably, in Iredell's phrase, "of a much more unequivocal nature than speculation and refined principles." Notwithstanding the fact that it had been "so vainly and confidently relied on" by their antagonists, that "beautiful theory in political discourses—the necessity of an absolute power residing somewhere in every state"—seemed, as Iredell wrote, to be wholly inapplicable to a situation involving "several distinct and independent legislatures, each engaged in a separate scale, and employed about different objects."[19]

Indeed, if the *imperium in imperio* argument had any relevance to the existing debate, the colonists had no doubt that it worked in favor of their argument in at least two senses. First, as Moses Mather noted in taking obvious delight in turning the conventional metropolitan argument on its head, because, in conjunction with the king, each of the "multiplicity of legislatures" in the empire already had full authority over their respective jurisdictions, it was impossible to subject the colonies "at the same time to the legislative power of parliament" without introducing "an *imperium in imperio,* one supreme power within another," which, he mockingly remarked in parroting his opponents, was obviously "the height of political absurdity." Second, and more seriously, as the Earl of Abingdon pointed out, the most blatant "solecism" in the contemporary debate was the assertion "that in a *limited* government [like that of Britain], there can be an *unlimited* power." No less than the executive authority of the crown, the "legislative power of Great Britain" was, they asserted in terms they had been using from the beginning of the debate, necessarily "limited to, and circumscribed by the constitution of the kingdom, and the fundamental laws thereof."[20]

With Jonathan Shipley, bishop of St. Asaph, colonial leaders called upon the metropolitan government to abandon its pursuit of the "vain phantom of unlimited sovereignty, which was not made for man," and content itself with "the solid advantages of a moderate, useful and intelligible authority." As long as all members of the empire adhered to the customary arrangements that had developed over the previous century and a half, as long as the king was the "supreme head of every legislature in the British dominions," he would always have it in his power to "guide the vast and complicated machine of government, to the reciprocal advantage of all his dominions" and, by his authority to veto laws, would on any occasion be able to "prevent the actual injury to the whole of any positive law in any part of the empire." As long as "the power of every distinct branch [of the empire was] . . . limited to itself" and the king, "the only sovereign of the empire," was "acknowledged, by every member," to have "Sovereign" authority "over the whole," Alexander Hamilton contended, there was absolutely no danger in having many legislatures in the same polity and no possibility that there would ever "be two sovereign powers, in the same state."[21]

That this entire line of argument applied to the relationship between Britain and all of its associated polities its proponents had no doubt. Every colony had within itself "the rights and the actual powers of legislation." The "West India islands, as well as the continental colonies," declared Cartwright, were exempt from Parliament's authority and "certainly have a right to their [legislative] independency, whenever they shall think proper to demand it." Parliament's authority, he contended, was "confined to the British Isles, and to the various *settlements and factories of our trade* in the different parts of the world, including *the government of Newfoundland;* together with the garrisons of *Gibralter* and *Minorca"*—those few British territories that did not "contain within themselves every necessary of legislation." Within the term *British Isles,* Cartwright meant to include Ireland, which, because of its proximity he thought was "naturally a dependent upon Great-Britain," albeit he did advocate a parliamentary union of the kind that had already been formed between England and Scotland. Others strongly disagreed. "The Representative Body of Ireland," wrote Rokeby, might be "called a Parliament; that of America, an Assembly. The term of kingdom" might obtain "in one country, and that of colony in the other," but, he asked rhetorically, "Is there any charm in the sound of these words, which makes a difference?" "By their own circumstances," Hamilton confidently predicted, "the Irish . . . will be taught to sympathise with us and commend our conduct."[22]

Other than the thirteen dissident colonies, however, the only overseas territory to align itself officially with the colonial point of view was Jamaica, where, ever since the Stamp Act crisis, there had been considerable support for the American cause. In December 1774, just a few weeks after the adjournment of the First Continental Congress, the Jamaica Assembly adopted a petition and memorial to the king that constituted a ringing endorsement of the emerging colonial view of the distribution of authority within the empire. Although this document began by pointing out that Jamaica's extensive slave population prevented it from offering any overt physical resistance to British authority, it subscribed to the argument that Parliament's legislative authority was confined to Britain. Following the example of the North American Congress, it "freely consent[ed] to the operation of all such Acts of the *British* Parliament, as are limited to the regulation of our external commerce only, and the sole object of which is the mutual advantage of *Great Britain* and her Colonies," obviously intending thereby to give the navigation acts constitutional standing in Jamaica. "By the principles of our Constitution, as it has arisen from colonization," however, it denied that its constituents or, for that matter, any other group of colonists, could be "bound by any other laws than such as they have themselves assented to, and are not disallowed by your Majesty" and prayed "that no laws shall be made and attempted to be forced upon them, injurious to their rights as Colonists, *Englishmen,* or *Britons*."[23]

The lack of formal endorsement from other colonies does not, however, mean an absence of extensive support for the American position. To be sure, in the fall of 1775, the Irish Parliament approved an address condemning the Americans as rebels. But it was vigorously opposed by the so-called Patriots, who throughout the previous decade of constitutional controversy had been sympathetic to the Americans and had emphasized the extent to which, as Henry Flood wrote the colonists in 1768, "your circumstances and ours" were "exactly the same." Praising Americans for being the true heirs of William Molyneux, the great exponent of Irish home rule at the end of the previous century, Patriot speakers predicted that if Parliament succeeded in forcing the colonies to acknowledge its taxing power over them, it would next turn its attention to Ireland. Similarly, when in early 1776 the Irish Parliament voted, again with strong Patriot opposition, to send four thousand troops from Ireland to the colonies, a group of dissenting lords denounced the action and declared that Parliament's claim to tax any part of the empire other than Britain was "not inherent in the general constitution of the empire." For the first time since 1749, a new Irish edition of Molyneux's *Case of Ireland* was published in 1776 with a preface calling upon Irishmen to "despise all authority which is not founded in justice and . . .to defend with their fortunes and their lives those constitutional rights which they inherit from their ancestors."[24]

In their efforts to explain—and to rationalize—existing constitutional relationships within the empire, colonial protagonists, between 1764 and 1776, had discovered that the locus of authority necessarily had to reside in each of the separate corporate entities that composed the empire. Contrary to metropolitan theory as it had developed following the Glorious Revolution and, more especially after 1740, authority, they now clearly understood, had never been concentrated in a sovereign institution at the center. Rather, it had always been dispersed among the several parliaments that routinely had been established to preside over—and express the collective will of—each new polity within the empire. Indeed, this proliferation of legislatures was the only way that those traditional English rights that had been confirmed to the inhabitants of the metropolis by the revolutionary settlement—especially that most fundamental right of no legislation without representation—could be extended to people in the peripheries of a large, extended polity like the early modern British Empire. For the inhabitants of those—by then—quite ancient corporate entities, English liberty and their specific local corporate rights were identical. Just as it had been throughout the colonial era, the integrity of those rights and of the constitutions and assemblies that embodied and protected them was thus, not surprisingly, the central theme of colonial constitutional protest during the 1760s and 1770s.

If, as Peter S. Onuf has pointed out, this insistence upon the "autonomy and integrity" of the several colonial constitutions was indeed a "defense of constitutional multiplicity" within the empire, the ancient and continuing association of its several separate polities clearly implied the existence of a larger imperial constitution. Though this constitution was obviously based upon and expressed the same fundamental principles, it was emphatically not identical to the British constitution. By the 1760s the British constitution had become the constitution of parliamentary supremacy. But the emerging imperial constitution, like the separate constitutions of Britain's many overseas dominions, remained a customary constitution in which, according to the colonial point of view, sovereignty resided not in an all-powerful Parliament but in the crown, the power of which had been considerably reduced over the previous century by the specific "gains made over the years in the direction of self-determination" by each representative body within the empire.[25]

When in 1774–75 colonial protagonists demanded the establishment of a new "Constitutional Charter" for the empire, what they had in mind was thus one in which these gains would be "recogniz'd and establish'd" on a secure foundation. Determined to be no longer governed "without known and stipulated rules," they were insistent that the "Extent of Power and Right" between metropolis and colonies be "explicitly stipulated" in such a way that, in Hamilton's words, "an *exact equality of constitutional rights,* among all His Majesty's subjects, in the several parts of the empire" would "be uniformly and invariably maintained and supported." If, by their constitutions, the colonies had long been enjoined "to make no law[s] repugnant to the law of England," thenceforth England would be "bound . . . to make no laws repugnant to the laws and rights of America." And such a parity of rights, they were persuaded, required local autonomy throughout the empire.[26]

To that end, they thought it necessary that Parliament repeal not simply all tax measures but the Declaratory Act and all measures, such as the Massachusetts Government Act and the Quebec Act, by which it had sought to alter the established constitutions of the colonies—measures that would signify both that Parliament had abandoned all pretensions to authority over the colonies and that the several "provincial legislatures" were "the only supreme authorities in our colonies." Moreover, they insisted that the new imperial constitution could not be established by the unilateral action of Parliament, which, having "no true authority for that purpose," would, as John Adams succinctly announced, never be "allow[ed] . . . any authority to alter their constitutions at all."[27]

But no one in a position of authority in Britain could take these demands seriously. The few "friends of America" in Parliament counseled conciliation and urged the abandonment of all measures that called attention to "the unlimited and illimitable nature of supreme sovereignty." By insisting upon establishing what William Dowdeswell called "a most ridiculous superiority," Parliament, they argued, effectively forced the colonists "to call that sovereignty itself in question" and thereby inadvertently "sophisticate[d] and poison[ed] the very source of government." The colonies, declared Charles James Fox, could only "be governed by . . . affection and interest," and, he warned, no people could be expected to "love laws, by which their rights and liberties are not protected." Only by "rendering it reciprocally and equally advantageous," such people suggested, could "the connection between Great Britain and the colonies be perpetuated."[28]

Repeating the old truism that all government was "founded on Opinion, and a Sense of Duty," an earlier analyst had quoted David Hume to the same effect: "Wherever the supreme Power by a Law, or positive Prescription, shocks *an Opinion regarded as fundamental*," Hume had written, "*the Principle is subverted by which Power is established, and Obedience can be no longer hoped for.*" "The *first* law of every government," the "*supreme law* of every society," such colonial writers as James Wilson and Alexander Hamilton had declared in applying to

the imperial crisis one of the central tenets of the new Scottish com-
mon-sense philosophy, was "*its own* happiness," and Burke, building
on the same theme, told Parliament, that, if "sovereignty and freedom" could not "be reconciled" in such a way as to make the colonists happy, they would not long hesitate to "cast your sovereignty in
your face." The metropolis would then have to resort to arms to enforce parliamentary sovereignty. But the idea of governing such pop-
ulous and extensive territories by force struck many metropolitan observers as entirely "visionary and chimerical." "That Country which
is kept by power," said one M.P., was "in danger of being lost every
day," and Isaac Barre predicted that Parliament would never be able to
"reduce to practice" the rights that it fancied it held "in theory."[29]

Regarding any diminution of parliamentary sovereignty as a prelude to the eventual loss of control of the colonies that seemed to be
so intimately associated with Britain's rise to world power, the vast
majority of the metropolitan political nation found it impossible to
heed such warnings. Besides, from the perspective of Britain's own
internal constitutional development during the previous century,
colonial theories about the organization of the empire seemed dan-
gerously retrograde. By placing the resources of Ireland and the colonies directly in the hands of the crown and beyond the reach of
Parliament, those theories appeared to strike directly at the root of the
legislative supremacy that, for them, was the primary legacy of the
Glorious Revolution.

In 1774, the Coercive Acts, which Johnstone denounced in Parliament as that "species of political phrenzy," had produced an astonishing union among the colonies. Though they were "divided in
customs, manners, climate, and communication," the colonies were
so alarmed that those measures would deprive them of "every essential privilege" that, as the Massachusetts Committee of Correspondence wrote Franklin in the spring of 1774, "the whole Continent"
was united "in Sentiment and . . . Measures." Already, in the initial
response to those measures, a few writers, notably Thomas Jefferson
and William Henry Drayton, had pointed out that many of the most
egregious colonial grievances were attributable directly to the crown.
By thus raising the old question of the extent of the king's authority in
the colonies, a question that had been given new force by the many
local controversies of the early 1770s, they thereby both issued a new
challenge to the crown's claim for "more extensive [prerogative] in

America, than it" was "by law limited in England" and, implicitly at least, questioned the wisdom of the emerging argument that a continuing connection with Britain through the crown would provide an adequate basis for the security of colonial rights.[30]

As it became increasingly clear in 1775-76 that Parliament would not abandon its "idle ideas of superiority" and that George III was every bit as committed to the idea of parliamentary sovereignty as was the rest of the metropolitan political nation, more colonials began to think of a new course of political action that included both independence from Britain and the creation of "an AMERICAN COMMONWEALTH." Notwithstanding the old conviction that every colony was "so fond of" its own "peculiarities" that they could "never unite into one state," they more and more came to the conclusion that there was no other way that was "likely to answer the great purpose of preserving our liberties." Whether independence would be the first step toward the establishment of a viable union that would enable them to resolve the problem that had brought the British Empire to grief, the problem of how in an extended polity authority should be distributed between center and peripheries, was still an open question when they opted for independence in July 1776.[31]

Over the past decade, several legal historians, including especially Barbara Black, John Phillip Reid, and Thomas C. Grey, have examined the legitimacy of the colonial case in the constitutional debates of the 1760s and 1770s. As Black has pointed out, "twentieth-century scholarship" has been "virtually unanimous in holding that," in this debate, "Americans . . . were 'wrong on the law,'" in Reid's words, that "American constitutional pretensions" should not be "tak[en] seriously because the constitution was what Parliament declared it to be." But Reid, Black, Grey, and others offer a powerful case against this conventional view. They argue that, so far from being right, that view is "really an incorrect conclusion of law."[32]

These scholars do not deny that London authorities thought "of the governance of their empire in terms of [a] . . . unicentric power applying one law laid down by parliament." But they do contend, as has been argued in this work, that the "imperial constitution of eighteenth-century British North America was not [nearly] as precise as today's historians insist [that] it must have been" and that it by no means "furnish[ed] definitive answers" about the scope of Parliament's authority within the empire. The doctrine of parliamentary supremacy, they argue, was still sufficiently new as not yet to be fully understood or accepted even within England itself, and the "old idea of a . . . fixed constitution standing above and limiting the working institutions of government . . . [still] remained a respectable idea in England in the 1760s." In fact, as Reid remarks, the very concept of the constitution was still so imprecise that "definition [was] more a matter of personal usage than of judicial certainty," and it was still possible even "to accept the new constitution of parliamentary supremacy while clinging to the old constitution of fixed restraints."[33]

In this fluid and unsettled situation, it is scarcely satisfactory to dismiss the American view as "an archaism." As Reid explains, the fact that "the seventeenth-century constitution of customary rights would never be reestablished as the constitution of Great Britain does not prove that the eighteenth-century constitution of parliamentary supremacy had been established in the North American colonies." Rather, Reid and Black both argue that the colonies operated under the aegis not of the British constitution but of an emerging imperial constitution that rested on solid legal foundations, the most important of which was the doctrine of usage.[34]

The primary "source of authority underlying both the seventeenth-century English constitution, and the contemporary American constitution[s] that colonial whigs were defending against the eighteenth-century British Constitution," writes Reid, "was custom." The eighteenth-century Cambridge natural law theorist Thomas Rutherforth agreed. "The content of a nation's constitution," he wrote in 1750, was largely "a question of fact, to be determined by considering the history and customs of a people." To a very important extent, the American case ultimately rested on the contention, first asserted during the Stamp Act crisis, that both "interference in local affairs by Parliament through legislation" and "direct parliamentary taxation" were "contrary to the principles of the contemporary" colonial constitutions, as those "constitution[s] had been established by long custom and as" that custom "was currently sanctioned by accepted usage."[35]

As historians have long recognized, evidence for these claims is by no means insubstantial. During the eighteenth century, as Black notes and as has been argued at length in this volume, Britain's various overseas dominions had been "much, if not equally, blessed by the extension of the benefits of government by consent." In theory, the crown's prerogative remained extensive in the colonies. Through a combination of statutes and custom, however, the assemblies in most colonies had managed largely to neutralize royal power. To an extraordinary degree, in fact, royal government in the colonies had come more and more to mean "government by the elected representatives of the people."[36]

The corollary to this diminution of royal power was the failure of Parliament to take an expansive role in colonial affairs. Precisely because Parliament thus played only a limited, "essentially conciliar" role in colonial matters, the fact "that the prerogative was at its height in the colonies reinforced the sense of" the colonies "as the king's dominions." As a result, Black observes, the "reduction of the king's power by English law, as well as by the ingenuity and effort of the colonial assemblies . . . irresistibly [suggested] the reduction in law of all external power"—that of Parliament as well as that of the king—and thereby gave legitimacy to the American claim that rights established through custom "were beyond modification by Parliament" as well as by the king. As far as the colonists were concerned, then, "the supremacy of Parliament," as Reid puts it, "had not yet been established as part of their customary constitution[s] and, now that the Stamp Act [had] exposed the danger[s] of parliamentary supremacy, it would never be [so] established."[37]

Most historians, including some earlier legal historians, have treated the disparity between the actualities of colonial self-government and metropolitan theory as a distinction between "fact and law" or, in the case of the present writer, between fact and theory. But, as the work of Black, Reid, and Grey makes clear, such distinctions seriously underestimate the legal force of custom in English law. The supposed "tension between fact and law," Black states, was actually a "tension within law." In English jurisprudence, as Reid explains, custom obtained "the force of law by a combination of time and precedent. Whatever had been done from time immemorial in a community was legal; whatever had been abstained from was illegal." "Historical fact was the source of constitutional custom," and, according to contemporary English practice well into the late eighteenth century, "rights established by custom and proven by time were legal rights" that, as Grey notes, were "*judicially* enforceable, even against the highest legislative and executive organs of government."[38]

The colonists, Grey observes, did not condemn British policies as "merely . . . unjust or untraditional or even 'unconstitutional' in the extra-legal sense of that term." They denounced them "as *illegal*—and the law" they invoked "was the unwritten fundamental law of reasonable custom and customary reason that [had traditionally] made [and still continued to make] up [so much of] the British constitution." Historians who have treated "custom as a source of or authority for 'law' that in fact" was "not law, or" was "something less than law" have thus been wrong. As Black insists, colonial "gains made over the years in the direction of self-determination" through usage were "gains made *in and by law*," and the "reduction of the king's power and the increase in the representative dimension of the imperial constitution" were developments "in law [as well]] as in fact."[39]

These legal historians thus underline the validity of the colonial argument that there was more than one constitution in the early modern British Empire. If by the 1760s the British constitution had become the constitution of parliamentary supremacy, the emerging imperial constitution, like the separate constitutions of Britain's many overseas dominions, remained a customary constitution. As Rutherforth noted in 1750, usage that had "obtained in any civil society [from] . . . time immemorial . . . may be presumed to have obtained with its consent." And just as, in Rutherforth's words, "whatever is consented to by a civil society, becomes a law of such society," so it was a hallowed English constitutional principle that nothing could become law without such consent.[40]

This principle lay at the heart of the familiar idea of a constitutional contract between the ruled and their rulers. According to that idea, neither party could change the contract without the consent of the other. No political and constitutional changes, in short, could take effect without the consent of *all* concerned parties as indicated either by long-standing acceptance through usage or by a formal legislative enactment by a representative body empowered to give such consent. Because historians have tended to trace the colonists' use of this argument to the writings of John Locke and various other natural law theorists, they have mostly failed to appreciate, as Reid writes, that it had also been "a central dogma in English and British constitutional law since time immemorial." Contract theory did not therefore rest only on philosophical grounds but, like the doctrine of usage, was also deeply rooted in "customary [English] jurisprudence" and had firm legal standing.[41]

Recognition of the legal status of the doctrines of consent and contract tends to give still further legal weight to the colonial argument that "parliament and the ministry in London, not they, [had] defied the ancient law" and attempted to violate their "old rights" by altering their "customary constitution[s]." At least before 1774, they admitted that it was legal for Parliament to regulate colonial trade because, as a *quid pro quo* for protection, they had through usage " 'chearfully' consented" to such regulations. But they vehemently argued that it was *illegal* for Parliament to tax the colonies or otherwise interfere in unaccustomed ways with their internal affairs because they had never given their consent to such exertions of parliamentary power. Through both formal parliamentary enactments in the wake of the Glorious Revolution and usage during succeeding decades, British people in Britain had obviously consented to the doctrine of parliamentary supremacy. In the colonies, however, neither the people at large through custom nor their representatives in the several colonial legislatures had given such consent. For Parliament to attempt to bind the colonies without that consent was nothing less than "a unilateral breach of an agreement that could properly be changed only by bilateral negotiation."[42]

However strong its case in law, colonial claims that the imperial constitution was one of "principled limitation" by which they were guaranteed "government by consent" of course found little support in Britain. There, constitutional theory was running in an entirely different direction, one, in Black's words, that "in theory involved the obliteration of every trace of principled limitation from law and its relegation to the precarious plane of practice." Once metropolitan officials had subjected the colonial claim to the test of this new theory, any hope of winning a favorable hearing for their case in London was "pretty much lost."[43]

But their refusal to take these claims seriously does not mean that metropolitan officials were "right about the law." As these legal historians have so cogently stressed, constitutional arrangements within the British Empire were far from precise, and each side could marshal effective legal arguments in behalf of its position. Nor, as Reid emphasizes, was there within the empire any "tribunal to which [such] a constitutional dispute could be taken for resolution except parliament itself—the very institution against which the colonists were contending." In this unsettled situation, questions "of sovereignty and legitimacy" were by no means so clear as they were said to be in London and as has been assumed by so many later historians. The *legal* question of "whether usage was . . . the authority for the [imperial] constitution," the primary issue "dividing American Whigs from their fellow subjects in Great Britain" during the 1760s and 1770s, was still very much open to debate.[44]

The picture of the prerevolutionary constitutional debate that emerges from the new legal history literature is thus one in which the quarrel was not over a right and a wrong interpretation of the constitution but a "struggle . . . between different levels of government," each of which had a legitimate constitutional case. By no means yet a modern unitary state, the early modern British Empire was directed by a "multicentric" rather than a "unicentric. . . authority." Imperial institutions in the colonies had little coercive power and depended for their effectiveness upon the consent of local populations. Authority within the empire was dispersed into the hands of authoritative, powerful, and "largely autonomous local institutions." Not dependent for their effectiveness "on the support or the acquiesence of a central authority" and highly "resistant to centralized control," these institutions were regarded, both by those who composed them and those whom they served, as largely "independent recipients of constitutional power and authority." In this "diffuse and decentralized" political entity local institutions invariably determined the nature of law and the constitution as much as did authorities at the center.[45]

Thus, in regard to extended polities in the era before the development of the modern consolidated state in the wake of the French Revolution, it should not automatically be assumed that the perspective of the center is the correct or even the dominant one. In any polity like the early modern British Empire in which the authority and ideology of the center are weak in the peripheries while local power and traditions are strong, local institutions and customs may be at least as important in determining existing legal and constitutional arrangements as those of the center. In such an entity, a *center* perspective will almost automatically be a *partisan* perspective. In the particular case of the British Empire at the time of the American Revolution, the antiquity of the notion of a customary imperial constitution of principled limitation and the strength of local institutions combined with the comparative recentness of the doctrine of parliamentary supremacy and weakness of metropolitan authority in the colonies to make the perspective of the center a "tory perspective." Perhaps even more important, the failure of the center to establish the legitimacy of its perspective in the peripheries rendered it an *anachronistic* perspective when applied to legal and constitutional arrangements within the empire as a whole.[46]

Book Three

A Problem
Resolved,
1776–1788

Chapter Eight

A Confederation of States, 1776–1783

For a century and a half before the American Revolution, metropolitans and colonials had wrestled with the difficult question of how, in the extended polity of the British overseas empire, to allocate authority between the center and the peripheries, between Britain and its distant colonies in America. Either explicitly or implicitly, this question, almost invariably, had been at the heart of the persistent tensions that beset constitutional relations between colonies and crown both before and after 1763. When people on both sides of the Atlantic confronted it for the first time in a sustained and systematic way between 1763 and 1776, they developed radically divergent views that ultimately led to the secession of thirteen of the North American colonies from the empire.

As James Madison later noted, for most colonial leaders, "the fundamental principle of the Revolution was, that the Colonies were coordinate members with each other and with Great Britain, of an empire united by a common executive sovereign, but not united by any common legislative sovereign." Maintaining that legislative authority was distributed broadly and equally among the several corporate entities that composed the empire, the colonists insisted both that the legislative power of "each American Parliament" was as "complete" as that of the British Parliament and that "the royal prerogative was in force in each Colony by virtue of its acknowledging the King for its executive magistrate, as it was in Great Britain by virtue of a like acknowledgement there." More than any other development, Madison correctly observed, "a denial of these principles by Great Britain, and the assertion of them by America, produced the Revolution."[1]

But separation from Britain by no means resolved this ancient question. To the contrary, it made it even more difficult by linking it inextricably with the equally vexing problem of how to forge a viable political and constitutional union out of thirteen distinct polities that previously had been formally tied together only by their common relationship to the British Empire through the emerging imperial constitution. To be sure, some colonial leaders had been considering a continental union at least since the Albany Congress in 1754. On several occasions during the prerevolutionary debates, some writers had proposed establishing "a general legislature . . . for the whole British empire in America, composed of delegates from each colony" to which "the several provincial legislatures would be necessarily subordinated." But the first general American constitution began to grow up around the institution of the Continental Congress beginning with the first meeting of that body in the fall of 1774. Like the metropolitan, colonial, and imperial constitutions of the empire, it was, in the beginning, very largely a customary constitution.[2]

Whether a more formal constitutional union could be achieved and what form it should take were two of the most important constitutional questions confronting American resistance leaders throughout the early years of war and independence. Far from being an inevitable development, the fabrication of such a union was highly problematic. From very early on, however, it had been apparent that the permanent establishment of such a union and the perpetuation of the new United States would be heavily dependent upon the resolution of the old problem of the allocation of authority in an extended polity composed of many distinct corporate entities.

John Witherspoon, the learned president of the College of New Jersey and a delegate to the second Continental Congress from New Jersey, emphasized the problematic character of the American national union in the summer of 1776 during the initial debates over what form that union should take. Reflecting upon the astonishing events of the previous two years, Witherspoon noted that "Honour, interest, safety and necessity" had conspired to produce "such a degree of union through these colonies, as nobody would have prophesied, and hardly any would have expected." As a result of this startling development, he declared, American political leaders had suddenly become aware that "a well planned confederacy among the states of America" would contribute enormously to "their future security and improvement." "A lasting confederacy," he predicted, would not only "hand down the blessings of peace and public order to many generations" of Americans. It would also serve as a model and an inspiration for the rest of the civilized world, which, he hoped, might eventually "see it proper by some plan of union, to perpetuate security and peace" over large portions of the globe.[3]

Witherspoon was by no means unique in either his surprise at the unity achieved by the colonies in their resistance to Britain in 1774–76 or his assessment of the promise of an American union. As Jack N. Rakove has recently emphasized, several short-range developments propelled Americans in that direction during those years. By far the most important of those developments, Rakove has shown, were the exigencies arising out of the necessity of coordinating an effective resistance and waging a war against the strongest military power then existing in the Western world. From the beginning, American leaders were aware that they had no chance of success unless they could maintain a high degree of "agreement on the principles and tactics of opposition" and avoid "the types of jealousy that had troubled American resistance in the early 1770's."[4]

Inexorably, this awareness pushed delegates to the Continental Congress in the direction of a customary arrangement in which Congress exerted extraordinarily extensive power and thereby constituted a de facto national government. As Peter Onuf has noted, "the states behaved as if Congress had a superintending jurisdiction," and many American leaders "simply assumed that Congress had succeeded to the authority of the British Crown." In this situation, Congress rapidly acquired "powers in an ad hoc fashion, as it responded to contingencies." In the process, it created an "informal constitution" that was largely sufficient to sustain some semblance of national government throughout most of the war.[5]

Under these conditions, Rakove has found, there was little interest during the first year of the war in creating "an enduring national state." But the surprising success of Congress in presiding over and organizing a coordinated defense effort rapidly yielded still a second short-term development that created additional pressures toward the formation of a continental union. This development was the emergence among delegates of the hope, expressed by Witherspoon, that the colonies might, despite many perceived differences among them, actually be able to achieve "a lasting Confederation." As they came to grasp the potential for such a union, especially as it was spelled out for them by Thomas Paine and others during the first half of 1776, they began to feel that it would be a great tragedy if they did not seize so favorable an opportunity to accomplish such a noble end.[6]

Yet, as Rakove has also revealed, two additional short-term developments combined both to delay codification and formal adoption of a continental confederation and to raise profound doubts about whether, as Joseph Hewes of North Carolina worried shortly after independence, delegates would ever be able to "modell it so as to be agreed to by all the Colonies." First and most decisive during the first two years after independence was simply the press of other more urgent business. "The immensity of business created by the war," lamented the Virginia delegate Richard Henry Lee in August 1777, necessarily meant that "the Confederation goes on but slowly."[7]

Second, and of even greater long-term significance, was the rapid identification in 1775–76 of the enormously complex issues involved in trying to bring thirteen separate political entities into a broad continental union. "In such a Period as this, Sir, when Thirteen Colonies unacquainted in a great Measure, with each other are rushing together into one Mass," John Adams wrote presciently in November 1775, "it would be a Miracle, if Such heterogeneous Ingredients did not at first produce violent Fermentations."[8]

The coming together of representatives from the several states inevitably produced not only a sense of common purpose in resisting Britain but also a far more intense awareness of the remaining differences in interest and orientation among the several colonies. Specifically, delegates discovered that they disagreed over certain fundamental and enormously difficult issues involving representation, expenses, and western lands. By and large, the division over these issues was not sectional. Rather, as Merrill Jensen has pointed out, the "large colonies were pitted against the small ones; colonies with many slaves were in opposition to those with fewer; colonies that had no western lands contended with those that did."[9]

But the delegates also quickly identified and articulated broad regional interests and contrasts between the southern and the eastern (New England) states, albeit no one initially seemed to be quite sure whether the middle states from Delaware to New York were closer to the southern or to the eastern states. Invariably, the differences among the colonies in orientation, interest, and issues operated to make confederation, as John Adams predicted in May 1776, "the most intricate, the most important, the most dangerous, and delicate Business of all."[10]

If as a result of Rakove's analysis we now understand better than ever before the short-term developments beginning in late 1774 that both pushed the American colonies toward a continental union and made it difficult for them to contrive one, no one has yet considered systematically the several long-term preconditions that lay behind and affected that process. This chapter examines those preconditions, including both those that inhibited and those that facilitated the formation of a permanent national union, as they operated to shape that union in its initial form in the Articles of Confederation.

Certainly one of the most powerful of the preconditions operating to make the achievement of a permanent union extremely difficult was the obvious dissimilarities among the colonies and the nearly ubiquitous judgment that those dissimilarities were far more impressive than any similarities. Such a perception had prevailed throughout the colonial period and had received widespread expression in the decades just before the Revolution. Thus, in 1760, less than fifteen years before the beginnings of American national union, Benjamin Franklin had informed British readers that Britain's "fourteen separate governments on the maritime coast of the [North American] continent" were "not only under different governors, but have different forms of government, different laws, different interests, and some of them different religious persuasions and different manners." These differences, Franklin observed, gave rise to mutual suspicions and jealousies that were "so great that however necessary and desirable an union of the colonies has long been, for their common defence and security against their enemies, and how sensible soever each colony has been of that necessity, yet they have never been able to effect such an union among themselves, nor even to agree in requesting the mother country to establish it for them."[11]

Franklin was writing for the express purpose of allaying growing fears in Britain that the increasingly valuable colonies might rise up and throw off British control, but he expressed the conventional wisdom of his time. Indeed, during the decades immediately preceding the Revolution, virtually every commentator on both sides of the Atlantic was entirely persuaded, with Franklin, that the extraordinary differences among the colonies made any form of union impossible.

The validity of this conclusion seemed to be dramatically underscored by the fate of the Albany Plan of Union in 1754. This proposal for a limited defensive confederation against the French was not ratified by a single colony. Even worse, during the Seven Years' War several colonies had shown very little concern for the welfare of their neighbors. When their assistance had "been demanded or implored by any of their distressed neighbours and fellow subjects," charged the metropolitan economist Malachy Postlethwayt in 1757, some colonies had "scandalously affected delays" and "by an inactive stupidity or indolence, appeared insensible to their distressed situation, and regardless of the common danger, because they felt not the immediate effect of it." "Being in a state of separation," each of the colonies, another metropolitan writer complained during the war, acted "solely for its own interest, without regard to the welfare or safety of the rest," a situation that unfortunately "naturally begat jealousies, envyings, animosities, and even the disposition to do one another mischief rather than good." It was an unfortunate fact, Henry Frankland admitted from Boston in September 1757, that the colonies were "all jealous of each other."[12]

How, contemporaries seem mostly to have thought, could it have been otherwise? In language very similar to that expressed by Franklin just four years earlier, Thomas Pownall, the former Massachusetts governor, in 1764 in his widely read treatise, *The Administration of the Colonies,* explained the deep and manifold differences among the colonies. He predicted that "the different manner in which they are settled, the different modes under which they live, the different forms of charters, grants, and frames of government they possess, the various principles of repulsion . . . the different interests which they actuate, the religious interests by which they are actuated, the rivalship and jealousies which arise from hence, and the impracticability, if not the impossibility, of reconciling and accommodating these incompatible ideas and claims" would "obviously for ever" keep them "disconnected and independent of each other," a mere "rope of sand," in the words of another writer, the individual strands of which were all too "peculiarly attached to their respective constitutions of Governments," forms of society, and interests ever "to relish a union with one another."[13]

So deep were the differences and animosities among the colonies thought to run that they became an important element in the calculations of both metropolitan officials and American resistance leaders during the controversies that preceded the American Revolution. "The mutual jealousies amongst the several Colonies," Lord Morton assured Chancellor Hardwicke in the early 1760s, "would always keep them in a state of dependence," and metropolitan strategy in the Coercive Acts, the measures that played such a crucial role in stimulating the final crisis that led to war and the American decision for independence, was based upon the supposition that colonial opposition could easily be diffused by a policy of divide and rule, a policy the British government continued to pursue throughout the nine years of war that followed.[14]

Nor prior to 1774 were many American leaders very sanguine about their capacity even to offer a united resistance, much less to weld themselves together into a single political society. The inability of the colonists to maintain economic sanctions against Britain during the crisis over the Townshend Acts between 1768 and 1770 provided an object lesson in the difficulties of united action and exacerbated long-standing fears of internal division and disunion. These experiences and fears were certainly one of the more important deterrents to colonial revolt right down into the mid-1770s.

Such fears and the perceptions of diversity that underlay them were not quickly dissipated once united resistance had begun in the mid-1770s. Rather, close associations in the Continental Congresses seem both to have sharpened those perceptions and to have intensified the suspicions and distrust that accompanied them. "The Characters of Gentlemen in the four New England Colonies," John Adams wrote to Joseph Hawley in November 1775, "differ as much from those in the others . . . as much as [in] several distinct Nations almost. Gentlemen, Men of Sense, or any Kind of Education in the other Colonies are much fewer in Proportion than in N. England," Adams thought, expressing his customary sectional pride: "Gentlemen, in the other Colonies have large Plantations of slaves, and the common People among them are very ignorant and very poor. These Gentlemen are accustomed, habituated to higher Notions of themselves and the distinction between them and the common People, than We are." Ever the realist, Adams thought that nothing less than "a Miracle" could produce "an instantaneous alteration of the Character of a Colony, and that Temper and those Sentiments which its Inhabitants imbibed with their Mother[']s Milk, and which have grown with their Growth and strengthened with their Strength."[15]

More cautious delegates especially continued to doubt that any effective or lasting union among such heterogeneous components could ever turn out well. "Their different Forms of Government—

Productions of Soil—and Views of Commerce, their different Religions—Tempers and private Interest—their Prejudices against, and Jealousies of, each other—all have, and ever will, from the Nature and Reason of things, conspire to create such a Diversity of Interests, Inclinations, and Decisions, that they never can [long] unite together even for their own Protection," predicted Joseph Galloway: "In this Situation Controversies founded in Interest, Religion or Ambition, will soon embrue their Hands in the blood of each other."[16]

Not just timid and future loyalists like Galloway but also ardent proponents of continental union like John Adams worried about the long-range prospects of a union of such apparently disparate parts. "I dread the Consequencies of this Disimilitude of Character" among the colonies, Adams wrote, "and without the Utmost Caution . . . and the most considerate Forbearance with one another and prudent Condescention . . . they will certainly be fatal." As the war went along, moreover, people became ever more aware of the extraordinary "difficulty of combining, in one general system, the various sentiments and interests of a continent, divided into so many sovereign and independent states . . . differing in habits, produce, manufactures, commerce, and internal police."[17]

These widespread perceptions of diversity among the separate states and regions and the many difficulties they created were not the only long-term source of anxiety that made people skeptical about the viability of a continental union. Bernard Bailyn has shown in detail the pervasiveness in early American politics of fears of the corrupting tendencies of power. The particular difficulties of bringing a distant power to account had been indelibly impressed upon Americans during the long controversy with Britain after 1763, and those painful lessons gave rise to a profound mistrust of central power that was readily transferable from the British government to an American national government and constituted a second precondition that delayed and affected the creation of a continental union.[18]

Having just separated from a strong central government in some major part because they had been unable to influence it in their favor, much less to control it, many American leaders were understandably wary, as Merrill Jensen has repeatedly emphasized, of creating something similar in America. More recently, Rakove has pointed out that this wariness rarely rose to the surface of public life during the early years of the War for Independence. But it was so deeply embedded in public consciousness as to be easily reactivated by those who, like North Carolina delegate Thomas Burke, had an especially intense fear of power and were anxious lest, in the absence of adequate restraints, the members of a national government "would make their own power as unlimited as they please." This suspicion and fear of central power meant that the grant of power to the central government in the first national union would necessarily be limited.[19]

The absence of positive examples in either theory or history constituted yet a third precondition that limited expectations and shaped attitudes about the form of a continental union. By 1787–88 assiduous scholars of the science of politics such as James Madison and James Wilson had analyzed existing literature on "Ancient & Modern Confederacies" exhaustively and systematically. By contrast, in the mid-1770s, no one was similarly prepared to put the problems of an extensive continental union in historical perspective. What American resistance leaders did know, however, discouraged all but a small minority from being very optimistic or thinking in grand terms.[20]

As Gordon S. Wood has observed, "few Americans thought that . . . an extensive continental republic, as distinct from a league of states, was feasible." This opinion derived in part from Montesquieu, the one reputable source of authority on the subject, who was of the opinion that liberty, as some later antifederalists phrased it, could not be preserved over an extensive territory "otherwise than by a confederation of republics, possessing all the powers of internal government, but united in the management of their general and foreign concerns," a theory that seemed to have been more than adequately borne out by the Americans' recent experience in the British Empire.[21]

Just as Montesquieu taught Americans that small republics linked together in a loose confederation had a better chance of surviving and preserving their citizens' liberty than large consolidated republics, so also did both historical and contemporary examples. The people who contrived the first American national union were familiar with the confederated governments of the United Provinces of the Netherlands and the league of Swiss cantons, each of which was a limited confederacy that reserved considerable local autonomy to its constituent parts. From the works of Sir William Temple and Abbé Reynall, they understood that each of these confederations had serious deficiencies. Yet their longevity constituted a strong recommendation for their limited grant of powers to the central government. Though some questioned the extent to which the Dutch had actually managed to preserve much liberty in their limited confederacy, these confederacies served as still further confirmation of the correctness of Montesquieu's belief that a confederation among republics was viable only with sharply restricted powers.[22]

A fourth precondition that inhibited the rapid formation of a permanent continental union was the almost total absence of any sense of American national consciousness. Right down to the actual break with Britain, colonial national consciousness had been intensely British. All over the colonies, Americans took pride in their incorporation into the larger Anglophone world. Their ability to identify themselves as "free Englishmen, inheriting the liberties," rights, and culture of all British subjects was, for them, essential to the maintenance of a positive sense of identity, and this "feeling of a community of values," traditions, language, religion, manners, interests, and identity between Britain and the colonies was powerfully enhanced by the colonies' close—and growing—commercial association with the metropolis. Certainly, as one contemporary observer remarked, even as late as the early 1760s the colonies were far more "directly connected with their Mother Country" than they were "with each other."[23]

It was therefore scarcely surprising, as Franklin observed in 1760, that the colonies "all love[d] Britain much more than they love[d] one another." By the middle decades of the eighteenth century, in fact, the colonists' pride in being British had, in Yehoshua Arieli's words, "all but obliterated" any "sense of separation and distinctiveness" that the colonists, especially New Englanders, might have felt earlier in the colonial period. There was not "a single true *New England* Man, in the whole Province," exclaimed the Reverend John Barnard in 1734 from Massachusetts, the colony that had been most resistant to the benefits of metropolitan imperialism, cultural as well as economic and political, during the seventeenth century, who did not "readily" subscribe to the belief that "that form of Civil Government is best for us, which we are under, I mean the *British Constitution*."[24]

This widespread identification with Britain and the British necessarily meant that, far from being exponents of American nationalism, the colonists exhibited "an intense personal affection, even reverence, for" British "leaders, institutions, and culture" and the most profound feelings of *British* nationalism. Nor were these feelings at any time more intense than in the 1760s during the wake of the Seven Years' War. That so much of that war had been fought in the colonies, that the metropolitan government had made such a major effort to defend the colonies, and that the colonies had themselves—for the very first time—made, as they were persuaded, a substantial contribution of money and manpower to such a great national cause increased the immediacy and strength of colonial ties with Britain and produced a surge of British patriotism among the colonists that found expression in the confident expectation that they were now finally— or would soon be—"upon an equal footing" with Englishmen at home.[25]

Even the long and bitter controversy during the 1760s and 1770s could not wholly eradicate this deep-seated American reverence for Britain. Throughout that controversy, as Samuel H. Beer has noted, the colonists "steadfastly claimed that they sought only freedom within the British empire, not freedom from it." "So strong has been their Attachment to Britain" that "the Abilities of a Child might have governed this country," Connecticut delegate Oliver Wolcott said in May 1776 in expressing his dismay over the ineptness of the British government's handling of the colonies over the previous few years.[26]

In early 1776, Thomas Paine endeavored in *Common Sense* to make Americans aware of the many social and cultural unities among them and to articulate a vision of America's potential as a united republican political society that would serve as an example for the rest of the world. But not even Paine's persuasive rhetoric and exhilarating vision of America's common destiny in occupying a place of the first importance in the unfolding course of human history could immediately produce a powerful, subsuming national consciousness of the kind usually connoted by the word *nationalism*. John Shy has shown that the War for Independence and, more especially, the behavior of the British army and the widespread popular participation in the war, contributed to a kind of "hothouse nationalism" and that the Revolution itself provided Americans with an instant common past. But it would be at least two further generations before most Americans would give a high priority to American, as opposed to their own state or regional, loyalties. Becoming visibly manifest only in the mid-1760s, the process by which Americans began to think of themselves as "a people" was still in a primitive stage of development between 1775 and 1787.[27]

The fifth, last, and in many respects most important precondition that significantly inhibited and affected the development of a continental union was the long existence of the several states as separate corporate entities. By the time of independence, every one of the thirteen colonies except Georgia had been in existence as a distinct corporate body for at least nine decades, and the oldest colonies in the Chesapeake and in New England went back to the early decades of the seventeenth century. Consisting of a well-defined body of territory, each of these colonies had its own peculiar constitution, institutions, laws, history, and identity, to which its inhabitants were, for the most part, both well socialized and strongly attached. As Andrew C. McLaughlin has remarked, the thirteen colonies were, in fact, "thirteen distinct groups of people."[28]

Throughout the colonial period, the members of each of these distinct groups identified and defined themselves not only as members of the greater British world of which they were a part but also by their common residence and collective experiences and associations as members of the clearly delineated and separate corporate bodies that each of the colonies was and had long been. If before the Declaration of Independence, none of these colonies was independent of Britain, they were, nonetheless, as many contemporary observers pointed out, wholly independent of each other.

That Americans thought of themselves as being organized into a series of independent corporate entities, each of which had its own specific identity and characteristics that it had every intention of preserving to the fullest possible extent, was evident throughout the controversy with Britain between 1764 and 1776. From the Stamp Act crisis onward, as McLaughlin has pointed out and as the three preceding chapters have underlined, Americans claimed both individual liberty and "local liberty within the British empire." They demanded recognition from the metropolitan government not just of the individual rights of Americans as Englishmen and as men but also "of the rights of the colonies, as bodies corporate, constituent members of the Empire."[29]

Similarly, delegates to the first and second Continental Congresses went off to defend not only individual rights but the corporate rights of the colonies—and they went as representatives not of the people at large but of the colonies, those ancient corporate entities that retained their distinctive identities and being through the rapid series of changes in government—from colonial to provisional revolutionary to state—in the mid-1770s. As Peter Onuf has emphasized, the integrity of the thirteen states as states was powerfully reinforced by the doctrine of state succession developed by revolutionary theorists to explain these changes. This doctrine saw the new independent state governments as successors to the old colonial governments in old political communities that, throughout the momentous events of 1775–76, remained fully intact. Far from producing a blank slate in politics, the transition from colony to state, according to this doctrine, actually reaffirmed the validity of the existing frameworks of statutory and customary law that had long defined the collective life of the colonies as distinct political communities.[30]

Historians have frequently cited Patrick Henry's famous declaration at the first Continental Congress in the fall of 1774 that "the distinctions between Virginians, Pennsylvanians, New Yorkers, and New Englanders are no more. I am not a Virginian, but an American." But few Americans managed to shed their provincial identities and acquire a new national one so rapidly. Their deep local patriotism, rooted in their intimate associations with their native or adopted colonies, continued to be manifest during the Revolution in a strong determination to preserve the identity, authority, and distinctiveness of the corporate entities to which they belonged. The difficulty of reconciling this determination with the desire to create a new national entity was perhaps the most perplexing single problem facing American resistance leaders in their efforts to create a lasting continental union.[31]

These five preconditions—(1) the widespread tendency to emphasize the differences among the colonies with a corresponding mutuality of suspicion among them, (2) fear of the aggrandizing tendencies of a remote central power, (3) existing theory about and contemporary examples of confederated republics, (4) the primitive state of American national consciousness, and (5) a strong sense in every colony of its identity as a distinctive corporate entity which it had an unquestioned commitment to preserve—either retarded the adoption of or set definite limits upon the shape and nature of a continental union during the late 1770s. At the same time, however, still other, and ultimately more powerful, long-range developments helped to predispose American leaders toward the creation of a new center in the form of a permanent national political union.

Certainly, the most important of those events was the remarkable social and cultural convergence experienced by the colonies beginning during the century before the Revolution. A series of diverse socioeconomic regions throughout most of the seventeenth and even into the early eighteenth century, the British settlements on the North American continent had moved ever closer together in the configuration of their socioeconomic and political life after 1720.

This growing convergence can be attributed to two overlapping processes that were simultaneously at work in all the colonies. For purposes of analysis, they may be crudely designated as processes of Americanization and Anglicization. Distance from Britain, the looseness of British controls, the (relatively) easy availability of land and other exploitable resources, and incorporation into the larger metropolitan economy and, increasingly, into the broad Atlantic trading system stretching from West Africa to the Caribbean in the south and North America to western Europe in the north all combined to produce levels of prosperity sufficient to support societies that were everywhere becoming more and more pluralistic, complex, differentiated, and developed. They also worked to stimulate the high levels of individual activity and expansiveness that underlay the remarkable economic and demographic growth that characterized all of the North American colonies through the middle decades of the eighteenth century.

If, as remarked Samuel Williams, whose *History of Vermont*, published during the last decade of the eighteenth century, was one of the first systematic analyses of the configuration of this emerging American society, a "similarity of situation and conditions" had gradually pushed the colonies toward a similitude of society and values, more specifically, toward "that natural, easy, independent situation, and spirit, in which the body of the [free] people were found, when the American war came on," still a second major influence—growing Anglicization—was important in helping to erode differences among the colonies.[32]

This development was partly the result of deliberate efforts by metropolitan authorities to bring the colonies under closer control after the Restoration. These efforts led both to the establishment of a common pattern of political institutions among the colonies and to an ever more intense involvement between metropolis and colonies in both the political and economic spheres. Together with an increasing volume of contacts among individuals and the improved communications that accompanied them, this growing involvement drew the colonists ever closer into the ambit of British life during the eighteenth century, provided them with easier and more direct access to English, Irish, and, increasingly, Scottish ideas and models of behavior, and tied them ever more closely to metropolitan culture.

As the ties with the metropolis thus tightened, the pull of metropolitan culture increased, and the standards of the metropolis more and more came to be the primary model for colonial behavior, the one certain measure of cultural achievement for these provincial societies at the outermost peripheries of the British world. Throughout the colonies, and especially among the emergent elites, there was a self-conscious effort to anglicize colonial life through the deliberate imitation of metropolitan institutions, values, and culture. Thus, before the mid-1770s, British-Americans thought of themselves primarily as Britons, albeit Britons overseas, and, contrary to the dominant opinion among earlier historians, colonial comparisons of the colonies with Britain did not usually come out in favor of the colonies. On the contrary, the colonists were far less interested in identifying and finding ways to express and to celebrate what was distinctively American about themselves than, insofar as possible, in eliminating those distinctions so that they might with more credibility think of themselves—and be thought of by people in Britain—as demonstrably British.[33]

As each of the colonies had become both more American and more British during the century previous to the American Revolution, as they increasingly assimilated to a common American social and behavioral pattern and to British cultural models, they became more and more alike. They shared similar institutions, a common identity as Britons overseas, a similar historical experience, a common political inheritance, the same political and social ideology, and similarly, though by no means equally, fragile structures of social and political authority. They were all becoming, to one degree or another, ever more complex and pluralistic societies, and they all had an upward trajectory of demographic and economic growth. As William Grayson would later remark, they also displayed a conspicuous "similarity of laws, religion, language, and manners."[34]

There were still obvious differences, many of them rooted in the distinctions between the slave-powered staple economies of the south and the mixed agricultural and commercial economies of the north, albeit when John Dickinson worried in July 1776 about the eventual dissolution of the American union, he drew the line not between north and south but between New England and the rest of the states. Whatever the continuing variety among the new American states and to whatever extent that variety continued to impress contemporaries, their interests, "Trade, Language, Customs, and Manners," Benjamin Rush could credibly insist in congressional debate during the summer of 1776, were by no means "more divided than they are among . . . people in Britain."[35]

This growing convergence was the single most important precondition for either the American Revolution or the emergence of an American national government and an American nationality. As the late David Potter has reminded us, however, social and "cultural similarities alone will not provide a basis of affinity between groups." Nationalism and similar collective loyalties, he points out, have to rest on "two psychological bases": the "feeling of a common culture *and* the feeling of common interest." "Of the two," he posits, "the concept of culture is, no doubt, of greater weight," but it cannot have its full effect without a mutual awareness of common interests.[36]

In the American case prior awareness of a common interest was a second necessary precondition even for a clear and full recognition of the existence of a common culture. As several scholars have argued, the emergence during the middle decades of the eighteenth century of intercolonial trading patterns and communications networks, an interlocking elite, closer interurban ties, and common participation between 1739 and 1763 in two wars against the neighboring colonies of foreign metropolitan powers resulted in the colonies becoming increasingly more interested in one another and perhaps even in the development of some nascent sense of American community. This development was in turn stimulated to some degree by the metropolitan penchant, especially evident during the midcentury intercolonial wars, for treating the continental colonies as a unit and describing them under the common rubric *American*. Perhaps the most important point that can be made about the Albany Plan of Union in the early 1750s, which seems not to have been appreciated by anybody at the time, was not that it was universally rejected but that it had been proposed and adopted by a conference of leaders in the first place. For its mere initiation manifested at least a rudimentary consciousness of the existence of some basis for an "American" union.[37]

But Americans did not yet fully understand nor attach any special importance to the many and growing commonalities among them— as opposed to the similarities that linked them all to Britain—until the metropolis vividly impressed upon them that they had a common interest by challenging their pretensions to an equal status with Britons at home by the new tax and other restrictive measures between 1763 and 1776. In pointing out the seemingly vast differences among the colonies and stressing the extent to which those differences made united action improbable, Franklin had warned metropolitans in 1760, in words echoed both by himself and by many later observers, that a "grievous tyranny and oppression" might very well drive the colonies to unite. During the 1760s, many Americans had pointed out, as did Richard Henry Lee of Virginia, that the colonists' attachment to Britain could be preserved "on no other terms . . . than by a free intercourse and equal participation of good offices, liberty and free constitution of government." But Lee's point was appreciated, virtually alone within Britain's political establishment, by Edmund Burke when he pointed out that America's affection for Britain had always been conditional upon its continuing ability to carry "the mark of a free people in all" its "internal concerns" and to retain at least "the image of the British constitution."[38]

Britain's insistence upon treating the colonies as separate and unequal in the 1760s and 1770s was thus the contingent development that, in the words of Yehoshua Arieli, provided the "point of observation and comparison from which" the colonists could finally come to appreciate the many unities among them. Increasingly during those years, they came to comprehend that, given existing attitudes among those in power in Britain, membership in the British Empire did not mean, for them, the equality as freeborn Englishmen to which they had so long aspired. Rather, it meant an inferior status equivalent, in the bitter words of Alexander Hamilton in 1774, only to those unworthy people in Britain who were "in so mean a situation" that they were "supposed to have no will of their own" and, according to Sir William Blackstone, therefore deserved no role in governing themselves.[39]

As the colonists slowly came to this comprehension, they gradually began to lose their British nationalism and to develop, as grounds for asserting their own worthiness against their metropolitan antagonists, an awareness of their common interest in resisting metropolitan efforts to place them in a subordinate, unequal, and un-British status. They developed as well an understanding of the common histories of the colonies as asylums for the oppressed and places where unfortunates could make new beginnings and of the many social and cultural similarities among them. Only then did they begin to acquire some sense of their possible "future power and imperial greatness" as a separate American people and to glimpse the potential for a comprehensive American political union.[40]

Still a third precondition that propelled leaders of American resistance toward a national union was their deep-seated and residual fear of disorder. Almost to a man, they took pride in the Anglo-Americans' devotion to liberty. But they knew from history and their own experience that the line between liberty and licentiousness was thin, and they worried that the notorious weakness of authority in America might under certain conditions lead to the breakdown of political institutions. Although the extent and depth of such fears varied from place to place according to the strength of local political institutions and the cohesiveness of local elites, they had clearly been in part behind the powerful anglicizing impulses among the colonies' emerging elites throughout the eighteenth century and had actually functioned as a powerful deterrent to revolution during the period from 1763 to 1776.[41]

One of the most evident manifestations of these fears in the pre-revolutionary period had been the belief that the British connection was essential to the continued political stability of the colonies. "We think ourselves happier . . . in being dependent on Great Britain, than in a state of independence," said an anonymous writer in the *New York Mercury* in 1764, "for then the disputes amongst ourselves would throw us into all the confusion, and bring on us all the calamities usually attendant on civil wars." Given the weakness of authority in the colonies, many people feared with John Dickinson that without Britain's central controlling power Anglo-America would quickly degenerate into "a multitude of Commonwealths, Crimes and Calamities—centuries of mutual Jealousies, Hatreds, Wars and Devastations, until at last the exhausted Provinces shall sink into Slavery under the yoke of some fortunate conqueror."[42]

During the uncertain situation that obtained after 1774, such anxieties quickly translated into powerful fears of division and disunion and pushed congressional delegates more and more toward the view that a national union was essential not simply to coordinate resistance and war against Britain but to prevent internal chaos. At the time of the first Continental Congress, Joseph Galloway, later a loyalist, was one of the few to voice openly his anxieties about the ill effects that might arise from the absence of a central controlling authority, without which, he observed in urging his fellow delegates to support his proposed plan of union, the colonies would be "destitute of any supreme direction or decision whatever, even to the settlement of differences among themselves."[43]

With war and independence, however, virtually all delegates from the most cautious to the boldest agreed that "Disunion among ourselves," as Witherspoon declared, was "the greatest Danger We have" and that a formal union was absolutely essential not just to prosecute the war but, in the words of Richard Henry Lee, to secure "internal peace." "Two contrary powers, of any kind whatever, that act against and oppose each other," warned the Connecticut minister Enoch Huntington in 1776, "can have no other tendency but to destroy each other's force": "In all bodies of men and civil communities whether great or small, whether considered as kingdoms, provinces, cities, towns, or still lesser societies, even particular private houses, and families," he observed, "their strength and stability is in proportion to their union; and disunion and division have the most fatal and destructive tendency."[44]

In the uncertain situation produced by independence, the threat of division and disunion seemed especially acute. "The Inhabitants of every Colony," complained Edward Rutledge, a delegate from South Carolina, "consider[ed] themselves at Liberty to do as they please[d] upon almost every occasion." Only a formal and lasting continental union, as Gouverneur Morris had earlier suggested, could be certain to "restrain the democratic spirit, which the constitutions and the local circumstances of the country had so long fostered in the minds of the people" throughout the colonies. If the colonies remained "separate and disunited, after this war," predicted Witherspoon in urging a formal confederation upon Congress, "we may be sure of coming off the worse." Victory over Britain would surely be followed by "a more lasting war, a more unnatural, more bloody, and more hopeless war, among the colonies themselves."[45]

A corollary of this fear of disunion and discord and still a fourth major precondition that strongly predisposed American resistance leaders toward a permanent continental union was the growing realization during the war that a national government with general superintending power was perhaps the only certain guarantee of the corporate territorial integrity of the individual states. A variety of conflicting interests over boundaries, land claims, navigation rights, and trade pitted the several states against one another, and revolutionary leaders quickly came to understand that no state could effectually claim any more than "other states were willing to recognize." To the rather great extent that, in Peter Onuf's words, "mutual recognition" thus became "the ultimate legitimating source of statehood claims," the very existence of the states as states, contemporaries slowly came to comprehend, depended upon their general association in Congress.[46]

Yet a fifth—and final—precondition pushing revolutionaries toward union was their long-standing involvement with the de facto federal system of government in the British Empire. Notwithstanding metropolitan theory that Britain and its colonies constituted a single unitary state in which sovereignty—ultimate unqualified authority—lay in the metropolitan government, the empire, as previous chapters have shown, had, throughout its first century and a half, functioned as a federal polity. As the New York lawyer William Smith, Jr., observed in the mid-1760s, constitutional arrangements within the empire had gradually drifted into a situation in which there was in fact a "*manifold . . . Partition,* of the *Legislative* Authority of the Empire" with virtually all internal matters being handled by the governments of the respective colonies and most external affairs by the metropolitan government. In the later words of John Witherspoon, the empire was "a federal" and not "an incorporating Union," the colonies having always been independent "of the people or Parliament of England."[47]

When American resistance leaders took their first concrete steps toward the creation of a continental political system in 1774–76, they simply followed this traditional distribution of authority. If, as many scholars have noted, "theory . . . powerfully directed" the work of the people who fashioned and pushed through the Federal Constitution of 1787–88, experience and exigency were much more evident in shaping the earliest national political system under both the Continental Congress and the Articles of Confederation. The Americans' experience in the old empire had accustomed them to living in a political system in which there were functionally two interdependent levels of government, each with its own sphere of authority. Reinforced beginning in 1775 by the palpable fact that resistance and war, general activities that "from the *necessity of the case* . . . . could not well be exercised" by the individual states, required central direction, this experience also produced a strong disposition to recreate in their new national situation a system in which political authority was similarly allocated.[48]

In view of their long experience with a divided structure of authority, it is not surprising, as Rakove has found, that, far from being "central to the burgeoning Revolutionary . . . controversy between anti-Federalists and continentalists," as Merrill Jensen and, more recently, Richard B. Morris have affirmed, the question of sovereignty, the question to which metropolitan protagonists had insisted on reducing the prerevolutionary debate over the nature of the constitution of the empire, "was never directly raised" in 1775–76. In fact, "political exigencies imposed [such] powerful limits on the sweep [and, one might add, depth] of formal constitutional thought" that not even the problem of the proper allocation of authority "was at first . . . carefully examined." Even the intense theoretical discussion in 1776–77 of the form of the new republican state governments included little consideration of the relationship of those governments to Congress or to a permanent national union. Indeed, by absorbing so much of the attention of resistance leaders it actually operated to ensure that "the precise nature of congressional power" would be given "relatively little" attention. "Basic issues," Rakove shows, "were neither clearly posed nor well understood," and congressional discussions of confederation "tended, like other issues, to be more deeply influenced by the demands of resistance."[49]

In this situation, the federal structure of the new nation simply evolved out of the colonists' experience in the empire and the need to meet the conditions of the war. Throughout this process, as Onuf has noted, "American experience in the empire remained paradigmatic." Much as in the history of the empire, a working division of power between Congress and the states along the lines that had obtained in the empire quickly took shape. In accord with the constitutional arguments Americans had articulated between 1764 and 1776, individual states retained full control over their "internal police or domestic concerns," and Congress exercised the general "superintending power" required "to adjust disputes between Colonies, regulate the affairs of trade, war, peace, alliances," and otherwise attend to the "many general regulations to which the provincial legislatures will not be competent."[50]

Indeed, as Rakove has shown, in view of the intense suspicion of a remote central power exhibited by American leaders both during the years preceding independence and in the 1780s, American leaders showed remarkably little aversion during the first years of the war to endowing Congress with "legislative and administrative responsibilities unprecedented in the colonial past." At that point, Rakove notes, Congress still commanded a degree of deference that "left it immune from close theoretical scrutiny." Perhaps more important, resistance leaders of all political persuasions seemed to have assumed, virtually without question, the continuation of the pragmatic division of power that had taken shape during the early years of resistance, a division that had evolved, like that of the British Empire, without formal codification and that saw the states handling all matters internal to them while Congress was "endowed with substantial authority over matters of general concern." The difference between a formal confederation and the existing union, John Adams blithely declared in April 1776, would be no greater than "that between an express and an implied Contract."[51]

In the mid-1770s, four powerful long-range preconditions—an increasing social and cultural convergence among the colonies; a developing awareness of a common interest in opposing metropolitan efforts to curtail colonial rights and privileges; fears of both disunion and the fragility of authority in American society; and an emerging recognition that a national government was necessary to guarantee the integrity of the several states—thus combined with short-term pressures created by war and the colonists' earliest experiences with united action to push American resistance leaders in the direction of a permanent national continental union, while a fifth precondition—their experience with a multitiered government in the empire—predisposed them toward a federal union. Simultaneously, the five preconditions discussed earlier—mutual suspicions and sharpened perceptions of differences, mistrust of distant power, available theories and models of federal organization, absence of national consciousness, and the long-standing existence of the states as distinctive corporate entities—made the actual codification of the ad hoc federal structure that had taken shape in 1774–76 extremely difficult.

Precisely how difficult was revealed with the very first effort to devise a suitable plan of confederation beginning in June 1776. On the surface, immediate issues involving representation, expenses, and western lands seemed to be most troublesome. Lurking behind all of these issues, however, was the old imperial problem of specifying a clear division of power among the two existing spheres of authority that would give the central government sufficient power to meet its responsibilities without compromising the political integrity of the individual states.

Although it clearly did not, as Edward Rutledge charged, destroy "all Provincial [state] Distinctions" and by no means sought to consolidate the states "into one unitary polity," the original plan of confederation drawn up by John Dickinson in mid-1776, which, in Rakove's words "clearly intended to use confederation as a vehicle not only for defining the powers of Congress, but also for limiting the authority of the states," gave much too extensive powers to Congress to satisfy the majority of the delegates. The changes in Dickinson's plan made by Congress in the summer of 1776 and subsequently incorporated into the draft of the Articles of Confederation approved by Congress for submission to the states in November 1777 signaled an intention to divide the "effective powers of government . . . into two general spheres of authority, with the respective functions of Congress and the states clearly and exclusively distinguished" roughly according to the by then familiar distinction between external and internal, general and provincial realms.[52]

What was remarkable throughout this initial phase in the creation of an American national union is that the location of sovereignty, the issue that has received so much stress from modern historians, was so little emphasized by contemporaries. Much more interested in the practical problem of allocating power between the national and the state governments, members of Congress failed "to give serious attention" to that issue. Even when Thomas Burke, the North Carolina delegate, raised it explicitly in Congress in early 1777, few of his colleagues exhibited much interest in pursuing it. Persisting fears of disunion and military exigencies continued to combine to produce a settled determination among the vast majority of delegates to avoid systematic consideration of the nature of the federal system they were creating. Indeed, by the time Congress took up the Articles for final adoption in June and July 1778, the dangers of not establishing a formal confederation appeared to be "of such momentous consequence" that it refused even to adopt any of the many amendments proposed by the states.[53]

Rakove concludes on the basis of this evidence that before the end of the War for Independence, few Americans seemed to be "deeply interested in the nature of the union they were forming." If, however, Congress "never directly raised" the question of sovereignty in 1775–76 and, in the interest of the war effort, systematically avoided it thereafter, the Articles of Confederation contained an implicit—and ambiguous—answer to that question. Article 2 specified that "Each State retains its sovereignty, freedom and independence." As Rakove has emphasized, however, the practical division of authority established by the Articles effectively "meant that, in their separate spheres, both Congress and the states were to exercise certain functions of sovereign government, and that a division of sovereignty was [therefore] implicit in the structure of American federalism from its very inception."[54]

Productive of enormous confusion, this ambiguity was always a potential source of conflict during the war. Optimists hoped that the states would continue to accept congressional authority and to put up with "considerable local Disadvantages" in return for the many benefits derived from confederation and that the Confederation would, in the words of David Ramsay, a young enthusiastic exponent of a "continental liberality," prove capable of providing "us the strength and protection of a power equal to the greatest [nation]; at the same time that, in all our internal concerns, we have the freedom of small independent Commonwealths." From 1778 on, however, there was a growing tendency among some delegates to Congress to emphasize the potential conflicts between congressional and state authority. They opposed acts of Congress on the grounds that they "step[ped] over that constitutional line which has been chaulked out to them" by the Confederation and, literally interpreting the language of Article 2, insisted upon regarding Congress as nothing more than "the united Council of the free, Independent, Sovereign States of America" whose resolutions could not possibly "superceed the Law of a *Sovereign* State."[55]

Nor during the closing years of the war did Congress offer much resistance to this tendency. By voluntarily giving up the power to emit paper money and "gradually surrendering or throwing upon the several States the exercise of powers they should have retained and to their utmost have exercised themselves," Congress, Ezekiel Cornell wrote Nathanael Greene in July 1780, was so far from manifesting "the most distant wish for more powers" that it seemed rather to "wish to see their States without control (as the term is) free, sovereign, and independent."[56]

Congress's growing deference to state authority resulted in a dramatic growth of state and a rapid decline in congressional power during the early 1780s. "The situation of Congress," James Madison wrote Thomas Jefferson in May 1780, "has undergone a total change from what it originally was. Whilst they exercised the indefinite power of emitting money on the credit of their constituents they had the whole wealth and resources of the continent within their command, and could go on with their affairs independently and as they pleased," Madison observed, but since Congress had eschewed that power it had become "as dependent on the States as the King of England is on the parliament." Joseph Jones wrote George Washington in a similar vein a month later that Congress had "scarce a power left but such as concerns foreign transactions." Even with regard to the army, he reported, Congress had become "little more than the medium through which the wants of the army are conveyed to the States." "All that Congress can do in future," Madison predicted, "will be to administer public affairs with prudence vigor and oeconomy." In Washington's phrase, "one head [was] gradually changing into thirteen."[57]

If, as Gordon Wood has noted, the war years yielded no theoretical advance over the formulations of Blackstone with regard to the problem of the location of sovereignty and if that problem was still only "imperfectly understood" at the end of the war, the direction of development thus seemed to be strongly toward predominance of the states over the national government. The American experiment in federal government seemed to be heading precisely in the direction metropolitan protagonists had predicted the British Empire would go if colonial constitutional claims were accepted: in the steady diminution of central authority and its progressive and centrifugal dissipation into the hands of the provincial governments. Whether this tendency could be altered, whether a viable balance between national and provincial authority ever could be achieved and the continental union preserved as something more than a tenuous alliance among independent states, was a paramount question confronting the leaders of the United States at the conclusion of the war in 1783.[58]

During most of the present century, historians have assumed that the national government was actually the creation of thirteen sovereign states which retained all those powers they did not delegate to Congress. Since the publication of a seminal article by Curtis P. Nettels in 1960, however, this "contract theory" of the formation of the American national union has been replaced by a new orthodoxy. Following Nettels, Richard B. Morris, Samuel H. Beer, and Jack N. Rakove have each in turn attested to the validity of a national theory of the origins of American federalism by which the national government "existed and functioned before the birth of any state" and "the source of authority for the various acts initiated by the congress was 'the inhabitants of the several colonies, whom we represent.'" According to this interpretation, Congress as well as the states were the creation of "a single sovereign power, the people of the United States," and Congress "alone possessed those attributes of external sovereignty which entitled" the United States "to be called a state in the international sense while the separate States, possessing a limited or internal sovereignty, may rightly be considered a creation of the Continental Congress, which preceded them in time and brought them into being."[59]

But neither the old nor the new orthodoxy on this point seems to be an adequate description of what happened. To be sure, Congress existed before any of the new independent state governments. But these new state governments were merely the creations and the newest political instruments of old corporate entities, each of which preserved its own well-defined territory and collective legal identity as it moved rapidly in 1775–76 through a series of statuses from colony to provincial revolutionary society to independent state. These distinctive corporate entities certainly preceded the existence of a new continental one.

Of course, Congress portrayed itself in various public documents from September 1774 onward as representing "the inhabitants of the several colonies," and during the debates over confederation a few delegates even argued that Congress should represent people rather than states. But this view was strongly and successfully opposed at the time by those who, with Roger Sherman, insisted that "we are rep[resentative]s of States, not Individuals." Behind this view of Congress as an assemblage of representatives of the states and not of the people at large was the assumption, made explicit by Witherspoon, that "Every Colony is a distinct Person." Congress may have directed the colonies to form new state governments. But, Witherspoon thus implied, each of them retained its ancient legal identity as a distinctive corporate entity. In all probability, this view was strongly reinforced by the actual process of state constitution making in 1776 and 1777, which had given explicit definition to and reaffirmation of the authority and legal identity of the states.[60]

The triumph of the view represented by Sherman and Witherspoon was evident as delegates to Congress continued to be selected by the state governments both before and after the adoption of the Articles of Confederation, which were ratified not by the people at large but by the states. The "Provincial Distinctions" cherished by so many of the delegates would not be obliterated by the Articles of Confederation, and the first American national union would thus be not, as Beer has argued, representational but territorial and corporate, its source of authority lying not, as recent scholars have suggested, in the people of the United States but in the states as corporate entities, which retained their separate identities and legal authority throughout the transition from colonies to states, from membership in the British Empire to membership in the new United States.[61]

As it had developed within the colonies before 1770, American government, as Beer has argued, was fundamentally government by consent as opposed to the "Old Whig constitution" in England, which was not representational but hierarchical and corporatist. To an important degree, however, America's first *national* government was to be a throwback to the old Whig constitution. It would represent the territorial and legal corporations of the states, not the people at large.[62]

But this is emphatically not to suggest that the older compact theory of the origins of American federalism whereby a group of sovereign states came together to create a national government is correct. If few in Congress before the early 1780s intended to annihilate the identities of the individual states, yet, as Rakove has argued with great cogency, Congress had all along been "a national government" exerting an extraordinary degree of authority over the separate states. Moreover, the framers of the Articles of Confederation revealed their conscious intention to perpetuate this arrangement by vesting "certain sovereign powers in Congress" and subordinating "the states to its decisions."[63]

During the war, most delegates probably agreed with William Henry Drayton that Congress should have no power that could "with propriety, be exercised by the several states." But the declaration in Article 2 of the Articles of Confederation that "Each State retained its sovereignty, freedom and independence" was, ultimately, a fiction. As Rufus King would point out in the Philadelphia Convention in 1787, the states, under the Articles, lacked many of the fundamental attributes of sovereignty: "They could not make war, nor peace, nor alliances, nor treaties." On paper at least, the Articles of Confederation, as Gordon Wood has correctly remarked, "made the league of states as cohesive and strong as any similar sort of republican confederation in history." In doing so, the Articles simply gave formal sanction to an existing arrangement.[64]

The process by which the American union was formed is thus too complicated to support either a national or a compact theory of its origins. The Continental Congress gathered to itself broad powers at the same time that the colonies as old and continuing corporate entities were changing themselves into states. What was clear throughout was that from the first Continental Congress on the national union had involved a division of authority in which Congress and the states both exercised powers normally associated with sovereign governments. Inherited from the British Empire, such a division was thus "inherent in the nature of American union from the start" and, as McLaughlin long ago pointed out, was perpetuated by the Articles of Confederation, which sought to specify the boundaries between Congress and the state governments "with considerable precision."[65]

Chapter Nine

In Quest of a Republican Empire: Creating a New Center, 1783–1788

"In the interval between the commencement of the Revolution and the final ratification of" the Articles of Confederation in 1781, observed James Madison in 1800, "the nature and extent of the Union was determined by the circumstances of the crisis, rather than by any accurate delineation of the general authority." The states retained full jurisdiction over their internal affairs, but throughout the early years of the war, power flowed into the center. Considering itself "as vested with full power *to preserve the republic from harm*," Congress, as Alexander Hamilton later noted, performed "many of the highest acts of sovereignty, which were always chearfully submitted too [by the states]—the declaration of independence, the declaration of war, the levying an army, creating a navy, emitting money, making alliances with foreign powers." To an important degree, the Articles of Confederation represented an attempt to codify this situation by investing Congress with broad general powers and leaving the several states in charge of all matters of local concern.[1]

But the Articles provided no mechanism by which Congress could force the states to comply with its authority, and, as the war dragged on, power tended to drain out of the center to the peripheries, from Congress to the state governments. Moreover, as the war wound down and the necessity for united efforts against an external power correspondingly diminished in 1781–82, this process was accelerated. In the early modern British Empire the peripheries had found themselves on the defensive against the aggressive power of the center; under the Articles, it was precisely the opposite: the center found itself without sufficient authority to preserve the general interests of the United States against the power of the several states.[2]

A PROBLEM RESOLVED, 1776–1788

Such an arrangement was, perhaps, the logical outcome of colonial constitutional arguments between 1764 and 1776. From the mid-1760s through 1787, "the emergence of the political community itself as the locus of authority" had been, as Peter Onuf has put it, "the central theme of American constitutionalism." "While independence was accompanied by the formal inversion of 'sovereignty' above—in the king-in-parliament—to below—in the community at large—the relation of [the colonial] assembly [or, after 1776, the state legislature] to [the] community," Onuf points out, "was not essentially altered." Through the Revolution and beyond, those legislatures "continued to defend and guarantee local rights" as well as to exert broad authority over all matters of local concern.[3]

Winning independence in 1783 thus effectively secured for Americans the original goal of the Revolution—local control over local affairs; but this achievement had not been accompanied by an effort even explicitly to confront, much less to resolve, "the underlying theoretical and practical problem of how to combine" the individual states "into an effective union." The Revolution, in short, had left the "organization of power in the United States" in a thoroughly ambiguous state. The effort to resolve this ambiguity, to solve the ancient problem of how in an extended polity to distribute authority between the center and the peripheries, was the primary focus of American constitutional thought during the 1780s. How that problem was perceived and resolved is the subject of this chapter.[4]

Well before the end of the war, between the adoption of the Articles in 1778 and their approval by the states in 1781, many men in Congress and other positions of responsibility in the central government had decided that the structure of governance established by the Articles was deeply flawed. The Connecticut delegate Jesse Root succinctly identified the major problem in December 1780. "The system of government over these States as at present exercised is extremely defective," he wrote Governor Jonathan Trumbull in words similar of those of many other congressmen: "Having no permanent funds in its possession, nor the means of establishing any," the "sovereign power of war and peace," Root observed, "must feel itself weak and prevent or defeat almost every measure however necessary and render the execution languid, tardy and oft times wholly abortive. The wealth of the States constitutes the great fund on which we must depend for credit abroad and for resources at home," he continued, but "while these are drawn forth at the volition of each State, by recommendatory requisitions only, it is in the power of any State to defeat the most important measure."[5]

To make them "adequate to the great objects of the Confederacy," the Articles obviously needed major amendments. "The existence of a power (if it can be called such) constituted for national purposes, especially for directing the affairs of a war, not possessing any constitutional authority to command the smallest portion of property," declared the Connecticut congressional delegation in January 1781, was "scarcely conceivable" and must, added Oliver Wolcott, be a complete "novelty in the history of mankind." "Power without revenue in political society," agreed Hamilton, was nothing more than "a name." The only solution, it seemed to these people, was to provide Congress with authority either to raise some revenues independent of the states or to coerce the states to comply with its revenue demands.[6]

For people at the center, both the problem and the solution seemed so obvious that it was difficult for them to conceive how it could fail of satisfactory resolution. As nothing more than a "great republic" of thirteen "States or political persons" formed for their own "mutual interest and security" in which each state constituted "one member or subject, over which Congress" had been "appointed to preside," the union, it seemed clear to such people, had to have "powers of coercion over the particular States for the general purposes of the confederacy." "So far from infringing upon the rights or sovereignty of the particular States," such powers, they believed, would give Congress no authority over the states that was not already exercised by each state over its "citizens for the weal of the State." For Congress to have at least that much authority appeared to be every bit "as necessary for the preservation of" the states as was "the union itself." Not enabling Congress "to draw forth in some Just proportion the Resources of the several Branches of the federal Union," James Duane predicted, could only "terminate in the common ruin." Either the state legislatures "must resign a portion of their Authority to the national Representative" or they might very well "cease to be Legislatures." Without "a strong federal Constitution," declared Richard Peters, there would be nothing "to keep the great States from destroying the lesser ones."[7]

As the more penetrating advocates of constitutional reform appreciated, however, the problem was not merely structural and not, therefore, easily resolved. The roots of congressional weakness went far deeper, and no one analyzed them with more penetration than Hamilton in his letters and in a series of essays entitled "The Continentalist" and published in the *New-York Packet, and the American Advertiser* in 1781–82. In Hamilton's view, one of the main lessons Americans should have learned as a result of their brief experiment with federal government was that its effects and tendencies were radically different from those that obtained in unitary states. Whereas in unitary states, the primary danger was that the sovereign would have "too much power to oppress the parts of which it" consisted, in a federal government, composed of different states, "each with a government completely organised within itself" and with "all the means to draw its subjects to a close dependence on itself," the danger was "directly the reverse": specifically, "that the common sovereign" would "not have power sufficient to unite the different members together, and direct the common forces to the interest and happiness of the whole."[8]

From his observations of the experience of the United States under the Articles, Hamilton cited several interrelated tendencies to explain why, in federal governments, member states exhibited a greater impulse to aggrandize power than did the central government. At the same time that each state showed itself to be far "more disposed to advance its own authority upon the ruins of that of the Confederacy, than to make any improper concessions in its favour," Hamilton noted, "the subjects of each member" were invariably "more devoted in their attachments and obedience to their own particular governments, than to that of the union." Added to these general tendencies, according to Hamilton, was the "excess[ive] . . . spirit of liberty which . . . made the particular states show a jealousy of all power not in their hands." A logical extension of the suspicions of the metropolitan government that had long animated colonial leaders and had been given even more intensity by developments between 1764 and 1776, this "extreme jealousy of power" had, moreover, evoked a corresponding desire on the part of the states "of monopolizing all power in themselves."[9]

In the views of Hamilton and people of similar persuasion the effects of these tendencies were all undesirable. By encouraging that "narrow disposition," that "attachment to State Views, State Interests and State Prejudices," they led directly to the progressive enervation of "the government of the union" and to a degree of "constitutional imbecillity" that, Hamilton was persuaded, "must be apparent to every man of reflection." No less important, the "numberless embarassments" caused by the states' repeated encroachments on the authority of Congress both vividly underlined the failure of the Articles to establish "a proper line" between state and national authority and made it clear that those "national principles from whence union and force" might "be derived" had not yet even been identified, much less "properly established."[10]

Whether such principles might ever be established, whether, in the words of Madison, "prosperity and tranquility, [or confusion and disunion]" would "be the fruits of the Revolution," was thus very much an open and—for people attached to the center and animated by a vision of American national greatness—a vital question at the end of the war. Some confidently believed that the "dangers and distresses" experienced during the war had so "opened the Eyes of the People" as to make constitutional reform inevitable. Others were far less optimistic. Madison worried as early as November 1781 lest "the present Union . . . but little survive the present war," and events immediately following the end of the war did not allay such fears. Because it had been founded on little more than "an occasional friendship, resulting from our being involved in a common calamity, and the necessity we were under of uniting in means and measures, for our mutual defence and deliverance," the union, an anonymous writer declared in 1784, "must necessarily dissolve" once the occasion that had produced it had been eliminated. Charles Thomson, longtime secretary to Congress, agreed with this assessment. "The common danger which has hitherto held these states together now being removed," he lamented in July 1783, "I see local prejudices, passions and views already beginning to operate with all their force. And I confess I have my fears, that the predictions of our enemies will be found true, that on the removal of common danger our Confederacy & Union will be a rope of sand."[11]

Peace was a signal for advocates of constitutional reform to press their case for giving, in George Washington's words, "such a tone to our federal government, as will enable it to answer the ends of its institution." Most important, they proposed to grant Congress authority to levy moderate land or capitation taxes or to levy duties on foreign imports, the last having the double advantage of both providing the federal government with an independent source of revenue and giving it sufficient power over trade regulations to prevent trade wars and other debilitating forms of economic competition among the states. As early as November 1784, delegates to Congress were discussing the possibility of a special convention to consider these and other measures designed "to enable Congress to execute with more energy, effect & vigor, the powers assigned to it, than it appears by experience that they can do under the present state of things."[12]

Although few political figures probably disagreed with the proposition that, as Madison phrased it, a "Union of the States" was "essential to their safety ag[ain]st foreign danger & internal contention," the immediate postwar years saw no exigencies sufficient to overcome the powerful centrifugal tendencies inherent in the American union and to propel the country in the direction of major constitutional reform. Congress frequently debated specific amendments to the Articles and twice proposed changes that would have given it authority to levy an impost. But both of these measures failed to obtain the unanimous consent of the states as required by the Articles. As a result, these years, as Gordon Wood has shown, were marked not by an augmentation of federal authority but by a strong reassertion of state power. In turn, this development produced an intensification of that traditional, one might almost say endemic, distrust of remote central power that had been so strongly manifest in the controversy with Britain in the 1760s and early 1770s and would be such a conspicuous feature of the debate over the Constitution of 1787.[13]

Advocates of constitutional reform found this fear of power both difficult to comprehend and misguided. "To *me*," declared Washington in October 1785, "it is a solecism in politics: indeed it is one of the most extraordinary things in nature, that we should confederate as a Nation, and yet be afraid to give the rulers of that nation, who are the creatures of our [own] making, appointed for a limited and short duration, and who are amenable for every action, and recallable at any moment, and are subject to all the evils which they may be instrumental in producing, sufficient powers to order and direct the affairs of the same." "Upon every occasion," Hamilton fumed fourteen months later, "we hear a loud cry raised about the danger of intrusting power to Congress, we are told it is dangerous to trust power any where; that *power* is liable to *abuse* with a variety of trite maxims of the same kind." Perhaps it was equally true, he added in reemphasizing one of his earliest insights into the defects of the Articles, "that too little power is as dangerous as too much, that it leads to anarchy, and from anarchy to despotism."[14]

Such proponents of the enhancement of central authority preferred to think of themselves as men who had risen above the "Illiberality, Jealousy, and local policy" represented by their opponents, and they depicted the contest in which they were engaged as one between responsible men of expansive vision and men of narrow experience who, "unaccustomed to consider the interests of the State[s] as they are interwoven with those of the Confederacy," opposed all measures for strengthening the union either because they did not understand the necessity for a more energetic union to guarantee the integrity of the separate states or because the defense of local authority was politically popular in the states. Notwithstanding all their doubts about "the perpetuity & efficacy of the present system" and all their railings against the "local and selfinteresting" behavior of their opponents, however, advocates of a stronger union could do little in the years just after the war to prevent the central government from degenerating into what Washington called "a name without substance" or to keep Congress from becoming little more than "a vagabond, strolling, contemptible Crew," a "nugatory body" whose ordinances bound the states no longer "than it suits *present* purposes."[15]

The result of these developments was "so great a relaxation in the Confoederal springs" that some people began to doubt whether "the machine [could] . . . be long kept in motion, unless great & effectual repairs are made." Although some leaders continued to emphasize the extent to which "the intimate connections of these states, the similitude of governments, situations, customs, [and] manners" worked in favor of a perpetuation of the union, others began to question "whether our Union is natural; or rather whether the Dispositions and Views of the several Parts of the Continent are so similar as that they can and will be happy under the same Form of Government." As men more and more considered the degree to which "the interests of the different parts of the Union were different from each other," supporters of the American experiment in federal government increasingly began to fear that the Confederation would soon break up into two or three small, rival, perhaps even warring, confederacies.[16]

If during the war Americans had "avoided debate about the nature of American federalism," the end of the war effectively removed all inhibitions to such discussions. As a consequence, the problem of the location of sovereignty, which had "remained academic" in the late 1770s, quickly became an important "practical issue" in the 1780s and throughout the decade remained at the center of the intensifying discussion of the desirability of constitutional reform.[17]

In this discussion, proponents of a stronger union might insist that sovereignty had always resided in Congress. In support of their claim, they pointed to the Declaration of Independence, which, in claiming for the United States "full power to . . . do all . . . acts and things that independent states may of right do," had "not even mentioned" the "several states . . . by name in any part of it." "As if it was intended to impress this maxim on America, that our freedom and independence arose from our union, and that without it we could neither be free nor independent," this omission seemed to prove, as Charles Pinckney subsequently declared, both that "the separate independence and individual sovereignty of the several states were not even thought of by the enlightened band of patriots who framed" that document and, as Hamilton argued, "that the United States had in their origin full power to do all acts and things which independent states may of right do; or, in other words, full power of sovereignty."[18]

Not just the language of the Declaration but the subsequent conduct of political affairs seemed, to people of this persuasion, to support their claims. Throughout the early years of the war, Congress had proceeded, with the full approval of the states, to "levy war, contract alliances, and exercise other high powers of sovereignty." Assuming, with John Witherspoon, that under the empire sovereignty had resided in the crown, they thus contended that the Revolution had been "begun and the war . . . carried on by the united and joint efforts of the thirteen States" and that "by their joint exertions and not by those of any one State the dominion of Great Britain" had been "broken, and consequently [that] the rights claimed and exercised by the crown," including the right of sovereignty, "devolved on the United States" as a whole, and not on the individual states.[19]

Although they admitted that the adoption of the Articles had brought about "an abridgment of the original sovereignty of the union," even that document, they insisted, had placed "the exclusive right of war and peace in the United States in Congress" as well as "the sole power of making treaties with foreign nations." Pointing out that these powers were "among the first rights of sovereignty," they argued that, by delegating them to Congress, the Articles had necessarily "abridge[d] the sovereignty of each particular state." Indeed, as Pelatiah Webster announced in a 1783 pamphlet, it seemed obvious that "a number of sovereign states uniting into one commonwealth, and appointing a supreme power to manage the affairs of the union, *do necessarily and unavoidably part with and transfer over [to] such supreme power, so much of their own sovereignty, as is necessary to render the ends of the union effectual.*"[20]

The contrary doctrine, the argument that sovereignty resided solely in the separate states, seemed, to the proponents of a stronger union, to be both erroneous and dangerous. In Europe, Benjamin Rush informed readers of the *Independent Gazeteer* in June 1786, the term sovereignty "applied only to those states which possess[ed] the power of making war and peace." Because that power belonged solely to the national government of the United States, Rush argued, the contention that sovereignty was located in the states revealed that "the people of America" had seriously "mistaken the meaning of the word *sovereignty.*" Ironically, they employed precisely the same arguments used by the metropolitan British political establishment in the 1760s and 1770s, contending that it was logically impossible for both the United States and the thirteen individual states "to be perfectly sovereign and independent at the same time." "The idea of each state preserving its sovereignty and independence in their full latitude, and yet holding up the appearance of a confederacy and a concert of measures," said Noah Webster in echoing Blackstone, was "a solecism in politics" that "sooner or later" must "dissolve the pretended union." "A species of political heresy" calculated only "to weaken this union," the idea that each state was "separately and individually independent," Charles Coatesworth Pinckney declared, could only "bring on us the most serious distresses."[21]

Even the most ardent advocates of increasing national authority had to admit, however, that Congress had been steadily losing power to the states throughout the early 1780s. "In proportion as the governments of the several states have acquired vigor and maturity," observed the author of an anonymous pamphlet in 1783, "the weight, the influence, and of course the efficient powers of" Congress "have been declining." In view of this development, it seemed entirely plausible to argue, as did the Virginian Arthur Lee in debate in Congress in August 1782, that "Congress had no authority but what it derived from the States." The "sovereignty of the Crown of G[reat] B[ritain]," Lee explained, could not possibly have "devolve[d up]on the U[nited] S[tates] in Congress assembled, before such an assembly existed." Rather, Lee argued, it devolved upon the states "individually [,which] were in existence before Congress . . . and retained all the rights of sovereign free and independent states, except what they voluntarily gave to Congress by the Confederation."[22]

That Lee's argument was not merely a debating position but an accurate description of the existing situation was fully underlined by the anonymous author of *The Political Establishments of the United States of America*, published in Philadelphia in 1784. No friend to a weak central government, this writer readily admitted that the "first principle of our national existence" was "the sovereignty and independence of the several states," which, he insisted, "makes us so many separate and distinct nations." "Thirteen sovereign and independent powers," he explained, "will have thirteen separate and independent interests to promote and secure, and for that purpose, will establish as many different systems of policy." As "so many greater divisions of the people, whose political interests are separate and opposed to one another, whose objects are different and measures various," and who were entirely "sovereign and independent," the states, he concluded, could not possibly "be controlled" by Congress. "Considering the nature and extent of their powers, the design of the institution, and the little regard paid . . . to their recommendations . . . by the states," Congress, "in whom [alone] we have any semblance of a union," was thus merely "a burlesque on government, and a most severe satire on the wisdom and sagacity of the people."[23]

Notwithstanding the extraordinary powers it had exercised throughout the early years of the war, Congress, from this new and later perspective, thus by no means appeared to be, as Ezra Stiles observed in 1783, "a body in which resides authoritative sovereignty." The Confederation, said Stiles, had obviously involved "no real cession of dominion, no surrender or transfer of sovereignty to the national council." Rather, "each state in the confederacy" had remained "an independent sovereignty." Congress, declared John Adams in spelling out the implications of this argument in the mid-1780s, was neither "a legislative assembly, nor a representative assembly, but only a diplomatic assembly" that, said another writer, had not authority "enough to prosecute any one particular purpose to effect, nor, to give a sufficient weight and dignity to national resolutions."[24]

Why the American political union had developed in this way seemed, in retrospect, entirely obvious and was fully and cogently analyzed by the author of *Political Establishments*. The colonies had, after all, been first settled and had continued throughout their existence in a "state of division." When the contest with Britain embroiled them "in one general calamity" and they found themselves "unanimously determined to make a defence" and "saw the necessity of some plan of union, whereby" their "efforts might be rendered the more efficacious and successful," they had simply appointed "a congress of delegates from the (then) several Colonies . . . to advise and direct in all matters relating to the whole so far as respected the war; which was (probably) all that was intended at the time of that appointment; for the powers they were invested with . . . were confined to that object." Along "with every other public measure" at the time, this action was, moreover, "grounded . . . on the presumption, that the state governments were as unalterably fixed, as the laws of the Medes and the Persians." Given these conditions and limitations, this author perceptively observed, it "would have been a matter of wonder" had American leaders managed "to pay that attention to the subject" that "its nature and importance required." Even had they "been ever so much inclined," they simply had not had "leisure . . . to deliberate on, and settle a[n adequate] constitution for the government of the whole."[25]

Nor had the subsequent efforts of Congress "to remedy the apparent defects of their institution" by the Articles of Confederation much improved the contingent arrangements that had been adopted in 1775–76. Fully understanding that the "foundation of our opposition to the unconstitutional measures of the British parliament" was the defense of the corporate rights and integrity of the states, the framers of the Articles had been especially careful in the ninth article, wrote longtime Connecticut delegate Roger Sherman, to reserve to the states all authority necessary to enable them to "retain their *sovereignty, freedom* and *independence*." If, as Sherman remarked, the "form of government planned by Congress, and adopted by the states," was thus "the only form we could [have] adopt[ed] under our circumstances," it was, nonetheless, a government in which, as the author of *Political Establishments* complained, the powers vested in Congress—"Circumscribed with regard to their objects, in some instances merely recommendatory, in others implied, and in but very few determinate"—had by "no means [proved] answerable to their proposed end," which he defined as the establishment of a perpetual union that was "competent to the purposes of national policy."[26]

The weakness of the American national union was, however, more easily analyzed than remedied, and there was a wide range of opinion over precisely what should be done about it. Some thought with Roger Sherman that the Articles should be kept "strictly . . . inviolate" until time and *"practice"* had made their defects more evident. Emphasizing that by their early decisions the American people had by no means "debar[red] themselves from the privilege of reconsideration," people at the other extreme advocated a radical redistribution of power in favor of the national government. On the grounds that all of the "political evils" of the United States derived from "the sovereignty of the states," they argued either that "the power of all the states must be reduced to a narrow compass" and Congress endowed with "complete sovereignty in all but the mere municipal law of each state" or that the states should be abolished and a constitution formed "whereby the whole nation" might "be united in one government."[27]

In between these two poles, most analysts wished simply to work out a more precise allocation of authority between the national and the state governments. Like their predecessors in the constitutional debates of the 1760s and early 1770s, they fell easily into commonplace distinctions between particular and general, local and national, internal and external, domestic and foreign spheres of government. "Whenever an object occurs, to the direction of which no particular state is competent," wrote James Wilson in 1785, "the management of it must, of necessity, belong to the United States in Congress assembled," and he pointed to "many objects of this extended nature," including the "purchase, the sale, the defence, and the government of lands and countries, not within any state." The United States as a whole, Wilson argued, had "general rights, general powers, and general obligations, not derived from any particular states, nor from all the particular states, taken separately; but resulting from the union of the whole." The very "Spirit of the Confederation," added Daniel Carroll, dictated "that all matters of a general tendency, shou'd be [vested] in the representative Body of the whole, or under its authority."[28]

As Pelatiah Webster shrewdly observed, however, "the great and most difficult part of this weighty subject" was how to constitute the general government so that it could "exercise with full force, and effect the vast powers" it required "for the good and well-being of the United States, and yet be . . . checked and restrained from exercising these powers to the injury and ruin of the states." For, as Hamilton repeatedly pointed out, it was virtually "impossible for Congress to do a single act which" did "not directly or indirectly affect the internal police of every state." "The truth is," declared Hamilton, "that no Foederal constitution can exist without powers, that in their exercise affect the internal police of the component members."[29]

For that reason, as Washington noted to many of his correspondents, almost every federal act was viewed with "*unreasonable* jealousies" by the states and, as Rufus King complained in 1786, "every man who wishes to strengthen the federal Government, and confirm the Union" was "represented as unfriendly to the liberties of the People." Like the colonial legislatures in the prerevolutionary crises and for the same reasons, the states thus "ardently contended for" their own "independent sovereignty" as the only basis on which they could maintain their power against that of the federal government. So long as this "tenacity of . . . power" and "*the bantling, I had liked to have said monster,* for sovereignty, which have taken such fast hold of the States individually," were so pervasive, Washington despaired, the states were unlikely to accede to changes that would enable the United States to resolve the classic problem of the distribution of authority in an extended federal polity. To paraphrase Madison's famous observation about republican government, the "great disideratum which has not yet been found for" federal governments was thus "some disinterested & dispassionate umpire in disputes between different" levels of government.[30]

The simple fact was that even after several years of discussion Americans in the mid-1780s had not yet discovered any "established principle" by which, in Noah Webster's words, "the several states, as to their own internal police, [could] be sovereign and independent, but as to the common concerns of all . . . mere subjects of the federal head," and the primary obstacle to their doing so was precisely the one that had brought the British Empire to grief a decade earlier, the problem of the location of final, sovereign authority. In 1783, a writer calling himself Tullius made a bold assault upon this problem in a pamphlet published in Philadelphia and entitled *Three Letters Addressed to the Public.* Distinguishing between *political* sovereignty and *juridical* sovereignty, Tullius argued that the former belonged to Congress and the latter to the states.[31]

Citing Vattel's definition of a sovereign state as one with "a right immediately to *figure* . . . in the universal society of nations," Tullius held that the United States was "one individual nation, whose moral personality resides in Congress." Just as "the safety of individuals is the foundation of civil societies," he wrote, "in like manner the safety of societies is the foundation of political confederations." Hence, he reasoned, the main "object of a political foederal union" like the United States was "the safety of the states who compose it." To enable it to achieve this object, such a union, he argued, had to have "a representative body" in which "reside[d] the sovereignty of the United States; the deputies of each state collectively, forming the moral representative and sovereign power of the whole." But that "Congress alone" thus held "the power of making war and peace, and treating in a sovereign capacity with other nations" did not, in Tullius's view, preclude the states from retaining "a separate, inferior, limited juridical sovereignty" over the "less splendid, tho' not less necessary objects" of "domestic policy within their own limits."[32]

Although this distinction between political and juridical sovereignty seemed to Tullius "plainly, and . . . naturally marked out, by the obvious purposes of a confederation," he nevertheless had to admit that there was "no parallel in history, by which . . . the political and juridical sovereignties" had been similarly "separated and rendered independent of each other." But he did not view this novel arrangement as a liability. Rather, he suggested that it might be especially well calculated to secure the two "primary objects of civil government," which he defined as public safety and private happiness. By depositing "the powers necessary for each, so happily separable in their nature . . . in distinct bodies, no way influenced by each other," the "frame of the American government," he believed, had "a peculiar felicity . . . for the attainment" of each. Because they "relate[d] more particularly to the safety of the nation," the "conduct of war, treaties, politics, and necessary revenue" were "the proper business of Congress," whereas "Laws, police, order, justice, the cultivation and improvement of the social virtues," and other things that "promote[d] private happiness" were "the proper objects of the legislative assemblies in the States: And in order to give efficacy to the measures adopted for those purposes, there" was "the sanction of sovereign power residing in each."[33]

Tullius's formulation had the virtue of investing Congress "with more extensive authority" while at the same time reserving to the states a "limited territorial" jurisdiction that catered to their "favourite and flattering idea" of state sovereignty, but it did not contain a formula for resolving the theoretical and practical problem of what to do in cases of jurisdictional disputes over the boundaries of authority between the two sovereign realms. Contrary to what Washington remarked, the American system of government under the Articles of Confederation, even as explained by Tullius, was emphatically not "more perfect in theory than [it was] in practice."[34]

As contemporaries also understood, this theoretical dilemma was compounded by the structural imperatives operating within the union. As acute political observers, American leaders of the 1780s all understood that interest was the "only permanent bond by which individuals, or communities can be united." Under the Articles of Confederation, however, the "political and civil interests" of the citizenry, as one writer pointed out in 1784, were "completely formed and established in each of the states," which subsequently considered them "their primary and fundamental objects," while "the general interests and concerns . . . of the confederation," which were "either matters of burden or advantage," tended, more often than not, to become "objects of subordinate consideration." So powerful were these centrifugal structural propensities within the American union that they strongly tended to fix "the ultimate power of governance in each of the states," thereby setting "up thirteen interests in opposition to one another" and rendering "the institution of Congress entirely subordinate, or rather useless."[35]

If, since the war had ended, the individual states had been largely "governed by their particular interests," advocates of constitutional reform hoped that those interests might once again come together to produce a demand for a stronger union. In the 1780s, two separate developments were working toward that end. First, as Peter Onuf has emphasized, was a growing awareness that the states were heavily dependent upon the national government for the maintenance of their corporate and territorial integrity against the claims both of other states and of separatist groups within them. So great was the potential for conflict in this area that many people feared civil war. As Onuf has noted, however, the states were too weak to go to war with each other, and this weakness effectively prevented them from behaving toward each other "as independent sovereign states were supposed to behave." None of them had the coercive resources necessary to stand alone.[36]

Once they had become aware that they could claim no more than "other states were willing to recognize" and that membership in the union and the "mutual recognition" that membership implied were the "ultimate legitimating source[s]" for their claims as states, the states slowly began to realize that, as William Grayson put it in June 1787, only a strong political union could "guaranty the limits of every State in the Confederation" and to accept what Onuf calls "an increasingly diminutive notion of statehood." As Onuf argues, this development was virtually complete by the mid-1780s and was essential for both the achievement of a satisfactory national policy for dealing with western territories in 1785–87—the one clear success achieved by the Confederation Congress during those years—and for "the radical expansion of national power" in the Constitution of 1787.[37]

A second development that helped to change the climate of opinion and give the states a renewed sense of common interest was the sudden emergence in the mid-1780s of a broadly diffused fear of anarchy and disorder among significant numbers of American political leaders. This fear derived from two main sources. First was the growing recognition that, as one member of Congress put it, by imbibing too heavily from the "intoxicating Draughts of Liberty" and "pursuing their own whimsical Schemes of dangerous Experiment, regardless of the federal System," the states were rapidly "destroying their own Strength." "The flagrant violations of the public faith . . . in the [many] Emissions of Paper money" in 1785–86 were merely the most egregious examples of this problem. Second was the perception, crystallized by Shays's Rebellion in 1786, that the states were virtually powerless to maintain internal order within their own boundaries, that, as Henry Knox wrote Washington in October 1786, they were almost wholly "without the essential concomitant of government, the power of preserving peace."[38]

"By juxtaposing and synthesizing different and previously unconnected kinds of violence and disorder and by treating them all as symptoms of an underlying constitutional problem" that could be solved only by augmenting the authority of the union, this rising fear of disorder, as Onuf has noted, "created a new reality" that, in Washington's words, finally persuaded the "greater part of the Union . . . of the necessity of foederal measures" to establish a secure political order. Although a few people continued to think that it might be sufficient merely to alter those parts of the Articles "where we are pretty clearly convinced of the defects," many others seem to have agreed with Madison that "the Present System neither has nor deserves advocates." By failing to provide the federal government with any coercive authority over the states, the Articles, Madison explained in a brilliant analysis of the "Vices" of the existing political system, had deprived the federal government of "the great vital principles of a Political Cons[ti]tution," made it possible for the states to encroach upon federal authority with impunity, and rendered it inevitable that, without a "systematic change" that would "strike . . . deeply at the old Confederation," the union could never be anything more than "a league of sovereign powers." If the American union were ever to achieve strength and energy, more and more people were coming to believe that it would have to be "on other principles" than those that underlay the Articles of Confederation.[39]

The Philadelphia Convention of 1787 quickly revealed that many American leaders had reached this conclusion. Acutely aware, as Madison later said, that "Public opinion sets bounds to every government," the delegates to that body realized that the depth of the public attachment to their several state governments and the extended character of the American polity rendered "a consolidation of the States into one simple republic" impossible and required that a significant amount of independent and "separate authority [be] reserved to the states." Similarly, they understood that public opinion reinforced their own determination that any changes would have to be in accord with "Republican Principles." Having also learned from their experiences with the Confederation that, as Madison said, "an individual independence of the States" was "utterly irreconcilable with the idea of an aggregate sovereignty" or an energetic and effective central government, the members of the convention found themselves engaged in what Madison described as a search for a "middle ground" that would "at once support a due supremacy of the national authority, and leave in force the local authorities so far as they can be subordinately useful."[40]

To an important degree, this search for a middle way that would subordinate the states to the federal government without either consolidating them into a single government or depriving them of authority over their own internal affairs was merely a continuation of the ancient quest, dating back to the earliest history of the colonies, to find a workable allocation of authority between the center and the peripheries, between the national government and the states. Indeed, the delegates had few other precedents to guide them in this effort. As both James Madison and James Wilson pointed out at the time, those few European states that were not unitary in structure— Poland, the Swiss cantons, and the Netherlands—were all loose confederations analogous to the Articles of Confederation, and the same was true of the ancient confederation of Grecian republics in the Amphictyonic Council. Two other Greek unions, the Archaen League and the Lycian Confederacy, seemed to have invested greater power in the central government. But too little was known about the details of their organization to provide a clear model. In this situation, the delegates could do no better than to turn for guidance to their own experience with overlapping authority in the British Empire and under the Articles.[41]

That experience had told them that it would be "easy to discover a proper and satisfactory principle on the subject," the principle inherent in the conventional distinction between general and local spheres, a distinction that, as Onuf has noted, had "a venerable pedigree in American efforts to define a safe place for the colonies in the British Empire" and had been explicitly incorporated into the Articles of Confederation. As the convention confessed to Congress in recommending the Constitution for consideration by the states, however, it was much less easy "to draw with Precision the Line between those Rights which must be surrendered [to the national government] and those which may be reserved" to the states.[42]

In their discussion of this problem, everyone agreed that public opinion and efficient governance dictated that the states be preserved as subdivisions responsible for all those "local objects" to which the "Nat[iona]l Gover[nmen]t could not descend." "All large Governments," declared Wilson, "must be subdivided into lesser jurisdictions." But there was considerably less agreement over precisely what authority should be left to the states. A few people thought that "the difficulty of drawing the line between" state and federal authority was so great that they despaired that any "boundary could be drawn between the National & State Legislatures," that, as Gunning Bedford of Delaware put it, "there was no middle way between a perfect consolidation and a mere confederacy of the States."[43]

For precisely this reason, several delegates from the small states argued that the state governments had to retain their superiority over the national government, the initial purpose of which, according to Bedford, was nothing more than "to defend the whole ag[ain]st foreign nations, in case of war, and to defend the lesser States ag[ain]st the ambition of the larger." "At the separation from the British Empire," insisted Maryland delegate Luther Martin, "the people of America [had] preferred the Establishment of themselves into thirteen separate sovereignties instead of incorporating themselves into one," and it was to these local governments that they still looked "for the security of their lives, liberties & properties." From the states alone, said Oliver Ellsworth of Connecticut, could Americans expect to derive "domestic happiness."[44]

At the other extreme, Hamilton was virtually alone in concluding that the difficulty of distinguishing state and national authority required that the national government be vested with "indefinite authority." As he later put it in *Federalist* 15, the Articles of Confederation had fully confirmed his belief that, "in every political association . . . formed upon the principle of uniting in a common interest a number of lesser sovereignties, there will be found a kind of excentric tendency in the subordinate or inferior orbs, by the operation of which there will be a perpetual effort in each to fly off from the common center." So powerful was this tendency, Hamilton was persuaded, that if the authority of the federal government "were limited at all, the rivalship of the States would gradually subvert it."[45]

If no other delegate agreed with Hamilton that the federal government should be given unlimited authority, a majority nonetheless believed that it should "have powers far beyond those exercised by the British Parliament, when the states were part of the British Empire" and should "be paramount to the state constitutions" in all matters relating to the general interest of the nation. Unless federal laws and courts were superior to those of the states, Madison observed, the federal government would never be able to resist the tendency, inherent in all confederations, for "the parts to encroach on the authority of the whole" or even to prevent the parts from encroaching upon each other. "Without a controuling power" in "the whole over the parts," said Madison, in adopting both the logic and the language of Blackstone, "our system" would involve "the evil of imperia in imperio."[46]

The basic and radical premise behind this majority position among the delegates was "that the United States constituted a single political community," that it "ought to be one Nation" and "for ever considered as one Body corporate and politic in law, and entitled to all the rights[,] privileges, and immunities, which to Bodies corporate do or ought to appertain." From this premise, it followed that the states had never "possessed the essential rights of sovereignty." In opposition to Luther Martin's contention that "when the Colonies became independent of G[reat] Britain, they became independent also of each other," Wilson argued that the very language of the Declaration strongly inferred that the states asserted their independence, "not *Individually* but *Unitedly*," and Elbridge Gerry insisted that "even on the principles of the Confederation," the states "never were independent States, were not such now, & never could be." "They did not possess [any of] the peculiar features of sovereignty," Rufus King declared in debate, "they could not make war, nor peace, nor alliances, nor treaties. Considering them as political Beings, they were dumb, for they could not speak to any foreign Sovereign whatever. They were deaf, for they could not hear any propositions from such Sovereign."[47]

Like the defenders of the colonies between the Stamp Act crisis and independence, however, these advocates of a stronger national union quickly sensed that, as Onuf has observed, they "had to abandon the language and logic of 'sovereignty' altogether" in favor of "new images of the union that would resolve the apparent paradox of sovereign states in a sovereign union." In pursuit of that goal, they developed four parallel and complementary strategies.[48]

First, they endeavored to found "the authority of the union" directly upon the people as individual citizens rather than upon the states or the people collectively as citizens of the states. "The great and radical vice in the construction of the existing Confederation," Hamilton asserted in *Federalist* 15, was "in the principle of LEGISLATION for STATES or GOVERNMENTS, in their CORPORATE or COLLECTIVE CAPACITIES . . . as contradistinguished from the INDIVIDUALS of which they consist." The two devices adopted by the convention to remedy this problem were to make the House of Representatives representational in the sense that it was both based upon population and elected by the citizens directly and to require that the new constitution be "ratified by the authority of the people, and not merely by that of the Legislatures." Only such "a change in the principle of representation" and "such a ratification by the people themselves," Madison had decided even before the convention met, could render the authority of the federal government "clearly paramount to" state "Legislative authorities," give the federal government the weight and energy it needed to secure the purposes of the union, and, as Hamilton said in debate, ensure that the individual rights of the citizenry would not be "sacrifice[d] . . . to the preservation of the [corporate] rights of an *artificial* being, called states."[49]

If these steps represented a radical move away from the constitutional tradition articulated in the prerevolutionary debate and incorporated in the Articles of Confederation, the tradition that the integrity of the corporate rights of the states was the best safeguard for the individual rights of the people who composed them, the convention tried to ensure that the corporate rights of the states would be maintained through a second major strategy, the incorporation into the Constitution of the principle of equal representation of the states in the Senate. If, as Madison explained to Jefferson, the House of Representatives represented "the people of the States in their individual capacity," the Senate, being "elected absolutely and exclusively by the state legislatures," represented "the States in their political capacity." Just as "the fundamental rights of individuals" were "secured by express provisions in the State Constitutions," so through the device of the Senate, which was "only another edition of [the Confederation] Cong[ress]," was "a like security . . . provided for the Rights of [the] States in the National Constitution."[50]

But the authority, integrity, and identity of the states was still further "secured ag[ain]st the general sovereignty & jurisdiction" of "the national Government" by a third major strategy: the extension to the federal Constitution of the principle—contended for against Britain in the 1760s and early 1770s and incorporated into all of the revolutionary state constitutions—that constitutions limited the governments they established. "To control the power and the conduct of the legislature by an overruling constitution," James Wilson announced proudly in the Pennsylvania ratifying convention, "was an improvement in the science and practice of government" that had been "reserved to the American States" and had now been included in the federal government.[51]

The result, Madison explained in the *Federalist*, was that the federal legislature would "possess a part only of that supreme legislative authority which is vested completely in the British Parliament; and which, with a few exceptions, was exercised by the colonial assemblies and the Irish legislature." Under the new Constitution, the "powers delegated . . . to the federal government" were "few and defined" and applied principally to "external objects, [such] as war, peace, negociation, and foreign commerce," whereas those which were "to remain in the state governments" were "numerous and infinite" and "extend[ed] to all the objects, which, in the ordinary course of affairs, concern[ed] the lives, liberties and properties of the people; and the internal order, improvement and prosperity of the State."[52]

The fourth, and probably the most important, strategy adopted by the proponents of the Constitution was to redefine the concept of sovereignty itself. Following the example of colonial protagonists between 1764 and 1776, supporters and defenders alike continued, throughout the debate over ratification, to speak in terms of concurrent or divided sovereignty. According to this doctrine, reiterated over and over again by Hamilton and Madison in the *Federalist*, the state governments by the new Constitution retained "all the rights of sovereignty which they had before had and which were not by that act *exclusively* delegated to the United States": "in all unenumerated cases"—which, the *Federalist* hastened to point out, were few—the states were to be "left in the enjoyment of their sovereign and independent jurisdiction."[53]

Opponents of the Constitution refused to be taken in by this argument, however. With their antagonists, they had learned from Blackstone and others that "two co-ordinate sovereignties would be a solecism in politics," that it was intellectually "Inconsistent . . . to have one sovereignty within another." "The idea of two distinct sovereigns in the same country, separately *possessed* of sovereign and supreme power, in the same matters at the same time," asserted Thomas Tredwell in the New York ratifying convention, was "as supreme an absurdity, as that two distinct separate circles can be bounded exactly by the same circumference." Dismissing the concept of coordinate sovereignty as nothing more than an artful contrivance to vest "all the essential characteristics of sovereignty . . . in the general government," they argued that the powers vested in Congress by the new Constitution "must necessarily annihilate and absorb the legislative, executive, and judicial powers of the several states, and produce from their ruins one consolidated government," and they reminded their readers that the defense of the corporate rights of the colonies against Parliament's attempts to gather all sovereign power to itself "was the leading principle of the revolution, and . . . an essential article in our creed."[54]

But the Constitution's supporters were ready with an answer to the imperium in imperio objection, one that had been unavailable to them in the 1760s and 1770s. For they were now able to legitimize the doctrine of coordinate sovereignty by founding it upon the concept of popular sovereignty, the idea that sovereignty resided not in governments but in the people themselves. This was by no means a new idea in 1787. Various commentators, including the English radical John Cartwright, had argued in the prerevolutionary debate that "the rights of sovereignty reside[d] in the people themselves," and the state constitutions both had been based upon and embodied this principle. By the mid-1780s, the notion that "ultimate authority, wherever the derivative may be found, resides in the people" had become a commonplace. Although by 1787 the discovery, in James Wilson's words, that the "dread and redoubtable sovereign, when traced to his ultimate and genuine source," was to be "found . . . in the free and independent man" was "nothing very astonishing," it nevertheless turned out to be "something very useful."[55]

Precisely how useful was revealed in the Federal Convention and its aftermath, for the contribution of the framers of the Constitution was to take this principle and use it as the basis for resolving the old question of by what principles the essential powers of sovereignty could be distributed between center and periphery. As Andrew C. McLaughlin pointed out more than a half century ago, the convention's solution to this question was both its "signal contribution . . . to the political life of the modern world" and the most important American contribution to political theory and practice. So original was the convention's solution that its members did not fully understand it until after the Constitution had been completed and they had—in the crucible of debate—to explain the principles behind the new government and how it would operate.[56]

As Gordon Wood has more recently explained, the idea of popular sovereignty provided the foundation for the crucial intellectual break-through that made the contrivance of a viable federal system possible. If, as the new Constitution assumed, sovereignty resided in the people, the "state governments could never lose their sovereignty be-cause they had never possessed it." Moreover, the sovereign people could delegate the basic powers of sovereignty to any government or governments they wished, and they could divide up those powers in any way they saw fit, delegating some to one level of government and others to another, while retaining still others in their own hands.[57]

James Wilson spelled out the new theory fully for his fellow dele-gates in the Pennsylvania ratifying convention in the fall of 1787. In the American political system, he explained, sovereignty did not re-side in the states or in any government. Those politicians who had "not considered, with sufficient accuracy, our political systems," said Wilson, might claim "that, in our governments, the supreme power was vested in the constitutions. This opinion," he admitted, ap-proached "a step nearer to the truth, but" did "not reach it. The truth is," he declared, "that, in our governments, the supreme, absolute, and uncontrollable power remains in the people. As our constitutions are superiour to our legislatures; so the people are superiour to our constitutions." Sovereignty, Wilson said, thus always resided "in the people; they have not parted with it; they have only dispensed such portions of power as were conceived necessary for the public wel-fare."[58]

Both the state and the national government, Edmund Pendleton declared in the Virginia ratifying convention, were thus equally crea-tures of the people: "both possessed of our equal confidence—both chosen in the same manner, and both equally responsible to us." "The federal and state governments," Madison wrote in *Federalist* 46, were "in fact but different agents and trustees of the people, con-stituted with different powers, and designed for different purposes." Although the supremacy clause in Article VI of the Constitution en-sured that federal laws would take precedence over state laws when-ever the two came into conflict, both the national government and the state governments would have full authority within their respective spheres, authority deriving directly from grants by the people—in whom sovereignty continued to reside.[59]

The framers had thus fashioned a government that was neither a consolidated government nor a mere confederation of states. In Hamilton's words in *The Federalist*, the former implied "an entire consolidation of the States into one complete national sovereignty," and the latter suggested simply "an association of two or more states" into one polity with all sovereignty remaining in the states. The new federal government was something in between. It aimed, said Hamilton in *Federalist* 32, "only at a partial . . . . consolidation" in which the states clearly retained all those rights of sovereignty that they had traditionally exercised, except for those that through the Constitution had been reallocated by the people to the federal government.[60]

In many respects, as McLaughlin long ago pointed out, in its organization, the United States after 1788 looked very much like the early modern British Empire. Certainly, in contriving the Constitution, the framers had clearly drawn, if in many cases half-consciously, upon the experience and precedents of the empire. Like the empire, the American federal system did not concentrate authority in a single government but distributed it among different levels. It thus "gave legal and institutional reality to the principle of diversification of powers and . . . crystallized a system much like that under which the colonists had" lived for a century and a half.[61]

But if the American federal system was not so radical in form, it was fundamentally so in principle. By locating sovereignty in the people rather than in the government or in some branch thereof, the framers of the Constitution had invented a radical new scheme of governance whereby the basic powers of sovereignty could be divided without dividing sovereignty itself. This intellectual—and political—invention not only finally made possible the solution of the old imperial problem of the constitutional relationship between center and periphery, between national and local authority, in its American context. By making "it possible to think of sovereignty itself, like population, as expansionable," the doctrine of popular sovereignty also served as a principle by which new states as they were formed could be united with the "Thirteen primitive States" in what Madison called the great "extended Republic of the United States."[62]

What was new and radical about the Constitution was thus its embodiment of the new American theory that sovereignty resided in the people at large and its incorporation of the idea of consent into the national government through the institutions of direct election of members to the House of Representatives. These steps made American federalism, the "new" federalism of 1787, *representational*. What was old about the Federal Constitution was its endorsement of the continued sanctity of the identity of each of the states as separate territorial and corporate entities and their representation in the Senate. That provision ensured that American federalism would continue to be, as it had been entirely under the Articles of Confederation, not merely representational, as Samuel H. Beer has recently argued, but also *territorial*.[63]

Throughout most of the 1780s, from the conclusion of the War for Independence in 1783 to the adoption of the Federal Constitution in 1788, the primary question facing the newly independent American political communities was how they should organize themselves politically and constitutionally. This question in turn involved a series of subordinate questions. How the states should relate to each other, whether they should have a common center at all, and, if so, how it should be created and organized were all questions that were powerfully thrust upon them by the problems, exigencies, and potentialities of their political situation. Given their long-standing relationship to Britain, especially as that experience had been redefined for them by the events of the 1760s and 1770s, the questions could not be considered apart from the deep-seated suspicions they all entertained of a distant central authority. Perhaps it was only because they had no preexisting dominant territorial center such as obtained in the early modern British Empire—because, in the sense that they were all peripheries without a center, the several states all enjoyed equal status as political communities—that the states were able even to ignore the well-known risks of creating a powerful new political center and to consider these questions at all.

What they discovered in the process of exploring them was that they could never hope either to relate to each other in a reasonably harmonious way or to protect themselves against external threats without a center and that only a center with sufficient strength and integrity to maintain its authority against the powerful centrifugal tendencies inherent in a federal political system could possibly secure those ends. The combination of representational and territorial elements in the central government, the framers hoped, would enable the United States to have an energetic center without depriving the states of the local autonomy and ancient corporate integrity and identity they had so jealously defended throughout the colonial era and had fought a revolution to preserve.

If, as one commentator remarked, the Revolution had "in a great measure" so "effaced . . . all former habits" that there existed in the new United States no "great reluctance to innovation" in political and constitutional arrangements, the same could not be said for the empire they had just left. Everywhere in the old outlying areas of the empire, in Ireland, the West Indian colonies, and even Nova Scotia, the revolt of the American colonies only intensified demands for greater home rule, for the preservation of local corporate rights over those of the center. No less than the revolting colonies, Lord Abingdon declared in 1778, "Every island in the West-Indies look[ed] upon" the Declaratory Act "with terror. All Ireland see it with a jealous eye: For who is the casuist," he asked, "that discriminate between a British Parliamentary right to tax America, and a British parliamentary right to tax Ireland?" But only in Ireland did the demand for constitutional reform force the metropolis to make any significant concessions, and those would not survive the end of the century.[64]

Even though Poyning's Law and the Declaratory Act of 1720 remained on the statute books, the Irish Parliament, as was pointed out in earlier chapters, had exerted considerable autonomy over Irish domestic affairs throughout the first half of the eighteenth century. Beginning with the money bill dispute of 1753, a controversy over the right of the Irish House of Commons to participate in the disposal of surplus funds in the treasury, and especially after 1761, a group of opposition politicians led by Henry Flood and known as the Patriots had "been pressing with increasing vociferousness for a series of reforms and the promotion of Ireland's interests as a distinct kingdom" wholly independent of the British Parliament. As various scholars have pointed out, however, it was only the American war and the formation of the Volunteers, a Protestant citizen army organized in the late 1770s ostensibly to defend Ireland against French and Spanish invasion, that made the achievement of Patriot goals possible.[65]

Their victory came in two phases, both heavily influenced by the disastrous results of the American war for Britain. First, with opposition support in Britain, the Patriots and the Volunteers combined to mobilize Irish Protestant opinion to persuade Lord North's government "to remove practically all restrictions on Irish commerce" in

1779–80. Second, in April 1782, the Patriots, led by Henry Grattan, managed to carry by a unanimous vote in the Irish House of Commons a resolution declaring that "the king's most excellent majesty, and the lords and commons of Ireland, are the only power competent to enact laws to bind Ireland." In the wake of that resolution, the British Parliament, now under the control of the opposition, quickly gave way and passed a bill repealing the Irish Declaratory Act. It thereby effectively recognized "the sole right of the Irish parliament to legislate for Ireland." At the same time, the Irish Parliament's passage of Yelverton's Act so far altered Poynings' Act as to abolish the crown's right to originate or alter, but not to veto, Irish laws. In associated reforms, "Irish courts were rendered free from final appeal to Britain's House of Lords in their verdicts; Irish judges were granted life tenure; [and] the army in Ireland was placed under Irish-legislated discipline passed biennially."[66]

If the new "Irish constitution" of 1782 effectively brought the legislative "subordination of Ireland . . . to an end" and thereby secured for Ireland the legislative autonomy achieved by the thirteen revolting states only by war and revolution, constitutional reform did not go deep enough to be lasting. As Joseph Lee has put it, "1782 merely marked a change in relations between the Irish parliament and the English parliament; it involved no change in relations between the Irish parliament and the Irish people." Representing almost exclusively the small Protestant establishment, the Irish Parliament remained "unreformed and unrepresentative," and when, inspired by the French Revolution, the Catholic Irish began to demand wider political rights in the 1790s and rose in rebellion in 1798, the Protestant establishment lost its nerve and in 1800 agreed to a formal legislative union with Britain by which the Irish Parliament was abolished and Ireland now sent members to the British Parliament. At least theoretically, Ireland had finally escaped the disabilities of the peripheries by being incorporated into the center, an arrangement that would last until the great Irish Revolution in the first decades of the twentieth century.[67]

Although it was not for want of trying, local legislative authorities elsewhere in the peripheries of the old empire did not manage to achieve even the fleeting taste of autonomy enjoyed by Ireland from 1782 to 1800. Throughout the "remaining colonies," in the newer colonies of Dominica, Grenada, New Brunswick, Prince Edward Island, St. Vincent, Tobago, the Virgin Islands, and, after the Constitutional Act of 1791 provided each of them with an assembly, Upper and Lower Canada as well as in the older colonies of Barbados, the Leeward Islands, Jamaica, and Nova Scotia, the old tensions between central authority and peripheral rights continued unabated. By promising "all the colonies, provinces, and plantations in North America and the West Indies" exemption from parliamentary taxation, the peace plan offered to the revolting colonies by the North ministry in 1778 clearly implied "a willingness to consider modifications of the Declaratory Act" of 1766, and Parliament did not in fact ever again attempt to tax any colony that had its own legislature. But the American rejection of that plan left the entire issue in abeyance. For all these colonies that continued in the British Empire, the American Revolution, as Chester Martin has observed, "left 'the American question'"—the question of how, constitutionally, the peripheries could safeguard their inhabitants' rights as Britons against the unlimited authority claimed by the metropolis—"still unsolved."[68]

In the decades during and immediately after the Revolution, the West Indian colonists were especially strident in claiming for themselves "those Invaluable Privileges of *English* Subjects, in being Taxable only by themselves, and of being bound by no Laws made without the Consent of their Ancestors or themselves" and in demanding full "exemption . . . from the Impositions and Oppression of any Internal Tax by the British parliament . . . so long as we Continue in Allegiance to our King, & the Constitution." Like the revolting colonies, they insisted that their connection to the metropolis was through the king. Although they agreed with the First Continental Congress that Parliament might need to exercise authority over all those general matters in which "the local jurisdiction of any one particular colony is not competent," they argued that Parliament was "not competent to judge" for the purely domestic affairs of the colonies and that a clear boundary should be drawn "between a constitutional, superintending, controuling power in the British parliament, and a system of perfect unqualified tyranny, *the power of binding the colonies in all cases whatsoever.*"[69]

The historian and member of the Jamaica Assembly Bryan Edwards succinctly stated the colonial position on this question in 1793 in his *History, Civil and Commercial, of the British Colonies in the West Indies.* In terms very similar to those employed by the continental colonies in the 1760s and 1770s and by the Jamaican Assembly in its 1774 petition to the king, Edwards argued that the British government was "a *limited* government" and that it was "therefore a gross and palpable contradiction and paradox to say, that a *limited* government can possess *unlimited* authority." What restrained the British government, Edwards contended, was "those ancient, fundamental, unwritten laws . . . called THE BIRTHRIGHT OF THE PEOPLE. These are the laws," said Edwards, "to which we allude, when we speak of the *English constitution*, in contradistinction to *English acts of parliament*." Indeed, Edwards insisted, Blackstone had been wrong in arguing that all societies had to have somewhere within them "an absolute and despotic jurisdiction." "The truth is," said Edwards in echoing recent American theory about the nature and location of sovereignty, "that this despotic and unlimited power is reserved by the people in their own hands."[70]

For the West Indian and other British colonies remaining in the empire, the American concept of popular sovereignty translated into local legislative autonomy. What they wanted was what English colonists settled in the distant parts of the empire had, since the early seventeenth century, always wanted: in the colorful language of the Jamaican historian Edward Long, "a mutual Confidence, founded rather on the Love and Gratitude of Free Subjects, confirmed in the fullest Enjoyment of their Birthrights, than on the Awe and Fear of mere wretched Slaves, stripped of their Rights and Franchises, and held in base Submission, by the sole Power, of unlimited Prerogative, of Military Force, or Parliamentary Tyranny." Without that mutual confidence, they believed in common with virtually all the settler colonists who had gone before them, residents of the peripheries of the empire would never enjoy the full rights, benefits, and security of those at the center.[71]

If, we can see in retrospect, these continuing demands for legislative autonomy and exemption from parliamentary authority pointed in the direction of "some form of responsible government for the dependencies" and a commonwealth system in which, as the North Americans had proposed in the late 1760s and early 1770s, the separate political entities of the empire were joined together through a common link with the British crown, these changes would not come rapidly. It would be another fifty years after the achievement of American independence before the development of responsible government, first in Nova Scotia in the 1830s and 1840s and then in the rest of British North America, and almost another thirty years before the metropolitan government would recognize the right of any segment of the empire to full legislative independence, a right that subsequently applied to many different areas of the empire. Only with those developments did the British Empire itself finally resolve the classic problems of the constitutional relationship between center and periphery. In the meantime, however, the constitutional history of the second British Empire, the empire that came into being in the wake of the American Revolution, would continue to be "not only reminiscent of the first but scarcely distinguishable from it."[72]

Epilogue

With ratification of the Federal Constitution in 1788, its framers cautiously hoped that they had finally resolved the old constitutional problem of the distribution of authority in an extended polity consisting of an association of distinctive states. They created a new, national level of government founded directly on the authority of the people and endowed it with sovereign authority coordinate with that of the states. In effect, both national and state governments held sovereign powers appropriate to their respective functions within the national political union. By grounding this system of coordinate sovereignty in the concept of popular sovereignty, the framers believed that they could eliminate the logical difficulty of imperium in imperio and in time solve the old problem of imperial governance by making it possible for the United States to achieve both a workable division of authority between states and nation and a satisfactory balance between local diversity and central unity. Indeed, they hoped that this division of authority between different levels of government would make the American political system even more effective in preventing abuses of power on the part of governors by providing still another level of checks and balances to augment the traditional partition of authority among legislative, executive, and judicial departments.[1]

But these hopes were only partially fulfilled. The attachment of the people to their respective states remained too strong; the distrust of a distant central authority ran too deep. From the beginning, some people worried that the federal capital would become a new London, a "center of revenue, and of business," to which "all the men of genius and wealth" would "resort" while "the extremes of the empire," "drained to fatten an overgrown capital," would "in a very short time sink into the same degradation and contempt with respect to the" capital "as Ireland, Scotland, & Wales, are in with regard to England." Ratification had been obtained at the price of catering to these fears from the peripheries, and the Tenth Amendment to the Constitution explicitly stipulated that all those "powers not delegated to the United States by the Constitution, nor prohibited by it to the States, are reserved to the States respectively, or to the people."[2]

Although the language of the Tenth Amendment clearly reiterated the Federalist doctrines of both coordinate and popular sovereignty, there was, throughout the early decades of the republic, an implicit tension between the two, and the notion of coordinate sovereignty in which the balance of authority lay with the states rapidly came to predominate over the concept of popular sovereignty. In practice, of course, the line between national and state authority rarely became a matter of serious dispute. Contrary to Antifederalist fears in 1787–88, the national government did not become a consolidated government. As Kenneth M. Stampp has remarked, the Constitution "created a union of the states—to be sure, a union with the powers of the federal government significantly augmented and the powers of the states curtailed, but a union rather than a consolidated government." "To some indeterminate degree," writes Stampp, the Tenth Amendment clearly "preserved the principle of state sovereignty."[3]

But it was a principle that did not often have to be affirmed. From the beginning, the national government was extremely cautious in asserting its jurisdiction. As Madison wrote in 1791, it had neither the competence to deal with a wide range of purely state and local affairs nor the public support necessary to extend its sphere of jurisdiction beyond the general objectives marked out in the Constitution. "Public opinion," said Madison in repeating the familiar British-American political aphorism, "sets bounds to every government, and is the real sovereign in every free one"; and, as contemporary leaders all were aware, "the force of public opinion" ran strongly in the direction of limited government—at the national as well as at the state level. Even those who, like Washington and other strong Federalists, believed that American society could never reach its full potential without an efficient central government had never disputed Antifederalist claims in 1787–88 that the rapid development and domestic happiness of the several American societies that composed the United States had arisen "from the freedom of our institutions and the limited nature of our government."[4]

After—as before—the adoption of the Constitution, the overwhelming majority of free Americans continued to associate the pursuit of happiness with the private, not the public, realm and to regard government as an instrument not for dominating the private realm but for facilitating the manifold activities carried on by the multitude of individual citizens who composed it. Jesse Root, a Connecticut del-

Epilogue

egate to the Continental Congress, put this philosophy succinctly in the early 1780s. The "prospect of advantage," he wrote Jonathan Trumbull, was "the spring of industry, and economy," and that prospect, he averred, was "more or less opperative according to the opinion the people have of the justice of the government under which they live, the security it affords to property, and the liberty it gives to every one to make the most of what they have to put off in an honest way."[5]

Washington explained how the new central government could gain the affections of the people and win the allegiance of the peripheries by operating in exactly this facilitative and nonthreatening way. By ensuring justice, security, and liberty, the federal government, Washington wrote Lafayette in June 1788, would provide the public stability that would help to bring Americans what he referred to as "the fruits of freedom." "Whereas many causes will have conspired to produce" those fruits, he wrote, the public would invariably attribute them "to the fostering effects of the new government," and that development, as Madison later predicted, could not fail to lead to a consolidation, not of power in the national government, but of the "interests and affections" of the people in support of that government and to a conviction that private happiness depended upon an energetic union and could never be maintained if the United States were "split into a number of unsocial, jealous, and alien sovereignties." The good opinion of the public would give the new central government authority.[6]

Although sentiment for the union, identified with the national government, developed in much the way Washington and Madison had envisoned, it took a full quarter of a century to do so; in the meantime, as Stampp has explained, the Tenth Amendment provided the basis for the development of an elaborate theory of states rights. Initially enunciated most fully by Madison and Jefferson in the Virginia and Kentucky Resolutions of 1798–99 against the Alien and Sedition Acts, this theory asserted the right of states to judge the constitutionality of federal laws on the grounds that the Constitution was "a compact to which 'each State acceded as a State'; that the states had reserved the right to judge when the federal government" exceeded "its powers; that such measures" were " 'unauthoritative, void, and of no force'; that states" could " 'interpose' their authority to arrest the evil of unconstitutional federal acts; and that nullification" of unconstitutional acts was "a 'rightful remedy.'" Reaffirmed by New England opponents of the War of 1812 and reiterated during the debate over the admission of Missouri to statehood in 1820, the theory and language of state sovereignty, according to Stampp, had already by the 1820s "become deeply embedded in the American [political] vocabulary" and was readily available for use by the South Carolina nullificationists during the crisis of 1830–33.[7]

By contrast, the counterargument that the union took precedence over the states emerged far more slowly, roughly following the rise of public sentiment for the union. Questioning the theory of states rights, a few people reiterated the Federalist argument of the 1780s that sovereignty resided in the broad body of the people and not in the states and contended that the union was formed by the people and not by the states. But the idea of the supremacy of the national government was poorly developed before 1815, perhaps, as Stampp has suggested, because most American political leaders continued to think of the union as a bold new experiment that might very well not succeed. Although Chief Justice John Marshall's Supreme Court decisions between 1810 and 1821 went far to establish the supremacy of the federal government over the states in all areas in which it had been empowered by the Constitution, a concept of a perpetual and indissoluble union from which no member could secede and whose laws and judicial rulings were supreme in all cases in which it had been accorded authority by the Constitution was only fully elaborated in response to the Nullification Crisis of the early 1830s.[8]

But the articulation of a theory of perpetual union did not of course resolve the problem of which level of government—national or local—was supreme whenever the two came into conflict. In essence, the theory of states rights, like the colonial theory of the integrity of local rights before the American Revolution, remained for the peripheries as the main line of defense of local peculiarities and interests against the center—as defined by the majority of the union.

Especially after 1830, the major local peculiarity that some peripheral areas thought needed to be defended was the institution of chattel slavery. This problem had been foreseen by the leaders of the revolutionary generation, who, notwithstanding the strong social and cultural convergence that had characterized the development of the several regions of British America during the eighteenth century, worried about the long-range effects of the many "differences pecu-

Epilogue

liar to [the] Eastern, Middle, and Southern States." "The great danger to our general government," Madison declared in the Federal Convention in June 1788, was not the varying size of the states but *"the great southern and northern interests of the continent, being opposed to each other. Look to the votes in congress,"* he recommended to his listeners, *"most of them stand divided by the geography of the country, not according to the size of the states."* As southerners continued to regard slavery as essential to their economic survival and way of life and inhabitants of other sections increasingly came to see it as a moral evil and a stain on American republicanism, this division became ever more serious between 1820 and 1860.[9]

In the end, slavery was a problem that could not be resolved by peaceable means within the framework of the constitutional arrangements established in 1787–88. When the debate over this problem reached its final phase in 1860–61, it turned around the question of the nature of the union that had been created by those arrangements, whether the Constitution had created "a union of sovereign states, each of which retained the right to secede at its own discretion" or "a union from which no state, once having joined, could escape except by an extra-constitutional act of revolution?" On a question of such fundamental importance, the ancient issue of the location of sovereignty in an extended federal polity could not be avoided. Because the Constitution offered no unequivocal guidance on this matter, it could not provide the basis for achieving a consensus that could bridge the gap among contending points of view. When, in this situation, the southern states denied the legitimacy—always a function of opinion—of the union, of the center's right to command the continued respect and obedience of those areas in the peripheries that no longer acknowledged its right to authority over them, the union was faced with the stark alternative of relinquishing that authority altogether or attempting to restore it by force.[10]

The resulting Civil War, "America's most acute constitutional crisis," thus made it clear that, notwithstanding the framers' hopes, the problem of the distribution of authority between center and peripheries, between national and state governments, had not been fully settled by the Constitution of 1787. Indeed, not even the victory of the center in 1865 resolved this problem. Throughout the subsequent history of the United States, as throughout the previous history of the early modern British Empire, it has remained an issue of major and enduring importance. Over and over again, the center has had to resort to sanctions and force to coerce recalcitrant areas in the peripheries to comply with statutes and judicial rulings that ran counter to local opinion. In an extended polity composed of separate states, the experience of the early modern British Empire and the United States thus seems to indicate, boundary disputes between the authority of the center and that of the peripheries apparently can be settled only by separation, force, or the threat thereof.[11]

Notes

Preface

1. Edward Shils, "Center and Periphery," first published in *The Logic of Personal Knowledge: Essays in Honour of Michael Polyani* (Glencoe, Ill., 1961), is the title essay in *Center and Periphery: Essays in Macrosociology* (Chicago, 1975), 3–16.
2. Jack P. Greene, "From the Perspective of Law: Context and Legitimacy in the Origins of the American Revolution. A Review Essay," *South Atlantic Quarterly* 85(1986): 56–77, provides an extended analysis of the work of these legal historians; Peter S. Onuf, *The Origins of the Federal Republic: Jurisdictional Controversies in the United States, 1775–1787* (Philadelphia, 1983).
3. Bernard Bailyn, *The Ideological Origins of the American Revolution* (Boston, 1967), 160–229; Gordon S. Wood, *The Creation of the American Republic, 1776–1787* (Chapel Hill, 1969). Also important in this regard is J. R. Pole, *Political Representation in England and the Origins of the American Republic* (London, 1966). J. G. A. Pocock, *The Machiavellian Moment: Florentine Political Thought and the Atlantic Republican Tradition* (Princeton, 1975), is the classic study of the civic humanist tradition as it migrated from Renaissance Italy to early modern England to revolutionary America.
4. Particularly, Andrew C. McLaughlin, *The Foundations of American Constitutionalism* (New York, 1932), and *A Constitutional History of the United States* (New York, 1935); Charles H. McIlwain, *The American Revolution: A Constitutional Interpretation* (New York, 1923). Also important is Randolph G. Adams, *Political Ideas of the American Revolution* (Durham, N.C., 1922).
5. In addition to the works cited in note 3 above, Jack N. Rakove, *The Beginnings of National Politics: An Interpretive History of the Continental Congress* (New York, 1979), has been especially important.
6. Particularly the introductions to *Great Britain and the American Colonies, 1606–1763* (New York, 1970) and *The Nature of Colony Constitutions: Two Pamphlets on the Wilkes Fund Controversy by Sir Egerton Leigh and Arthur Lee* (Columbia, S.C., 1970) and "Political Mimesis: A Consideration of the Historical and Cultural Roots of Legislative Behavior in the British Colonies in the Eighteenth Century," *American Historical Review* 75(1969): 337–67; "William Knox's Explanation for the American Revolution," *William and Mary Quarterly*, 3d ser. 30(1973): 293–306; " 'A Posture of Hostility': A Reconsideration of Some Aspects of the Origins of the American Revolution," *American Antiquarian Society Proceedings* 87(1977): 27–68; "The Background to the Articles of Confederation," *Publius* 12(1982): 15–44; and "The Imperial Roots of American Federalism," *This Constitution*, no. 6 (1985), 4–11.

Prologue

1. Speech of Wilson, June 19, 1787, in Max Farrand, ed., *The Records of the Federal Convention of 1787*, 4 vols. (Washington, 1911–37), 1:322–23, 328, 330.
2. Madison to Jefferson, Oct. 24, 1787, in Julian P. Boyd, ed., *The Papers of Thomas Jefferson*, 19 vols. to date (Princeton, 1950–), 12:273.
3. Ibid., 271.
4. See Norman J. G. Pounds and Sue Simons Ball, "Core-Areas and the Development of the European State System," *Annals of the Association of American Geographers* 54(1964): 24–40.
5. Michael Hechter, *Internal Colonialism: The Celtic Fringe in British National Development, 1536–1966* (Berkeley and Los Angeles, 1975).
6. The concept of a satellite state is sensibly developed in Stale Dyrvik, Knut Mykland, and Jan Oldervoll, eds., *The Satellite State in the 17th and 18th Centuries* (Bergen, 1979).
7. *A Letter from Mr. Burke, to John Farr and John Harris, Esqrs. Sheriffs of the City of Bristol; on the Affairs of America* (1777), in *The Works of Edmund Burke*, 16 vols. (London, 1826), 3:187.

Chapter One

1. The best discussion of England's medieval empire and the relationships among its various parts is A. F. M. Madden, "1066, 1776, and All That: The Relevance of English Medieval Experience of 'Empire' to Later Imperial Constitutional Issues," in J. E. Flint and G. Williams, eds., *Perspectives of Empire* (London, 1973), 9–16. On the Welsh experience, see B. E. Howells, "Society in Early Modern Wales," in Stale Dyrvik, Knut Mykland, and Jan Oldervoll, eds., *The Satellite State in the 17th and 18th Centuries* (Bergen, 1979), 80–98.
2. On the Elizabethan and Jacobean plantations in Ireland see a series of recent articles by Nicholas Canny: "The Ideology of English Colonization: From Ireland to America," *William and Mary Quarterly*, 3d ser., 30(1973): 575–98; "Dominant Minorities: English Settlers in Ireland and Virginia, 1550–1650," in A. C. Hepburn, ed., *Minorities in History* (London, 1978), 51–69; and "The Permissive Frontier: The Problem of Social Control in English Settlements in Ireland and Virginia, 1550–1650," in K. R. Andrews, N. P. Canny, and P. E. H. Hair, eds., *The Westward Enterprise: English Activities in Ireland, the Atlantic, and America, 1480–1650* (Detroit, 1979), 17–44.
3. See among many similar characterizations of Greek and Roman colonization, Samuel Estwick, *A Letter to the Reverend Josiah Tucker, D.D., . . .* (London, 1776), 92–93. The most extensive contemporary analysis of the bearing of the colonial experience in antiquity upon that of the early modern British is by James Abercromby, a Scottish lawyer and member of

Parliament. See Jack P. Greene, Charles F. Mullett, and Edward C. Papen-
fuse, Jr., eds., *"Magna Charta for America": James Abercromby's "An Examination of the Acts of Parliament Relative to the Trade and the Government of our
American Colonies" (1752) and "De Jure et Gubernatione Coloniarum, or An
Inquiry into the Nature, and the Rights of Colonies, Ancient, and Modern"
(1774)* (Philadelphia, 1986).

4. See Stephens Saunders Webb, *The Governors-General: The English Army and
the Definition of the Empire, 1569–1681* (Chapel Hill, 1979), which provides
an extended discussion of the ways metropolitan experience with garrison government affected English official thought about the colonies.

5. John Trenchard and Thomas Gordon, *Cato's Letters*, 4 vols. (London,
1724), 3:283–84; William Douglass, *Summary, Historical and Political, of the
first Planting, progressive Improvements, and present State of the British Settlements in North-America*, 2 vols. (Boston, 1749–51), 1:205–7; Malachy
Postlethwayt, *The Universal Dictionary of Trade and Commerce*, 2 vols. (London, 1757), 2:471; Estwick, *Letter to Josiah Tucker*, 92–93; and Anthony
Stokes, *A View of the Constitution of the British Colonies . . .* (London, 1783),
1–3, all contain contemporary discussion of the nature of colonies. An
interesting short modern analysis is M. I. Finley, "Colonies—An Attempt
at a Typology," *Transactions of the Royal Historical Society*, 5th ser., 26 (1976):
167–88.

6. W. L. Grant and J. Munro, eds., *Acts of the Privy Council, Colonial Series*, 6
vols. (London, 1908–12), 1:49. For the confusion over whether the colonies were "foreign" or "home," see the description of the House of Commons debate over whether Sir George Somers, admiral of the fleet that
sailed for Virginia in May 1609, should lose his seat in Parliament for
having left the realm in Wilcomb E. Washburn, "Law and Authority in
Colonial Virginia," in George A. Billias, ed., *Law and Authority in Colonial
America* (Barre, Mass., 1965), 121.

7. William Smith, *Mr. Smith's Opinion Humbly Offered to the General Assembly
of the Colony of New-York* [New York, 1734], 17; James Knight, "The Natural, Moral, and Political History of Jamaica, and the Territories thereon
depending," 2:112, in Long Papers, Additional Manuscripts 12,419, British Library, London; Jeremiah Dummer, *A Defence of the New-England
Charters* (London, 1726), 56; John Vaughan, *The Reports and Arguments of
that Learned Judge Sir John Vaughan* (London, 1677), 401–2; Opinion of
Henley and Yorke, May 18, 1757, in George Chalmers, ed., *Opinions of
Eminent Lawyers* (Burlington, Vt., 1858), 209.

8. Stokes, *View of the Constitution*, 12. The definitions in this paragraph and
throughout this volume are taken from Samuel Johnson, *A Dictionary of
the English Language*, 8th ed., 2 vols. (London, 1799).

9. Grant and Munro, eds., *Acts of the Privy Council, Colonial*, 1:48–49; "The
Watchman, Letter IV," *Pennsylvania Journal and Weekly Advertiser* (Philadelphia), Apr. 27, 1758; Michael Hechter, *Internal Colonialism: The Celtic
Fringe in British National Development, 1536–1936* (Berkeley and Los Angeles, 1975), 62–63.

10. Kenneth R. Andrews, *Trade, Plunder and Settlement: Maritime Enterprise and the Genesis of the British Empire, 1480–1630* (Cambridge, 1984), 16–17; Mark A. Kishlansky, "Community and Continuity: A Review of Selected Works on English Local History," *William and Mary Quarterly*, 3d ser., 37(1980): 140, 146.

11. Opinion of Harcourt and Montague, Dec. 23, 1707, in Chalmers, ed., *Opinions of Eminent Lawyers*, 345; Assembly Proceedings, Oct. 25, 1722, in William H. Browne et al., eds., *Archives of Maryland*, 72 vols. (Baltimore, 1883–), 34:442; *The Case of William Penn, Esq; As to the Proprietary Government of Pennsylvania* [London, 1701].

12. Vaughan, *Reports and Arguments*, 402; "A Proclamation for Settlinge the Plantations of Virginia," May 13, 1625, in Thomas Rymer, ed., *Foedera, Conventiones, Literal, Acta Publica, Regis Anglicae*, 2d ed., 20 vols. (London, 1726), 18:72–73; Herman Merivale, *Lectures on Colonization and Colonies* (London, 1861), 75; N. Darnell Davis, *The Cavaliers and Roundheads of Barbados, 1650–1652* (Georgetown, British Guiana, 1883), 197–200.

13. The most thorough modern treatment of the navigation measures is Lawrence A. Harper, *The English Navigation Laws: A Seventeenth-Century Experiment in Social Engineering* (New York, 1939). The quotation is from a report of royal commissioners sent to investigate the New England colonies, [April 30,] 1661, in W. Noel Sainsbury et al., eds., *Calendar of State Papers, Colonial*, 44 vols. (London, 1860–), *1661–68*, 25.

14. These efforts may be followed in detail in several excellent modern works: A. P. Thornton, *West-India Policy under the Restoration* (Oxford, 1956); Philip Haffenden, "The Crown and the Colonial Charters, 1675–1688," *William and Mary Quarterly*, 3d ser., 14 (1958): 297–311, 452–66; Michael G. Hall, *Edward Randolph and the American Colonies, 1676–1703* (Chapel Hill, 1960); Richard S. Dunn, "Imperial Pressures on Massachusetts and Jamaica, 1675–1700," in Alison Gilbert Olson and Richard Maxwell Brown, eds., *Anglo-American Political Relations, 1675–1775* (New Brunswick, N.J., 1970), 52–75; David S. Lovejoy, *The Glorious Revolution in America* (New York, 1972); Webb, *Governors-General*, 151–459, and *1676: The End of American Independence* (New York, 1984); J. M. Sosin, *English America and the Restoration Monarchy of Charles II: Trans-Atlantic Politics, Commerce, and Kinship* (Lincoln, Neb. 1980), and *English America and the Revolution of 1688: Royal Administration and the Structure of Provincial Government* (Lincoln, Neb., 1982); and Richard R. Johnson, *Adjustment of Empire: The New England Colonies, 1675–1715* (New Brunswick, N.J., 1981).

15. As quoted by Agnes M. Whitson, *The Constitutional Development of Jamaica, 1660 to 1729* (Manchester, 1929), 162. On the pretensions and powers of the early colonial legislative assemblies, see Michael Kammen, *Deputyes & Libertyes: The Origins of Representative Government in Colonial America* (New York, 1969), 3–68.

16. As quoted by George Dargo, *Roots of the Republic: A New Perspective on Early American Constitutionalism* (New York, 1974), 58. See also Kammen, *Deputyes & Libertyes*, 58–64.

17. These efforts are treated in detail in Lovejoy, *Glorious Revolution in Amer-ica*. But see also the excellent documentary collection, Michael G. Hall, Lawrence H. Leder, and Michael G. Kammen, eds., *The Glorious Revolution in America* (Chapel Hill, 1964).

18. Caleb Heathcote to Board of Trade, Sept. 7, 1719, as quoted by Dixon Ryan Fox, *Caleb Heathcote, Gentleman Colonist* (New York, 1926), 186–89.

Chapter Two

1. N. Darnell Davis, *The Cavaliers and Roundheads of Barbados, 1650–1652* (Georgetown, British Guinea, 1883), 198–99.

2. Edward Littleton, *The Groans of the Plantations* (London, 1689), 15–17. For additional references to colonial resistance to the Navigation Acts, see the references in Chapter 1, note 13.

3. Jack P. Greene, ed., "William Knox's Explanation for the American Revolution," *William and Mary Quarterly*, 3d ser., 30(1973): 302; [Nicholas Bourke], *The Privileges of the Island of Jamaica Vindicated with an Impartial Narrative of the late Dispute between the Governor and House of Representatives* (London, 1766), 8; Bernard Bailyn, *The Origins of American Politics* (New York, 1968), 66–71; "Of the American Plantations," [Feb. 23, 1715], in William L. Saunders, ed., *The Colonial Records of North Carolina*, 10 vols. (Raleigh, 1886–90), 2:166.

4. [Benjamin Harrison III], *An Essay upon the Government of the English Planta-tions on the Continent of America (1701); An Anonymous Virginian's Proposals for Liberty under the British Crown, with Two Memoranda by William Byrd*, ed. Louis B. Wright (San Marino, Calif., 1945), 17; *The Groans of Jamaica, Ex-press'd in a Letter from a Gentleman Residing there, to his Friend in London* (London, 1714), iv.

5. *A Letter to S[ir] C. M. a Member of Parliament from an Inhabitant of the Island of Barbados* (Bridgetown, [1700]), 1–2; *The Case of William Penn, Esq; As to the Proprietary Government of Pennsylvania* [London, 1701], "Of the American Plantations," [Feb. 23, 1715], Saunders, ed., *Colonial Records of North Car-olina*, 2:159–60; [William Cleland], *The Present State of the Sugar Plantations Consider'd . . .*(London, 1713), 8; [Harrison], *Essay upon the Government of the English Plantations*, 11; *Some Considerations on the Consequences of the French Settling Colonies on the Mississippi* (London, 1720), 41–42; *Some In-stances of the Oppression and Male Administration of Col. Parke, late Governor of the Leeward Islands, with an Account of the Rise and Progress of the Insurrec-tion at Antegoa . . .* (N.p., n.d.); *The Humble Representation of the General Assembly of . . . New-Jersey to His Excellency Robert Hunter* (New York, 1710), 1; *The Deplorable State of New England by Reason of a Covetous and Treacherous Governor* (Boston, 1720); Lewis Morris to secretary of state, Feb. 9, 1707, in E. B. O'Callaghan and Berthold Fernow, eds., *Documents Relative to the Colonial History of the State of New York*, 15 vols. (Albany, 1856–87), 5:37.

6. *A Letter to S[ir] C. M.*, 4–5; *A Pattern for Governours: Exemplify'd in the Character of Scroop Late Lord Viscount Howe, Baron of Clonawly; and Governour of Barbados* (London, 1735); James Otis, *A Vindication of the Conduct of the House of Representatives of the Province of the Massachusetts-Bay* (Boston, 1762), 18, 20; [William Gordon], *A Representation of the Miserable State of Barbados* (London, 1719), 22–23; Speech of Sir John Randolph, Aug. 6, 1736, in John Pendleton Kennedy and Henry R. McIlwain, eds., *Journals of the House of Burgesses of Virginia, 1727–1740* (Richmond, 1910), 242; *Pennsylvania Gazette* (Philadelphia), Apr. 22, 1736; A New-England Man, *A Letter to the Freeholders and Qualified Voters, Relating to the Ensuing Election* (Boston, 1742), 5; *American Magazine & Monthly Chronicle for the British Colonies* 1 (1758): 227.

7. *The Liberty and Property of British Subjects Asserted* (London, 1726), 28, 32; Samuel Nadgorth to Secretary Morrice, Oct. 26, 1666, in W. Noel Sainsbury et al., eds., *Calendar of State Papers, Colonial*, 44 vols. (London, 1860–), *1661–68*, 417–18; Davis, *Cavaliers and Roundheads*, 198–99; Littleton, *Groans of the Plantations*, 15–17, 23, 26; *A State of the Present Condition of the Island of Barbados* (London, 1698), 3; *Maryland Gazette* (Annapolis), Mar. 16, 1748; *The Case of the Inhabitants and Planters in the Island of Jamaica* (London, [1714]).

8. A New-England Man, *Letter to the Freeholders*, 5; [Thomas Nairne], *A Letter from South Carolina* (London, 1710), 22.

9. The contemporary discussion of the legal status of the colonies and the questions of under what circumstances what sorts of English law applied there may be traced in A. Berriedale Keith, *Constitutional History of the First British Empire* (Oxford, 1930), 9–17, 182–86; Sir William Searle Holdsworth, *A History of English Law*, 16 vols. (London, 1922–66), 11:229–48; and, especially, in the excellent analysis by Joseph Henry Smith, *Appeals to the Privy Council from the American Plantations* (New York, 1950), 464–522. The quotations are from Smith, *Appeals*, 468, 472; and Peere Williams, *Reports*, 3 vols. (London, 1740), 2: 75–76.

10. Sir William Blackstone, *Commentaries on the Laws of England*, 4 vols. (London, 1822), 1:112; Greene, ed., "Knox's Explanation for the American Revolution," 302; Anthony Stokes, *A View of the Constitution of the British Colonies . . .* (London, 1783), 10–12; [Edward Long], *The History of Jamaica*, 3 vols. (London, 1774), 1:160.

11. Agnes M. Whitson, *The Constitutional Development of Jamaica, 1660 to 1729* (Manchester, 1929), 60–167; St. George Leakin Sioussat, *The English Statutes in Maryland* (Baltimore, 1903); Keith, *Constitutional History*, 141; Duke of Portland to [Lord Carteret], Dec. 7, 1723, in *Calendar of State Papers, Colonial, 1722–23*, 385.

12. Keith, *Constitutional History*, 185–86; Stokes, *View of the Constitution*, 10; Jeremiah Dummer, *A Defence of the New-England Charters* (London, 1726), 56–57.

13. [Lewis Morris], *Some Observations upon the Charge Given by the Honourable James De Lancey, Esq. . . .* (New York, 1734), 9–11; [Harrison], *Essay upon the Government of the English Plantations*, 23.

14. Richard West to Board of Trade, June 20, 1720, *Calendar of State Papers, Colonial, 1720–21*, 53; Peere Williams, *Reports*, 2:75; [Morris], *Some Observations upon the Charge*, 10.

15. Greene, ed., "Knox's Explanation for the American Revolution," 302–3; Isaac Norris, *The Speech Delivered from the Bench in the Court of Common Pleas held for the City and Court of Philadelphia* (Philadelphia, 1727), 2; Sir John Randolph to Captain Pearse, [1734–35], in William Smith, Jr., *The History of the Province of New-York*, ed. Michael Kammen, 2 vols. (Cambridge, Mass., 1972), 1:264–67; Smith, *Appeals to the Privy Council*, 476–85; Thomas Nairne to [Earl of Sunderland], July 28, [1708], *Calendar of State Papers, Colonial, 1708–9*, 433; Daniel Dulany, *The Right of the Inhabitants of Maryland to the Benefit of the English Laws* (Annapolis, 1728); Sir William Keith, "A Short Discourse on the Present State of the Colonies in America," [1726], in Jack P. Greene, ed., *Great Britain and the American Colonies, 1606–1763* (New York, 1970), 191–92.

16. Smith, *Appeals to the Privy Council*, 520–22; Edward Long, "On the Constitution and Government of Jamaica," [ca. 1770s–1780s], Long Papers, Additional Manuscripts 12,402, British Library, London, f. 42b. Gooch's remarks, written in the late 1720s, are reprinted in Greene, ed., *Great Britain and the American Colonies*, 196–212. The quotations are from p. 203.

17. [Harrison], *Essay upon the Government of the English Plantations*, 23; Keith, "Discourse," in Greene, ed., *Great Britain and the American Colonies*, 192; Christopher Codrington, Jr., to Board of Trade, Nov. 10, 1701, *Calendar of State Papers, Colonial, 1701*, 602, 604–5; Browne et al., eds., *Archives of Maryland*, 61:330–31.

18. [Harrison], *Essay upon the Government of the English Plantations*, 23–24.

19. Smith, *Appeals to the Privy Council*, 465; Leonard W. Labaree, ed., *Royal Instructions to British Colonial Governors*, 2 vols. (New York, 1935), 2:818–19; Edward Northey to Board of Trade, May 31, 1703, *Calendar of State Papers, Colonial, 1702–3*, 470–71.

20. Robert Raymond to Board of Trade, Aug. 19, 1713, *Calendar of State Papers, Colonial, 1712–14*, 222; Board of Trade to king, Sept. 8, 1721, ibid., *1720–21*, 444–49; Board of Trade to House of Lords, Jan. 23, 1734, ibid., *1734–35*, 12; William Douglass, *Summary, Historical and Political, of the First Planting, Progressive Improvements, and Present State of the British Settlements in North America*, 2 vols. (Boston, 1749–51), 1:207; *An Account of the Present-State of Nova-Scotia* (London, 1756), 2–7; Opinion of Murray and Lloyd, Apr. 29, 1755, in George Chalmers, ed., *Opinions of Eminent Lawyers* (Burlington, Vt., 1858), 263–64.

21. Labaree, ed., *Royal Instructions*, 2: 819; Board of Trade to House of Lords, Jan. 23, 1734, *Calendar of State Papers, Colonial, 1734–35*, 11–13.

22. Jonathan Law to Jonathan Belcher, June 18, 1728, "The Talcott Papers," *Collections of the Connecticut Historical Society*, 42 vols. (Hartford, 1860–), 4: 121; Jeremiah Dummer, *A Defence of the New-England Charters* (London, 1726), 56–57; Governor and Company of Rhode Island, Reply to Charges, Feb. 1, 1706, *Calendar of State Papers, Colonial, 1706–8*, 33–35; [Morris], *Some Observations upon the Charge*, 8–10. Smith, *Appeals to the Privy Coun-*

cil, 523–653, is a superb general discussion of the processes of legislative and judicial review by the Privy Council and of the various issues involved in those processes. Though it was not exempt by charter, Delaware, which was under the jurisdiction of the Penn family, also seems usually not to have submitted its laws for review in London.

23. [Nairne], *Letter from South Carolina,* 21–22; Douglass, *Summary, Historical and Political,* 1:213–14; Henry Worsley to Duke of Newcastle, Aug. 4, 1727, *Calendar of State Papers, Colonial, 1726–27,* 325–26; *Remarks on the Proceedings of some Members of Assembly at Philadelphia: April 1728* [Philadelphia, 1728], 1–2. In this connection, see also Jack P. Greene, "Political Mimesis: A Consideration of the Historical and Cultural Roots of Legislative Behavior in the British Colonies in the Eighteenth Century," *American Historical Review* 75(1969): 337–60.

24. James Knight, "The Natural, Moral, and Political History of Jamaica, and the Territories thereon depending," 1:193, 206, in Long Papers, Additional Manuscripts 12, 419, British Library, London; [Bourke], *Privileges of the Island of Jamaica Vindicated,* 3, 33–34; [Nairne], *Letter from South Carolina,* 21–22; [Joseph Galloway], *A True and Impartial State of the Province of Pennsylvania* (Philadelphia, 1759), 36; Otis, *Vindication of the Conduct of the House of Representatives,* 15; Massachusetts House of Representatives to the king, June 17, 1724, *Calendar of State Papers, Colonial, 1724–25,* 210–14; *The Case of the Colony of Connecticut, upon its Present Establishment under the Charter of K. Charles II* (London, [1701]); *Votes and Proceedings of the General Assembly of the Colony of New-York, June 27, 1749 to August 4, 1749* (New York, 1749), 14–17. See also Jack P. Greene, *The Quest for Power: The Lower Houses of Assembly in the Southern Royal Colonies, 1689–1763* (Chapel Hill, 1963).

25. [Harrison], *Essay upon the Government of the English Plantations,* 17; [Gordon], *Representation of the Miserable State of Barbados,* 32–33; [Nairne], *Letter from South Carolina,* 21–22, 26–27; A New-England Man, *Letter to the Freeholders,* 5; William Duke, *Some Memoirs of the First Settlement of the Island of Barbados and Other the Caribbee Islands* (London, 1743), 63; "Reasons offer'd by the . . . Council," n.d., in Samuel Keimer, *Caribbeana,* 2 vols. (London, 1741), 2: 312–15; Stokes, *View of the Constitution,* 23–24, 243; [Galloway], *True and Impartial State,* 23.

26. Lords of Trade to Privy Council, May 28, 1679, *Calendar of State Papers, Colonial, 1677–80,* 368; Sir William Beeston to Board of Trade, Aug. 19, 1701, ibid., *1701,* 424–25; Robert Lowther to Board of Trade, Aug. 16, 1712, ibid., *1712–14,* 29; Board of Trade to king, Aug. 10, 1721, ibid., *1720–21,* 386–87; Samuel Shute to king, [Aug. 16, 1723], ibid., *1722–23,* 324–30; *The Representation and Memorial of the Council of the Island of Jamaica to the Right Honourable The Lords Commissioners for Trade and Plantations* (London, 1716), ii, iv, 14.

27. Lowther to Board of Trade, Aug. 16, 1712, *Calendar of State Papers, Colonial, 1712–14,* 29; Cadwallader Colden, "Observations on the Balance of Power in Government," [1744–45], in Greene, ed., *Great Britain and the American*

Colonies, 252–58; James Glen to Board of Trade, Oct. 10, 1748, in ibid., 261–67; George Clinton to Board of Trade, Oct. 20, 1748, O'Callaghan and Fernow, eds., *Documents of Colonial New York*, 6:456–57; Thomas Pownall, "State of the Government of Massachusetts Bay as it stood in the Year 1757," Colonial Office Papers 941, ff. 363–73, Public Record Office, London; [Archibald Kennedy], *An Essay on the Government of the Colonies* (New York, 1752), and *A Speech Said to Have been Delivered Some Time before the Close of the Last Sessions* ([New York], 1755), 5, 36–37; [William Smith], *A Brief State of the Province of Pennsylvania*, 3d ed. (London, 1756), 10–12.

28. Lords of Trade to Privy Council, May 28, 1679, *Calendar of State Papers, Colonial, 1677–80*, 369.

29. Opinions of Edward Northey and Samuel Harcourt, Feb. 1, 1705, Robert Raymond, Sept. 16, 1723, Francis Fane, July 20, 1738, July 1, 1746, Dudley Ryder and William Murray, Mar. 18, 1747, July 20, 1753, in Chalmers, ed., *Opinions of Eminent Lawyers*, 270–92, 295; Sir William Beeston to Thomas Barrow, [1701], *Calendar of State Papers, Colonial, 1701*, 427; Henry Worsley to Duke of Newcastle, Aug. 4, 1727, ibid., *1726–27*, 325–26; [Kennedy], *Essay on the Government of the Colonies*, 14–17; *Some Considerations on the Consequences of the French Settling Colonies*, 41; John Palmer, *The Present State of New-England Impartially Considered* (Boston, 1689), 10–11; Lewis Morris, Speech to the New Jersey Assembly, Mar. 15, 1739, in *Pennsylvania Gazette* (Philadelphia), Apr. 19, 1739; [Lewis Morris], *Extracts from the Minutes and Votes of the House of Assembly of the Colony of New Jersey . . . to which are added Some Notes and Observations on the said Votes* ([Philadelphia], 1743), 7–8, 37–38; [Edward Horne], *A Defence of the Legislative Constitution of Pennsylvania As it now stands Confirmed and Established, by Law and Charter* (Philadelphia, 1728), 3–5; *South Carolina Gazette* (Charleston), June 5, 1756.

30. Zacharius Plaintruth, *New-York Gazette Revived in the Weekly Post-Boy* (New York), Jan. 27, 1752; George Clinton, *A Message from His Excellency the Honourable George Clinton . . . of New-York . . . on . . . the Thirteenth of October, 1747* ([New York, 1747]), 2; Lewis Morris to Board of Trade, Jan. 28, 1745, in "The Papers of Lewis Morris," *Collections of the New Jersey Historical Society* 4 (1852): 225–26; Palmer, *Present State of New-England*, 10–11; "Colonel Coddrington's Opinion," n.d., and "Reasons offer'd by the . . . Council," n.d., Keimer, ed., *Caribbeana*, 2: 97, 313–14; Greene, ed., "Knox's Explanation for the American Revolution," 301.

31. Keith, "Short Discourse," in Greene, ed., *Great Britain and the American Colonies*, 189–91; *Case of the Colony of Connecticut*; Opinions of William Rawlins, [ca. 1715], Richard West, May 27, 1719, Lewis Morris, [1730s], and Charles Pratt, [1757–58], in Chalmers, ed., *Opinions of Eminent Lawyers*, 239–43, 249–57, 264–67, 373–82; *New-York Gazette* (New York), Oct. 8, 1739; *Remarks upon a Message Sent by the Lower House to the Upper House of Assembly Apr. 4, 1762* ([Philadelphia], 1764), 13; *The Proceedings of Some Members of Assembly, at Philadelphia, April 1728, Vindicated* [Philadelphia, 1728], 1–2; Sir John Harvey to Secretary Windebank, July 14, 1635, in

Calendar of State Papers, Colonial, 1575–1660, 212; Board of Trade to Viscount Cornbury, Feb. 4, 1706, ibid., *1706–8*, 45; Instructions to Sir Nathaniel Lawes, Jan. 1, 1718, ibid., *1717–18*, 66–67; Shute to king, [Aug. 16, 1723], ibid., *1722–23*, 324–30; *Representation and Memorial of the Council of Jamaica*, iv, 14; *Some Instances of Oppression and Male Administration of Col. Parke*, 1; Watchman, #1, *Pennsylvania Journal & Weekly Advertiser* (Philadelphia), Feb. 23, 1758; *The Honest Man's Interest As he Claims any Lands In the Counties of New-Castle, Kent, or Sussex, on Delaware* ([Philadelphia, 1726]), 1; [Smith], *Brief State of the Province of Pennsylvania*, 12–13; [Kennedy], *Essay on the Government of the Colonies*, 10–20; Isaac Norris, *Friendly Advice to the Inhabitants of Pennsylvania* (Philadelphia, 1710), 2.

32. Zacharius Plaintruth, *New-York Gazette Revived*, Jan. 27, 1752; [Bourke], *Privileges of the Island of Jamaica Vindicated*, 45; Thomas Prince, *A Sermon on the Sorrowful Occasion of the Death of His Late Majesty King George* (Boston, 1727), 26; Thomas Foxcroft, *God the Judge, putting down One, and setting up Another* (Boston, 1727), 27, 39; Jared Eliot, *Give Cesar his Due; or, The Obligation the Subjects are under to Their Civil Rulers* (New London, 1738), 36–37; *New-England Weekly Journal* (Boston), Mar. 18, 1728; Norris, *Speech Delivered from the Bench*, 2; A Freeholder, *Maryland Gazette* (Annapolis), Mar. 10, 1748; The Inhabitant, *South Carolina Gazette* (Charleston), Dec. 10, 1764; [Edward Rawson], *The Revolution in New England Justified* (Boston, 1691), 42–43; [Increase Mather], *The Declaration of the Gentlemen, Merchants, and Inhabitants of Boston, and the Countrey Adjacent* (Boston, 1689), 2; *New York Gazette*, Aug. 19, 1728; Americanus, *A Letter to the Freeholders and other Inhabitants of the Massachusetts-Bay* ([Boston], 1739), 5; [Richard Jackson], *An Historical Review of the Constitution of Government of Pennsylvania* (London, 1759), 7; Thomas Pownall, *The Administration of the Colonies* (London, 1764), 40–41.

33. William Bollan's Petition to the House of Commons, Aug. 6, 1749, Massachusetts Archives (Boston), 20:501–6; [Bourke], *Privileges of the Island of Jamaica Vindicated*, 28; [William Smith], *Mr. Smith's Opinion Humbly Offered to the General Assembly of the Colony of New York* (New York, 1734), 13, 34, 45; Opinions of Richard West, 1720, and Charles Pratt and Charles Yorke, n.d., Chalmers, ed., *Opinions of Eminent Lawyers*, 206–7; Otis, *Vindication of the Conduct of the House of Representatives*, 51–52; Pennsylvania Assembly Journals, *Pennsylvania Archives* (Harrisburg, 1852–1935), 8th ser., 5:4176–77; *Boston Evening Post* (Boston), Apr. 27, 1761; [Rawson], *Revolution in New England Justified*, 42–43.

34. Smith, *Mr. Smith's Opinion Humbly Offered*, 34; [Rawson], *Revolution in New England Justified*, 42–43; Smith, *History of New York*, 256–58; The Inhabitant, *South Carolina Gazette*, Dec. 10, 1764; [William Blathwayt] to Chief Justice North, [Oct. 20, 1680], *Calendar of State Papers, Colonial, 1677–80*, 616; Cornbury to Board of Trade, Feb. 19, 1705, ibid., *1704–6*, 386; Board of Trade to Privy Council, Nov. 13, 1711, ibid., *1711–12*, 146–47; Knight, "History of Jamaica," 2:110–18; Christopher Gadsden, *South Carolina Gazette*, Feb. 5, 1763; "Remarks on the Maryland Government,"

American Magazine, or, a Monthly Review of the Political State of the American Colonies 1 (1741): 29–30; Dalby Thomas, *An Historical Account of the Rise and Growth of the West-India Colonies* (London, 1690), 32; John Webb, *The Great Concern of New-England* (Boston, 1731), 28; Pownall, *Administration of the Colonies*, 40.

35. Joseph Murray, *Mr. Murray's Opinion Relating to the Courts of Justice in the Colony of New-York* [New York, 1734], 5–6; Sir John Davies, *Irish Reports* (London, 1674), preface; Opinion of Charles Pratt, [1757–58], Chalmers, ed., *Opinions of Eminent Lawyers*, 265–66; George Petyt, *Lex Parliamentaria: or a Treatise of the Law and Custom of the Parliaments of England* (London, 1689), 9, 36–37, 81–82, 87, 139.

36. J.G.A. Pocock, *The Ancient Constitution and the Feudal Law: English Historical Thought in the Seventeenth Century* (New York, 1967), 30–38, 50–51, 170–78, 233–43; Thomas Rutherforth, *Institutes of Natural Law; being the Substance of a Course of Lectures on Grotius' de Jure Belli ac Pacis*, 2 vols. (Cambridge, 1754–56). The Rutherforth quotations are from the second American edition (Baltimore, 1832), 63, 65, 296–97, 326, 396, 566.

37. Murray, *Mr. Murray's Opinion*, 7, 15.

38. Thomas Lynch to Lords of Trade, Dec. 18, 1678, and Lord Carlisle's Charges against Samuel Long, [Sept. 16, 1680], *Calendar of State Papers, Colonial, 1677–80*, 457, 603; [Rawson], *Revolution in New England Justified*, 6; Jonathan Law to Jonathan Belcher, June 18, 1728, and Instruction to Belcher, [1728], "Talcott Papers," *Collections of the Connecticut Historical Society*, 4: 122–23, 143–44; Maryland Assembly Proceedings, Oct. 8, 1722, Browne, et al., eds., *Archives of Maryland*, 34:442; [Cleland], *Present State of the Sugar Plantations*, 12–13.

39. Knight, "History of Jamaica," 2:110–16; Christopher Gadsden, *South Carolina Gazette*, Dec. 17, 1764; [Bourke], *Privileges of the Island of Jamaica Vindicated*, 31; Elisha Cooke, *Mr. Cooke's Just and Seasonable Vindication Respecting some Affairs transacted by the late General Assembly at Boston, 1720* [Boston, 1720], 9; Henry Wilkinson, "The Governor, the Council & Assembly in Bermuda during the First Half of the Eighteenth Century," *Bermuda Historical Quarterly* 2 (1945): 81–84; "Vindication of the Council," *South Carolina Gazette*, June 5, 1756; [Jonathan Blenman], *Remarks on Several Acts of Parliament Relating More especially to the Colonies abroad* (London, 1742), 17; *Pennsylvania Gazette*, Mar. 30, 1738, Oct. 2, 1755; [Nairne], *Letter from South Carolina*, 25; David Lloyd, *A Vindication of the Legislative Power, Submitted to the Representatives of all the Free-men of the Province of Pennsylvania, now sitting in Assembly* ([Philadelphia,] 1725), 3; Americanus, *Letter to the Freeholders*, 5; *American Magazine*, 1:26–27, 30–31.

40. Christopher Gadsden, *South Carolina Gazette*, Dec. 3, 1764; Board of Trade to William Mathew, Oct. 22, 1730, *Calendar of State Papers, Colonial, 1730*, 327–28; Opinions of Philip Yorke and Charles Talbot, Aug. 1, 1730, Dudley Ryder and William Murray, July 20, 1753, and Murray and Richard Lloyd, Apr. 29, 1755, Chalmers, ed., *Opinions of Eminent Lawyers*, 291–93, 341–42, 352–53; [John Pownall], "General Propositions: Form and Constitution to

230

Notes to Pages 44–47

be established in the new Colonies," [1763], Shelburne Papers, 90:559–60, William L. Clements Library, Ann Arbor, Mich.; James Logan, *The Charge Delivered from the Bench to the Grand-Jury* (Philadelphia, 1723), 5; Alexander Forrester's Argument, in Jack P. Greene, ed., "The Case of the Pistole Fee: The Report of a Hearing on the Pistole Fee Dispute before the Privy Council, June 18, 1754," *Virginia Magazine of History and Biography* 66 (1958): 418; *Pennsylvania Gazette*, Oct. 2, 1755.

Chapter Three

1. Charles D'Avenant, *Political and Commercial Works*, 4 vols. (London, 1771), 2:35, 55; [Benjamin Harrison III], *An Essay upon the Government of the English Plantations on the Continent of America (1701); An Anonymous Virginian's Proposals for Liberty under the British Crown, with Two Memoranda by William Byrd*, ed. Louis B. Wright (San Marino, Calif., 1945), 15–24; *The Groans of Jamaica, Expressed in a Letter from a Gentleman Residing there, to his Friend in London* (London, 1714), iv; William Wood, *A Survey of Trade*, 2d ed. (London, 1719), 177.
2. John Trenchard and Thomas Gordon, *Cato's Letters*, 4 vols. (London, 1724), 3:286.
3. James Madison, "Public Opinion," Dec. 19, 1791, in Gaillard Hunt, ed., *The Writings of James Madison*, 9 vols. (New York, 1900–1910), 6:70; Edmund Burke, "Letter to the Sheriffs of Bristol," in *The Works of Edmund Burke*, 16 vols. (London, 1826), 3:179; A Merchant, *A Discourse of the Duties on Merchandize, more Particularly of that on Sugars* (London, 1695), 6–7.
4. Archibald Kennedy, *Observations on the Importance of the Northern Colonies under Proper Regulations* (New York, 1750), 12, 30–31; The Watchman, #4, *Pennsylvania Journal & Weekly Advertiser*, Apr. 27, 1758; George Chalmers, *An Introduction to the History of the Revolt of the American Colonies*, 2 vols. (Boston, 1845), 1:16; Malachy Postlethwayt, *The Universal Dictionary of Trade and Commerce*, 2 vols. (London, 1757), 1:535; Josiah Tucker, *A Brief Essay on the Advantages and Disadvantages . . .* (London, 1750), 95–96; Adam Smith, *An Inquiry into the Nature and Causes of the Wealth of Nations* (Chicago: Encyclopedia Britannica, 1952), 246.
5. Joshua Gee, *The Trade and Navigation of Great-Britain* (London, 1729), 98; Charles Delafaye to Francis Nicholson, Jan. 16, 1722, in Jack P. Greene, ed., *Settlements to Society, 1584–1763* (New York, 1966), 231–32.
6. William Gooch, "Some Remarks on a Paper transmitted into America . . . ," in Jack P. Greene, ed., *Great Britain and the American Colonies, 1606–1763* (New York, 1970), 196–97, 208, 212; Chalmers, *Introduction to the History of the Revolt*, 2:354. See also Bernard Bailyn, *The Origins of American Politics* (New York, 1968), 72–80.
7. "Of the State of the British Plantations in America," in Joseph E. Johnson, ed., "A Quaker Imperialist's View of the British Colonies in America:

1732," *Pennsylvania Magazine of History and Biography* 60 (1936): 114; Gabriel Johnston to Lord Wilmington, Feb. 10, 1737, Historical Manuscripts Commission, *The Manuscripts of the Marquess of Townshend* (London, 1887), 262–64.

8. *The Charter of Maryland Together with the Debates and Proceedings of the . . . Assembly* (Annapolis, 1725), iii; Gooch, "Some Remarks on a Paper," in Greene, ed., *Great Britain and the American Colonies*, 200; Burke, "Letter to the Sheriffs of Bristol," in *Works*, 3:189; Ferdinand John Paris to Jeremiah Allen, July 26, 1738, "Talcott Papers," *Collections of the Connecticut Historical Society* 5 (1896): 83.

9. Opinions of Rawlins, n.d., and Pratt, [1757–58], George Chalmers, ed., *Opinions of Eminent Lawyers* (Burlington, Vt., 1858), 267, 376; Gooch, "Some Remarks on a Paper," and Sir John Randolph's Speech, [Aug. 6, 1737], in Greene, ed., *Great Britain and the American Colonies*, 200, 244–45; Burke, "Letter to the Sheriffs of Bristol," in *Works*, 3: 189; [Nicholas Bourke], *Privileges of the Island of Jamaica Vindicated with an Impartial Narrative of the Late Dispute between the Governor and House of Representatives* (London, 1766), 31; *Remarks upon a Message Sent by the Lower House to the Upper House of Assembly Apr. 4, 1762* ([Philadelphia], 1764), 14; J.N., *The Liberty and Property of British Subjects Asserted* (London, 1726), 22; James Otis, *A Vindication of the Conduct of the House of Representatives of the Province of Massachusetts-Bay* (Boston, 1762), 52; *Charter of Maryland Together with the Debates*, iii.

10. Gooch, "Some Remarks on a Paper," in Greene, ed., *Great Britain and the American Colonies*, 198; Jack P. Greene, ed., "William Knox's Explanation for the American Revolution," *William and Mary Quarterly*, 3d ser., 30 (1973): 302.

11. Anonymous letter, ca. early 1730s, in Greene, ed., *Great Britain and the American Colonies*, 268–69; Board of Trade to king, Sept. 8, 1721, and Joshua Gee to Board of Trade, [Oct. 27, 1721], W. Noel Sainsbury et al., eds., *Calendar of State Papers, Colonial*, 44 vols. (London, 1860–), 1720–21, 444–49, 475. See also John Bumstead, " 'Things in the Womb of Time': Ideas of American Independence, 1633 to 1763," *William and Mary Quarterly*, 3d ser., 31 (1974): 533–64.

12. A fuller analysis of this new metropolitan campaign will be found in Jack P. Greene, " 'A Posture of Hostility,': A Reconsideration of Some Aspects of the Origins of the American Revolution," *American Antiquarian Society Proceedings* 87 (1977): 5–46.

13. See, on this point, Leonard W. Labaree, *Royal Government in America: A Study of the British Colonial System before 1783* (New Haven, 1930), 420–48, and Jack P. Greene, *The Quest for Power: The Lower Houses of Assembly in the Southern Royal Colonies, 1689–1763* (Chapel Hill, 1963), 13–14, 52, 129, 380–87, 439–40.

14. Opinion of William Rawlin, n.d., Chalmers, ed., *Opinions of Eminent Lawyers*, 376; Greene, ed., "Knox's Explanation for the American Revolution," 301.

15. Greene, ed., "Knox's Explanation for the American Revolution," 301–2.
16. Samuel Shute to Board of Trade, [Sept. 8, 1721], Oct. 29, 1722, *Calendar of State Papers, Colonial, 1720–21*, 407, *1722–23*, 157–58; [Joseph Galloway], *A True and Impartial State of the Province of Pennsylvania* (Philadelphia, 1759), 31–32; *Pennsylvania Gazette*, Sept. 18, 1729; *Boston Weekly News-Letter* (Boston), Jan. 27, 1732; William Douglass, *Summary, Historical and Political, of the First Planting, Progressive Improvements, and Present State of the British Settlements in North America*, 2 vols. (Boston, 1749–51), 2: 33–34; *The Reply of the House of Representatives of the Province of New Jersey* [New York, 1707], 8.
17. C.G., *South Carolina Gazette*, Dec. 3, 1764; T.W., ibid., May 13, 1756; The Inhabitant, ibid., Dec. 10, 1764; Lewis Morris to Board of Trade, Jan. 28, 1745, in "The Papers of Lewis Morris," *Collections of the New Jersey Historical Society* 4 (1852): 221; Thomas Pownall, *The Administration of the Colonies* (London, 1764), 40–41.
18. Benjamin Franklin to the Proprietors, Aug. 20, 1757, in Leonard W. Labaree et al., eds., *The Papers of Benjamin Franklin*, 23 vols. to date (New Haven, 1959–), 7: 249–50; to Isaac Norris, Mar. 19, 1759, ibid., 8: 293.
19. Franklin to Norris, Mar. 19, 1759, ibid., 8: 293–95.
20. Greene, ed., "Knox's Explanation for the American Revolution," 302; [Bourke], *Privileges of the Island of Jamaica Vindicated*, 2, 27–28, 42, 66; Pennsylvanus, *Pennsylvania Journal* (Philadelphia), Supplement, Mar. 25, 1756.
21. The Inhabitant, *South Carolina Gazette*, Dec. 10, 1764; [Galloway], *True and Impartial State*, 11; C.G., *South Carolina Gazette*, Dec. 17, 1764.
22. Opinion of Yorke and Wearg, May 18, 1724, Chalmers, ed., *Opinions of Eminent Lawyers*, 216; William Smith, Jr., *The History of the Province of New-York*, ed. Michael Kammen; 2 vols. (Cambridge, Mass., 1972), 1: 259; Virginia Committee of Correspondence to Edward Montague, July 28, 1764, "Proceedings of the Virginia Committee of Correspondence," *Virginia Magazine of History and Biography* 12 (1905): 5–14; Robert Hunter Morris to William Pitt, [1758–59], Miscellaneous Manuscripts, Clements Library; Benning Wentworth to Board of Trade, Dec. 23, 1755, Colonial Office Papers, 5/926, Public Record Office, London.

Chapter Four

1. "An Act Declaring and Constituting the People of England to be a Commonwealth and Free-State," [May 19, 1649], in C. H. Firth and R. S. Rait, eds., *Acts and Ordinances of the Interregnum, 1642–1660*, 2 vols. (London, 1911), 2: 122; N. Darnell Davis, *The Cavaliers and Roundheads of Barbados, 1650–1652* (Georgetown, British Guiana, 1883), 198; Samuel Nadhorth to Secretary Morrice, Oct. 26, 1666, in W. Noel Sainsbury et al., eds., *Calendar of State Papers, Colonial*, 44 vols. (London, 1860–), *1661–68*, 418. See also, A. Berriedale Keith, *Constitutional History of the First British Empire* (Oxford, 1930), 104–6.

2. Robert L. Schuyler, *Parliament and the British Empire* (New York, 1929), 1–39; A. Donaldson, "The Application in Ireland of English and British Legislation Made before 1801" (Ph.D dissertation, Queen's University, Belfast, 1952), 357, as quoted by Barbara A. Black, "The Constitution of Empire: The Case for the Colonists," *University of Pennsylvania Law Review* 124 (1976): 1183.

3. See Leo Francis Stock, ed., *Proceedings and Debates of the British Parliaments respecting North America*, 5 vols. (Washington, 1924–41), 1: 31; A.F.M. Madden, "1066, 1776 and All That: The Relevance of English Medieval Experience of 'Empire' to Later Imperial Constitutional Issues," in J. E. Flint and G. Williams, eds., *Perspectives of Empire* (London, 1973), 10–11, 13, 15.

4. Madden, "1066, 1776, and All That," 24; Black, "Constitution of Empire," 1193; H. T. Dickinson, "The Eighteenth-Century Debate on the 'Glorious Revolution,'" *History* 61 (1976): 42–43; John Phillip Reid, *In Defiance of the Law: The Standing-Army Controversy, the Two Constitutions, and the Coming of the American Revolution* (Chapel Hill, 1981), 3; Quentin Skinner, "History and Ideology in the English Revolution," *Historical Journal* 8 (1965): 151; Corinne C. Weston, "Co-ordination—a Radicalising Principle in Stuart Politics," in Margaret Jacob and James Jacob, eds., *The Origins of Anglo-American Radicalism* (London, 1984), 85–104.

5. Jennifer Carter, "The Revolution and the Constitution," in Geoffrey Holmes, ed., *Britain after the Glorious Revolution, 1689–1715* (New York, 1969), 39–40, 47, 55; Edmund Burke, "Letter to the Sheriffs of Bristol," in *The Works of Edmund Burke*, 16 vols. (London: 1826), 3: 188; H. T. Dickinson, "The Eighteenth-Century Debate on the Sovereignty of Parliament," *Transactions of the Royal Historical Society*, 5th ser., 26 (1976): 189; Black, "Constitution of Empire," 1210–11; Dickinson, "Eighteenth-Century Debate on the Glorious Revolution," 33, 39.

6. See, for instance, the essay signed "Z" in *Pennsylvania Gazette*, Apr. 8, 1736.

7. William Molyneux, *The Case of Ireland's Being Bound by Acts of Parliament in England Stated* (Dublin, 1698). Caroline Robbins, *The Eighteenth-Century Commonwealthman: Studies in the Transmission, Development and Circumstance of English Liberal Thought from the Restoration of Charles II until the War with the Thirteen Colonies* (Cambridge, Mass., 1961), 137–43, contains an excellent short discussion of Molyneux and his treatise.

8. *An Account of the Rise, Progress, and Consequence of the Land Bank* (Boston, 1744), 39–40; Deposition of Samuel Peabody, Sept. 15, 1758, Rhode Island Manuscripts, 12:21, Rhode Island Historical Society, Providence; Loudoun to Earl of Halifax, Dec. 26, 1756, Loudoun Papers 2416C, Huntington Library, San Marino, Calif.

9. George Larkin to Board of Trade, Oct. 14, 1701, *Calendar of State Papers, Colonial, 1701*, 576; [Francis Mackemie], *A Narrative of a New and Unusual American Imprisonment* ([New York], 1707).

10. *The Melancholy State of this Province Considered in a Letter from a Gentleman in*

Boston to his Friend in the Country (Boston, 1736), 4; William Douglass, *A Discourse Concerning the Currencies of the British Plantations in America* (Boston, 1740), 20–21, 41; Sir William Beeston to Board of Trade, July 30, 1701, *Calendar of State Papers, Colonial, 1701,* 379–80; [Jonathan Belcher], *Extracts from the Political State of Great Britain, December, 1730* [Boston, 1731], 14; Declaration of the House of Commons, May 10, 1733, in Stock, ed., *Proceedings and Debates,* 4:214–15.

11. Board of Trade to King, Feb. 26, 1698, Sept. 2, 1714, *Calendar of State Papers, Colonial, 1697–98,* 121–22, *1714–15,* 19–20; Board of Trade to Queen, Mar. 26, 1701, Jan. 10, 1706, ibid., *1701,* 141–43, *1706–8,* 3–6; House of Commons Committee to Board of Trade, Aug. 17, 1715, ibid., *1714–15,* 269; Opinion of Edmund Northey, July 22, 1714, George Chalmers, ed., *Opinions of Eminent Lawyers* (Burlington, Vt., 1858), 338–41. See also the documents in Stock, ed., *Proceedings and Debates,* 3: 16–17, 114, 118, 361–65.

12. Board of Trade to Privy Council, Mar. 1, 1711, in W. L. Grant and J. Munro, eds., *Acts of the Privy Council, Colonial Series,* 6 vols. (London, 1908–12), 2:641–42; Board of Trade to Dartmouth, Apr. 1, 1713, *Calendar of State Papers, Colonial, 1712–14,* 168. See also Board of Trade to Gov. Robert Lowther of Barbados, July 20, 1713, and Gov. Lord Archibald Hamilton of Jamaica, Mar. 22, 1714, ibid., 207–9, 322.

13. Board of Trade to Newcastle, Mar. 27, 1729, and Newcastle to William Burnett, June 26, 1729 (two letters), *Calendar of State Papers, Colonial, 1728–29,* 339–40, 412–14; Jonathan Belcher to Newcastle, June 11, 1734, and Board of Trade to king, Aug. 29, 1734, ibid., *1734–35,* 130–131, 194–95; *Acts of the Privy Council, Colonial,* 3: 259–64; *Boston Gazette,* Sept. 1, 1729; *Boston Weekly News-Letter,* Sept. 18, 1729; *Pennsylvania Gazette,* Sept. 18, 1729.

14. See Stock, ed., *Proceedings and Debates,* 4: 236–37, 5: 183–87, 298, 360–66; William Cobbett and T. C. Hansard, eds., *The Parliamentary History of England from the Earliest Period to 1803,* 36 vols. (London, 1806–20), 14: 563–64.

15. Jack P. Greene, ed., "Martin Bladen's Blueprint for a Colonial Union," *William and Mary Quarterly,* 3d ser., 17 (1960): 522.

16. J. C. Beckett, "The Irish Parliament in the Eighteenth Century," *Belfast National History and Philosophical Society Proceedings,* 2d ser., 4 (1955): 22–23, and "Anglo-Irish Constitutional Relations in the Later Eighteenth Century," *Irish Historical Studies,* 14 (1964–65): 20–23.

17. Beckett, "Anglo-Irish Constitutional Relations," 21–22; J. L. McCracken, "The Conflict between the Irish Administration and Parliament, 1753–6," *Irish Historical Studies,* 3 (1942–43): 169, 179; F. G. James, "Irish Smuggling in the Eighteenth Century," ibid., 12 (1961): 299–317.

18. Alison Gilbert Olson, "Parliament, Empire, and Parliamentary Law, 1776," in J. G. A. Pocock, ed., *Three British Revolutions: 1641, 1688, 1776* (Princeton, 1980), 289; Carter, "Revolution and the Constitution," 53, 56; T. H. Breen, *Puritans and Adventurers: Change and Persistence in Early Amer-*

ica (New York, 1980), 4–24; Edward Shils, *Center and Periphery: Essays in Microsociology* (Chicago, 1975), 10. See also Norma Landau, *Justices of the Peace, 1679–1760* (Berkeley and Los Angeles, 1984), on the continuing independence of county elites in regard to the internal affairs of the counties, and E. P. Thompson, "The Grid of Inheritance: A Comment," in Jack Goody, Joan Thirsk, and E. P. Thompson, eds., *Family and Inheritance: Rural Society in Western Europe, 1200–1800* (Cambridge, 1976), 328–60, on the "tenacity and force of local custom" in determining patterns of social and legal relations in English local society.

19. Beckett, "Irish Parliament in the Eighteenth Century," 18–20.
20. Burke, "Letter to the Sheriffs of Bristol," in *Works*, 3: 188–89; Beckett, "Irish Parliament in the Eighteenth Century," 17–28.
21. Clayton Roberts, "The Constitutional Significance of the Financial Settlement of 1690," *Historical Journal* 20 (1970): 59–76; Herman Merivale, *Lectures on Colonization and Colonies* (London, 1861), 74; Christopher Gadsden to the Gentlemen Electors of the Parish of St. Paul, Stono, *South Carolina Gazette*, Feb. 5, 1763; *Remarks upon a Message Sent by the Lower House to the Upper House of Assembly Apr. 4, 1762* ([Philadelphia], 1764), 14.
22. Burke, "Letter to the Sheriffs of Bristol," in *Works*, 3: 190; Sir George Saville to [Mr. Acklom], [Aug. 1768], Saville Papers, William L. Clements Library, Ann Arbor, Mich.
23. John Phillip Reid, "In Accordance with Usage: The Authority of Custom, the Stamp Act Debate, and the Coming of the American Revolution," *Fordham Law Review* 45 (1976): 341; Richard Koebner, *Empire* (Cambridge, 1961), 61–193; Burke, "Letter to the Sheriffs of Bristol," in *Works*, 3:190; Andrew C. McLaughlin, *The Foundations of American Constitutionalism* (New York, 1932), 138.
24. Burke, "Letter to the Sheriffs of Bristol," in *Works*, 3:190; *American Magazine* 1 (Jan. 1741): viii; Black, "Constitution of Empire," 1202–3. The colonists were not the only people in the empire who believed that jurisdiction over the colonies was largely the concern of the crown. In a House of Commons debate in December 1754 Henry Fox argued against passage of "a particular and distinct Mutiny Bill" for the colonies on those grounds. Because the colonies were "more immediately under the eye of the crown than any other part of the British dominions," Fox declared, such a bill would be "too great an encroachment upon the prerogatives of the crown, or at least . . . would be intermeddling in an affair with which we have no call to have any concern" (R. C. Simmons and P.D.G. Thomas, eds., *Proceedings and Debates of the British Parliament Respecting North America, 1754–1783*, 3 vols. to date, [New York, 1982–], 1:36).
25. *A Letter to a Gentleman chosen to be a Member of the Honourable House of Representatives* ([Boston,] 1732), 15; Gov. Robert Hunter to Sec. St. John, Sept. 12, 1711, *Calendar of State Papers, Colonial, 1711–12*, 103–4; Benjamin Franklin, "On the Tenure of the Manor of East Greenwich," 1766, in Verner W. Crane, ed., *Benjamin Franklin's Letters to the Press* (Chapel Hill, 1950), 48.

26. A Freeholder, *Maryland Gazette*, Mar. 16, 1748; C.G., *South Carolina Gazette*, Dec. 17, 1764; *New York Gazette*, Oct. 21, 1734.
27. Cobbett and Hansard, eds., *Parliamentary History of England*, 14: 563; Lewis Morris to Board of Trade and to Newcastle, Jan. 28, 1745, "The Papers of Lewis Morris," *Collections of the New Jersey Historical Society* 4 (1852): 220–21, 226–28; Opinion of Edmund Northey, July 22, 1714, in Chalmers, ed., *Opinions of Eminent Lawyers*, 339; Sir Nathaniel Lawes to Board of Trade, Nov. 13, 1720, Apr. 20, June 12, Oct. 30, 1721, *Calendar of State Papers, Colonial, 1720–21*, 194, 290, 334, 480; Robert Hunter Morris to William Pitt, [1758–59], Miscellaneous Mss., William L. Clements Library; William Douglass, *Summary, Historical and Political, of the First Planting, Progressive Improvements, and Present State of the British Settlements in North-America*, 2 vols. (Boston, 1749–51), 1:212, 2:34; *Weekly News-Letter* (Boston), Sept. 11, 1728; Richard Jackson's Opinion on Changing the Pennsylvania Constitution, [1758], in Carl Van Doren, ed., *Letters and Papers of Benjamin Franklin and Richard Jackson, 1753–1785* (Philadelphia, 1947), 83–84; *Some Observations on the [Excise] Bill . . .* (Boston, 1754), 7–8; *New York Gazette Revived in the Post-Boy*, Jan. 18, 1748.
28. Thomas Pownall to Halifax, Oct. 29, 1757, Force Papers, vol. 9 Box 7, Library of Congress, Washington, D.C.; Thomas C. Barrow, "A Project for Imperial Reform: 'Hints Respecting the Settlement for our American Provinces,' 1763," *William and Mary Quarterly*, 3d ser., 24 (1967): 118; Charles Townshend to Newcastle, Nov. 7, 1754, Newcastle Papers, Additional Manuscripts, 32737, ff. 57–58, British Library, London; William Shirley to Sir Thomas Robinson, Feb. 4, 1755, in C. H. Lincoln, ed., *Correspondence of William Shirley*, 2 vols. (New York, 1912), 2: 123–24; Robert Dinwiddie to Robinson, Feb. 12, 1755, in Robert A. Brock, ed., *The Official Records of Robert Dinwiddie*, 2 vols. (Richmond, 1883-84), 1: 493; [Henry McCulloh], *Proposals for Uniting the English Colonies on the Continent of America* (London, 1757), 15–16; *State of the British and French Colonies in North America* (London, 1755), 57, 67–68; Malachy Postlethwayt, *Britain's Commercial Interest Explained and Improved*, 2 vols. (London, 1757), 424–25, and *The Universal Dictionary of Trade and Commerce*, 2 vols. (London, 1757), I, 373; T——s W——t, *South Carolina Gazette*, Supplement, May 13, 1756.
29. *Journals of the House of Commons* (London), 27: 910–11 (May 23, 1757); John Pownall to governors, June 3, 1757, Colonial Office Papers, 324/6, Public Record Office, London; "Some Instances of Matters relating to the Colonies in which the House of Commons have interfered," 1757, Hardwicke Papers, Add. Mss. 35909, ff. 275–80, British Library, London.
30. A New-England Man, *A Letter to the Inhabitants of the Province of the Massachusetts-Bay* (Boston, 1751), 4; [Archibald Kennedy], *Serious Considerations on the Present State of the Affairs of the Northern Colonies* (New York, 1754), 23–24; *American Magazine* 1 (Jan. 1741): viii; Cadwallader Colden's "Observations on the Balance of Power in Government," 1744/45, in *The Letters and Papers of Cadwallader Colden, New-York Historical Society Collections*, 68 (1937): 257; *New-York Post-Boy*, Apr. 9, 1745; Douglass, *Summary*,

Historical and Political, 1: 243–44; *South Carolina Gazette,* June 5, 1756; William Smith, *A Brief State of the Province of Pennsylvania,* 3d ed. (London, 1756), 41–42.

31. Jeremiah Dummer, *Defence of the New-England Charters* (London, 1721), 76, 78.

32. Cadwallader Colden to Archibald Kennedy, Apr. 4, 1745, *Colden Papers, New-York Historical Society Collections,* 67 (1934): 310–12; William Bollan to Massachusetts Speaker, July 12, 1751, Bollan Papers, Manuscript A B62, New England Historical and Genealogical Society, Boston; Petition of Eliakin Palmer, Mar. 5, 1749, in Stock, ed., *Proceedings and Debates,* 5: 304–6; William Greene to Richard Partridge, [June 18, 1749], in Gertrude S. Kimball, ed., *Correspondence of the Colonial Governors of Rhode Island, 1723–1775,* 2 vols. (Cambridge, Mass., 1902–3), 2: 94.

33. *New-York Post-Boy,* Apr. 9, 1745; Daniel Neal, *The History of New-England,* 2 vols. (London, 1720), 2: 479.

34. A Freeholder, *Maryland Gazette* (Annapolis), Feb. 10, 1748; *Boston Gazette or Country Journal,* May 10, 1756; The Watchman, #1, *Pennsylvania Journal and Weekly Advertiser* (Philadelphia), Feb. 23, 1758. For an example of the contrary view, see *Pennsylvania Gazette,* Apr. 8, 1736.

35. Philanthropos, *Maryland Gazette,* Apr. 27, May 18, 1748; Americano-Britannus, ibid., June 4, 1748; A Native of Maryland, ibid., May 11, 1748; *Pennsylvania Journal and Weekly Advertiser,* July 4, 1754, Feb. 23, 1758; [Daniel Fowle], *An Appendix to the Late Eclipse of Liberty* (Boston, 1756), 20–21, 24.

36. Henry Beekman to Henry Livingston, Jan. 7, 1745, as quoted by Philip L. White, *The Beekmans of New York in Politics and Commerce, 1674–1877* (New York, 1956), 190; Isaac Norris to Benjamin Franklin, May 18, 1765, Leonard W. Labaree et al., eds., *The Papers of Benjamin Franklin,* 23 vols. to date (New Haven, 1959–), 12:130–31; *A Letter to a Gentleman,* 15; William Smith, Jr., to Thomas Clap, [1757–1759], as quoted in William Smith, Jr., *History of the Province of New York,* ed. Michael Kammen, 2 vols. (Cambridge, Mass., 1972), xxxiv; Watchman, #2, *Pennsylvania Journal and Weekly Advertiser,* Mar. 26, 1758; C.G., *South Carolina Gazette,* Dec. 17, 1764.

37. The Inhabitant, *South Carolina Gazette,* Dec. 7, 1764; *A Letter to a Gentleman . . . 1731,* 8–9; Colden to Kennedy, Apr. 4, 1745, *Colden Papers,* 67:310–12; Benjamin Franklin, *Autobiography,* ed. W. MacDonald (London, 1908), 149; Franklin to Isaac Norris, Mar. 19, 1759, Labaree et al., eds., *Franklin Papers,* 8:296.

38. Jack P. Greene, ed., "William Knox's Explanation for the American Revolution," *William and Mary Quarterly,* 3d ser. 30(1973): 301; Barrow, ed., "Project for Imperial Reform," 117.

39. Charles H. McIlwain, *The American Revolution: A Constitutional Interpretation* (New York, 1923), 14.

40. Franklin, "On the Tenure of the Manor," in Crane, ed., *Franklin's Letters to the Press,* 48.

41. McLaughlin, *Foundations of American Constitutionalism,* 132–33, 138;

McLaughlin, *A Constitutional History of the United States* (New York, 1935), 14.

Chapter Five

1. Francis Bernard to Richard Jackson, Aug. 18, 1764, in Edmund S. Morgan, ed., *Prologue to Revolution: Sources and Documents on the Stamp Act Crisis, 1764–1766* (Chapel Hill, 1959), 29.
2. Bernard to Lord Barrington, Nov. 23, 1765, in Edward Channing and Archibald Cary Coolidge, eds., *The Barrington-Bernard Correspondence* (Cambridge, Mass., 1912), 96.
3. Commons Proceedings, Mar. 8, 1764, in R. C. Simmons and P. D. G. Thomas, eds., *Proceedings and Debates of the British Parliament Respecting North America, 1754–1783*, 3 vols, to date (New York, 1980–), 1:492; Bernard to Barrington, Nov. 23, 1765, Channing and Coolidge, eds., *Barrington-Bernard Correspondence*, 94.
4. [William Knox], *The Claim of the Colonies to an Exemption from Internal Taxes Imposed by Authority of Parliament Examined* (London, 1765), 30; Commons Proceedings, Feb. 6, 1765, in Simmons and Thomas, eds., *Proceedings and Debates*, 2:11.
5. [Thomas Whateley], *The Regulations Lately Made Concerning the Colonies and the Taxes Imposed upon Them, Considered* (London, 1765), 100–114. Examples of metropolitan calls for colonial representation in Parliament may be found in *Reflexions on Representation in Parliament* (London, 1766), 41–42, and [Thomas Crowley], *Letters and Dissertations on Various Subjects* (London, 1776), 8–9, 16.
6. Commons Proceedings, Mar. 8, 1764, in Simmons and Thomas, eds., *Proceedings and Debates*, 1:492.
7. The Earl of Clarendon [John Adams] to William Pym, Jan. 1766, in Charles F. Adams, ed., *The Works of John Adams*, 10 vols. (Boston, 1856), 3: 477; [Thomas Fitch, et al.], *Reasons Why the British Colonies, in America, Should Not Be Charged with Internal Taxes* (New Haven, 1764), in Bernard Bailyn, ed., *Pamphlets of the American Revolution, 1750–1776* (Cambridge, Mass., 1965), 404; John Dickinson, *Letters from a Farmer in Pennsylvania to the Inhabitants of the British Colonies* (Philadelphia, 1768), in Forrest McDonald, ed., *Empire and Nation* (Englewood Cliffs, N.J., 1962), 26; *New York Gazette & Post-Boy*, May 22, 1766; [Kenneth Morrison], *An Essay towards the Vindication of the Committee of Correspondence in Barbados* (Barbados, 1766), 9.
8. New York Petition to the House of Commons, Oct. 18, 1764, in Morgan, ed., *Prologue to Revolution*, 9–10; Barbados Assembly to Gov. Charles Pinfold, Nov. 26, 1765, as quoted in David H. Makinson, *Barbados: A Study of North-American–West-Indian Relations* (The Hague, 1964), 72; [Fitch], *Reasons Why*, in Bailyn, ed., *Pamphlets*, 385, 387.

9. Maurice Moore, *The Justice and Policy of Taxing the American Colonies in Great Britain, Considered* (Wilmington, 1765), in William S. Price, Jr., ed., *Not a Conquered People: Two Carolinians View Parliamentary Taxation* (Raleigh, 1975), 44–46; *Candid Observations on Two Pamphlets Lately Published* (Barbados, 1766), 22; *The Crisis, or, A Full Defence of the Colonies* (London, 1766), 5–7.

10. *Candid Observations*, 19–22, 30.

11. Ibid., 12.

12. Robert W. Tucker and David C. Hendrickson, *The Fall of the First British Empire: Origins of the War of American Independence* (Baltimore, 1982), 162, 187–88.

13. *Letter to G.G.* (London, 1767), 27; Pownall's speech, May 15, 1767, in Simmons and Thomas, eds., *Proceedings and Debates*, 2:482.

14. [Fitch], *Reasons Why*, in Bailyn, ed., *Pamphlets*, 393–94.

15. Ibid., 392; [Morrison], *Essay towards the Vindication*, 10–11; Barbados Committee of Correspondence to London agent, [1765], in John Dickinson, *An Address to the Committee of Correspondence in Barbados* (Philadelphia, 1766), in Paul Leicester Ford, ed., *The Writings of John Dickinson* (Philadelphia, 1895), 255–56; *Letter to G.G.*, 35–36; Aequus, letter from the *Massachusetts Gazette*, Mar. 6, 1766, in Charles S. Hyneman and Donald S. Lutz, eds., *American Political Writing during the Founding Era, 1760–1805*, 2 vols. (Indianapolis, 1983), 1:63, 65; Richard Bland, *The Colonel Dismounted: or the Rector Vindicated* (Williamsburg, 1764), in Bailyn, ed., *Pamphlets*, 323; John Gay Alleyne, *A Letter to the North American, On Occasion of his Address to the Committee of Correspondence in Barbados* (Barbados, 1766), 4.

16. Tucker and Hendrickson, *Fall of the First British Empire*, 73; Richard Bland, *An Inquiry into the Rights of the British Colonies* (Williamsburg, 1766), in William J. Van Schreeven and Robert L. Scribner, eds., *Revolutionary Virginia: The Road to Independence*, 4 vols. to date (Charlottesville, 1973–), 1:42; Massachusetts House to Bernard, Oct. 23, 1765, in Harry Alonzo Cushing, ed., *The Writings of Samuel Adams*, 4 vols. (New York, 1904–8), 1:16.

17. *Candid Observations*, 26–31.

18. [William Goddard?], *The Constitutional Courant: Containing Matters Interesting to Liberty, and No Wise Repugnant to Loyalty* ([Burlington, N.J.?], 1765), in Merrill Jensen, ed., *Tracts of the American Revolution, 1763–1776* (Indianapolis, 1967), 87, 90; Aequus, in Hynemann and Lutz, eds., *American Political Writing*, 1:64; Philalethes, in *New York Gazette*, May 8, 1766.

19. James Otis, *The Rights of the British Colonies Asserted and Proved* (Boston, 1764), in Bailyn, ed., *Pamphlets*, 457; [Fitch], *Reasons Why*, in ibid., 395; Daniel Dulany, *Considerations on the Propriety of Imposing Taxes in the British Colonies* (Annapolis, 1765), in ibid., 619.

20. Dulany, *Considerations*, in Bailyn, ed., *Pamphlets*, 619; Bland, *Inquiry*, in Van Schreeven and Scribner, eds., *Revolutionary Virginia*, 1:41, 43.

21. Edmund S. Morgan, "Colonial Ideas of Parliamentary Power," *William and Mary Quarterly*, 3d ser., 5(1948): 311–41. The quotation is from p. 326.

22. [Fitch], *Reasons Why*, in Bailyn, *Pamphlets*, 391, 406; Virginia Petition, Dec. 18, 1764, Virginia Resolutions, May 30, 1765, Rhode Island Resolves, Sept. 1765, Maryland Resolves, Sept. 28, 1765, Connecticut Resolves, Oct. 25, 1765, in Morgan, ed., *Prologue to Revolution*, 14, 48, 50–51, 53, 55; Massachusetts House to Bernard, Oct. 23, 1765, in Cushing, ed., *Writings of Samuel Adams*, 1:17–18.

 Of the nine colonies whose assemblies passed resolutions against the Stamp Act (those of Georgia, North Carolina, Delaware, and New Hampshire did not), four claimed exclusive jurisdiction over both taxation and internal legislation. If, on the basis of its letter to Bernard, the Massachusetts Assembly is added to this list, that makes five—or a majority—of the nine assemblies that subscribed to this more sweeping assertion. Indeed, except for that of Pennsylvania, all of the assemblies that passed resolutions before the Massachusetts Resolves of October 29, 1765, followed the Virginia formula, and all of those who acted after that date limited their explicit claims to an exemption from taxation. This temporal differentiation would seem to support the argument suggested above that the colonists' initial impulse was to adhere to a more expanded conception of their rights and that they only gradually focused their protests exclusively upon taxation. All of the assembly resolutions are conveniently collected in Morgan, ed., *Prologue to Revolution*, 47–62.

23. Bernard Bailyn, *The Ideological Origins of the American Revolution* (Boston, 1967), 213, n. 55.

24. Bland, *Colonel Dismounted*, in Bailyn, ed., *Pamphlets*, 320.

25. Bland, *Inquiry*, in Van Schreeven and Scribner, eds., *Revolutionary Virginia*, 1:38–39; Jack P. Greene, ed., " 'Not to be Governed or Taxed, But By . . . Our Representatives': Four Essays in Opposition to the Stamp Act by Landon Carter," *Virginia Magazine of History and Biography* 76(1968): 259–300.

26. Massachusetts House to Bernard, Oct. 23, 1765; Samuel Adams to Reverend G[eorge] W[hitfield], Nov. 11, 1765; James Otis, et al., to Dennys De Berdt, Dec. 20, 1765, in Cushing, ed., *Writings of Samuel Adams*, 1:20, 28–29, 67.

27. Stephen Hopkins, *The Rights of the Colonies Examined* (Providence, 1765), in Bailyn, ed., *Pamphlets*, 512, 519.

28. [William Hicks], *Considerations upon the Rights of the Colonies to the Privileges of British Subjects* (New York, 1765), 11; [Fitch], *Reasons Why*, in Bailyn, ed., *Pamphlets*; 395, 406.

29. *A Vindication of the Rights of the Americans* (London, 1765), 10–11.

30. Tucker and Hendrickson, *Fall of the First British Empire*, 175–76; [Fitch], *Reasons Why*, in Bailyn, ed., *Pamphlets*, 390–91, 394–95; [Hicks], *Considerations*, 10–11; *Letter to G.G.*, 38–39.

31. *A Letter to the Gentlemen of the Committee of London Merchants trading to North America* (London, 1766), 9–10; "Remarks on the Maryland Government," *American Magazine* 1 (1741): 30; Bailyn, *Ideological Origins*, 203.

32. *Candid Observations*, 20; F.L., in *Pennsylvania Journal* (Philadelphia), Mar. 13, 1766, in Morgan, ed., *Prologue to Revolution*, 91.

33. Tucker and Hendrickson, *Fall of the First British Empire*, 196; Philalethes, *New York Gazette & Post Boy*, May 8, 1766.

34. A Letter from a Plain Yeoman, *Providence Gazette*, May 11, 1765, in Morgan, ed., *Prologue to Revolution*, 73; Hopkins, *Rights of the Colonies*, in Bailyn, ed., *Pamphlets*, 518–19; *New York Gazette*, July 25, 1765.

35. Bland, *Inquiry*, in Van Schreeven and Scribner, eds., *Revolutionary Virginia*, 1:35–38. Benjamin Franklin employed precisely the same argument in his essay "On the Tenure of the Manor of East Greenwich," Jan. 11, 1766, in Verner W. Crane, ed., *Benjamin Franklin's Letters to the Press* (Chapel Hill, 1950), 48.

36. Philalethes, *New York Gazette*, May 8, 1766; Bland, *Inquiry*, in Van Schreeven and Scribner, eds., *Revolutionary Virginia*, 1:38–39; Bland, *Colonel Dismounted*, and Otis, *Rights of the British Colonies*, in Bailyn, ed., *Pamphlets*, 318, 323, 458; Landon Carter to *Maryland Gazette* (Annapolis), May 8, 1766, in Greene, ed., " 'Not to be Governed or Taxed,' " 272; Letter from a Plain Yeoman, *Providence Gazette*, May 11, 1765, in Morgan, ed., *Prologue to Revolution*, 73; *New York Gazette & Post Boy*, July 25, 1765.

37. Britannus Americanus, *Boston Gazette*, Mar. 17, 1766, in Hyneman and Lutz, eds., *American Political Writings*, 1:89–91; *Candid Observations*, 23–24; C.P., *A Letter to his Most Excellent Majesty, George the Third* . . . (New York, 1765), 1.

38. Franklin, "On the Tenure of the Manor of East Greenwich," Jan. 11, 1766, in Crane, ed., *Franklin's Letters to the Press*, 48; Earl of Clarendon [John Adams] to William Pym, Jan. 27, 1766, in Adams, ed., *Works of John Adams*, 3:477; Bland, *Inquiry*, in Van Schreeven and Scribner, eds., *Revolutionary Virginia*, 1:34; J.M., *The Legislative Authority of the British Parliament with respect to North America and the Privileges of the Assemblies there, briefly considered* (London, 1766), 11.

39. Bland, *Inquiry*, in Van Schreeven and Scribner, eds., *Revolutionary Virginia*, 1:43; Thomas Rutherforth, *Institutes of Natural Law*, 2d American ed. (Baltimore, 1832), 296.

40. Letter from a Plain Yeoman, *Providence Gazette*, May 11, 1765, in Morgan, ed., *Prologue to Revolution*, 73.

41. Tucker and Hendrickson, *Fall of the First British Empire*, 344.

42. J.M., *Legislative Authority of the British Parliament*, 4, 6, 8–10, 13; *The Justice and Necessity of Taxing the American Colonies, Demonstrated* (London, 1766), 26–27, 32; F. J. Hinkhouse, *The Preliminaries of the American Revolution as Seen in the English Press, 1763–1775* (New York, 1926), 120.

43. *The Late Occurrences in North America, and Policy of Great Britain Considered* (London, 1766), 5; *What should be Done: Or, Remarks on the Political State of Things* (London, 1766), 16–19; *Letter to G.G.*, 74, 84.

44. Camden's speeches, Feb. 6, Mar. 7, 1766; Beckford's speech, Feb. 3, 1766, in Simmons and Thomas, eds., *Proceedings and Debates*, 2:127, 147, 320–22; Rutherforth, *Institutes of Natural Law*, 399.

45. Camden's Speech, Mar. 7, 1766; Pitt's Speech, Jan. 14, 1766, in Simmons and Thomas, eds., *Proceedings and Debates*, 2:81–92, 320–22.

46. See, in this connection, [John Fothergill], *Considerations relative to the North*

American Colonies (London, 1765); *Vindication of the Rights; Late Occurrences.*

47. [Knox], *Claim of the Colonies,* 3–4, 8; *Late Occurrences,* 1–2; [Soame Jenyns], *The Objections to the Taxation of our American Colonies, by the Legislature of Great Britain, Briefly Consider'd* (London, 1765), 9; *Letter to G.G.,* 74; Northington's speech, Feb. 3, 1766, in Simmons and Thomas, eds., *Proceedings and Debates,* 2:129.

48. *The General Opposition of the Colonies to the Payment of the Stamp Duty* (London, 1766), 25–26; *A Letter to a Member of Parliament, Wherein the Power of the British Legislature, and the Case of the Colonists are Briefly and Impartially Considered* (London, 1765), 21; [Knox], *Claim of the Colonies,* 2.

49. [Jenyns], *Objections to the Taxation of our American Colonies,* 9–10; [Charles Jenkinson], Notes on the Right to Tax the Colonies, [1765], Additional Manuscripts 38339, ff. 133–35, British Library, London; *Letter to a Member of Parliament,* 12–13.

50. Blackstone, *Commentaries on the Laws of England,* 1:50; Grenville's and Townshend's speeches, Feb. 6, 1765, in Simmons and Thomas, eds., *Proceedings and Debates,* 2:9, 13.

51. Mansfield's and Northington's speeches, Feb. 3, 1766, in Simmons and Thomas, eds., *Proceedings and Debates,* 2:128–30; *Justice and Necessity of Taxing the American Colonies,* 21.

52. J.M., *Legislative Authority of the British Parliament,* 11; Sir William Blackstone, *Commentaries on the Laws of England,* 4 vols. (London, 1822), 1:50–51, 178–80; Grenville's speech, Feb. 6, 1765, in Simmons and Thomas, eds., *Proceedings and Debates,* 2:9; Ingersoll to Thomas Fitch, Feb. 11, 1765, in Morgan, ed., *Prologue to Revolution,* 30. Bailyn, *Ideological Origins,* 198–202, provides an excellent brief account of the development of the concept of sovereignty in early modern Britain.

53. *Letter to G.G.,* 74; Lyttelton's and Egmont's speeches, Feb. 3, Mar. 7, 1766, in Simmons and Thomas, eds., *Proceedings and Debates,* 2:126–27, 320–21; *Justice and Necessity of Taxing,* 21; *Protest against the Bill to Repeal the American Stamp Act* (Paris, 1766), 16; *The Rights of Parliament Vindicated, on the Occasion of the Late Stamp-Act* (London, 1766), 10–11, Several people, of course, charged that the colonists were aiming at independence. See, for instance, [Josiah Tucker], *A Letter from a Merchant in London to His Nephew in North America* (London, 1766), 42.

54. *A New and Impartial Collection of Interesting Letters, from the Public Papers* (London, 1767), 138; *New York Gazette & Post-Boy,* May 22, 1766.

55. Barre's speech, Feb. 24, 1766, in Simmons and Thomas, eds., *Proceedings and Debates,* 2:296; *The Political Balance, in which the Principles and Conduct of the Two Parties are weighed* (London, 1765), 45; J.M., *Legislative Authority of the British Parliament,* 11; Tucker and Hendrickson, *Fall of the First British Empire,* 175, 179.

56. [Fothergill], *Considerations,* 46–47; [Joshua Steele], *An Account of a Late Conference on the Occurrences in America* (London, 1766), 24–27, 33–40; Robert M. Calhoon, ed., "William Smith Jr.'s Alternative to the American

Revolution," *William and Mary Quarterly*, 3d ser., 22 (1965): 105–18; Speeches of Charles Yorke, Feb. 15, 1765, and Edmund Nugent and Welbore Ellis, Jan. 27, 1766, in Simmons and Thomas, eds., *Proceedings and Debates*, 2:111; Bernard to Barrington, Nov. 23, 1765, in Channing and Coolidge, eds., *Barrington-Bernard Correspondence*, 95; *New York Gazette & Post-Boy*, May 22, 1766.

Chapter Six

1. William Hicks, *The Nature and Extent of Parliamentary Power Considered* (New York, 1768), in Merrill Jensen, ed., *Tracts of the American Revolution, 1763–1776* (Indianapolis, 1967), 177; Jonathan Shipley, *A Sermon Preached before the Incorporated Society for the Propagation of the Gospel in Foreign Parts* (London, 1773), in Paul H. Smith, comp., *English Defenders of American Freedoms, 1774–1778* (Washington, 1972), 25; *An Inquiry into the Nature and Causes of the Present Disputes between the British Colonies in America and Their Mother Country* (London, 1769), 46; "Valerius Poplicola" [Samuel Adams] to *Boston Gazette*, Oct. 28, 1771, in Henry Alonzo Cushing, ed., *The Writings of Samuel Adams*, 4 vols. (New York, 1904–8), 2:257; Benjamin Franklin to Thomas Crowley, Oct. 21, 1768, and to Thomas Cushing, Feb. 5, 1771, in Leonard W. Labaree et al., eds., *The Papers of Benjamin Franklin*, 23 vols. to date (New Haven, 1959–), 15:241, 18:28; Thomas Pownall's speech, May 8, 1770, in R. C. Simmons and P. D. G. Thomas, eds., *Proceedings and Debates of the British Parliament Respecting North America, 1754–1783*, 3 vols. to date (New York, 1982–), 3:284.
2. Henry Seymour Conway's speech, Feb. 8, 1769, Richard Hussey's speech, Jan. 26, 1768, Rockingham's speech, May 18, 1770, Edmund Burke's speech, May 9, 1770, in Simmons and Thomas, eds., *Proceedings and Debates*, 3:69, 98, 323, 338; William Samuel Johnson to William Pitkin, Nov. 10, 1768, in ibid., 13. The Jamaican William Beckford was almost the only MP after 1766 even to suggest that there might be constitutional limitations upon Parliament's colonial authority. See his remark in a speech of December 7, 1768, that "Acts of Parliament are not like the laws of the Medes and Persians. An Act of Parliament against common right is a nullity, so says Lord Coke" (ibid., 32).
3. Allan Ramsay, *Thoughts on the Origin and Nature of Government* (London, 1768), 53; [Richard Phelps], *The Rights of the Colonies, and the Extent of the Legislative Authority of Great-Britain* (London, 1769), 3–4; [William Knox], *The Controversy Between Great Britain and her Colonies Reviewed* (London, 1769), 50–51.
4. Hillsborough's speech, Dec. 15, 1768, Hussey's speech, Jan. 26, 1769, in Simmons and Thomas, eds., *Proceedings and Debates*, 3:48, 70; Ramsay, *Thoughts*, 29, 52; *The Constitutional Right of the Legislature of Great Britain, to Tax the British Colonies in America, Impartially Stated* (London, 1768), 11; William Samuel Johnson to William Pitkin, Feb. 13, 1768, in "The Trum-

bull Papers," *Massachusetts Historical Society, Collections*, 5th ser., 9(Boston, 1885): 257.

5. Hillsborough's speeches, Dec. 15, 1768, May 18, 1770, in Simmons and Thomas, eds., *Proceedings and Debates*, 3:48, 334; *Constitutional Right of the Legislature*, 6–7, 12; [Knox], *Controversy*, 50–51; [Phelps], *Rights of the Colonies*, 11.

6. *Constitutional Right of the Legislature*, 27–28; Lord North's speech, Dec. 7, 1768, and Hans Stanley's speech, Nov. 8, 1768, in Simmons and Thomas, eds., *Proceedings and Debates*, 3:4, 32.

7. Stanley's speech, Nov. 8, 1768, in Simmons and Thomas, eds., *Proceedings and Debates*, 3:3; Ramsay, *Thoughts*, 60–62; *Constitutional Right of the Legislature*, 2–3.

8. Hillsborough's speech, May 18, 1770, in Simmons and Thomas, eds., *Proceedings and Debates*, 3:336; Ramsay, *Thoughts*, 49–51; Thomas Pownall, *The Administration of the Colonies*, 4th ed. (New York, 1971), 172–73; *A Letter to the Right Honourable The Earl of Hillsborough on the Present Situation of Affairs in America* (London, 1769), 100–101.

9. *Constitutional Right of the Legislature*, 12–13, 53, 57.

10. Pownall's speech, Apr. 19, 1769, in Simmons and Thomas, eds., *Proceedings and Debates*, 3:156.

11. John Dickinson, *Letters from a Farmer in Pennsylvania to the Inhabitants of the British Colonies* (Philadelphia, 1768), in Forrest McDonald, ed., *Empire and Nation* (Englewood Cliffs, N.J., 1962), 6.

12. Ibid., 7, 67; Dickinson, *An Address Read at a Meeting of Merchants to Consider Non-Importation*, Apr. 25, 1768, in Paul Leicester Ford, ed., *The Writings of John Dickinson*, (Philadelphia, 1895), 413.

13. Dickinson, *Letters*, in McDonald, ed., *Empire and Nation*, 7–8, 27.

14. Virginia legislature to George III, Apr. 16, 1768, in William J. Van Schreeven and Robert L. Scribner, eds., *Revolutionary Virginia: The Road to Independence*, 4 vols. (Charlottesville, 1973), 1:55.

15. Cushing to Franklin, May 6, 1773, in Labaree et al., eds., *Franklin Papers*, 20:204; Franklin to William Franklin, Mar. 13, 1768, in ibid., 15:75–76; Hicks, *Nature and Extent of Parliamentary Power*, 12.

16. [Gervase Parker Bushe], *The Case of Great Britain and America* (London, 1768), 27; [George Canning], *A Letter to The Right Honourable Wills Earl of Hillsborough, On The Connection Between Great Britain and Her American Colonies* (London, 1768), 9–10; *A Letter to the Right Honourable The Earl of H——b——h* (London, 1769), 2–3.

17. Franklin to Lord Kames, Feb. 25, 1767, in Labaree et al., eds., *Franklin Papers*, 14:68; [Thomas Hollis], *The True Sentiments of America* (London, 1768), 16; Edward Bancroft, *Remarks on the Review of the Controversy Between Great Britain and Her Colonies* (London, 1769), 44–45.

18. [Bushe], *Case of Great Britain and America*, 3–4.

19. Bancroft, *Remarks*, 44–45; Franklin to Lord Kames, Feb. 25, 1767, in Labaree et al., eds., *Franklin Papers*, 14: 68; [Thomas Pownall], *State of the*

Constitution of the Colonies [London, 1769], 2; William Samuel Johnson to William Pitkin, Feb. 13, 1768, and Pitkin to Johnson, June 10, 1768, in "Trumbull Papers," 259, 286–87; Silas Downer, *A Discourse at the Dedication of the Tree of Liberty* (Providence, 1768), in Charles S. Hyneman and Donald S. Lutz, eds., *American Political Writings during the Founding Era, 1760–1805*, 2 vols. (Indianapolis, 1983), 1:100.

20. Franklin to Lord Kames, Feb. 25, 1767, and to William Strahan, Nov. 29, 1769, in Labaree et al., eds., *Franklin Papers*, 14:68, 16:244; *Letter to H——b——h*, 12–13, 57, 99.

21. *Letter to H——b——h*, 15–16; Franklin's Marginalia to [Tucker], *Letter from a Merchant in London*, and to Matthew Wheelock, *Reflections Moral and Political on Great Britain and Her Colonies* (London, 1770), in Labaree et al., eds., *Franklin Papers*, 17:353, 396; Bancroft, *Remarks*, 44–45; Franklin to William Strahan, Nov. 29, 1769, in Labaree et al., eds., *Franklin Papers*, 16:244.

22. *Letter to H——b——h*, 13, 99; Franklin to *London Chronicle*, Oct. 18–20, 1768, in Labaree et al., eds., *Franklin Papers*, 15:234–35.

23. William Samuel Johnson to William Pitkin, Feb. 13, 1768, in "Trumbull Papers," 258; Bancroft, *Remarks*, 44–45; [Bushe], *Case of Great Britain and America*, 3–4; *Letter to H——b——h*, 13.

24. *Letter to H——b——h*,, 109; Wm. Pitkin to Richard Jackson, June 10, 1768, in "Trumbull Papers," 286–87; Hicks, *Nature and Extent of Parliamentary Power*, in Jensen, ed., *Tracts*, 171; "Valerius Poplicola" [Samuel Adams] to *Boston Gazette*, Oct. 28, 1771, in Cushing, ed., *Writings of Samuel Adams*, 2:261; "Massachusettensis" [Daniel Leonard] to "All Nations of Men," *Massachusetts Spy*, Nov. 18, 1773, in Hyneman and Lutz, eds., *American Political Writings*, 1:210.

25. "Mucius Scevola" [Joseph Greenleaf] to *Boston Gazette and Country Journal*, Mar. 4, 1771; John Joachim Zubly, *An Humble Enquiry Into the Nature of the Dependency of the American Colonies upon the Parliament of Great-Britain* (Charleston, 1769), in Randall M. Miller, ed., *"A Warm & Zealous Spirit": John J. Zubly and the American Revolution, A Selection of His Writings* (Macon, Ga., 1982), 57; Franklin, "Subjects of Subjects," Jan. 1768, Franklin to Jacques Barbeu-Duborg, Oct. 2, 1770, and Franklin, Marginalia to *An Inquiry into the Nature and Causes of the Present Disputes* (London, 1769), in Labaree et al., eds., *Franklin Papers*, 15:36–37, 17:233, 320.

26. "Massachusettensis" [Daniel Leonard] to "All Nations of Men," *Massachusetts Spy*, Nov. 18, 1773, in Hyneman and Lutz, eds., *American Political Writings*, 1:212; Franklin, Marginalia in Protests of the Lords against Repeal of the Stamp Act, Mar. 11, 1766, Franklin, "Subjects of Subjects," Jan. 1768, Franklin to *London Chronicle*, Oct. 18–20, 1768, Franklin to Samuel Cooper, June 8, 1770, Franklin to Barbeu-Duborg, Oct. 2, 1770, Franklin, Marginalia to *An Inquiry*, 1769, and Franklin, Marginalia to Wheelock, *Reflections*, 1770, in Labaree et al., eds., *Franklin Papers*, 13:219, 15:36–37, 233–34, 17:162–63, 233, 325, 333, 388; Massachusetts House of Represen-

tative to Dennys De Berdt, Jan. 11, 1768, in Cushing, ed., *Writings of Samuel Adams*, 1:134.

27. [Francis Maseres], *Considerations on the Expediency of Admitting Representatives from the American Colonies into the British House of Commons* (London, 1770), 5; Franklin, Marginalia to *An Inquiry*, 1770, in Labaree et al., eds., *Franklin Papers*, 17:320.

28. Franklin to William Strahan, Nov. 29, 1769, and Franklin, Marginalia to *An Inquiry*, 1770, in Labaree et al., eds., *Franklin Papers*, 16:246, 17:322; Hicks, *Nature and Extent of Parliamentary Power*, in Jensen, ed., *Tracts*, 171.

29. Benjamin Prescott, *A Free and Calm Consideration of the Unhappy Misunderstandings and Debates . . .* (Salem, 1774), 30; Franklin to *London Chronicle*, Oct. 18–20, 1768, in Labaree et al., eds., *Franklin Papers*, 15:233. Though not published until 1774, the Prescott pamphlet was written in 1768.

30. Franklin to Kames, Feb. 25, 1767, Franklin to *London Chronicle*, Oct. 18–20, 1768, and Franklin, Marginalia to *An Inquiry*, 1769, in Labaree et al., eds., *Franklin Papers*, 14:68–69, 15:233, 17:321; Hicks, *Nature and Extent of Parliamentary Power*, in Jensen, ed., *Tracts*, 170–71.

31. Franklin, Marginalia to Wheelock, *Reflections*, 1770, in Labaree et al., eds., *Franklin Papers*, 17:385; Bancroft, *Remarks*, 6–7; *Letter to H——b——h*, 26–27; Prescott, *Free and Calm Consideration*, 11; Hicks, *Nature and Extent of Parliamentary Power*, in Jensen, ed., *Tracts*, 175–76; Downer, *Discourse*, in Hyneman and Lutz, eds., *American Political Writings*, 1:102.

32. Franklin to Thomas Cushing, Dec. 24, 1770, and to William Franklin, Sept. 1, 1773, in Labaree et al., eds., *Franklin Papers*, 17:308, 20:386; Bancroft, *Remarks*, 75.

33. William Pitkin to William Samuel Johnson, June 6, 1768, "Trumbull Papers," 280; Massachusetts House of Representatives to Dennys De Berdt, Jan. 12, 1768, to Shelburne, Jan. 15, 1768, and to the king, Jan. 20, 1768, Alfred [Samuel Adams] to *Boston Gazette*, Oct. 2, 1769, Candidus [Samuel Adams] to *Boston Gazette*, Jan. 27, 1772, in Cushing, ed., *Writings of Samuel Adams*, 1:134, 156, 164, 390, 2:325–26; Zubly, *An Humble Enquiry*, in Miller, ed., *"A Warm & Zealous Spirit*," 58.

34. Shipley, *Sermon*, in Smith, comp., *English Defenders of American Freedoms*, 22; Franklin to William Strahan, Nov. 29, 1769, in Labaree et al., eds., *Franklin Papers*, 16:244; Bancroft, *Remarks*, 76; *Letter to H——b——h*, 29, 104.

35. [Sir Hercules Langrishe], *Considerations on the Dependencies of Great Britain* (London, 1769), 52–53; Franklin to Lord Kames, Feb. 25, 1767, in Labaree et al., eds., *Franklin Papers*, 14:69; Massachusetts House to king, Jan. 20, 1768, in Cushing, ed., *Writings of Samuel Adams*, 1:164.

36. Pownall's speech, Feb. 8, 1769, in Simmons and Thomas, eds., *Proceedings and Debates*, 3:109.

37. *Letter to H——b——h*, 80; Pitkin to William Samuel Johnson, June 6, 1768, in "Trumbull Papers," 280; Zubly, *An Humble Enquiry*, in Miller, ed., *"A Warm & Zealous Spirit*," 66.

38. Hicks, *The Nature and Extent of Parliamentary Power Considered* (New York, 1768), xiv, 170; *An Inquiry into the Nature and Causes of the Present Disputes*, 29; [Bushe], *Case of Great Britain and America*, 15–16; Downer, *Discourse*, in Hyneman and Lutz, eds., *American Political Writings*, 1:101; Hicks, *Nature and Extent of Parliamentary Power*, in Jensen, ed., *Tracts*, 170; Franklin, Marginalia in Protests of the Lords, Mar. 11, 1766, in Labaree et al., eds., *Franklin Papers*, 13:232.

39. Franklin to Kames, Feb. 25, 1767, in Labaree et al., eds., *Franklin Papers*, 14:65; Pownall, *Administration of the Colonies*, 4th ed., 164–75; *An Inquiry into the Nature and Causes of the Present Disputes*, 23; [Maseres], *Considerations*, 9–15; Hicks, *Nature and Extent of Parliamentary Power*, 14; *Observations and Propositions for an Accommodation between Great-Britain and her Colonies* ([New York], 1768).

40. Franklin, Marginalia in Protests of the Lords, Mar. 11, 1766, Franklin to Joseph Galloway, Jan. 11, 1770, in Labaree et al., eds., *Franklin Papers*, 13:224, 17:24; Bancroft, *Remarks*, 115.

41. Burke's speeches, Nov. 8, 1768, May 9, 1770; Cavendish's speech, Dec. 7, 1768; Pownall's speech, Apr. 19, 1769, in Simmons and Thomas, eds., *Proceedings and Debates*, 3:7, 38, 154, 303.

42. James Otis, *A Vindication of the Conduct of the House of Representatives of the Province of Massachusetts-Bay* (Boston, 1762); Milton M. Klein, "Prelude to Revolution in New York: Jury Trials and Judicial Tenure," *William and Mary Quarterly*, 3d ser., 17(1960): 439–62.

43. Jack P. Greene, "The Gadsden Election Controversy and the Revolutionary Movement in South Carolina," *Mississippi Valley Historical Review* 46(1959): 469–92; George Metcalf, *Royal Government and Political Conflict in Jamaica, 1729–1783* (London, 1965), 157–65.

44. Otis, *Vindication of the House of Representatives*, 51; [Nicholas Bourke], *The Privileges of the Island of Jamaica Vindicated with an Impartial Narrative of the Late Dispute between the Governor and House of Representatives* (London, 1766), 47, 64; John Dickinson, *A Speech Delivered in the House of Assembly of the Province of Pennsylvania, May 24th, 1764* (Philadelphia, 1764), in Paul Leicester Ford, ed., *The Writings of John Dickinson*, (Philadelphia, 1895), 40.

45. Jack P. Greene, *The Quest for Power: The Lower Houses of Assembly in the Southern Royal Colonies, 1689–1763* (Chapel Hill, 1963), 420–24, 433–36; Peter S. Onuf, ed., *Maryland and the Empire, 1773: The Antilon–First Citizen Letters* (Baltimore, 1974); Donald C. Lord and Robert M. Calhoon, "The Removal of the Massachusetts General Court from Boston, 1769–1772," *Journal of American History* 55(1969): 735–55; Jack P. Greene, "Bridge to Revolution: The Wilkes Fund Controversy in South Carolina, 1769–1775," *Journal of Southern History* 29 (1963): 19–52.

46. Franklin to James Bowdoin, Jan. 13, 1772, in Labaree et al., eds., *Franklin Papers*, 19:11; William Bollan, *The Free Britons Memorial* (London, 1769), 25; First Citizen's Third Letter, May 6, 1773, in Onuf, ed., *Maryland and the Empire*, 149.

47. See Jack P. Greene, ed., *The Nature of Colony Constitutions: Two Pamphlets on the Wilkes Fund Controversy by Sir Egerton Leigh and Arthur Lee* (Columbia, S.C., 1970), 49–55; Onuf, ed., *Maryland and the Empire*, 29.

Chapter Seven

1. *Colonising, or Plain Investigation of That Subject* (London, 1774), 8; [Jonathan Boucher], *A Letter from a Virginian to the members of the Congress* (Boston, 1774), 17–19.
2. [James Macpherson], *The Rights of Great Britain Asserted Against the Claims of America* (London, 1776), 3–5, 11.
3. [Macpherson], *Rights of Great Britain*, 3, 11; Nathaniel George Rice's speech, Mar. 7, 1774, and Charles Cornwall's speech, Apr. 19, 1774, in William Cobbett and T. C. Hansard, eds., *The Parliamentary History of England from the Earliest Period to 1803*, 36 vols. (London, 1806–20), 17:1149, 1214; Josiah Tucker, Tract V, *The Respective Pleas and Arguments of the Mother Country, and of the Colonies, Distinctly Set Forth* (Gloucester, 1775), 38.
4. Jonathan Shipley, *A Sermon Preached before the Incorporated Society for the Propagation of the Gospel in Foreign Parts* (London, 1773), in Paul H. Smith, comp., *English Defenders of American Freedom, 1774–1778* (Washington, 1972), 30; *An Argument in Defence of the Exclusive Right Claimed by the Colonies to Tax Themselves* (London, 1774), 5–6.
5. Matthew Robinson-Morris, Baron Rokeby, *Considerations on the Measures Carrying on with Respect to the British Colonies in North America* (London, 1774), in Smith, comp., *English Defenders of American Freedom*, 56, 65; Thomas Pownall, *The Administration of the British Colonies*, 2 vols., 5th ed. (London, 1774), 2:37–38, 78.
6. Pownall, *Administration of the Colonies*, 5th ed., 2:36–37, 100; *An Argument in Defence of the Exclusive Right*, 131.
7. John Cartwright, *American Independence, the Interest and Glory of Great Britain* (Philadelphia, 1776), in Smith, comp., *English Defenders of American Freedom*, 169; *America Vindicated from the High Charge of Ingratitude and Rebellion* (Devizes, 1774), 6, 40–41. For American expressions of similar views, see [Joseph Galloway], *A Candid Examination of the Mutual Claims . . .* (New York, 1775), 53, and William Henry Drayton, *A Letter from "Freeman" of South Carolina to the Deputies of North America, Assembled in the High Court of Congress at Philadelphia* (Charleston, 1774), in Robert W. Gibbes, ed., *Documentary History of the American Revolution* (New York, 1855), 18–19.
8. *A Letter to a Member of Parliament on the Unhappy Dispute Between Great-Britain and Her Colonies* (London, 1774), 6; James Iredell, "The Principles of an American Whig," [1775–76?], and "Causes of the American Revolution," June 1776, in Don Higginbotham, ed., *The Papers of James Iredell*, 1 vol. to date (Raleigh, 1976), 1:333, 375; Cartwright, *American Independence*, in Smith, comp., *English Defenders of American Freedom*, 157; Rokeby, *Con-*

siderations on the Measures, in ibid., 58, and *A Further Examination of our Present American Measures* (London, 1776), 115.

9. William Hicks, *The Nature and Extent of Parliamentary Power Considered,* in Merrill Jensen, ed., *Tracts of the American Revolution, 1763–1776* (Indianapolis, 1967), 177; Drayton, *Letter from "Freeman,"* in Gibbes, ed., *Documentary History,* 1:32.

10. *An Answer to a Pamphlet, Entitled Taxation no Tyranny* (London, 1775), 6; John Dickinson, *An Essay on the Constitutional Power of Great Britain over the Colonies in America* (Philadelphia, 1774), in Samuel Hazard, et al., eds., *Pennsylvania Archives,* 138 vols. (Philadelphia and Harrisburg, 1852–), 2d ser., 3:601; *An Argument in Defence of the Exclusive Right,* 104; [Arthur Lee], *An Appeal to the Justice and Interests of the People of Great Britain* (London, 1774), 20–21.

11. Dickinson, *Essay on the Constitutional Power,* in *Pennsylvania Archives,* 2d ser., 3:565; *An Argument in Defence of the Exclusive Right,* 104; "An Apology for the Late Conduct of America," *London Gazetteer,* Apr. 7, 1774, in Peter Force, ed., *American Archives,* 9 vols. (Washington, 1837–53), 4th ser., 1:242; "To the Freemen of America," May 18, 1774, in ibid., 336; [Hugh Baillie], *Some Observations on a Pamphlet Lately Published* (London, 1776), 2–3.

12. Cartwright, *American Independence,* in Smith, comp., *English Defenders of American Freedom,* 159–60; *An Answer to a Pamphlet, Entitled Taxation no Tyranny,* in Force, ed., *American Archives,* 4th ser., 1:1455; Moses Mather, *America's Appeal to the Impartial World* (Hartford, 1774), 34.

13. [Thomson Mason], "The British American," nos. VI–VII, July 7, 14, 1774; "A Brief Examination of American Grievances," July 28, 1774; "To the Inhabitants of New-York," Oct. 6, 1774, in Force, ed., *American Archives,* 4th ser., 1:522, 541, 658, 821.

14. [Sir John Dalrymple], *The Address of the People of Great Britain to the Inhabitants of America* (London, 1775), in Force, ed., *American Archives,* 4th ser., 1:1423; James Wilson, *Considerations on the Nature and Extent of the Legislative Authority of the British Parliament* (Philadelphia, 1774), in Robert Green McCloskey, ed., *The Works of James Wilson,* 2 vols. (Cambridge, Mass., 1967), 2:741, 745–46; Thomas Jefferson, *A Summary View of the Rights of British-America* (Williamsburg, 1774), in Julian P. Boyd, ed., *The Papers of Thomas Jefferson,* 19 vols. to date (Princeton, 1950–), 1:125; Alexander Hamilton, *The Farmer Refuted* (New York, 1775), in Harold C. Syrett and Jacob E. Cooke, eds., *The Papers of Alexander Hamilton,* 26 vols. (New York, 1961–79), 1:122; John Adams, "Novanglus," 1775, in Charles F. Adams, ed., *The Works of John Adams,* 10 vols. (Boston, 1856), 4:113–14.

15. Pownall, *Administration of the Colonies,* 5th ed., 2:100; Cartwright, *American Independence,* in *English Defenders of American Freedom,* 138; Wilson, *Considerations,* in McCloskey, ed., *Works of Wilson,* 2:745; *An Answer to a Pamphlet, Entitled Taxation no Tyranny,* 8; Mather, *America's Appeal,* 47; Iredell, "To the Inhabitants of Great Britain," Sept. 1774, in Higginbotham, ed., *Papers of Iredell,* 1:264; John Adams, "Novanglus," in Adams,

ed., *Works of John Adams*, 4:123; Franklin, Marginalia to Wheelock, *Reflections Moral and Political*, 1770, in Leonard Labaree et al., eds., *The Papers of Benjamin Franklin*, 23 vols. to date (New Haven, 1959–), 17:393.

16. Jonathan Shipley, *A Speech Intended to have been Spoken by the Bishop of St. Asaph*, in Smith, comp., *English Defenders of American Freedom*, 31; Cartwright, *American Independence*, in ibid., 144; Dickinson, *Essay on the Constitutional Power*, in *Pennsylvania Archives*, 2d ser., 3:578; Edmund Burke, *Speech on Conciliation with America* (New York, 1907), 25–26.

17. *Gov. Johnston's Speech on American Affairs on the Address in Answer to the King's Speech* (Edinburgh, 1776), 7–8; Johnstone's speeches, June 6, 8, 1774, in Sir Henry Cavendish, *Debates on the House of Commons in the Year 1774, on the Bill For Making More Effectual Provision for the Government of the Province of Quebec* (London, 1839), 187, 242.

18. Rokeby, *Considerations on the Measures*, in Smith, comp., *English Defenders of American Freedom*, 103; Cartwright, *American Independence*, in ibid., 134.

19. Iredell, "To the Inhabitants of Great Britain," Sept. 1774, and "The Principles of an American Whig," [1775–76], in Higginbotham, ed., *Papers of Iredell* 1:254, 264–67, 332; *Gov. Johnston's Speech*, 5–7.

20. Mather, *America's Appeal*, 44; Hamilton, *Farmer Refuted*, in Syrett and Cooke, eds., *Hamilton Papers*, 1: 164; *An Answer to a Pamphlet, Entitled Taxation no Tyranny*, 8; Willoughby Bertie, Earl of Abingdon, *Thoughts on the Letter of Edmund Burke, Esq., to the Sheriffs of Bristol, on the Affairs of America* (Oxford, 1778), in Smith, comp., *English Defenders of American Freedom*, 219–20; *Resistance No Rebellion* (London, 1775), 46–47; Granville Sharp, *A Declaration of the People's Natural Right to a Share in the Legislature* (London, 1774), 233, 238–39.

21. Shipley, *Sermon*, in Smith, comp., *English Defenders of American Freedom*, 38; Hamilton, *Farmer Refuted*, in Syrett and Cooke, eds., *Hamilton Papers*, 1:99; Iredell, "To the Inhabitants of Great Britain," Sept. 1774, in Higginbotham, ed., *Papers of Iredell*, 1:266.

22. Cartwright, *American Independence*, in Smith, comp., *English Defenders of American Freedom*, 149–52; Rokeby, *Considerations on the Measures*, in ibid., 65; Hamilton, *A Full Vindication of the Measures of the Congress* (New York, 1774) in Syrett and Cooke, eds., *Hamilton Papers*, 1:60.

23. Jamaica Assembly's Petition to king, Dec. 28, 1774, in Force, ed., *American Archives*, 4th ser., 1: 1072–74; George Metcalf, *Royal Government and Political Conflict in Jamaica, 1729–1783* (London, 1965), 167–91; Richard B. Sheridan, "The Jamaican Slave Insurrection Scare of 1776 and the American Revolution," *Journal of Negro History*, 61 (1976): 299–301.

24. The best existing published account of the Irish response to the American revolutionary argument is J. G. Simms, *Colonial Nationalism, 1698–1776* (Cork, 1976), 48–71. But see also Maurice R. O'Connell, *Irish Politics and Social Conflict in the Age of the American Revolution* (Philadelphia, 1965), 25–36; Francis G. James, *Ireland in the Empire, 1688–1770* (Cambridge, Mass., 1973), 307–12; and David N. Doyle, *Ireland, Irishmen and Revolutionary America* (Dublin, 1981), 152–61. The quotations are from Simms, *Colonial Nationalism*, 69, 71, and James, *Ireland in the Empire*, 311.

In Barbados, a section of the assembly also endeavored, albeit unsuccessfully, to address the king in support of the Americans. See Agnes M. Whitson, "The Outlook of the Continental American Colonies on the British West Indies, 1760–1775," *Political Science Quarterly*, 45(1930): 83–84, and S.H.H. Carrington, "West Indian Opposition to British Policy: Barbadian Politics, 1774–82," *Journal of Caribbean History*, 17 (1982): 30. The assembly of Nova Scotia, one of the weakest, least developed, and most dependent colonies, used the occasion of an address to the crown not to deny parliamentary authority but to secure crown recognition of local rights against prerogative power in the colony. See J. Bartlett Brebner, "Nova Scotia's Remedy for the American Revolution," *Canadian Historical Review* 15(1934): 171–81, and *An Essay on the Present State of the Province of Nova Scotia* [Halifax, 1774] for an exploration of many of the issues that lay behind the assembly's petition.

25. Peter S. Onuf, ed., *Maryland and the Empire, 1773: The Antilon–First Citizen Letters* (Baltimore, 1974), 29; Barbara A. Black, "The Constitution of the Empire: The Case for the Colonists," *University of Pennsylvania Law Review* 124 (1976): 1203.

26. Massachusetts Committee of Correspondence to Franklin, Mar. 31, 1774, Franklin to Thomas Cushing, Sept. 3, 1774, and to Joseph Galloway, Feb. 25, 1775, in Labaree et al., eds., *Franklin Papers*, 21:166–67, 280, 509–10; Hamilton, *Farmer Refuted*, in Syrett and Cooke, eds., *Hamilton Papers*, 1:163; [John Allen], *The American Alarm, Or the Bostonian's Plea, For the Rights, and Liberties, of the People* (Boston, 1773), 5.

27. Adams, "Novanglus," in Adams, ed., *Works of John Adams*, 4: 105, 118; "To the Inhabitants of New York," Oct. 6, 1774, in Force, ed., *American Archives*, 4th ser., 1: 826.

28. Burke's speech, Apr. 19, 1774, Dowdeswell's speech, Apr. 15, 1774, in Cobbett and Hansard, eds., *Parliamentary History*, 17:1198, 1265; Fox's speeches, May 26, June 8, 1774, in Cavendish, *Debates on the House of Commons in the Year 1774*, 62, 246; *A Letter to the Right Honourable The Earl of H——b——h* (London, 1769), 111.

29. *Candid Observations on Two Pamphlets Lately Published* (Barbados, 1766), 33–34; Burke's speech, Apr. 19, 1774, Cavendish's speech, Mar. 14, 1774, in Cobbett and Hansard, eds., *Parliamentary History*, 17:1169, 1265; Barre's speech, May 31, 1774, in Cavendish, *Debates on the House of Commons in the Year 1774*, 89; Shipley, *Sermon*, in Smith, comp., *English Defenders of American Freedom*, 36; Hamilton, *Farmer Refuted*, in Syrett and Cooke, eds., *Hamilton Papers*, 1:90; Wilson, *Considerations*, in McCloskey, ed., *Works of Wilson*, 2:723.

30. *Gov. Johnston's Speech*, 8; Massachusetts Committee of Correspondence to Franklin, Mar. 31, 1774, in Labaree et al., eds., *Franklin Papers*, 21:165–66; Jefferson, *Summary View*, in Boyd, ed., *Jefferson Papers*, 1:129–35; Drayton, *Letter from "Freeman,"* in Gibbes, ed., *Documentary History*, 1:17.

31. Cavendish's speech, Mar. 14, 1774, in Cobbett and Hansard, eds., *Parliamentary History*, 17:1169; "Z," in *Providence Gazette*, Oct. 16, 1773; Wm. Pitkin to William Samuel Johnson, June 6, 1768, in "The Trumbull Pa-

pers," *Massachusetts Historical Society, Collections*, 5th ser., 9 (Boston, 1885): 283.

32. Black, "Constitution of Empire," 1157; John Phillip Reid, *In Defiance of the Law: The Standing Army Controversy, the Two Constitutions, and the Coming of the American Revolution* (Chapel Hill, 1981), 168–69, and "The Irrelevance of the Declaration," in Hendrik B. Hartog, ed., *Law in the American Revolution and the Revolution in the Law* (New York, 1981), 60. This literature is explored in more detail in Jack P. Greene, "From the Perspective of Law: Context and Legitimacy in the Origins of the American Revolution. A Review Essay," *South Atlantic Quarterly* 85 (1986), 56–77.

33. John P. Reid, *In a Defiant Stance: The Conditions of Law in Massachusetts Bay, the Irish Comparison, and the Coming of the American Revolution* (University Park, Pa., 1977), 70; Reid, *In Defiance of the Law*, 25, 33, 36, 205; Reid, "The Ordeal by Law of Thomas Hutchinson," *New York University Law Review* 49(1974): 602; Black, "Constitution of Empire," 1210–11; Thomas C. Grey, "Origin of the Unwritten Constitution: Fundamental Law in American Revolutionary Thought," *Stanford Law Review* 30(1978): 858.

34. John P. Reid, "The Apparatus of Constitutional Advocacy and the American Revolution: A Review of Five Books," *New York University Law Review* 42 (1967): 194; Reid, "In the First Line of Defense: The Colonial Charters, the Stamp Act Debate and the Coming of the American Revolution," ibid. 51(1976): 177, 208–9, 211; Black, "Constitution of the Empire," 1203.

35. Reid, *In Defiance of the Law*, 79–80, 160; Reid, "In an Inherited Way: English Constitutional Rights, the Stamp Act Debates, and the Coming of the American Revolution," *Southern California Law Review* 49(1976): 1127; Reid, "In Accordance with Usage: The Authority of Custom, the Stamp Act Debate, and the Coming of the American Revolution," *Fordham Law Review* 45 (1976): 341; Grey, "Origins of the Unwritten Constitution," 863.

36. Black, "Constitution of Empire," 1193, 1198, 1200, 1203; Reid, "Ordeal by Law of Thomas Hutchinson," 599; Reid, "In Accordance with Usage," 366.

37. Reid, *In Defiance of the Law*, 162, 169; Reid, "In Accordance with Usage," 357, 364; Black, "Constitution of Empire," 1202.

38. Black, "Constitution of Empire," 1202; Reid, *In Defiance of the Law*, 81, 160, 165; Reid, "In Accordance with Usage," 356–57; Reid, "Irrelevance of the Declaration," 61; Grey, "Origins of the Unwritten Constitution," 850.

39. Grey, "Origins of the Unwritten Constitution," 850, 853–54, 890; Reid, "In Accordance with Usage," 344; Black, "Constitution of Empire," 1203, 1210.

40. Grey, "Origins of the Unwritten Constitution," 863–64; Reid, "Irrelevance of the Declaration," 65.

41. Reid, "Irrelevance of the Declaration," 72; Reid, "'In Our Contracted Sphere': The Constitutional Contract, the Stamp Act Crisis, and the Coming of the American Revolution," *Columbia Law Review* 76(1976): 22.

42. Reid, "Irrelevance of the Declaration," 83; Reid, "In Our Contracted Sphere," 31, 40; Reid, "In a Defensive Rage: The Uses of the Mob, the

Justification in Law, and the Coming of the American Revolution," *New York University Law Review* 49(1974): 1087; Black, "Constitution of Empire," 1202–3.

43. Reid, "In Accordance with Usage," 344; Black, "Constitution of Empire," 1203, 1210.

44. Reid, "In a Defensive Rage," 1063; Reid, *In a Defiant Stance*, 162; Reid, "A Lawyer Acquitted: John Adams and the Boston Massacre Trials," *American Journal of Legal History* 18(1974): 191; Reid, "In Accordance with Usage," 344.

45. Reid, *In a Defiant Stance*, 2, 161; Reid, "In a Defensive Rage," 1091; Hendrik B. Hartog, "Losing the World of the Massachusetts Whig," in Hartog, ed., *Law in the American Revolution*, 146–47, 152–53, 160.

46. Reid, *In a Defiant Stance*, 162.

Chapter Eight

1. Madison, "Notes on the Resolutions," 1799–1800, in Gaillard Hunt, ed., *The Writings of James Madison*, 9 vols. (New York, 1900–1910), 6:373.

2. See F.L. to *Pennsylvania Journal*, Mar. 13, 1766, in Edmund S. Morgan, ed., *Prologue to Revolution: Sources and Documents on the Stamp Act Crisis, 1764–1766* (Chapel Hill, 1959), 91.

3. John Witherspoon's speech in Congress, [July 30, 1776], in Paul H. Smith et al., eds., *Letters of Delegates to Congress* (Washington, D.C., 1976–), 4:584–87.

4. Jack N. Rakove, *The Beginnings of National Politics: An Interpretive History of the Continental Congress* (New York: 1979), 136–45.

5. Peter S. Onuf, *The Origins of the Federal Republic: Jurisdictional Controversies in the United States, 1775–1787* (Philadelphia, 1983), 7.

6. Rakove, *Beginnings of National Politics*, 145; Silas Deane to Patrick Henry, Jan. 2, 1775, in Smith, ed., *Letters of Delegates*, 1:291; Edmund Cody Barnett, *The Continental Congress* (New York, 1964), 136–37.

7. Joseph Hewes to Samuel Johnston, July 28, 1776; Richard Henry Lee to Thomas Jefferson, Aug. 25, 1777, in Smith, ed., *Letters of Delegates*, 4:555, 7:551.

8. John Adams to Samuel Osgood, Nov. 14, 1775, ibid., 2:342.

9. Merrill Jensen, *The Articles of Confederation: An Interpretation of the Social-Constitutional History of the American Revolution, 1774–1781* (Madison, 1959), 56.

10. See John R. Alden, *The First South* (Baton Rouge, 1961), 33–73; John Adams to James Warren, May 15, 1776, in Smith, ed., *Letters of Delegates*, 3:678.

11. Benjamin Franklin, *Interest of Great Britain Considered* (London, 1760) in Leonard W. Labaree et al., eds., *The Papers of Benjamin Franklin*, 23 vols. to

date (New Haven, 1959–), 9:90. On Britain's growing fear of losing the colonies, see especially Jack P. Greene, " 'A Posture of Hostility': A Reconsideration of Some Aspects of the Origins of the American Revolution," *American Antiquarian Society Proceedings* 87 (1977): 5–46.

12. Malachy Postlethwayt, *Britain's Commercial Interest*, in Jack P. Greene, ed., *Great Britain and the American Colonies, 1606–1763* (New York, 1970), 298; *State of the British and French Colonies in North America* (London, 1755), 54; Henry Frankland to Thomas Pelham, Sept. 1, 1757, Add. Mss., 33087, f. 353, British Library, London.

13. Pownall, *Administration of the Colonies* (1764), in Greene, ed., *Great Britain and the American Colonies,* 306; "Some Thoughts on the Settlement and Government of Our Colonies in North America," Mar. 10, 1763, Add. Mss. (Liverpool Papers) 38335, ff. 74–77, British Library.

14. As quoted by Sir Lewis Namier, *England in the Age of the American Revolution* (London, 1963), 276.

15. John Adams to Joseph Hawley, Nov. 25, 1775, in Smith, ed., *Letters of Delegates,* 2:385.

16. Joseph Galloway to [Samuel Verplanck], Dec. 30, 1774, ibid., 1:288.

17. Adams to Hawley, Nov. 25, 1775, ibid., 2:385–86; [Luther Martin], *To the People of Maryland* [(Baltimore, 1779)].

18. Bernard Bailyn, *The Ideological Origins of the American Revolution* (Boston, 1967), 55–93, and *The Origins of American Politics* (New York, 1968), 41–58, 135–61.

19. See Jensen, *Articles of Confederation,* and "The Articles of Confederation," in *Fundamental Testaments of the American Revolution* (Washington, 1973), 49–80; Rakove, *Beginnings of National Politics,* 1–239; Thomas Burke to Richard Caswell, Apr. 29, 1777, in Smith, ed., *Letters of Delegates,* 6:672.

A later corollary of this fear that a central government would run roughshod over the rights and powers of the constituent components of the union was that in America, as in Britain, not only power but wealth and talent, attracted by the great influence of a central government, would all flow from the peripheries to the center. Agrippa later articulated this fear succinctly during the debate over the Constitution in 1787, predicting that the northern and southern states would "in a very short time sink into the same degradation and contempt with respect to the middle state(s) as Ireland, Scotland, & Wales are in regard to England. All the men of genius and wealth will resort to the seat of government, that will be [the] center of revenue, and of business, which the extremes will be drained to supply" Letter to Agrippa [James Winthrop], in Cecelia M. Kenyon, ed., *The Antifederalists* (Indianapolis, 1966), 157.

20. See James Madison, "Ancient & Modern Confederacies," in William T. Hutchinson, et al., eds., *The Papers of James Madison,* 15 vols. (Chicago, 1962–), 9:4–24; Benjamin F. Wright, ed., *The Federalist* (Cambridge, 1961), 171–85; Wilson, "Lectures on Law," in Robert Green McCloskey, ed., *The Works of James Wilson,* 2 vols. (Cambridge, Mass., 1967), 1:247–69.

21. Gordon S. Wood, *The Creation of the American Republic, 1776–1787* (Chapel Hill, 1969), 58, 356, 499; Address and Reasons of Dissent of the Minority

of the Convention of the State of Pennsylvania, 1787, in Kenyon, ed., *Antifederalists*, 39. See also Samuel H. Beer, "Federalism, Nationalism, and Democracy in America," *American Political Science Review* 72 (1978): 13.

22. See Josiah Bartlett's notes, [June 12–July 12, 1776], John Adams's notes of debate, July 30, Aug. 1, 1776, John Witherspoon's speech, [July 30, 1776], and Benjamin Rush's notes for a speech, [Aug. 1, 1776], in Smith, ed., *Letters of Delegates*, 4:199–200, 568, 587, 592, 598–99; William Henry Drayton's speech, Jan. 20, 1778, in Hezekiah Niles, ed., *Principles and Acts of the Revolution in America* (New York, 1876), 563.

23. Yehoshua Arieli, *Individualism and Nationalism in American Ideology* (Cambridge, 1964), 45–49; "Some Thoughts on the Settlement and Government of Our Colonies," ff. 74–77.

24. Franklin, *Interest of Great Britain Considered*, in Labaree et al., eds., *Franklin Papers*, 9:90; Arieli, *Individualism and Nationalism*, 45–49; John Barnard, *The Throne Established by Righteousness* (Boston, 1734), as quoted by Paul A. Varg, "The Advent of Nationalism, 1758–1776," *American Quarterly* 16 (1964): 172.

25. Edwin Burrows and Michael Wallace, "The American Revolution: The Ideology and Psychology of National Liberation," *Perspectives in American History* 6 (1972): 275–76; *State of the British and French Colonies*, 63–64.

26. Beer, "Federalism, Nationalism, and Democracy," 11; Oliver Wolcott to Samuel Lyman, May 16, 1776, in Smith, ed., *Letters of Delegates*, 4:17.

27. Jack P. Greene, "Paine, America, and the 'Modernization' of Political Consciousness," *Political Science Quarterly* 93 (1978): 73–92; John Shy, "The American Revolution: The Military Conflict Considered as a Revolutionary War," in Stephen G. Kurtz and James H. Hutson, eds., *Essays on the American Revolution* (Chapel Hill, 1973), 155.

28. Andrew C. McLaughlin, *The Confederation and the Constitution, 1783–1789* (New York, 1962), 41.

29. Andrew C. McLaughlin, *The Foundations of American Constitutionalism* (New York, 1932), 132–33, 138; Jack P. Greene, *The Quest for Power: The Lower Houses of Assembly in the Southern Royal Colonies, 1689–1763* (Chapel Hill, 1963), 438–53.

30. Onuf, *Origins of the Federal Republic*, 21–22.

31. John Adams's notes of debates, [Sept. 6, 1776], in Smith, ed., *Letters of Delegates*, 1:28.

32. Samuel Williams, *The Natural and Civil History of Vermont*, 2 vols. (Walpole, N.H., 1794), 2:429–31.

33. A fuller discussion of this subject may be found in Jack P. Greene, "Search for Identity: An Interpretation of the Meaning of Selected Patterns of Social Response in Eighteenth-Century America," *Journal of Social History* 3 (1970): 189–224. The contrary view is succinctly stated in Max Savelle, "Nationalism and Other Loyalties in the American Revolution," *American Historical Review* 67 (1962): 904.

34. Grayson's observation may be conveniently found in Kenyon, ed., *Antifederalists*, 282.

35. John Dickinson's notes for a speech in Congress, July 1, 1776, John

Adams's notes in debates, Aug. 1, 1776, and Benjamin Rush's notes for a speech in Congress, [Aug. 1, 1776], in Smith, ed., *Letters of Delegates*, 4:356, 592, 599.

36. David M. Potter, "The Historians' Use of Nationalism and Vice Versa," *American Historical Review* 67(1962): 935, 949.

37. See Albert Harkness, Jr., "Americanism and Jenkins' Ear," *Mississippi Valley Historical Review* 37(1950): 61–90; Richard L. Merritt, *Symbols of American Community, 1735–1775* (New Haven, 1966); Michael Kraus, *Intercolonial Aspects of American Culture on the Eve of the Revolution with Special Reference to the Northern Towns* (New York, 1928): and Carl Bridenbaugh, *Cities in Revolt: Urban Life in America, 1743–1776* (New York, 1955).

38. Franklin, *Interest of Great Britain Considered*, in Labaree, et al., eds., *Franklin Papers*, 9:90; Richard Henry Lee to Arthur Lee, July 4, 1763, in James C. Ballagh, ed., *Letters of Richard Henry Lee*, 2 vols. (New York, 1911–14), 1:11; Burke, "Speech on American Taxation," Apr. 19, 1774, in Thomas H. D. Mahoney, ed., *Edmund Burke: Selected Writings and Speeches on America* (Indianapolis, 1964), 79. See also, among many expressions of beliefs similar to those of Lee, Robert M. Calhoon, ed., "William Smith Jr.'s Alternative to the American Revolution," *William and Mary Quarterly*, 3d ser., 22 (1965): 117.

39. Arieli, *Individualism and Nationalism*, 45; Alexander Hamilton, *The Farmer Refuted*, [Feb. 23], 1774, in Harold C. Syrett and Jacob E. Cooke, eds., *The Papers of Alexander Hamilton* 26 vols. (New York: 1961–79), 1:106–7.

40. Arieli, *Individualism and Nationalism*, 67–68.

41. On the differential effects of such fears in the 1760s and 1770s, see Jack P. Greene, "Social Context and the Causal Pattern of the American Revolution: A Preliminary Consideration of New-York, Virginia and Massachusetts," in Claude Fohlen and Jacques Godechot, eds., *La Révolution Américaine et l'Europe* (Paris, 1979), 25–63.

42. *New York Mercury*, Aug. 27, 1764, as quoted by Burrows and Wallace, "American Revolution," 191; Dickinson to William Pitt, Dec. 21, 1765, Chatham Papers, PRO 30/8/97, Public Record Office, London.

43. Joseph Galloway, *Historical and Political Reflections on the Rise and Progress of the American Rebellion* (London, 1780), 77, as quoted by Jensen, *Articles of Confederation*, 69.

44. Adams's notes of debate, July 30, 1776, in Smith, ed., *Letters of Delegates*, 4:568; Richard Henry Lee to Landon Carter, June 2, 1776, in Ballagh, ed., *Letters of Richard Henry Lee*, 1:198; Enoch Huntington, *The Happy Effects of Union, and the Fatal Tendency of Disunion* (Hartford, 1776), 11.

45. Edward Rutledge to John Jay, [June 8, 1776] and speech of Witherspoon, [July 30, 1776], in Smith, ed., *Letters of Delegates*, 4:175, 584–85; Jared Sparks, *The Life of Gouverneur Morris*, 3 vols. (Boston, 1832), 1:26–27, as cited by Merrill Jensen, "The Articles of Confederation," in *Fundamental Testaments of the American Revolution*, 57. On the general way the fear of disunion operated in favor of continental confederation in the mid-1770s, see the excellent analysis in Rakove, *Beginnings of National Politics*, 135–215.

46. Onuf, *Origins of the Federal Republic*, 22–23.

47. Calhoon, ed., "Smith's Alternative to Revolution," 114; Thomas Jefferson's notes of proceedings in Congress, [June, 1776], and John Adams's notes of debates, Aug. 1, 1776, in Smith, ed., *Letters of Delegates*, 4:161, 593.
48. Beer, "Federalism, Nationalism, and Democracy," 12; McLaughlin, *Foundations of American Constitutionalism*, 138. See also John C. Ranney, "The Bases of American Federalism," *William and Mary Quarterly*, 3d ser., 3 (1946): 8–9.
49. Richard B. Morris, "The Forging of the Union Reconsidered: A Historical Refutation of the State Sovereignty over Seabeds," *Columbia Law Review* 74 (1974): 1062; Jensen, *Articles of Confederation;* Rakove, *Beginnings of National Politics*, xvi, 136, 162, 190; Onuf, *Origins of the Federal Republic*, 12.
50. Carter Braxton, *An Address to the Convention of the Colony and Ancient Dominion of Virginia* (Philadelphia, 1776), 23–24; Onuf, *Origins of the Federal Republic*, 21–22.
51. Rakove, *Beginnings of National Politics*, 136, 148–49, 151, 172, 184–85; John Adams to James Warren, Apr. 16, 1776, in Smith, ed., *Letters of Delegates*, 3:536.
52. Edward Rutledge to John Jay, June 29, 1776, ibid., 4:338; Rakove, *Beginnings of National Politics*, 155–57, 160.
53. Rakove, *Beginnings of National Politics*, 164–73; Onuf, *Origins of the Federal Republic*, 150; Thomas Burke to Richard Caswell, Apr. 29, 1778, Maryland Delegates to Maryland Assembly, June 22, 1778; Connecticut Delegates to Jonathan Trumbull, Sr., July 9, 1778, and Nathaniel Scudder to John Hart, July 13, 1778, in Smith, ed., *Letters of Delegates*, 9:527, 529, 10:175, 242, 272–73.
54. Rakove, *Beginnings of National Politics*, 164, 166, 174, 185; Jensen, *Articles of Confederation*, 263.
55. Thomas Burke to North Carolina Assembly, [Apr. 29, 1778], and Nathaniel Scudder to John Hart, July 13, 1778, John Mathews to Thomas Bee, Aug. 30, 1778, in Smith, ed., *Letters of Delegates*, 9:534, 10:273, 533; David Ramsay, *An Oration or the Advantages of American Independence* (Charleston, 1778), 19–20; William Floyd to George Clinton, Jan. 3, 1779, James Duane to George Clinton, Feb. 20, 1779, William Whipple to Josiah Bartlett, Mar. 7, 1779, and John Jay to George Clinton, Sept. 25, 1779, in Edmund Cody Burnett, ed., *Letters of Members of the Continental Congress*, 8 vols. (Washington, 1921–38), 4:5, 78, 91, 433.
56. Joseph Jones to George Washington, [June 19, 1780], and Ezekiel Cornell to Nathanael Greene, [July 21, 1780], in Burnett, ed., *Letters of Members*, 5:227, 281.
57. James Madison to Thomas Jefferson, May 6, 1780, and Jones to Washington, [June 19, 1780], in ibid., 5:128–29, 227.
58. Wood, *Creation of the American Republic*, 353; Rakove, *Beginnings of National Politics*, 174.
59. Curtis P. Nettels, "The Origin of the Union and of the States," *Proceedings of the Massachusetts Historical Society* 72 (1957–60), 68–83; Morris, "Forging of the Union," 1067, 1089; Beer, "Federalism, Nationalism, and Democ-

racy," 12; Rakove, *Beginnings of National Politics*, 173–74. For the tradi-
tional view, see, especially, in addition to Jensen, *Articles of Confederation*,
C. H. Van Tyne, "Sovereignty in the American Revolution: An Historical
Study," *American Historical Review* 12 (1907): 529–45.

60. Morris, "Forging of the Union," 1067; John Adams's notes of debates, July
30, Aug. 1, 1776; Benjamin Rush's notes for a speech, [Aug. 1, 1776]; in
Smith, ed., *Letters of Delegates*, 4:568, 592–93, 599–601; "Of the Present
State of America," Oct. 10, 1776, in Peter Force, comp., *American Archives*,
9 vols. (Washington, 1837–53), 5th ser., 2:967–70; Rakove, *Beginnings of
National Politics*, 167.

61. Edward Rutledge to John Jay, June 29, 1776, in Smith, ed., *Letters of Delegates*, 3:138.

62. Beer, "Federalism, Nationalism, and Democracy," 10, 12.

63. Rakove, *Beginnings of National Politics*, 184–85.

64. William Henry Drayton's speech, Jan. 20, 1778, in Niles, ed., *Principles
and Acts*, 363; Jensen, *Articles of Confederation*, 263; Morris, "Forging of the
Union," 1064; Wood, *Creation of the American Republic*, 359.

65. Rakove, *Beginnings of National Politics*, 162, 172; McLaughlin, *Foundations
of American Constitutionalism*, 140.

Chapter Nine

1. Madison, "Notes on the Resolutions," 1799–1800, in Gaillard Hunt ed.,
The Writings of James Madison, 9 vols. (New York, 1900–1910), 6:375; Hamilton to James Duane, [Sept. 3, 1780], in Harold C. Syrett and Jacob E.
Cooke, eds., *The Papers of Alexander Hamilton*, 26 vols. (New York, 1961–
79), 2:401.

2. Peter S. Onuf, *The Origins of the Federal Republic: Jurisdictional Controversies
in the United States, 1775–1787* (Philadelphia, 1983), 201.

3. Peter S. Onuf, ed., *Maryland the Empire, 1773: The Antilon–First Citizen
Letters* (Baltimore, 1974), 38–39.

4. Onuf, *Origins of the Federal Republic*, 154, 158.

5. Root to Trumbull, Dec. 27, 1780, in Edmund Cody Burnett, ed., *Letters of
Members of the Continental Congress*, 8 vols. (Washington, 1921–38), 5:504.

6. Joseph Jones to George Washington, Feb. 27, 1781, Root to Trumbull, Dec.
27, 1780, Wolcott to Trumbull, Jan. 9, 1781, and Connecticut Delegates to
Trumbull, Jan. 16, 1781, in Burnett, ed., *Letters of Members*, 5:504, 526, 536,
584; Hamilton, "The Continentalist," No. IV, Aug. 30, 1781, in Syrett and
Cooke, eds., *Hamilton Papers*, 2:670–71.

7. Root to Trumbull, Dec. 27, 1780, Duane to Washington, Jan. 29, 1781,
Richard Peters to Oliver Wolcott, July 15, 1783, in Burnett, ed., *Letters of
Members*, 5:504, 551, 7:225.

8. Hamilton to James Duane, [Sept. 3, 1780], and Hamilton, "The Continentalist," No. II, [July 19, 1781], in Syrett and Cooke, eds., *Hamilton Papers*,
2:403, 654.

9. Hamilton to James Duane, [Sept. 3, 1780]; Hamilton, "The Continentalist," No. I, [July 12, 1781], No. II [July 19, 1781], and No. III, [August 9, 1781], in Syrett and Cooke, eds., *Hamilton Papers*, 2:401, 650, 655, 663; Hamilton to John Jay, July 25, 1783, in Burnett, ed., *Letters of Members*, 7:233.

10. Hamilton, "The Continentalist," No. V, [April 18, 1782]; Hamilton, "Defense of Congress," [July 1783], in Syrett and Cooke, eds., *Hamilton Papers*, 3:82, 427; Connecticut Delegates to Trumbull, Jan. 16, 1781, John Mathews to William Livingston, [Mar. 6, 1781], and Jacob Read to George Washington, Aug. 13, 1784, in Burnett, ed., *Letters of Members*, 5:537, 6:15, 7:583.

11. Duane to Washington, Jan. 29, 1781, Madison to Jefferson, November 18, 1781, and to Edmund Randolph, Feb. 25, 1783, in Burnett, ed., *Letters of Members*, 5:551, 6:265, 7:58; *The Political Establishments of the United States of America* (Philadelphia, 1783), 10–11; Charles to Hannah Thomson, July 25, 1783, in Eugene R. Sheridan and John M. Murrin, eds., *Congress at Princeton: Being the Letters of Charles Thomson to Hannah Thomson, June–October 1783* (Princeton, 1985), 29–30.

12. Washington's Circular Letter to the States, June 8, 1783; John Francis Mercer to Madison, Nov. 26, 1784; and James Monroe to Thomas Jefferson, June 16, 1785, in Burnett, ed., *Letters of Members*, 7:218, 616, 8:143; Hamilton, "The Continentalist," No. IV, [Aug. 30, 1781], and "Unsubmitted Resolutions Calling for a Convention," [July 1783], in Syrett and Cooke, eds., *Hamilton Papers*, 2:669–71, 3:420–26; Richard Henry Lee to James Madison, Nov. 26, 1784; Joseph Jones to Madison, June 12, 1785; Madison to Jefferson, Oct. 3, 1785; Madison, "Draft of Resolutions on Foreign Trade," [Nov. 12, 1785] in William T. Hutchinson, et al., eds., *The Papers of James Madison*, 15 vols. (Chicago, 1962–), 8:151, 293, 373–74, 409.

13. Madison to Richard Henry Lee, Dec. 15, 1784, in Hutchinson, et al., eds., *Madison Papers*, 8:201; Jack W. Rakove, *The Beginnings of National Politics: An Interpretive History of the Continental Congress* (New York, 1979), 289–96, 313–16, 337–38, 345–49, 365–68, 370–72, 381–82; Gordon S. Wood, *The Creation of the American Republic, 1776–1787* (Chapel Hill, 1969), 464.

14. Washington to James Warren, Oct. 7, 1785, in J. C. Fitzpatrick, ed., *The Writings of George Washington*, 39 vols. (Washington, 1931–44), 28:290; Hamilton, speech to the New York Legislature, [Jan. 19, 1787], in Syrett and Cooke, eds., *Hamilton Papers*, 4:11; Thomas Rodney's report on speech of Thomas Burke, Mar. 5, 1781, in Burnett, ed., *Letters of Members*, 6:5.

15. Madison to Richard Henry Lee, Dec. 25, 1784, and to James Monroe, Aug. 7, 1785, in Hutchinson et al., eds., *Madison Papers*, 8:201, 335–36; John Francis Mercer to Jacob Read, Sept. 23, 1784, in Burnett, ed., *Letters of Members*, 7:591; Washington to Henry Knox, Dec. 5, 1784, and to James Warren, Oct. 7, 1785, in Fitzpatrick, ed., *Washington Writings*, 28:5, 290.

16. James Francis Mercer to Madison, Nov. 26, 1784, and James Monroe to Madison, July 18, 1785, in Hutchinson et al., eds., *Madison Papers*, 8:152, 330;

Samuel Osgood to John Adams, [Jan. 14, 1784], in Burnett, ed., *Letters of Members*, 7:415; Hamilton, "The Continentalist," No. V, (Apr. 18, 1782], in Syrett and Cooke, eds., *Hamilton Papers*, 3:81; Charles Thomson to Hannah Thomson, July 25, 1783, in Sheridan and Murrin, eds., *Congress at Princeton*, 29–30.

17. Onuf, *Origins of the Federal Republic*, 150; Willi Paul Adams, *The First American Constitutions: Republican Ideology and the Making of the State Constitutions in the Revolutionary Era* (Chapel Hill, 1980), 50.

18. Hamilton, Remarks to the New York Assembly, [Feb. 15, 1787], in Syrett and Cooke, eds., *Hamilton Papers*, 4:77; Charles Coatesworth Pinckney's speech, Jan. 18, 1788, in Jonathan Elliott, ed., *The Debates of the Several State Conventions on the Adoption of the Federal Constitution*, 5 vols. (Philadelphia, 1901), 4:301–2.

19. Hamilton, remarks to the New York Assembly, [Feb. 15, 1787], in Syrett and Cooke, eds., *Hamilton Papers*, 4:77; Charles Thomson's notes on John Witherspoon's speech, Aug. 27, 1782, in Burnett, ed., *Letters of Members*, 6:458–59.

20. Hamilton, *A Letter from Phocion to the Considerate Citizens of New York*, [Jan. 1–27, 1784], and Remarks to the New York Assembly, [Feb. 15, 1787], in Syrett and Cooke, eds., *Hamilton Papers*, 3:489, 4:77; Nathan Dane, Address to Massachusetts House of Representatives, [Nov. 9, 1786], in Burnett, ed., *Letters of Members*, 8:502–3; Pelatiah Webster, *A Dissertation on the Political Union and Constitution of the Thirteen United States, of North America* (Philadelphia, 1783), 3–4.

21. Noah Webster, *Sketches of American Policy* (Hartford, 1785), 31–33; Nestor to *Independent Gazeteer* (Philadelphia), June 3, 1786, and Stephen Higginson to Henry Knox, Feb. 8, 1787, as quoted by Onuf, *Origins of the American Republic*, 7–8, 150; Pinckney's speech, Jan. 18, 1788, in Elliott, ed., *Debates*, 4:301–2; Hamilton, *Letter from Phocion*, [Jan. 1–27, 1784], in Syrett and Cooke, eds., *Hamilton Papers*, 3:489.

22. Tullius, *Three Letters Addressed to the Public* (Philadelphia, 1783), 11; Charles Thomson's notes on Lee's speeches, Aug. 20, 27, 1782, in Burnett, ed., *Letters of Members*, 6:448, 457.

23. *Political Establishments*, 10, 17–18.

24. Ezra Stiles, *The United States Elevated to Glory and Honor* (New Haven, 1783), in John Wingate Thornton, ed., *The Pulpit of the American Revolution* (Boston, 1876), 419; and John Adams, *A Defence of the Constitutions of Government of the United States of America* (Boston, 1787), in Charles F. Adams, ed., *The Works of John Adams*, 10 vols. (Boston, 1856), 4:579; *Political Establishments*, 17–18.

25. *Political Establishments*, 10, 16.

26. Roger Sherman, *Remarks on a Pamphlet, Entitled A Dissertation on the Political Union and Constitution of the Thirteen United States of North-America* (New Haven, 1784), 15, 39; *Political Establishments*, 10.

27. Sherman, *Remarks on a Pamphlet*, ix, 12–13, 39; N. Webster, *Sketches of*

American Policy, 35; *Political Establishments*, 21; John Jay to John Adams, May 4, 1786, in Burnett, ed., *Letters of Members*, 8:355; Hamilton to Robert Morris, Apr. 1781, in Syrett and Cooke, eds., *Hamilton Papers*, 2:630.

28. James Wilson, *Considerations on the Bank of North America* (1785), in Robert Green McCloskey, ed., *The Works of James Wilson*, 2 vols. (Cambridge, Mass., 1967), 2:829; P. Webster, *Dissertation on the Political Union*, 37; N. Webster, *Sketches of American Policy*, 35; Jefferson to Madison, Feb. 8, Dec. 16, 1786, and Daniel Carroll to Madison, Mar. 13, 1786, in Hutchinson et al., *Madison Papers*, 8:486, 496, 9:211; Charles Pinckney's speech to the New Jersey Assembly, [Mar. 13, 1786], in Burnett, ed., *Letters of Members*, 8:322–23.

29. P. Webster, *Dissertation on the Political Union*, 17–18; Hamilton, "Report on a Letter from the Speaker of the Rhode Island Assembly," Dec. 16, 1782, and *Letter from Phocion*, [Jan. 1–27, 1784], in Syrett and Cooke, eds., *Hamilton Papers*, 3:216, 218–19, 490.

30. Washington to James McHenry, Aug. 22, 1785, to Henry Knox, Feb. 3, 1787, to secretary for foreign affairs, Mar. 10, 1787, to David Stuart, July 1, 1787, in Fitzpatrick, ed., *Washington Writings*, 28:228–29, 19:153, 176, 238; Rufus King to Elbridge Gerry, in Burnett, ed., *Letters of Members*, 8:393; Madison to Washington, Apr. 16, 1787, in Hutchinson et al., eds., *Madison Papers*, 9:384.

31. *Political Establishments*, 17–18; N. Webster, *Sketches of American Policy*, 35; Tullius, *Three Letters*, 12.

32. Tullius, *Three Letters*, 7–10.

33. Ibid., 9–10, 12.

34. Ibid., 7–8; Washington to secretary for foreign affairs, Mar. 10, 1787, in Fitzpatrick, ed., *Washington Writings*, 29:176.

35. *Political Establishments*, 11.

36. Thomas Stone to James Monroe, Dec. 15, 1784, and Rufus King to Jonathan Jackson, Sept. 3, 1786, in Burnett, ed., *Letters of Members*, 7:629, 8:459; Onuf, *Origins of the Federal Republic*, 3–5.

37. Onuf, *Origins of the Federal Republic*, 21, 23, 33, 46; William Grayson to Edmund Randolph, June 12, 1787, in Burnett, ed., *Letters of Members*, 8:609.

38. Charles Pettit to Jeremiah Wadsworth, May 27, 1786, and James Manning to Nathan Miller, June 12, 1786, in Burnett, ed., *Letters of Members*, 8:369–70, 391; Henry Knox to Washington, Oct. 23, 1786, as cited by Onuf, *Origins of the Federal Republic*, 6.

39. Onuf, *Origins of the Federal Republic*, 184–85; Washington to Chevalier de la Luzerne, Aug. 1, 1786, in Fitzpatrick, ed., *Washington Writings*, 28:500; Nathan Dane to John Choate, Jan. 31, 1786, and Madison to Edmund Pendleton, Feb. 24, 1787, in Burnett, ed., *Letters of Members*, 8:292–93, 547; Madison, "Vices of the Political System of the United States," Apr. 1787, and Madison to Edmund Randolph, Apr. 8, 1787, in Hutchinson et al., eds., *Madison Papers*, 9:348–52, 369; *Political Establishments*, 11.

40. Madison to Edmund Randolph, Apr. 8, 1787, and to Washington, Apr. 16, 1787, in Hutchinson et al., *Madison Papers*, 9:369–71, 383; Madison, "Consolidation," and "Charters," *National Gazette*, Dec. 5, 1791, Jan. 19, 1792, in Hunt, ed., *Madison Writings*, 6:68–70, 83, 85.

41. Madison, "Federalist Nos. 18–20," in Benjamin F. Wright, ed., *The Federalist* (Cambridge, 1961), 171–86; Wilson, "Lectures on Law," in McCloskey, ed., *Works of Wilson*, 1:247–60; Onuf, *Origins of the Federal Republic*, 158, 172, 207. Earlier examples of writers who questioned the appropriateness of either ancient or contemporary models for the political organization of the United States include Hamilton, "Continentalist," No. IV, [July 4, 1782], in Syrett and Cooke, eds., *Hamilton Papers*, 3:103; and William Grayson to Madison, Mar. 21, 1786, in Hutchinson et al., eds., *Madison Papers*, 8:510.

42. James Wilson, *Speech Delivered on 26th November, 1787, in the Convention of Pennsylvania* (Philadelphia, 1787), in McCloskey, ed., *Works of Wilson*, 2:764; Onuf, *Origins of the Federal Republic*, 198; Convention to Congress, Sept. 12, 1787, in Max Farrand, ed., *Records of the Federal Convention of 1787*, 4 vols. (Washington, 1911–37), 2:584; Madison, *Federalist* 37, in Wright, ed., *Federalist*, 361–63.

43. Wilson's speech, June 19, 1787, George Mason's speech, June 20, 1787, and Bedford's and Oliver Ellsworth's speeches, June 30, 1787, in Farrand, ed., *Records of the Federal Convention*, 1:322–23, 340, 490, 492; Hamilton's speech, June 19, 1787, in Syrett and Cooke, eds., *Hamilton Papers*, 4:211.

44. Luther Martin's speech, June 20, 1787, Bedford's and Ellsworth's speeches, June 30, 1787, in Farrand, ed., *Records of the Federal Convention*, 1:340–41, 490, 492.

45. Hamilton's speech, June 19, 1787, and Hamilton, *Federalist* 15, in Syrett and Cooke, eds., *Hamilton Papers*, 4:211, 362.

46. Madison, "Vices of the Political System," Apr.–June 1787, to Randolph, Apr. 8, 1787, "Reply to the New Jersey Plan," June 19, 1787, and "Rule of Representation," [June 29, 1787], in Hutchinson et al., eds., *Madison Papers*, 9:348–57, 369–70, 10:55–59, 86; Edmund Randolph's speech, May 29, 1787, in Farrand, ed., *Records of the Federal Convention*, 1:18; Madison to Jefferson, Oct. 24, 1787, in Julian P. Boyd, ed., *The Papers of Thomas Jefferson*, 19 vols. to date (Princeton, 1950–), 12:273.

47. Onuf, *Origins of the Federal Republic*, 191; Edmund Randolph's speech, May 29, 1787; Madison's speech, June 9, 1787; Rufus King's and James Wilson's speeches, June 19, 1787; Elbridge Gerry's and Madison's speeches, June 29, 1787; Convention Proceedings, Aug. 20, 1787, in Farrand, ed., *Records of the Federal Convention*, 1:27, 180, 323–24, 467, 471, 2:342; Madison's speech, June 21, 1787, in Hutchinson et al., eds., *Madison Papers*, 67–68.

48. Onuf, *Origins of the Federal Republic*, 198.

49. Madison to Jefferson, Mar. 19, 1787, to Randolph, Apr. 8, 1787, "Reply to the New Jersey Plan," June 19, 1787, and *Federalist* 45, Jan. 16, 1788, in Hutchinson et al., eds., *Madison Papers*, 9:55–56, 318–19, 370, 430; Hamil-

ton, *Federalist* 15, in Wright, ed., *Federalist*, 158–59; Hamilton's speech, June 29, 1787, in Farrand, ed., *Records of the Federal Convention*, 1:473.

50. Wilson's speech, June 21, 1787; Wilson's, Madison's, and Rufus King's speeches, June 30, 1787, in Farrand, ed., *Records of the Federal Convention*, 1:355, 490, 493; Madison to Jefferson, Oct. 24, 1787, in Boyd, ed., *Jefferson Papers*, 12:275; *Federalist* 45, in Hutchinson et al., eds., *Madison Papers*, 10:430.

51. William Samuel Johnson's speech, June 21, 1787, in Farrand, ed., *Records of the Federal Convention*, 1:355; Wilson, *Speech Delivered, on 26th November, 1787*, in McCloskey, ed., *Works of Wilson*, 2:770.

52. Madison, *Federalist* 14, Nov. 30, 1787, 45, Jan. 26, 1788, in Hutchinson et al., eds., *Madison Papers*, 10:286, 431; *Federalist* 52, in Wright, ed., *Federalist*, 363.

53. George Mason's speech, Aug. 20, 1787, in Farrand, ed., *Records of the Federal Convention*, 2:347; Hamilton, *Federalist* 32, [Jan. 2, 1788], in Syrett and Cooke, eds., *Hamilton Papers*, 4:461–62; Madison, *Federalist* 40, Jan. 18, 1788, and 44, Jan. 25, 1788, in Hutchinson et al., eds., *Madison Papers*, 10:387, 425.

54. "Dissent of the Minority of the Pennsylvania Convention," Dec. 18, 1787, in Herbert J. Storing and J. Murray Dry, eds., *The Complete Anti-Federalist*, 7 vols. (Chicago, 1982), 3:155, and in Merrill Jensen, ed., *The Documentary History of the Ratification of the Constitution by the States*, 2 vols. (Madison, Wisc., 1976), 2:626; "The Fallacies of the Freeman," Apr. 1788, and "Essays by Cato," 1788, in Storing and Dry, eds., *Complete Anti-Federalist*, 3:190, 5:138; Agrippa's Letter, [Dec. 3, 1787], and Thomas Tredwell's Speech, July 2, 1788, in Cecelia M. Kenyon, ed., *The Antifederalists* (Indianapolis, 1966), 134, 401.

55. John Cartwright, *American Independence*, in Paul H. Smith, comp., *English Defenders of American Freedom, 1774–1778* (Washington, 1972), 139; Onuf, *Origins of the Federal Republic*, 22; N. Webster, *Sketches of American Policy*, 4; Hamilton, "Remarks," [Feb. 15, 1787], in Syrett and Cooke, eds., *Hamilton Papers*, 4:73; Madison, *Federalist* 46, Jan. 29, 1788, in Hutchinson et al., eds., *Madison Papers*, 10:439; Wilson, "Lectures on Law," 1790–91, in McCloskey, ed., *Works of Wilson*, 1:81.

56. Andrew C. McLaughlin, *A Constitutional History of the United States* (New York, 1935), 154, and *The Foundations of American Constitutionalism* (New York, 1932), 135.

57. Wood, *Creation of the American Republic*, 531.

58. Wilson, *Speech Delivered, on 26th November, 1787*, in McCloskey, ed., *Works of Wilson*, 2:770; Wilson, speech, Dec. 1, 1787, in Jensen, ed., *Documentary History*, 2:448.

59. Wood, *Creation of the American Republic*, 545–46, quoting Edmund Pendleton's speech, June 12, 1788, in Elliott, *Debates*, 3:301; Madison, *Federalist* 46, in Wright, ed., *Federalist*, 330.

60. Hamilton, *Federalist* 9 and 32, in Wright, ed., *Federalist*, 148, 241.

61. McLaughlin, *Foundations of American Constitutionalism*, 140.

62. Onuf, *Origins of the Federal Republic*, 207; Madison to Jefferson, Oct. 24, 1787, and, Madison, *Federalist*, 14, in Hutchinson et al., eds., *Madison Papers*, 10:214, 287.

63. Samuel H. Beer, "Federalism, Nationalism, and Democracy in America," *American Political Science Review* 72 (1978): 12, 14–15.

64. Centinel I, *Independent Gazeteer*, Oct. 5, 1787, in Jensen, ed., *Documentary History*, 1: 159; Willoughby Bertie, Fourth Earl of Abingdon, *Thoughts on the Letter of Edmund Burke, Esq., To the Sheriffs of Bristol on the Affairs of America* (Oxford, 1778), in Smith, comp., *English Defenders of American Freedom*, 223–24.

65. J. C. Beckett, "The Irish Parliament in the Eighteenth Century," *Belfast National History and Philosophical Society Proceedings*, 2d ser., 4 (1955): 22–24, and "Anglo-Irish Constitutional Relations in the Later Eighteenth Century," *Irish Historical Studies* 4 (1964–65): 26; J. L. McCracken, *The Irish Parliament in the Eighteenth Century* (Dundalk, 1971), 19; David N. Doyle, *Ireland, Irishmen and Revolutionary America* (Dublin, 1981), 152–55; Declan O'Donovan, "The Money Bill Dispute of 1753," in Thomas Bartlett and D. W. Hayton, eds., *Penal Era and Golden Age: Essays in Irish History* (Belfast, 1979), 55–87; P.D.H. Smyth, "The Volunteers and Parliament, 1779–84," in ibid., 113–36.

66. McCracken, *Irish Parliament*, 19–20; Doyle, *Ireland, Irishmen and Revolutionary America*, 156–57; J. G. Simms, *Colonial Nationalism, 1698–1776* (Cork, 1976), 76–77; Owen Dudley Edwards, "The Impact of the American Revolution in Ireland," in *The Impact of the American Revolution Abroad* (Washington, 1976), 123–41; Maurice R. O'Connell, *Irish Politics and Social Conflict in the Age of the American Revolution* (Philadelphia, 1965), 319–48.

67. Beckett, "Anglo-Irish Constitutional Relations," 28; Joseph Lee, "Grattan's Parliament," in Brian Farrell, ed., *The Irish Parliamentary Tradition* (New York, 1973), 150; Simms, *Colonial Nationalism*, 76; McCracken, *Irish Parliament*, 22–23; Edith M. Johnston, *Great Britain and Ireland, 1760–1800* (London, 1963).

68. Weldon A. Brown, *Empire or Independence: A Study in the Failure of Reconciliation, 1774–1783* (Baton Rouge, 1941), 215–16, 250–51; Bryan Edwards, *The History, Civil and Commercial, of the British Colonies in the West Indies*, 2 vols. (Dublin, 1793), 2:339; Chester Martin, *Empire and Commonwealth: Studies in Governance and Self-Government in Canada* (Oxford, 1929), 148; S.H.H. Carrington, "West Indian Opposition to British Policy: Barbadian Politics, 1774–82," *Journal of Caribbean History* 17 (1982): 26–49; George Metcalf, *Royal Government and Political Conflict in Jamaica, 1729–1783* (London, 1965), 199–237.

69. Long, "On the Constitution and Government of Jamaica," [1770s–1780s], Long Papers, Add. Mss. 12,402, ff. 2, 43; Edwards, *History*, 2:339–40, 343, 347.

70. Edwards, *History*, 2:340–41.

71. Long, "Constitutional Remarks on the Government of Jamaica," [ca. 1770s–1780s], Add. Mss. 12,402, f. 76.

72. Metcalf, *Royal Government and Political Conflict in Jamaica*, 228; Martin, *Empire and Commonwealth*, 148.

Epilogue

1. James Madison, "Government of the United States," *National Gazette*, Feb. 6, 1792, in Gaillard Hunt, ed., *The Writings of James Madison*, 9 vols. (New York, 1900–1910), 6:91–92.
2. [John Winthrop], "Letters of Agrippa," [Jan. 14, Feb. 5, 1788], in Cecelia M. Kenyon, ed., *The Antifederalists* (Indianapolis, 1966), 143, 157.
3. Kenneth M. Stampp, "The Concept of a Perpetual Union," *Journal of American History* 65(1978): 11.
4. Madison, "Consolidation," "Public Opinion," and "British Government," *National Gazette*, Dec. 5, 19, 1791, Jan. 30, 1792, in Hunt, ed., *Madison Writings*, 6:67–68, 70, 87; Washington to Richard Henderson, June 19, 1788, in J. C. Fitzpatrick, ed., *The Writings of George Washington*, 39 vols. (Washington, 1931–44), 29:522; [Winthrop], "Letters of Agrippa," [Jan. 14, 1788], in Kenyon, ed., *Antifederalists*, 140.
5. Jesse Root to Jonathan Trumbull, Jan. 8, 1781, in Edmund Cody Burnett, ed., *Letters of Members of the Continental Congress*, 8 vols. (Washington, 1921–38), 5:520. For an expansion of this argument see Jack P. Greene, "The Pursuit of Happiness: The Private Realm, Commerce, and the Constitution," *This Constitution*, No. 8 (Fall 1985), 40–42.
6. Washington to Lafayette, June 19, 1788, in Fitzpatrick, ed., *Washington Writings*, 29:525–26; Madison, "Consolidation," *National Gazette*, Dec. 5, 1791, in Hunt, ed., *Madison Writings*, 6:68; John Jay, *Federalist* 2, in Benjamin F. Wright, ed., *The Federalist* (Cambridge, 1961), 94.
7. Stampp, "Concept of a Perpetual Union," 5, 20–23, 26, 28–29.
8. Ibid., 20–33.
9. Madison's speech, June 29, 1787, in William T. Hutchinson et al., eds., *The Papers of James Madison*, 15 vols. (Chicago, 1962–), 10:88; [Richard Henry Lee], *Letters from the Federal Farmer* (1787–88) in Kenyon, ed., *Antifederalists*, 218. See also John R. Alden, *The First South* (Baton Rouge, 1961), 33–127.
10. Stampp, "Concept of a Perpetual Union," 5; Michael Hechter, *Internal Colonialism: The Celtic Fringe in British National Development, 1536–1966* Berkeley and Los Angeles, 1975), 64.
11. Stampp, "Concept of a Perpetual Union," 5.

Index

Abingdon, Earl of, 138
Abingdon, Lord, 207
Act of Union, 8
Adams, John, 95, 135, 142, 156, 159–60, 174, 190
Adams, Samuel, 88, 89–90, 116
Addison, Joseph, 82
Albany Congress of 1754, 154
Albany Plan of Union, 157, 168
Alien Act, 214
Americanization: as cultural process, 166–67
American Parliament, 132
American Revolution, xi, 3, 149, 158, 167, 209
Andrews, Kenneth R., 11
Anglicization: as cultural process, 166–67
Arieli, Yehoshua, 162, 169
Articles of Confederation, 3, 157, 172, 198, 199, 201, 206; adoption, 175–78; deficiencies, 182–97; factors facilitating revision, 195–96; nature of, 175–82; proposals for reform, 185–97
Assemblies, colonial: authority equated with corporate rights of colonies, 83–97; authority of, 28–42, 139–41; cease demanding explicit guarantees of rights, 47–49; colonial conception of, 30–42, 48–49, 83–87, 139–41; effect of Glorious Revolution upon development of, 63; exclusive taxing power over colonies asserted, 82–97; metropolitan conception of, 33–35, 48–49, 100–101; oppose expanded use of royal instructions, 51–54; sources of authority, 28–42; status as parliaments, 14, 30–42, 48–49, 52, 64, 67, 139–41
Authority: allocation of, in the empire, 33, 65–66, 75–76, 88–93, 111–12, 120–36, 138–39, 172–74; mistrust of central, 15, 75–76, 160–61, 186–87, 193
Autonomy, local: in colonies, 11–12, 92; in England, 11; in Ireland, 58; metropolitan efforts to restrict, in colonies, 12–18, 46–47, 49–54. See also Assemblies, colonial; Local

foundations of legislative authority; Local rights; Self-government

Bacon's Rebellion, 44
Bailyn, Bernard, x, 88, 92, 160
Bancroft, Edward, 119–20
Barbados Assembly, 81
Barnard, John, 162
Barre, Isaac, 103, 143
Beccaria, Cesare, 136
Beckett, J. C., 61, 62, 63
Beckford, William, 80
Bedford, Gunning, 199
Beer, Samuel H., 163, 178, 179, 206
Beeston, Sir William, 59
Bernard, Francis, 79, 80, 88, 104, 125
Bill of Privileges, 16
Black, Barbara A., x, 66, 144–48
Blackstone, Sir William, 24, 169, 177, 189, 200, 202, 210; Commentaries of the Law of England, 101
Bladen, Martin, 61
Bland, Richard, 86, 87, 90, 94–96, 112, 121; An Inquiry into the Rights of the British Colonies, 89; The Colonel Dismounted, 88–89
Blenman, Jonathan, 41
Board of Trade, 16, 41, 45–46, 59–60
Bollan, William, 70
Boone, Thomas, 125
Border Areas of England: as precedents for colonies, 9, 11
Boston Gazette, 95
Britannus Americanus, 95
British Empire: constitutional development after 1776, 207–11
Burke, Edmund, 2, 38, 44, 48, 57, 64–66, 106, 123, 124, 130, 136, 143, 169
Burke, Thomas, 161, 175
Burnett, William, 36
Bushe, Gervase Parker, 113, 116, 122

Camden, Lord, 98, 99, 101, 107
Canada: constitutional development after 1776, 208–11
Carroll, Charles, 127

Index

Carroll, Daniel, 192
Carter, Jennifer, 57, 62
Carter, Landon, 88, 89
Cartwright, John, 134, 136, 139, 203
Cavendish, Lord John, 124
Center: definition of, ix
Charles I, 19, 62, 63
Charles II, 14; restoration of, 13, 37, 59, 63
Charter of Liberties, 16
Charters: as basis for colonial claims to rights of Englishmen, 15; as basis for colonial constitutions, 12, 36; as basis for opposing parliamentary legislation, 84–85; denied as basis for colonial exemption from parliamentary taxation, 99–100; as property, 12
Civil War, 216
Clarendon, Earl of, 72–73
Coercive Acts, 132, 143, 159
Coke, Sir Edward, 36, 41; and *Calvin's Case*, 23–24
Colden, Cadwallader, 125
Colonies, British: as commercial enterprises, 9–10; as conquests, 9, 23–24, 28, 113; as settler societies, 9–10, 23–24; attitudes of inhabitants towards Parliament before 1763, 58–59, 69–76; colonial conceptions of, as distinct corporate entities, 10, 89–91, 93–94, 97, 114–24, 135–44; definitions, 7–12; growth, 45; law-making powers of, 12; metropolitan conceptions of, 100–101, 106–10, 129–31; metropolitan policy towards, 12–18, 20–42, 44–47; relations with Crown before 1763, 7–54; relations with Parliament before 1763, 55–76. *See also* Assemblies
Colonies: in antiquity, 9; in Spanish Empire, 9
Colonization: English objectives in, 10–11
Commissions, royal: as basis for colonial constitutions, 33–36, 50–57, 73
Common interest: developing colonial perceptions of, after 1763, 168–70
Compacts: charters and settlements as evidence of, with Crown, 12, 36, 113–14. *See also* Consent
Conciliation: desire for, during Townshend Acts crisis, 105–6, 110–12;

desire for, during crisis of independence, 130–32
Confederation. *See* Articles of Confederation; Union, American national
Confederation Congress, 196
Connecticut Assembly, 84, 87
Consent: as foundations of constitutional authority, 85–86, 119–22; custom as evidence of, 39–41, 92; as necessary for constitutional change, 39; nature of, analyzed by legal historians, 147–48; *See also* Opinion
Constitution, American, 196, 201–5, 213–16; article V, 204; tenth ammendment, 213–14
Constitution, British: xi, 1, 67; not a model for colonial or imperial constitutions, 112–13, 141
Constitution, imperial: ix, 68; analyzed by legal historians, 144–50; colonial demand for, 43; colonial interpretations of, before 1763, 70–72, 75–76; customary basis of, 44–54, 65–68, 75–76; defined by Thomas Pownall in 1774, 131–32; definitions of, during crisis of Independence, 138–41; definitions of, during Stamp Act crisis, 95, 103–4; definitions of, during Townshend Acts crisis, 116–24; influence on American national union, 172–74, 178–80; proposals to make explicit, 132–33, 141–42; tendency to conflate with British constitution, 65; theory of, 153; unsettled character of, 43–44, 54, 65–67
Constitution, Irish; 8–9, 23, 61–65, 68, 117, 139; development after 1776, 207–8
Constitutions: as superior to governmental institutions, 85, 98–99, 120, 201–2
Continental Congress, 129, 133, 155, 159, 164, 165, 172, 178, 180, 214; first, 139, 171; second, 154
Contract: theory of formation of union, 178–80; *See also* Compacts; Consent
Convergence: social and cultural, among colonies, 166–70
Coordination principle: defined, 57:

inapplicable to imperial constitution, 118–19
Cornell, Ezekiel, 177
Corporate entities: colonies as, 75–76, 164–65, 172–73; effect of colonies' long-term existence as, upon the American union, 164–65; rights of states as, institutionalized in Senate, 201, 206–7
Corporate rights: of colonies asserted in Stamp Act crisis and equated with assembly rights, 83–97
Craw v. Ramsay, 23
Crown: as connecting link between colonies and Britain, 94–95, 113–18, 134; as sovereign authority over colonies, 119, 128, 138, 141; authority of, over colonies questioned after 1774, 143–44; relationship to colonies, 7–18, 20–54, 124–28; right to grant colonies separate political status affirmed, 113–14; role in colonization, 10–11
Currency Act, 69
Cushing, Thomas, 112
Custom: as basis for accepting parliamentary jurisdiction over external colonial affairs, 92; as basis for all British constitutions, 64–66; as basis for British constitution, 38–39; as basis for colonial constitutions, 12–13, 37–41; as basis for denying aspects of crown authority in colonies, 126–29; as basis for denying parliamentary jurisdiction over internal colonial affairs, 84–85, 96, 113–22; as superior to written law, 38; legitimacy of colonial, denied in Britain, 100; used by assemblies to secure rights and justify constitutional change, 47–49; validity of, confirmed by parliamentary inaction, 115–16; validity of, emphasized by legal historians, 144–50

Dalrymple, Sir John, 134
Davies, Sir John, 38–39
Declaration of Independence, 2, 164, 188
Declaration of Rights of 1689, 16
Declatory Act, 106–7, 108, 122, 124, 134, 142, 207, 209
Delafaye, Charles, 46

Dependence: colonial conceptions of, 93–94; theory of colonial, 10, 18, 86
De Vattel, Emmerich, 120
Dickinson, H. T., 56–57
Dickinson, John, 81; *Letters from a Farmer in Pennsylvania*, 110–12, 124, 136, 168, 170, 175
Disorder, fear of: role in affecting national union, 170–72, 196–97
Divisions, among colonies: role in affecting national union, 156–60
Douglass, Dr. William, 29
Dowdeswell, William, 142
Downer, Silas, 122
Drayton, William Henry, 143, 180
Duane, James, 183
Dulany, Daniel, 86–87
Dummer, Jeremiah, 30; *A Defence of the New England Charters*, 70
Dutton v. Howell, 24

Edwards, Bryan: *History, Civil and Commercial, of the British Colonies in the West Indies*, 209
Egmont, Lord, 102
Elizabeth I, 8
Ellsworth, Oliver, 199
Emigration, right of: as basis for colonial claims to rights of Englishmen, 22–23, 36, 94, 113
English Civil War, 19, 62
Enumerated powers: in Constitution, 202–3
Extended polity: as a new political phenomenon, 2; definition, ix, 1; dispersion of authority necessary in, 136
External polity, of colonies: colonial conceptions of Parliament's role in, 88–93, 111–12, 120–23, 134–35

Fairfield, William, 58
Federal Constitution, ix, 3, 172, 206, 212
Federal Convention, 1, 197–204, 216
Federalism: colonial experience with before 1763, 172–74; concept as developed during debate over constitution, 198–207; concept implicit in colonial arguments against parliamentary authority, 91, 103
Federalist 15, 199

Flood, Henry, 140, 207
Force: as basis for metropolitan control over colonies, 44
Fox, Charles James, 142
Frankland, Henry, 158
Franklin, Benjamin, 52–53, 66–67, 73–74, 95, 113–20, 122–23, 127, 129, 135, 143, 157, 162, 169
French Revolution, 149

Gadsden, Christopher, 64, 72
Galloway, Joseph, 160, 171
Garrison government: as mode of controlling English border areas, 9
George III, 56, 107, 121, 144
Georgia Commons, 126
Gerry, Elbridge, 200
Glorious Revolution, 126, 140, 143, 148; as a stimulus for exertion of local authority throughout British Empire, 62–63; as a stimulus to the growth of parliamentary institutions throughout British Empire, 63–65; colonial interpretations of, 16; does not extend restrictions on prerogative to colonies, 20–22; effect on British Constitution, 57–58; effects on Irish constitutional development, 63–65; fails to extend Parliament's jurisdiction over colonies, 115; invoked by colonists to support claims against parliamentary jurisdiction in colonies, 133–34; meaning for colonies, 58, 62–81; restrictions on royal prerogative in Britain produced by, 20
Gooch, Sir William, 27
Gordon, Thomas, 44
Governors, colonial: colonial attitudes towards, 21–22, 32; defend prerogative, 34–42; domesticated by colonists under Walpole, 46–47; patronage, 46–47
Grace and favor: as basis for colonial constitutions, 33–35, 50–54
Granville, Lord, 52
Grattan, Henry, 208
Grayson, William, 167, 196
Greene, Nathaniel, 177
Grenville, George, 79–81, 83, 93, 101–2, 106
Grey, Thomas C., x, 144–46

Hamilton, Alexander, 135, 138–39, 141–42, 169, 181, 184–86, 188, 193, 199, 201; Federalist, 202, 205; and Federalist 15, 200
Hanover: as model for colonial relationship to Britain, 95, 117–18
Happiness: as best promoted by state governments, 194–95, 213–14
Hardwicke, Chancellor, 158
Hawley, Joseph, 159
Hechter, Michael, 2
Hendrickson, David C., 83, 91
Henry VIII, 56
Henry, Patrick, 88, 165
Hewes, Joseph, 156
Hicks, William, 90, 116, 118–19, 122–23
Hillsborough, Lord, 107–8
History. See Custom
Hopkins, Stephen, 58, 88, 90, 93, 94, 112
House of Commons, 14, 31, 32, 35, 38, 48, 56, 59–61, 69, 72, 73, 80, 86, 98, 103, 107, 125, 126, 130
House of Lords, 24, 29, 31, 38, 56, 61, 64, 86, 98, 101, 115, 130, 208
House of Representatives, 201, 206
Hume, David, 83, 142
Hunter, Robert, 60
Huntingdon, Enoch, 171
Hussey, Richard, 107
Hyde, Edward, 21

Incorporation: as a mode of governing extended polities, 1–2, 10; colonies not incorporated as part of Britain, 116, 172–73; proposals for, during pre-Revolutionary crises, 122–23
Independence: charges that colonies aim at, 33, 108–9; metropolitan fears of colonial, 49; See also Autonomy, Self-government
Ingersoll, Jared, 102
Inheritance: as basis for colonial claims to rights of Englishmen, 15. See also Rights of Englishmen
Instructions, royal: as basis for colonial constitutions, 33, 50–51, 73; legal status of, 50–53, 126–28; metropolitan use of, to control colonies, 50–54; proposals for Parliament to give legal status to, 61, 73

Interest, community of: as basis for legislative authority, 82–83
Internal polity, jurisdiction over: claimed by colonists, 37, 88–93, 112, 121, 133–35, 138–39; left to assemblies in colonies, 65–66
Ireland: as a distinct state with control over internal affairs, 117, 139; attitude of inhabitants towards colonial resistance, 140; constitutional development after 1776, 207–8; relation of, to British Parliament, 61–62; relation to England, 8–9, 23
Irish Declatory Act, 74, 103, 208
Irish House of Commons, 207, 208
Irish Parliament, 140

Jamaica: assembly of, 16, 48, 59, 69, 73, 126; assembly endorses colonial view of imperial constitution in 1774, 139–40; constitutional development after 1776, 209–10
James I, 8, 63
James II, 13, 15, 29, 59, 63
Jefferson, Thomas, 1, 135, 143, 177, 201
Jensen, Merrill, 156, 160, 173
Johnson, Dr. Samuel: dictionary, 10
Johnson, William Samuel, 107
Johnstone, George, 136–37
Jones, Joseph, 177
Jones, Sir William, 37

Kames, Lord, 119
Keith, Sir William, 27
Kentucky Resolution of 1798–99, 214
King, Rufus, 180, 193, 200
Knight, James, 40
Knox, Henry, 196
Knox, William, 24, 26, 27, 33, 50, 73; and *The Controversy Between Great Britain and her Colonies Reviewed*, 107–8

Langrishe, Sir Hercules, 121
Law, British: colonial efforts to secure benefits of, 23–28; nature of English law, 25–26; role of colonial legislature and courts in determining scope of, in colonies, 26–28
Law, Jonathan, 40
Lee, Arthur, 190

Lee, Joseph, 208
Lee, Richard Henry, 156, 169, 171
Legal historians: analyze legal basis of colonial constitutional claims, 144–50
Legislation, none without representation: claimed by Barbados, 57, 70–71; claimed by colonists, 36–42, 87–97, 112–24, 131–34
Legislative authority: extent and sources of colonial, 28–42, 48–49; granted to colonies by charter, 12; metropolitan efforts to restrict, 12–18, 49–54
Liberty: as basis for successful colonies, 44–46
Littleton, Edward: *The Groans of the Plantations*, 19
Local foundations of legislative authority, 82–83, 91; examined by legal historians, 144–50
Localism: in English governance, 11; strengthened by Glorious Revolution, 62–63; in colonies, 11–12
Local rights: colonial attempt to secure against Crown, 23–42; view of Revolution as defense of colonial, 182, 191–92
Locke, John, 72, 94, 147
London Chronicle, 115
Long, Edward, 210
Long, Samuel, 40
Lords of Trade, 13–14, 16, 33
Loudoun, Earl of, 58
Lyttelton, William Henry, 125
Lyttleton, Lord, 101–2

McIlwain, Charles H., x, 74
McLaughlin, Andrew C., x, 65, 75, 164, 180, 203, 205
Macpherson, James, 130
Madden, A. F. M., 56
Madison, James, 1, 153, 161, 177, 181, 185–86, 193, 197–201, 205, 213–14, 216; and *Federalist*, 202, 204
Magna Charta, 25, 35–36, 71
Mansfield, Lord, 101
Marshall, John, 215
Martin, Chester, 209
Martin, Luther, 199–200
Maryland Assembly, 15
Maryland Gazette, 71

272

Index

Maseres, Francis, 123
Mason, Thomson, 134
Massachusetts Committee of
    Correspondence, 143
Massachusetts Government Act, 142
Massachusetts House of Representatives,
    49, 58, 60, 85, 89–90, 121
Mather, Moses, 138
Medieval empire: of England, 7–8
Molasses Act of 1733, 17
Molyneux, William: *The Case of Ireland's
    Being Bound by Acts of Parliament in
    England Stated*, 58, 140
Morgan, Edmund S., 87
Morris, Lewis, 26, 70
Morris, Richard B., 171, 173, 178
Morton, Lord, 158
Murray, Joseph, 39

Nationalism: American, early
    development of, 162–63; British,
    among colonists, 162–63, 167
Nationalist theory: of the formation of
    American union, 178–80
Navigation acts, 13, 16–17, 29; colonial
    attitude towards, 19–20, 55; selective
    colonial compliance with, 17, 62;
    selective Irish compliance with, 62
Navigation Laws, 135
Neal, Daniel: *History of New England*, 71
Nelson, William E., x
Nettels, Curtis P., 178
New Jersey Assembly, 51, 70–71
New York Assembly of 1683, 16, 60
New York Mercury, 170
*New York Packett, and the American
    Advertiser* (1781–82), 184
Nicholson, Francis, 46
Non-repugnancy clause: as basis for
    metropolitan review of colonial
    legislation, 29–30
North, Lord, 207
North Carolina Assembly, 126
Northington, Lord, 101
Nova Scotia: constitutional development
    after 1776, 109–11, 207
Nullification Crisis, 215

Onuf, Peter S., ix, xii, 128, 141, 155, 165,
    172–73, 182, 195–98, 200
Opinion: appreciation of importance of

as basis for government, 44–45, 74–75,
    110, 124, 136, 142–43, 197, 213, 216; as
    limit on parliamentary jurisdiction in
    Ireland and colonies, 61–62, 68, 72
Otis, James, 21, 22, 37, 49, 89, 94

Paine, Thomas, 155; *Common Sense*, 163
Parke, Daniel, 21
Parliament, British: as model for colonial
    assemblies, 31–32, 35–37; asserts
    jurisdiction over whole British Empire,
    98–104, 107–10; authority limited by
    constitutions, 70–72, 85, 98–99, 120;
    colonial conceptions of authority of,
    55, 114–15, 122–23; colonies oppose
    efforts to tax, 82–97, 110–24; confirms
    colonists' title to rights of Englishmen,
    37; economic regulations of colonies
    by, 13, 16–17, 19–20, 55–56, 59–61, 80;
    metropolitan officials propose
    intervention in colonial internal affairs,
    55, 68–69; proposals for colonial
    representation in, 80–81; range of
    colonial legislation before 1763, 61;
    relation to colonies, 55–76, 125,
    129–50; relation to Crown, 55; relation
    to Ireland and Irish Parliament, 56,
    61–62, 65–66, 98; relationship to
    colonies analyzed by legal historians,
    144–50; supremacy, development of
    doctrine of, in England, 38–39;
    supremacy over Britain gained as a
    result of Glorious Revolution, 56–59,
    62, 74; supremacy over colonies,
    asserted after 1763, 100–4, 107–10;
    supremacy over colonies, assumed in
    Britain, 68; supremacy over colonies,
    opposed by colonists, 71, 74
Parliament, Irish: development after
    Glorious Revolution, 98; development
    after 1776, 207–8; relation to British
    Parliament, 98
Patronage: engrossed by London
    authorities, 47; employed by colonial
    governors, 46–47
Pendleton, Edmund, 204
Penn, William, 12, 14–15, 16
Pennsylvania Assembly, 110
Peripheries: definition, ix
Peters, Richard, 183
Petition of Right, 25, 71

Phelps, Richard, 107–8
Philadelphia Convention, 197
Philalethes, 93
Pinckney, Charles Coatesworth, 188–89
Pitkin, William, 121
Pitt, William, 98–99
Pocock, J. G. A., 38
The Political Establishments of the United States of America (1784), 190–92
Portland, Duke of, 25
Post Office Act, 80
Postlethwayt, Malachy, 158
Potter, David, 168
Power: colonial conceptions of, 32; mistrust of central, 160–61, 186–87, 193. *See* Authority
Pownall, Thomas, 84, 109, 121, 123, 131–32; *The Administration of the Colonies*, 158
Poyning's Act, 208
Poyning's Law, 14, 33, 40, 64, 207
Prerogative, royal: as asserted in colonies, 20–22, 32; as diminished in Britain, 56; colonial fears of 72–73; conflicts over in colonies, 49–54, 124–28, 142–43; undermined by assemblies, 32–33, 47–49
Prescription. *See* Custom
Privy Council: 24, 26, 30, 52, 60; program of, 13–15; relation to medieval empire, 56

Quebec Act, 142
Queen Anne's War, 60

Rakove, Jack N., 160, 173–74, 176, 178, 180; American developments, 155–57
Ramsay, Allan, 107, 109
Ramsay, David, 176
Rawson, Edward, 36
Reid, John Phillip, x, 144–48
Representational basis of federal union, 205–6
Republican character of colonial governments: charged, 33
Republics: effect of history of, upon formation of American union, 161–62
Revenue: crown's quest for permanent, in colonies, 14
Reynall, Abbe, 161

Rights of Englishmen: as basis for colonial constitutions, 36–37, 39; as confirmed by characters, 15; as confirmed by crown law officers, 37; as confirmed by Parliament, 37; as equal in Britain and colonies, 36–37; as grounds for opposing parliamentary taxation, 83–85, 96; as part of colonial inheritance, 15; as secured for colonists by custom, 37–41, 48–49; colonial claims to, 15–16, 18, 22–42; defined, 36
Rokeby, Baron, 132, 139
Root, Jesse, 182, 213
Rush, Benjamin, 168; and *Independent Gazeteer* in 1786, 189
Rutherford, Thomas, 38–39, 96, 99, 145, 147
Rutledge, Edward, 171, 175

Salutory neglect: as policy towards colonies, 45–46
Saville, Sir George, 65
Schuyler, Robert L., 56
Sedition Act, 214
Self-government, colonial: as secret for success of British Empire, 135–37; extent of, 92. *See also* Autonomy
Seven Year's War, 24, 68, 79, 113, 158, 163
Shay's Rebellion, 196
Sherman, Roger, 179, 191–92
Shils, Edward, ix, 63
Shipley, Jonathan, 105, 130, 138
Shower, Sir Batholomew, 24
Shy, John, 163
Slavery: and development of American union, 215–27
Smith, Adam: and *The Wealth of Nations*, 45
Smith, William, 37
Smith, William, Jr., 172
Sovereignty: ambiguous nature of under Articles, 176–78; as located in colonial constitutions, 128; discussions of during Confederation, 188–96; disinterest in during early years of union, 173, 175–76; dispute over evaluated by legal historians, 144–50; doctrine of coordinate, 202–5, 213; doctrine of juridical, as distinct from political, 194–95; doctrine of popular,

Sovereignty (*continued*)
203–6, 213; doctrine of state, 189–96,
200, 213; issue raised by Grenville, 81;
metropolitan conceptions of, 57; of
king over colonies, admitted by
colonial supporters, 119, 138; of king
over colonies, asserted in Britain,
99–103, 106–10, 118, 130, 142–43, and
denied by colonial supporters, 114,
118–19, 133–39; redefined by Federal
Constitution, 202–7
Stamp Act of 1765, 79–81, 89, 91, 97, 101,
103, 110, 111, 118, 126–27, 132, 146,
164; congress, 87, 104; crisis, 66,
79–105, 106, 107, 112–13, 119, 121, 124,
125, 129, 139, 145, 200; declaration of,
111
Stampp, Kenneth M., 213–15
Stanley, Hans, 109
States: adopt constitutions, 173;
attachment of people to governments
of, 212–13; increase in power of
governments of, after 1778, 176–78,
181–97; sovereignty, of, 188–97, 213
States Rights: development of theory,
213–17
Stiles, Ezra, 190

Taxation of colonies, by Britain:
distinguished from legislation, 87–88,
98–101, 111–112; introduced by
Grenville, 79–81; opposed by
colonists, 82–97, 110–24, 134–135;
supported in Britain, 97–110
Tea Act, 129
Temple, Sir William, 161
Territorial basis of federal union of 1787,
206–7
Thomson, Charles, 185
Townshend Acts, 129, 131, 132, 134, 159;
crisis over, 105–27
Townshend, Charles, 101
Treaty of Paris, 24
Tredwell, Thomas, 202
Trenchard, John, 44
Trumbull, Jonathan, 182
Tucker, Josiah, 130
Tucker, Robert W., 83, 91
Tullius: *Three Letters Addressed to the
Public*, 194–95

Union, American national: customary
basis of initial, 155, 172, 174;
development of sentiment for, after
1788, 214–17; historical precedents for,
198; long-term preconditions for,
157–74; nature of before and after
Confederation, 178–80, 182–85,
187–97; process of formation of, 153–
78; proposals for, before the
Revolution, 154; sentiment for, in
1774–76, 144; short-range
developments affecting, 154–57
Usage. *See* Custom

Vaughan, John, 23
A Vindication of the Rights of the Americans,
91
Virginia Assembly, 88, 112
Virginia House of Burgesses, 88–89
Virginia Resolution of 1798–99, 214
Virtual representation, doctrine of:
devised by Thomas Whateley, 80–81;
opposed by colonists, 82, 112

Walpole, Sir Robert, 17; policies towards
colonies, 45–46
War of 1812, 215
War for Independence, 160, 163, 176, 206
Washington, George, 177, 185–87, 193,
195, 213–14
Webster, Noah, 189, 193
Webster, Pelatiah, 189, 193
West, Richard, 26
West Indies: constitutional development
after 1776, 207–11
Weston, Corinne C., 57
Whateley, Thomas, 80
William III, 16
Williams, Samuel: *History of Vermont*, 166
Wilson, James, 135, 142, 161, 192, 198,
201, 204
Witherspoon, John, 154, 155, 171, 172,
179, 188
Wolcott, Oliver, 163, 183
Wood, Gordon, x, 177, 180, 186, 203

Yelverton's Act, 208

Zubly, Johan Joachim, 117, 120, 122